Handbook of e-Business Security

T0225372

Handbook of e-Business Security

Edited by
João Manuel R.S. Tavares, Brojo Kishore Mishra,
Raghvendra Kumar, Noor Zaman, Manju Khari

CRC Press
Taylor & Francis Group
Boca Raton London New York

CRC Press is an imprint of the
Taylor & Francis Group, an **informa** business

CRC Press
Taylor & Francis Group
6000 Broken Sound Parkway NW, Suite 300
Boca Raton, FL 33487-2742

First issued in paperback 2020

© 2019 by Taylor & Francis Group, LLC
CRC Press is an imprint of Taylor & Francis Group, an Informa business

No claim to original U.S. Government works

ISBN-13: 978-1-138-57130-3 (hbk)
ISBN-13: 978-0-367-65718-5 (pbk)

Library of Congress Cataloging-in-Publication Data

Names: Tavares, Joao Manuel R.S., editor.
Title: Handbook of e-business security / editors, Joao Manuel
R.S. Tavares [and three others].
Description: Boca Raton, FL : CRC Press, 2018.
Identifiers: LCCN 2018013131 | ISBN 9781138571303 (hb : alk. paper)
Subjects: LCSH: Business enterprises—Computer networks—Security
measures. | Computer security.
Classification: LCC HD30.38 .H36 2018 | DDC 658.4/78—dc23
LC record available at https://lccn.loc.gov/2018013131

Visit the Taylor & Francis Web site at
http://www.taylorandfrancis.com

and the CRC Press Web site at
http://www.crcpress.com

Contents

Key Features

1. Identifies, discusses, and addresses real threats and security risk, which occurs in e-commerce treats;
2. Contains contributions from some of the world's leading researchers, scientists, business analytics, and academicians;
3. Includes interdisciplinary chapters that are based on engineering, economics, management, and security laws;
4. Covers different security risks, protocols, and solutions in national and international markets.

About the Book

This edited book deals with the current issues highly relevant in the business world. The wide range of topics covered is quite impressive and useful for today's life. Therefore, this book is not only useful for leaders and strategists in the business enterprises, but also for specialists in the business fields; additionally, executives in the state administration and research institutes will profit from the viewpoints and suggested solutions presented in this edited book.

Preface

An information system is not only about simple computers, but also about how businesses can make the best use of computer technology to provide the information needed to achieve their goals. In the same way as one's needs and priorities are unique, each organization has different goals and requirements, and successful implementation of the information system requires a thorough understanding of the business issues involved as well as different technologies that are available. Most of the time, there is no single correct answer, and one needs to draw on their own knowledge and judgment when planning or using an information system. Business makes use of the information system so that accurate and up-to-date information are available when required. Since it is not always possible to predict what information will be needed in the future, most organizations use computers to record and store the details of all their business transactions. When a query arises or a standard business report must be produced, this data can be retrieved and manipulated to produce the required information.

Providing recommendations to the users of web services is an emerging field. These recommendations help the user to make final decisions based on other user preferences. When any service provider publishes their details and interface information on the web, it is known as "web service". The client and the service provider can communicate over the web. Web services are designed with the aim of reusing whenever and wherever required. Web services are discovered based on user's requirement. Users face problems when the web service provides a list of options based on requirements; however, by using recommendation system, this problem is resolved. Herein, this book presents the various techniques used for web service recommendations. To provide recommendations according to user requirements, an efficient method is required. Collaborative filtering is used as a method to provide recommendations according to the user's need.

It is a growing technique used in making recommendations, which make use of web service. This book presents a view on different techniques in this field and elaborates the framework of collaborative filtering used for recommendations of web service for business transactions. Mobile cloud computing is being anticipated as the infrastructural basis of tomorrow's IT industry and continues to be a topic of interest of many new emerging IT firms. The cloud can deliver resources and services to computers and devices through the Internet. Since cloud computing involves outsourcing sensitive data and critical information, the security aspects of the cloud need to be dealt with carefully. Strong authentication, focusing mainly on user authentication, acts as a prerequisite for access control in the cloud environment. Hence, efficient authentication mechanisms to deal with the security threats that are faced by the cloud are discussed in this book. For example, by preventing the confidential data and information of end users stored in a private cloud from unauthorized access, a two-factor authentication involving shared image concept in addition to encrypted key authentication for business transactions is used.

A business is an organizational system where economic resources are transferred by various organization processes into goods and services. The information system provides information on the operations of the system to management for the direction and maintenance of the system, as it exchanges input and output with environments.

Within any single organization, executives at different levels in the management hierarchy have different information requirements, and different types of information systems have evolved to meet their needs. A common approach is to categorize information system applications by the role they play at various levels in the organizational structure. The information system depends upon the resources of people, hardware, software, data, and network to perform input, processing, storage, and control activities, which convert data resources into information products.

Web services are self-contained, modular business process applications that are based on the industry standard technologies of Web service definition language (WSDL), Universal Description, Discovery, and Integration (UDDI), and Simple Object Access Protocol (SOAP). Web services provide a means for different organizations to connect their applications with one another to conduct business across a network in a platform and language-independent manner. Transactions are a fundamental concept in building reliable distributed applications. A transaction is a mechanism that ensures all participants in an application achieve a mutually agreed outcome. The business transaction scenario provides an illustration of an implementation of a long-running transaction using web service transaction. The task within a business transaction generally consists of a number of automatic transactions. The resources updated by the automatic transaction must be undone should the overall business transaction fail, and comparison is a common methodology for dealing with transactions and implementing a business transaction protocol.

This book is organized into 15 chapters.

Chapter 1 describes in detail the advantages of security and trades in the online business fragment. Since sweeping open money is locked in with the trades, the piece of information assurance and security is not amplified in this business. In the wake of taking a look at the developments used as a piece of online business, the part proceeds to perceive the security essentials of web business structures from saw perils and vulnerabilities. By then, online business security is viewed as a building organization issue and a presence cycle approach is progressed.

Chapter 2 discusses the Internet, their security prospective and cryptography along with its principles, models, and modern algorithms. It also provides a brief actualization of the existing encryption algorithm in cryptography, their benefits, drawbacks, and the future of cryptography.

Chapter 3 discusses the support vector machine (SVM) due to usage of data mining techniques that we have successfully applied for attaining cybersecurity. Data mining is widely used in customer relationship management, medical analysis, diagnostic, supply chain management, fraud detection, and detecting criminal activities. Data mining is the way in the direction of posing queries and removing designs, regularly previously unidentified from large amounts of information utilizing design coordinating or other reasoning strategies. Data mining has frequent applications in security, including national security and cybersecurity. The threats to national security incorporate attacking structures and wrecking basic frameworks, for example, control matrices and telecommunication systems. Data mining methods are being explored to find out who the suspicious individuals are and who is equipped for fear monger exercises. Cybersecurity is included by protecting the computer and network systems against debasement, worms, and viruses. Data mining is likewise being connected to give arrangements, for example, interruption detection and inspection by using the SVM technique, it demonstrates a good speculation execution on some real-life data, and the approach is properly motivated hypothetically, and it has been connected extensively for a variety of uses. This chapter describes a concise detail of SVMs and attains the cybersecurity with the maximum accuracy of classifier and gave the report of the phishing attack and the distributed denial-of-service (DDoS) attack in our society.

Chapter 4 discusses the smart network-controlled, location-based, vitality-controlled systems that use the smart phone platform inspired by "vitality proportion computing" in modern computers. Real-world experiments are carried out on Internet of Things (IoT) network and the control system prototype, which clearly demonstrate the effective implementation of the suggested solution. Application of the proposed solution will not only be helpful in vitality saving, network intelligence, and economic benefits, but also lead to a social implication regarding global sustainability.

Chapter 5 discusses the Distributed Denial-of-Service (DDoS) as a rapidly growing attack that poses a tremendous threat to the future generation of Internet technology. A multitude of this attack is quickly becoming more and more complex. With the advancement of network technologies, the software-defined network (SDN) increases the chances to defeat DDoS attacks caused by several points of the network. In one way, the centralized control provisioning and enhanced visibility into an organization's network make it easier for SDN to detect DDoS attacks. On the other hand, it becomes a victim of DDoS attacks due to the potential vulnerabilities existing across various SDN layers. Moreover, this chapter focuses on the basic architectural design of SDN paradigms, different security threats that arise due to architectural shift from traditional networks to SDN, the purpose of DDoS threats with techniques, the possibility of DDoS threats to SDN, and various research efforts to detect this threat in different layers of SDN.

The objective of Chapters 6 and 8 is to traditional security model based on firewalls and local security mechanism are incapable of handling security in the Big Data infrastructure as it needs to be stretched out of the perimeter of the organization's network to handle the structured/unstructured streaming data. Based on these scenarios, the security issue for big data can be classified into four domains such as infrastructure-based security that concerns the secure layers in big data system's infrastructure, data privacy, integrity of data, and management of huge volume of data.

In Chapter 7, the presented research is based on the deep analysis of generic architecture of IoT and its security features based upon which key security threats are outlined.

Chapter 9 focuses on the identification of the key indicators of behavioural analytics (BA) and its applications. It classifies elements affecting the performance of BA, and discovers the role of big data in applying and identifying various statistical findings between BA and market trends.

Chapter 10 illustrates the understanding of cybercrime, recent trends in cybercrime, and the measures by which these cybercrimes can be eliminated to a considerable extent. The authors discuss various emerging cybercrime techniques, including steganography, next-generation malwares, next-generation ransom wares, social engineering attacks, and attacks using machine learning and IoT devices.

Chapter 11 concludes that lack of regulations dealing specifically with e-waste is the major problem in managing e-waste. Without proper implementation of regulation, no individual or private agency can work efficiently for e-waste. In the context of Developing Nations, lack of budget is the major barrier to carry out the activities related to e-waste management. For proper handling of e-waste, every organization needs a procedure by which large generation of e-waste could be minimized and as a result, there could be better management of e-waste.

Chapter 12 demonstrates the Ernst and Young (EY) Global Information Security Survey of 2017 and points out that the majority of organizations are expecting to be attacked at any time, and hence, they have started to pursue cyberresilience. The three essential components of cyberresilience are "sense", "resist", and "recover". The presented study also has thrown up a fascinating statistic: most of the organizations place the top priority on "resist", which deals with mechanisms of defense. The ability to recover from the disruption ("recover") is often taken as the lowest priority. The major focus of the chapter is to discuss the methods for building cyberresilience as a subset of organizational resilience. Furthermore, the chapter also aims to describe the metrics to measure cyberresilience.

Chapter 13 explains how in healthcare, the IoT offers enormous benefits for various stakeholders. One of its applications is remote monitoring of patients' health through healthcare wearable devices. Hence, a thorough understanding of the current trends in this segment is desirable for everyone interested in IoT deployment. However, the IoT remains in its introductory stage of product life cycle in the health-care field, especially in developing countries like India. Given the amount and sensitivity of health-related data, security and privacy need the utmost attention, especially if it is being exchanged with other devices, people, and organizations. The IoT deployment in healthcare raises numerous challenges such as identity management, interoperability, authentication, authorization, and management of several wearable connected devices. To understand the adoption of IoT in healthcare wearable devices, it is necessary not only to take cognizance of these challenges but also to devise pragmatic strategies to overcome them. This chapter makes an attempt to elucidate various sociotechnical challenges followed by possible solutions.

Chapter 14 briefs that any device that is a part of the IoT network can collect and transmit data, actuate devices based on triggers, receive information, and provide communication assistance. The device working on the concept of IoT usually comprises of sensors, communication modules (GSM, Bluetooth, WiFi, etc.), a control unit, and a power source. The main objective of this chapter is to throw light on implementing the concept of IoT in some home automation system by means of interfacing a microcontroller "Arduino Uno" with GSM Module "SIM 900A", so as to control the working of various home appliances connected with the help of a relay. This can be done with the help of short message service. The primary concern is to provide ease and convenience to a large number of users. With the advent of "Smart Home Technology", it is plausible to control, monitor, or access any device over the network and further make it possible to manage all devices from one place, even in remote areas. Hence, home automation has quickly paved its way in today's world for its simplicity and sense as well as the networking capability of the devices. The concept of IoT can be extended to various home applications, industries, as well as security systems such as guard alert systems, flood alert systems, and other smart systems. The data collected by the sensors, such as temperature, humidity, pressure, etc., can be accessed by the user via a browser or a mobile application, thus providing easy access to the devices in a user-friendly manner. With advancements in technology taking place at an accelerated pace, the day is not far when people are less concerned about their work because automation would have overpowered humans by then. A smart house should also be made secure and well connected with the owner. The main foundation is based on IoT. It also serves as a key component in home automation control systems using wireless technology. To ensure safety and security, electronic security systems are used.

Chapter 15 is devoted to defining the digital signature (DS), the security services provided by it, and the various schemes associated with DS as well as some of the relevant applications of DS. Basically, signature represents a combination of letters or figures written in a distinguished way that acts as a form of identification while conjointly authorizing a document or a formal letter. Every one of us is quite familiar with the notion of signature.

There have been several influences from our family and friends who have sacrificed a lot of their time and attention to ensure that we are kept motivated to complete this crucial project. To them, our deep thank you!

The editors are also thankful to all the members of CRC Press, especially Richard O'Hanley and Stephanie Place, for the opportunity to edit this book.

João Manuel R.S. Tavares
Brojo Kishore Mishra
Raghvendra Kumar
Noor Zaman
Manju Khari

Editors

João Manuel R.S. Tavares, Ph.D., graduated in mechanical engineering from the University of Porto, Portugal (1992). He also earned his M.Sc. and Ph.D. in electrical and computer engineering from the University of Porto in 1995 and 2001, respectively, and the habilitation in mechanical engineering in 2015. He is a senior researcher and project coordinator at the Instituto de Ciência e Inovação em Engenharia Mecânica e Engenharia Industrial (INEGI) and an associate professor at the Department of Mechanical Engineering of the Faculty of Engineering of the University of Porto (FEUP). He is a coeditor of more than 40 books, coauthor of more than 30 book chapters, 600 articles in international and national journals and conferences, and 3 international and 2 national patents. He has been a committee member of several international and national journals and conferences, is cofounder and coeditor of the book series *Lecture Notes in Computational Vision and Biomechanics* published by Springer, founder and editor-in-chief of the journal *Computer Methods in Biomechanics and Biomedical Engineering: Imaging & Visualization* published by Taylor & Francis, and cofounder and cochair of the international conference series: CompIMAGE, ECCOMAS VipIMAGE, ICCEBS, and BioDental. Also, he has been (co)supervisor of several M.Sc. and Ph.D. theses and supervisor of several postdoc projects, and has participated in many scientific projects both as researcher and as scientific coordinator. His main research areas include computational vision, medical imaging, human posture and gait, computational mechanics, scientific visualization, human–computer interaction, and new product development. (More information can be found at www.fe.up.pt/~tavares).

Brojo Kishore Mishra, Ph.D., is an associate professor (IT) and an institutional IQAC coordinator at the C.V. Raman College of Engineering (Autonomous), Bhubaneswar, India. He received his M.Tech. and Ph.D. degrees in computer science from Berhampur University in 2008 and 2012, respectively. Currently, he is guiding 5 Ph.D. research scholars at Biju Pattnaik University of Technology, Odisha. He has been selected as a state student coordinator (Odisha) and regional student coordinator (CSI Region—IV) of Computer Society of India in 2015–16 and 2016–17, respectively. He has been elected as the National Nomination

Committee Member (2017–18) for Computer Society of India. Similarly, he has been selected as the IEEE Day Ambassador for Kolkata Section of IEEE Region—10 for 2015 and 2016, respectively. He was the Jury Coordination Committee Member of All IEEE Young Engineers' Humanitarian Challenge (AIYEHUM 2015) project competition organized by IEEE Region 10 (Asia Pacific). His research interests included at a mining and big data analysis, machine learning, soft computing, and evolutionary computation. He has already published more than 40 research papers in internationally reputed journals and referred conferences, 7 book chapters, has edited 1 book, and is acting as a member of the editorial board/associate editor/guest editor for various international journals. He served in the capacity of keynote speaker, plenary speaker, program chair, proceeding chair, publicity chair, and special session chairperson, and as member of program committees of many international conferences. He was associated with a CSI-funded research project as a principal investigator. He is a life member of ISTE, CSI, and member of IEEE, ACM, IAENG, UACEE, and ACCS.

Raghvendra Kumar, Ph.D., is working as an assistant professor in Computer Science and Engineering Department, L.N.C.T Group of College Jabalpur, Madhya Pradesh, India. He received his B. Tech. in computer science and engineering from SRM University, Chennai (Tamil Nadu), India, M.Tech. in computer science and engineering from KIIT University, Bhubaneswar, (Odisha) India, and Ph.D. in computer science and engineering from Jodhpur National University, Jodhpur (Rajasthan), India. He has published 86 research papers in international/ national journal and conferences, including IEEE, Springer, and ACM as well as served as session chair and cochair, and as technical program committee member in many international and national conferences and served as guest editors in many special issues from reputed journals (Indexed By: Scopus, ESCI). He also received the Best Paper Award in IEEE Conference 2013 and Young Achiever Award2016 by IEAE Association for his research work in the field of distributed database. His research areas are computer networks, data mining, cloud computing, and secure multiparty computations, theory of computer science and design of algorithms. He authored 12 computer science books in the field of data mining, robotics, graph theory, and Turing machine by IGI Global Publication, USA, IOS Press Netherland, Springer, Lambert Publication, Scholar Press, CRC Press, Springer, dupedia Publication, Chand Publication, and Laxmi Publication.

Noor Zaman, Ph.D., has completed his Ph.D. in IT from University Technology Petronas (UTP), Malaysia. He has 16 years of teaching and administrative experience internationally. He has an intensive background of academic quality in higher education besides scientific research activities. He had worked for academic accreditation for more than a decade and earned ABET accreditation twice for three programs at College of Computer Sciences and IT, King Faisal University Saudi Arabia. He also worked for the National Commission for Academic Accreditation and Assessment (NCAAA), Education Evaluation Commission Higher Education Sector (EECHES), formerly NCAAA Saudi Arabia, for institutional level accreditation. He also worked for National Computing Education Accreditation Council (NCEAC) Pakistan. He has experience in teaching advanced era technological courses, including android programming, mobile computing, and.Net programming.

He has authored several research papers in indexed and impact factor research journals/international conferences, edited six international reputed computer science area books, focused on research students, and has many publications to his credit. He has successfully completed more than 18 international research grants. He is associate editor, regional editor, editorial board member, PC member, and reviewer for several reputed international journals and conferences around the globe. He also chaired international conference sessions and presented session talks internationally. He has strong analytical, problem solving, interpersonal, and communication skills. His areas of interest include wireless sensor network, IoT, mobile application programming, ad hoc networks, cloud computing, Big Data, mobile computing, and software engineering.

Manju Khari, Ph.D., is an assistant professor at Ambedkar Institute of Advanced Communication Technology and Research, under Govt. of NCT Delhi, affiliated with Guru Gobind Singh Indraprastsha University, India. She is also a professor in-charge of the IT Services of the Institute and has more than 12 years of experience in network planning and management. She holds a Ph.D. in computer science and engineering from the National Institute of Technology Patna and received her master degree in information security from Ambedkar Institute Technology of Advanced Communication Technology and Research, Delhi, India. Her research interests include software testing, software quality, software metrics, information security, and nature-inspired algorithms. She has published 60 papers in refereed national and international journals and conferences, and has authored six book chapters and coauthored two books. She is a life member of various international and national research societies (SDIWC, IAENG, etc.). She is also a guest editor of *International Journal of Advanced Intelligence Paradigms*, reviewer for *International Journal of Forensic Engineering*, and Editorial Board Member of *International Journal of Software Engineering and Knowledge Engineering*.

Contributors

M. Alam
Department of Software
  Engineering and Computer
  Information System
Institute of Business Management
  (IoBM)
Ilma University
Karachi, Pakistan

Rohit Anand
Department of ECE
G.B. Pant Government Engineering
  College
New Delhi, India

Amiya Bhusan Bagjadab
Department of Computer Science and
  Engineering
Veer Surendra Sai University of
  Technology
Burla, India

Ranjan Kumar Behera
Department of Computer Science and
  Engineering
National Institute of Technology
Rourkela, India

Nityesh Bhatt
Institute of Management
Nirma University (IMNU)
Ahmedabad, India

Sukant Kishoro Bisoy
Department of Computer Science
  and Engineering,
C.V. Raman College of
  Engineering
Bhubaneswar, India

Jyotirmoy Chatterjee
Department of Computer Science
  and Engineering
GD-RCET
Bhilai, India

Apurv Singh Gautam
Symbiosis Institute of Technology
Symbiosis International (Deemed
  University)
Pune, India

Ravika Gupta
Department of Electronics &
  Communication Engineering
G.B. Pant Government Engineering
  College
New Delhi, India

Sudan Jha
School of Computer Engineering
Kalinga Institute of Industrial
  Technology
Bhubaneswar, India

Pooja Kamat
Symbiosis Institute of Technology
Symbiosis International (Deemed
    University)
Pune, India

Manju Khari
Department of Computer Science &
    Engineering
AIACT&R
New Delhi, India

Raghvendra Kumar
Computer Science and Engineering
    Department
LNCT College
Bhopal, India

Sambit Mahapatra
Department of Computer Science and
    Engineering
National Institute of Technology
Rourkela, India

Mirjana Maksimovic
Faculty of Electrical Engineering
University of East Sarajevo
East Sarajevo, Bosnia and Herzegovina

Anjana Mishra
Department of Information
    Technology
C.V. Raman College of Engineering
Bhubaneswar, India

Brojo Kishore Mishra
Department of Information
    technology
C. V. Raman College of Engineering
Bhubaneswar, India

Gaurav Mishra
Development Management Institute
Patna, India

Mamta Mittal
Department of Computer Science
    and Engineering
G.B. Pant Govt Engineering College
New Delhi, India

Ramesh C. Poonia
Amity Institute of Information
    Technology
Amity University
Jaipur, India

Sushree Bibhuprada B. Priyadarshini
Department of Computer Science and
    Engineering
Institute of Technical Education and
    Research (ITER)
Bhubaneswar, India

Jayanthi Ranjan
IT Department
IMT Ghaziabad
Ghaziabad, India

Santanu Kumar Rath
Department of Computer Science and
    Engineering
National Institute of Technology
Rourkela, India

Soobia Saeed
Department of Software
    Engineering and Computer
    Information System
Institute of Business Management
    (IoBM)
Ilma University
Karachi, Pakistan

Bibhudatta Sahoo
Department of Computer Science and
    Engineering
National Institute of Technology
Rourkela, India

Kshira Sagar Sahoo
Department of Computer Science and
   Engineering
National Institute of Technology
Rourkela, India

Rohit Sharma
Department of ECE
SRM University
Ghaziabad, India

Gulshan Shrivastava
Department of Computer Science
   and Engineering
National Institute of Technology Patna
Patna, India

Archana Singh
ASET, Amity University Uttar Pradesh
Noida, India

Pankaj Singh
Department of ECE
SRM University
Ghaziabad, India

Le Hoang Son
VNU University of Science
Vietnam National University
Hanoi, Vietnam

Mayank Tiwary
Product and Innovation Team
SAP Labs, Bangalore, India

Tina Tomažič
Faculty of Electrical engineering and
   computer science
University of Maribor
Maribor, Slovenia

Balakrishnan Unny
Institute of Management
Nirma University (IMNU)
Ahmedabad, India

Chapter 1

Security Threats in e-Commerce

Rohit Sharma and Pankaj Singh

SRM University Ghaziabad

Contents

1.1 Introduction to e-Commerce

For the majority of people, the term electronic business (as a less than dependable term assigned to site-based business) infers shopping at a part of the site called the World Wide Web. In any case, site-based business has an essentially broader degree and connects various business practices other than, basically, site shopping. A couple of individuals and electronic businesses use the term e-business when they are examining site-based business in a broader sense. In this chapter, we use the term site-based business in its broadest definition.

Website-based business infers the utilization of electronic information transmission to execute or improve any business procedure. A few people use the expression "website business" to mean online business, which specifically uses a website as its information transmission medium. IBM has characterized electronic business as "the change of key business forms using Internet innovations" [1,2].

Equipment security incorporates any gadgets used as part of running the website-based business site like system gadgets, website servers, database servers, and a customer's personal computer (PC). Securing the system with a legitimately arranged firewall that is just permitting ports required to get to the website-based business is a fundamental piece of system security. The website server and database server ought to be confined from different systems utilizing a system demilitarized zone (DMZ) to diminish any conceivable interruption traded off PCs on different systems behind the firewall. A DMZ or neutral territory is a different system included between an ensured organization and an outside system, with a specific goal to provide an extra layer of security.

Any product used as part of running a website-based business framework, for example, the working framework, website server program (Internet information services (IIS), Apache), and database and website programs, are pieces of programming security. The working framework is the fundamental part of security that ought to be arranged appropriately to deal with security helplessness. Programming and routinely discharged security patches ought to be frequently refreshed to fill gaps in security. The site improvement itself ought to guarantee assurance against assaults like treat harming, shrouded field control, parameter altering, support flood, and cross-site scripting. Site pages, where secret data is being entered, ought to be secured with a solid cryptography calculation [3].

Dependably, there has been obstructions and issues caused by various reasons in the realm of business. A website has an exceptionally huge part in the present exchange exercise. Many organizations utilize website-based businesses as the main method of working together or as one of the ways. As the utilization of website-based business develops, so do the hindrances and issues inside internet businesses. The issues of trust and security have been thoroughly examined, and are the essential and unsolved factors in website-based business. Numerous, both private and entrepreneurial, organizations don't feel secured or guaranteed by working together or as individuals inside website-based business. The absence of trust and security causes genuine hindrances in online business, which needs to be truly considered.

In spite of the fact that establishments in various countries try to reduce the hoodwinking or manhandle of credit cards by using Mastercard, purchasers go out on a limb while cooperating on the site. Establishments raise the assertion of clients, yet the likelihood for coercion is never zero.

An essential audit, which happened in United States among educators and experts, was about the security issues in site-based businesses. The survey's result showed that a majority of educators and authorities were worried about their online individual information, in view of the lack of trust with respect to security issues inside the website-based business. They are unable to find offensive long mailing list from better places, which could cause varieties of disease strike, spread of their own information, and their visa number.

Trust and security issues could be found both inside electronic businesses that associate with free organizations and electronic businesses accomplishing broader associations. Jonathan (2003) infers that the culprits every now and then attempt to trim the information of online purchasers by working up claimed "spoof goals," which are phony website regions. He suggests that such website districts are being made by using the Hypertext Markup Language (HTML) code of the website goals that are honest. By doing this, the wrongdoers make sense of how to make a site that looks exactly like the true-blue electronic business's site [3].

1.1.1 The Background of e-Commerce

Consistently, 1990s was a period when people considered online business as a site-based business. The site-based business started before the 1990s. The designers suggest that site-based businesses had, and continue to have, a constant, strong relationship with the Internet. The site-based business' genesis goes back to the Internet's establishment that started with military research during the 1970s. The wander name was Advanced Research Project Agency Network (DARPANET). It is superior than the normal results, four schools in the USA got the commitment of working up the thought recalling a genuine goal to trade the examination happening, security, between the colleges [3].

Designers declare that the first email was sent in 1972, and now looking into the foreseeable future, the relationship between the USA and Europe was made on the site. Concurrent with the designers, it was this affiliation that made site-based business a reality for most of the branches. After that, site-based businesses began to develop slowly in the beginning of 1990s, during which the online business had its own triumphs.

1.1.2 Delimitation

There are numerous segments that are imperative inside web business, which should be developed. Regardless, considering our limited resources, we have focused on trust and security inside web businesses. The assessment is required for quite recently in online business associations, i.e. trust and security issues and responds in due order regarding them would be thought about from the perspective of business to purchasers (B2C). This examination will be tied in with finding ways to make trust and security for customers while doing associations inside online business. As e-portion issue is a champion among the most fundamental factors inside online business, this examination will have a minor focus on it.

1.2 Advantages and Disadvantages of e-Commerce

1.2.1 Advantages of e-Commerce

The upsides of web business for business substances can be condensed as follows: site-based business can grow bargains and with less costs. A firm can use web business as far as possible and feature parcels that are comprehensively scattered geologically.

The probability of the little electronic businesses equals the broad electronic businesses due to little expenses realized by a virtual shop, and little electronic businesses are running up against with one less prevention in penetrating the business segments viably charged by gigantic electronic businesses. In view of the versatility and insight towards new ones, the little electronic business has an important position in examination with a generous one governed by bureaucracy and conservatism [4].

General market intrusion of working environment in the world structure is not restricted by outskirts, and it doesn't have a place with anybody, and the get to and era costs are tremendously low. The correspondence with a client on the opposite side of the world is as clear as the correspondence going on with some person in the same room. Any maker can now offer his products in any nation by the systems for the site, and no contacts with near to affiliations or wide speculations are basic any more.

Reduction of working expenses —These expenses might be undeniably diminished by the automatic of the requesting philosophy. There is likewise the likelihood of aggregate automatics by the mix with the affiliation structure thus actuating the expansion of the general benefit of the affiliation.

New conceivable outcomes for playing out a speedy publicizing (balanced)— Compared with an individual, the PC may hold not only the name and individual information of all clients but also their inclinations, which the site can use to alter what they are offered and introduced to compared to other clients. The examination of the clients on location might be refined using every single piece of accessible information, for example, locale, sort of program, and operation structure, the site where they do start from course slants and the clients won't grasp at all that they are subject to such examination. This is the reason why many consider this as an encroachment of the individual closeness.

■ Electronic business diminishes the cost of making, preparing, disseminating, securing, and recovering paper-based data. For instance, by showing an electronic secure framework, affiliations can cut the regulatory expenses by 85 percent.

- Ability for making certain affiliations. For instance, puppy toys which can be sold just in pet shops or division and physical world discount stores, are now sold in a specific www.dogtoys.com.
- Electronic business licenses reduced inventories and overhead by enabling "draw"-sort stock framework association. In a power sort framework, the system begins from client requests and uses without a moment to information gathering.
- The power sort preparation empowers costly customization of things and electronic businesses, which gives high ground to its implementers. An unbelievable case is Dell Computer Corp, whose case will be depicted later.
- Electronic trade diminishes the time between the cost of capital and the receipt of things and electronic businesses.

1.2.2 Benefits to Consumers

The advantages of electronic commerce (EC) to purchasers are as follows [5]:

- Electronic trade empowers clients to shop or do different exchanges in 24 hours consistently, persisting as the year advanced, from any range.
- Electronic trade outfits clients with more decisions; electronic business always equips clients with more sensible things and electronic businesses by engaging them to shop in many places and leads to close examinations.
- From time to time, particularly with digitized products, EC permits fast development.
- Customers can get essential and isolated data in seconds, rather than days or weeks.
- Electronic business makes it conceivable to partake in virtual offers.
- Electronic business engages clients to interface with different clients in electronic social affairs and trade contemplations and analyze encounters.
- Electronic business engages rivalry, which acknowledges huge rebates.

1.2.3 Benefits to Society

The upsides of EC to society are indicated as follows:

- Electronic trade draws in more people to work from home and hence less transportation needed to go shopping and working, which leads to less activity in the city and lower air pollution.
- Electronic trade engages some stock to be sold at lowered costs, so less well-to-do individuals can purchase intelligently and increment their way of life.
- Electronic trade empowers individuals in Third World nations and country regions to recognize things and electronic businesses that generally are not open to them.

- This connects chances to learn explanations behind living and increment higher instructions.
- Electronic trade underpins development of open associations, for example, remedial organizations, planning, and spread of government social associations at a decreased cost. Helpful organizations, electronic businesses, for instance, can fulfill patients in like manner locales.

1.2.4 e-Commerce Disadvantages

Notwithstanding the way that the summary of web business purpose of intrigue is long, the online business condition has not yet come full circle. Likewise, the development is not impeccable. In addition, the thin and slimmer site-based business edges suggest that staying in business can transform into a reliably creating fight. Perhaps the best concern incorporates security, loss of assurance, low and remote organization levels, and complex genuine issues. We will take a look at each of these issues next [5].

1.2.4.1 Shrouded Costs

Notwithstanding the way that acquiring online is helpful, the accommodation cost is not clear at the front end. For instance, online purchases are often accompanied by high transportation and restocking costs, nonappearance of affirmation scope, and prohibited development times. The online purchases must be passed on, and the transportation charges might be immense. Some online business officials argue that the additional charges are genuinely a path for them to recuperate compensation they lost in the perspective of additional thin net livelihoods with which they traditionally work. This contention gives inadequate comfort to the client.

1.2.4.2 System Unreliability

With more than 100 million customers in North America alone, the Internet is an incredibly clamoring information thoroughfare. Regardless of the way that the Internet is planned to overcome the single reason for dissatisfaction issues, there have been a couple of particularly propelled scenes of framework disillusionments for the past couple of years. Right when an online business webpage can't profit off any customer since its Internet affiliation is down, there is an option that is other than a momentary interruption. A site-based business site that can't serve its customers loses arrangements, acceptability, and even customers. In fact, a framework dissatisfaction can appear differently in relation to having a zone at a prohibitive strip mall that is in focal point of no place and has no facing streets that incite it.

1.2.4.3 The Cost of Remaining in Business

We included operational cost funds and lower points of confinement of section in the rundown of online business positive conditions. That is, getting into business is generally less troublesome in an online business condition. Shockingly, the inverse side of the coin is that remaining in business might be more troublesome. To be profitable, e-affiliations must keep up high courses of action volumes—which along these lines propose making and keeping up an important and continuing client base. Drawing in clients and changing them into go over purchasers is the best way to deal with productivity. For instance, since its creation in 1997, CheapTickets. com has constructed a client base of more than 7 million enrolled clients that have engaged the relationship to stay as such. To survive and stay commanding, affiliations must place unequivocally in exorbitant progression [6].

The presentation of PC progression inside a business robotizes the business procedure and furthermore changes the way the affiliation collaborates inside and remotely. (The level of change is a part of the affiliation's status to get and sort out improvement.) Such joint exertion among progression and business operations makes the affiliation more subject to advancement, making it frailer against the pace and speed with which improvement occurs. Along these lines, affiliations have a tendency to get on an improvement meander treadmill, recalling a definitive target to stay focused. For instance, Delta Airlines contributed around 1 billion dollars on the movement of its Delta Nervous System (DNS) headway to overhaul its operations [7].

Unmistakably, headway is a blended present for any business in the online business condition; its appropriate utilization can position the relationship to get epic prizes and its utilization can induce the affiliation's quick passing. The essential concern progression a boss can ensure is the closeness of steady mechanical change and every single one of the costs related with such change. More shocking, in light of the way that site-based business is respectably new and changes constantly, there is no game plan of perceived models to take after. Most site-based attractive systems of action depend on a development of an extraordinary degree of trapped courses of action, and the majority of them are untested and unproved.

1.2.4.4 Absence of Human Contact

One of the central blockades to the wide affirmation of web business by electronic businesses and clients alike is the evident nonappearance of acceptable security in online trades. For example, buyers are dynamically exhausted about giving their Mastercard information over the Internet. In the past couple of years, the press has been stacked with reports about developers breaking into e-business destinations and assuming responsibility of card information. Generally speaking, the break-ins passed unnoticed for some time before either the merchant or the buyer found the issue.

1.2.4.5 Absence of Security

Guaranteeing the security of the data is of superior importance to clients and to the worthiness of the business. Clients additionally stress over the security repercussions of information amassed by relationships of various sorts and sizes. The amazing information storing process is a blended gift to clients. Definitely, even and not any clearer information level, deals data is secured in databases related with site servers, subsequently showing the data to mechanized lawbreakers. Since information assembling on the site is so customary, databases routinely contain data about clients acquiring affinities, estimation information, credit data, etc. Most of the time, affiliations offer client database data to publicizing affiliations. Accordingly, publicizing affiliations take an interest in gigantic email battles to pull in new clients. It doesn't take years for the client's email box to be stacked with bothersome and unconstrained emails (known as "spam"). The many offers of individual firewalls and the high number of "hits" for help with security issues are a declaration of how clients are consistently stressed over their online protection, and their search for approaches to shield themselves from mechanized aggressors [8].

1.2.4.6 Low Organization Levels

Another major dissent about coordinating online is the low level of client advantage that online affiliations tend to give. Despite the way that progression has robotized business exchanges to a colossal degree, there remains a bona fide essential for the human touch. Thus, client advantage has changed into a basic separating component. Since the site purchasing learning is altogether more nonexclusive than the conventional one, giving exceptional client advantage is fundamental to the survival of any e-business. Along these lines, site-based business goals must give

- A stunning and issue-free prerequesting and requesting establishment. The site building is a significant interface.
- Instantly accessible feasibly use input choices. Veritable client differences join the nonappearance of contact data on areas and the burden of accomplishing a client advantage pro.
- Convenient and beneficent strife affirmation.
- Consummate—and immaterial effort—transport and impel development of stock to clients.

1.2.4.7 Legitimate Issues

Good old fashioned issues experienced in the web business condition cement programming and copyright infringements. The measure of illegal substances available on the Internet appears as indicated by the Napster case. Napster, an acclaimed music webpage, was sued by the Recording Industry Association, since it upheld a noteworthy number of unlawful moved copies of copyrighted tunes that were uninhibitedly downloaded by various customers around the globe. After court action, Napster was obliged to change its course of action of development and to wipe out all unlawful material from its site.

Charge card coercion and stolen identities. The nonattendance of security we said before has put Mastercard terrorizing on the acclaimed front burner. Also, nonappearance of security makes it genuinely easy to remember another person's character to make counterfeit trades. Loss of trust in the security of online trades is a brake in the e-business outline.

1.2.4.8 Technical Limitations of EC

The specific necessities of EC are as indicated by the following [9]:

- Nonattendance of structure security, unfaltering quality, tenets, and some correspondence conventions.
- There is a deficiency with regard to media transmission and data transmission.
- The change instruments are so far advancing and growing quickly.
- Vendors may require stand-out website servers and different structures, regardless of system servers.
- Some EC programming will not fit with some equipment or with some working structures or different parts. Over the long haul, these constraints will decrease or be beaten; true-blue coordination can restrict their effect.

1.2.4.9 Nontechnical Limitations

The basic nontechnical limitations that direct the spread of EC are as follows:

- Security and prosperity: Following issues are essential in the B2C space, particularly security threats which are accepted to be more true blue than they really are when proper encryption is used. Affirmation measures are reliably best in class. In any case, the clients see these issues as objectives, and the e-commerce business has a long undertaking of convincing clients that online exchanges and protection are, truly, phenomenally secure.
- Other convincing portions. Nonattendance of touch and feel on the site. Two out of three clients value the chance to touch things, for example, bits of garments and get a kick out of the chance to know completely what they are procuring.
- Many lawful issues are so far faulty, and government headings and gages are not refined enough for a couple of conditions.
- Electronic business is 'as of recently making and progressing quickly.' Various individuals are chasing down a predictable zone before they go into it.

As experience assembles and advancement improves, the extent of EC points of interest to costs will increase, realizing a more critical rate of EC gathering. The potential points of interest may not be inducing enough inspirations to start EC workout.

1.3 e-Commerce Technologies

A couple of advances are required for a web business to exist. The clearest one is the site. Past that plan of interconnected frameworks, various other present-day programming and gear parts are relied upon to give the required help structure: database programming, arrange focuses, encryption hardware, programming, and the web. Procedures to partner all items and hardware segments in just the right way to deal with electronic business are changing and propelling standards. The rate of advancement is quick for all segments that assist electronic business. Any business that partakes in online business and needs to battle later on must change in accordance with new site progression. The normal web business over trouble anticipates that electronic businesses will find faster and more capable ways to deal with the routinely extending surge of online clients and the growing movement between electronic businesses [10].

Two sorts of encryption procedures offer tried and true protection to e-exchange associations. They are symmetric and unbalanced.

1.3.1 Symmetric Encryption

Symmetric encryption may likewise be recommended as a single key. In symmetric encryption, the same key is used both to encode and decode messages. Reliable symmetric encryption checks join Advanced Encryption Standard (AES), Data Encryption Standard (DES), Triple Data Encryption Algorithm (3DES), and Rivest Cipher 4 (RC4). Calculations of symmetric encryption can be to a staggering degree lively and less complex, which considers direct use in equipment.

1.3.2 Asymmetric Encryption

Asymmetric encryption is mostly called open-key cryptography or two-key encryption, in which two keys are used: one for encryption and the other for interpretation. The most comprehensive open-key encryption tally is Rivest–Shamir–Adleman (RSA).

1.3.3 Secure Socket Layer

The e-exchange business is tied in with benefitting and finding ways to deal with benefit. Regardless, it is hard if the customers don't feel safe executing a trade on your website. The server, which is basically another name for a PC, stores information about your site for overview by the customers and others must have a modernized Secure Sockets Layer (SSL) support. SSL gives these verifications and can read them. SSL announcements begin from a trusted pariah that can guarantee the encryption process. The SSL underwriting is a proof that the server is the thing that it says it is. Having an SSL makes it harder for fraudsters to put on a show to be another server [10].

1.3.4 Digital Signature

In the perspective of individuals when all is said and done, key cryptographic techniques joined with data hashing limits, for instance, MD-5 and SHA-1 mechanized imprints, are executed to check the beginning stage and substance of the online trade, which means purchasers showing their identity to shippers in the trade give nondisavowal features.

A propelled signature capacity with regard to an electronic record like a composed by hand signature enhances the circumstance printed reports. The physically composed check is an unforgeable piece of data that announces that a named individual formed or by and large agreed to the file to which the stamp is associated. A mechanized mark truly gives a more essential level of security than the physically composed check. The recipient of a painstakingly stamped message can affirm that the message started from the person whose check is joined and that the message has not been changed either deliberately or accidentally since it was settled upon. Additionally, secure automated imprints can't be denied, and this suggests that the endorser of a record can't later surrender it by ensuring that the stamp was delivered. Toward the day's end, propelled marks engage "approval" of modernized messages, ensuring that the recipient of a propelled message of both the identity of the sender and the respectability of the message [11].

1.3.5 Electronic Certificates

Automated Certificate is a technique for showing the character of people in electronic trades, much like a driver allow or a universal ID does in eye-to-eye collaboration. With a Digital Certificate, you can ensure business accomplices, mates, and online organizations that the electronic information they get from you is real. Propelled Certificates join a personality to a few electronic keys that can be utilized to encode and sign the modernized data. A Digital Certificate makes it possible to affirm an individual's claim that they have the benefit to use a given key, shielding customers from using misrepresentation keys to imitate distinctive customers. Certification Authority is issued a Digital Certificate and checked using the Certification Authority's private key. Propelled Certificates can be used for an arrangement of electronic trades that consolidates email, electronic exchange, groupware, and electronic resource trades.

1.3.6 Wise Cards

A wise card can be described as a plastic card with estimations like traditional charge/Mastercards, into which an electronic contraption has been solidified to allow information to amass. Moreover, it prudently has an organized circuit chip with data dealing with constraint. Clever cards are regularly detached into two orders: chip cards and memory cards are typically named keen cards for their capacity to take care of data and the propelled estimations embedded in them. The nonattendance of security and fear of software engineers are some of the reasons that have caused the direct improvement of online natural business trades among individuals and wanders, all things considered to be called consumer-to-business web business. Despite the amount of the bursts, charge cards are being used as one of the portion instruments over the Internet. For whatever period of time that business trades over the Internet are not exceptionally marvelous in the number and have a little individual money related regard, the honest-to-goodness threat could be considered at a low or satisfactory risk. At the point when this kind of trade gets client conviction and the volume grows, it will pull in more blackmail work out, in this manner, extending the level of risk presentation. One of the framework that has begun to be used as a piece in France and diverse countries is the sagacious card with a Chip-Secure Electronic Transaction (C-SET) tradition for online confirmation. This affirms both the card and the customer, and in this way offers a portion guarantee without customer's nonrefusal [11].

1.3.7 Electronic Money

Electronic money or mechanized cash (DC) is an electronic methodology portion on the Internet, with the result that money is traded beginning with one record and then onto the following. One can imagine a DC trade as a remote exchange grandstand, as real money is changed over to DC before it can be spent. When making a purchase, a buyer will send a "propelled coin" message mixed with its private key containing his identity, the measure of the coin, Internet address, its serial number, and expiry date. A record is kept of that trade to ensure that the coin is not spent twice. The propelled coin is also encoded with the shipper's open key. The merchant unscrambles the propelled coin with his private key and affirms the message. The sponsor must check the serial number of the propelled coin to certify that it is up until now present and has not been starting as now spent. The benefactor by then credits the dealer's budgetary adjustment with the cash and a while later crosses out the serial number.

1.4 Characteristics of e-Commerce Technologies

The following are the qualities of internet business advancements [2]:

1. *Ease of robotized preparation:* A payer has the ability to effectively mechanize the era and handling of different installments with negligible exertion and cost. Earlier, the reliance upon banks to deal with most installments and the absence of a shoddy, universal correspondence innovation made robotization of installment forms costly and hard to set up.
2. *Immediacy of result:* Payment happens instantaneously on account of mechanization and the capacity of the middle of the road frameworks and suppliers to process installments progressively. Manual paper-based frameworks cause a period delay because of the prerequisite of human mediation all the while.
3. *Openness:* The openness of poor enlisting and trades advancement, and fitting programming engages little attempts and individuals to get to or give an extent of portion benefits that were in advance recently available to far-reaching relationship by methods for conferred frameworks or the esteem-based dealing with units of bank.
4. *Loss of guarantee data:* The new innovation gets rid of, or modifies, security data going on with exchanges. This data has customarily been a piece of exchange and depends on the executing gatherings to approve singular installments. Insurance data can be characterized as data
   - which is not basic to the significance and expectation of an exchange.
   - which is regularly accidental to the idea of the interchange channel over which the exchange is directed; yet by and by gives helpful logical data to at least one of the gatherings to the exchange.
5. *Globalization:* The minimization of land factors in making portions is an unquestionable piece of the new portion structure. Its effect is upon ranges, for instance, size of the portion's business focus, precariousness as to legitimate domain if there should arise an occurrence of verbal confrontation, zone and the limit of a portion want to rapidly change in accordance with authoritative organizations constrained by one country.
6. *New plans of action:* New plans of action are being created to misuse the new installment advancements, specifically to address or exploit the disintermediation of clients from customary installment suppliers, for example, banks. Disintermediation is the place the innovation empowers an outsider to intercede between the client and the keeping money framework, adequately exchanging the client's put stock in association with the bank to the new party.

1.5 Security Threats to e-Commerce

Electronic business security requirements can be considered by taking a look at the general method, beginning with the buyer and finishing with the exchange server. Considering each sound association in the "business chain," the advantages that must be secured to ensure secure online business consolidate client PCs, the messages going on the correspondence channel, and the site and exchange servers including any gear added to the servers. While communicate correspondences are undeniably one of the genuine preferences to be guaranteed, the media interchange connects are not by any method the main stress in PC and site-based business security. For instance, if the correspondence connects were attempted secure, yet no wellbeing endeavors were executed for either client PCs or exchange and site servers, no trade security would exist for any extent of the creative energy [8,12].

1.5.1 Client Dangers

Until the introduction of executable site content, website pages were principally static. HTML-coded, static pages could do negligible more than indicate substance. In any case, the extensive usage of dynamic substance has changed this perception.

A. *Active substance:* Active substance implies programs that are introduced clearly in website pages and that reason action to happen. Dynamic substance can indicate moving outlines, download and play sound, or complete online spreadsheet programs. Dynamic substance is used as a piece of online business to put things one wishes to become tied up with a shopping wicker bin and to enlist the total receipt aggregate, including bargains cost, dealings, and shipping costs.

B. *Malicious codes:* Computer diseases, worms, and trojan stallions are instances of noxious code. A trojan stallion is a program that plays out an important limit, and plays out a startling movement as well.

Server-side camouflaging: Masquerading traps a setback into assuming that the substance with which it is passing on is a substitute component. For example, if a customer tries to sign into a PC over the site, yet rather accomplishes another PC to be the desired one, the customer has been caricatured. This may be a reserved attack (in which the customer does not attempt to approve the recipient, yet rather basically gets to it), yet it is ordinarily a dynamic strike (in which the impostor issues responses to trick the customer about its character).

1.5.2 Communication Channel Perils

The site fills in as the electronic chain accomplice a buyer (client) to a web business resource (exchange server). Messages on the site travel a whimsical course from a source center point to an objective core of interest. The message experiences various captivating PCs on the structure before accomplishing the last objective. It is hard to guarantee that every PC on the site through which messages pass is safe, secure, and nonadversarial.

A. Confidentiality dangers: Secrecy is the retaliation of unapproved information presentation. Shooting enigma on the site isn't troublesome. Recognize when one logs onto a site—say www.anybiz.com—that contains an edge with content boxes for name, address, and email address. When one changes those substance boxes and taps the submit, the information is sent to the site server for orchestrating. One commanding framework for transmitting data to a site server is to gather the substance box responses and place them toward the whole of the goal server's URL. On getting the data, the HTTP request to send the data to the server is then sent. A little later, the customer adjusts his choice, picks not to sit tight for a response from the anybiz.com server, and bobs to another site rather—say www.somecompany.com. The server at somecompany.com may hoard site monetary perspectives and log the URL from which the customer just came (www.anybiz.com). By doing this, somecompany.com has broken security by recording the flabbergast information the customer has begun to enter.

B. Integrity dangers: A faithfulness chance exists when an unapproved gathering can modify a message stream of information. Unprotected dealing with a record trade is in the risk to dependability encroachment. Automated vandalism is an event of trustworthiness encroachment. Motorized vandalism is the electronic harming of a present site page. Camouflaging or epitomizing—putting on a show to be some individual you are not or watching out for a site as an extraordinary when it is genuinely fake—is a procedure for making annihilation on objectives. Using a security opening in a space name server (DNS), obligated social affairs can substitute the address of their site set up of the tenable one to spoof site visitors. Steadfast dangers can change essential cash related, medicinal, or military information. It can have an honest approach for affiliations and people.

C. Availability dangers: The illumination behind openness threats, generally called deferral or sensible irregularity perils, is to outrage standard PC overseeing or to deny getting ready totally. For example, if the organizing pace of a specific ATM trade moderates from conceivably a couple of moments to 30 seconds, customers will leave ATMs completely. So likewise, planning any system access will drive customers to contenders' site or business destinations.

1.5.3 Server Risks

The server is the third relationship in the customer website server trio, epitomizing the web business route between the client and a business server. Servers have vulnerabilities that can be mistreated by anyone and can make arrangements to cause decimation or to unlawfully get data.

A. *Website-server perils:* Site server composing PC programs is wanted to pass on-site pages by reacting to HTTP asks. While site server composing PC programs is not naturally high shot, it has been portrayed out with site association and settlement as the lead plan objective. The more impulsive the thing is, the higher the likelihood that it contains coding mess-ups (bugs) and security gaps—security lacks that give openings through which blackguards can enter.

B. *Commerce server risks:* The exchange server, close to the site server, responds to requests from site programs through the HTTP custom and Common Gateway Interface (CGI) substance. A few bits of programming contain the two-way server programming, which includes a File Transfer Protocol server, an email server, a login server, and working structures on machines. Each of these can have security openings and bugs.

C. *Common entryway interface threats:* A regular door interface (CGI) executes the exchange of data from a site server to another program, for example, a database program. CGI and the undertakings to which they exchange information give dynamic substance to site pages. Since CGIs are programs, they exhibit a security risk if misused.

D. *Password hacking:* The most direct trap against a secret key-based structure is to figure out passwords. Guessing passwords requires that entrance to the supplement, as far as possible, to be gotten. In the event that none of these have changed when the secret key is guessed, the assailant can utilize the watchword to get to the framework.

1.6 Security Necessities and Security Approach

1.6.1 Security Necessities

Amidst this stage, the security needs of an undertaking are recognized. These requirements are represented by the need to ensure the accompanying security qualities [12,13]:

1.6.1.1 Authentication

Authentication is the capacity to state that an e-correspondence does really originate from who it implies to. Without close and personal contact, passing oneself off as another person is not troublesome on the website.

In e-trade, the best barrier against being misdirected by a fraud is given by unforgeable computerized authentications from a put stock in specialist (for example, VeriSign). Despite the fact that anybody can produce computerized declarations for themselves, a trusted expert requests true evidence of character and checks its legitimacy before issuing an advanced testament. Just testaments from trusted specialists will be consequently perceived and trusted by the real website program and email customer programming.

1.6.1.2 Privacy

In e-business, insurance is the ability to prove that data is gotten to and changed just by endorsed social events. Frequently, this is proficient by methods of encryption. Delicate data (for instance, charge card purposes of enthusiasm, prosperity records, bargain figures, etc.) are encoded before being transmitted over the open site by methods for email or the site. Data which has been secure with strong 128-piece encryption may be obstructed by software engineers, however, can't be decoded by them in a short time span. Afresh, propelled supports are used here to encode email or set up an ensured HTTP relationship with a site server. For extra security, data can be likewise secured in a mixed association.

1.6.1.3 Approval

Authorization enables a man or PC framework to decide whether somebody has the expertise to ask for or support an activity or data. In the physical world, confirmation is normally accomplished by frames requiring marks, or bolts where just approved people hold the keys.

1.6.1.4 Integrity

Trustworthiness of data proposes guarantee that a correspondence has not been changed or irritated. All things considered, this issue has been regulated by tight control over access to paper records and requiring avowed officers to start all developments made a framework with obvious downsides and objectives. In the event that some individual is enduring delicate data on the site, he not only wants to guarantee that it is beginning from who he presumes that it will (endorse), yet likewise that it hasn't been gotten by a product build while in travel and its substance adjusted. The speed and parcels attracted with online correspondences require an outright different way to deal with this issue from standard methods [13].

Nonrefusal: Nondissent is the capacity to ensure that once some individual has asked for an association or verified an activity, they can't turn and say, "I didn't do that!" Nonrefusal engages one to truly show that a man sent an email or influenced a buy to help from a website. For the most part, nondenial has been capable by having parties sign contracts and after that have the assertions confirmed by place stock in outsiders. Sending reports fused the use of enlisted mail, and stamps and record the arrangement of transmission and attestation. In the space of site-based business, noncontradict is capable by utilizing pushed marks. Mechanized engravings that have been issued by a confided genius (for example, VeriSign) can't be outlined, and their genuineness can be checked with any basic email or site program. A pushed stamp is lately introduced in the PC of its proprietor, who is routinely required to give a riddle key to make utilization of motorized check to encode or purposely sign their correspondences. On the off chance that an affiliation gets a buy sort out by strategies for email that has been decisively stamped, it has an indistinct true-blue assertion on receipt of a physical checked contract.

1.6.2 Security Policy

The essential stroll in securing an electronic business structure is making and executing a dynamic archive called a security course of action, which sees framework edges, for example, security objectives and risks. It is fundamental to set up who the confirmed clients may be, the path by which they will get to the framework and information, how unapproved clients will be denied get to, and how information will be secured inside the alliance and furthermore outside the connection.

A security approach must address a connection's particular hazards. To comprehend dangers, a fitting player should play out a security review that sees vulnerabilities and rates, both the genuineness of each peril and its probability of happening. The present modernized economy offers more zones for peril to be presented through the relationship of different social events, for example, providers, wholesalers, clients, and aides. Scientists feature the impelling need to address enter examine issues in force security movement strategies. Particular difficulties to approach examine raised by Lichtenstein solidify the need to address the not especially depicted substance and dealing with of substance in course of action progress [14].

1.6.2.1 Privacy

Security is an idea that is not effortlessly characterized, but rather it is frequently thought of as a good or legitimate right. Clarke depicts security as the "intrigue people have in supporting individual space free from obstruction by other individuals and associations." Protection along these lines influences electronic business customers and additionally shoppers, or partners, in different spaces. Consider, for instance, the part of a patient's data protection in the medicinal services industry, as investigated in a recent report. The examination measured protection impression of representatives having everyday introduction to data preparing exercises. The discoveries reasoned that workers are torn between their regard for individual protection and the need, regardless of whether forced by administration or through individual consideration to gather individual data. Correspondingly, there exists a need to investigate the same issues inside the setting of creating electronic trade applications.

Accordingly, security seals (e.g. TRUSTe, BBBonline, and WebsiteTrust) recommend to keep the presentation of enactment if organizations cannot viably accomplish self-direction. On the other hand, the P3P extend (Platform for Privacy Practices Project) offers a way to empower Internet clients to practice inclinations over Website protection hones. Data protection is affected by hierarchical capacities, for example, electronic business, database administration, security methods, broadcast communications, collective frameworks, and framework usage. Designers of electronic business frameworks should know about this association and understand the requirement for early protection arrangement. Plainly, it is important to consider these elements throughout the necessities assurance and programming outline of electronic business frameworks.

Security Policy: A protection approach is characterized as an exhaustive portrayal of a Website practice, which is situated in one place on the website page and might be effectively gotten to [10].

Each electronic business engaged with electronic trade exchange has a duty to embrace and execute a strategy for ensuring the security of separately identifiable data. electronic businesses additionally need to consider different associations with which they connect and make strides that cultivate the selection and usage of powerful online protection arrangements by those electronic businesses. In spite of the fact that associations with electronic exchanges ought to uncover a security arrangement that depends on reasonable data rehearses, the Georgetown Internet Privacy Policy Survey found that Internet protection divulgences did not generally reflect reasonable data hones.

This features the requirement of electronic business experts to pick up involvement in creating legitimate protection arrangements and for specialists to approach prescriptive direction for indicating the comparison of framework necessities.

1.6.2.2 Security Infrastructure

The security system is the execution of the security technique. The security structure is the development that secures the electronics-business and the protocols by which it works. A couple of instances of this include

A. Implementing mystery word developing and distroy
B. Implementing the flightiness of passwords
C. Blocking limited outbound relationship from the firewall
D. Requiring mechanized revelations to check remote get to relationship with an organization
E. Requiring recognizable pieces of proof for physical access to building
F. In a made log, it is required to record all physical access to servers.

Moreover, the security framework involves dealing with the conduct of both IT and human assets.

It ought to be routinely policed:

A. Who checks composed logs?
B. How regularly are firewall reports checked?

For durability, it must be authorized. The punishments for ruptures of the security strategy must be clarified to all representatives and accomplices and must be upheld if approach prerequisites are broken or disregarded.

1.7 Solution for Trust

As trust is a basic factor to get the feelings of purchasers to make web business a completely tried and true business focus, a couple of factors are displayed as answers for the place stock in issues inside site-based business. Four trusting feelings and seven essential variables are listed.

1.7.1 Four Trusting Convictions

The essential trusting conviction is Belief in the sympathetic actions of the website shipper, which is about the purchaser understanding the traits of the merchant, for instance, careful, concern, agreeable mentality, etc. The makers infer that the way buyers are being managed and treated by the online business merchants hugely influences the customer's trust towards web business [15].

The third conviction, Belief in the limit of the website merchant, is the thing and electronic business the sellers oblige the purchasers. The fashioners guarantee that the electronic business wires from the minute a buyer enters a website page to the very end, which would never end. Exceptional association is required under the entire strategy (conveying, requesting, transporting, advantage after the course of action, dealing with customers' stress, and whatnot). The things' condition ought to be as staggering, accepting more unfortunate, as it appeared on the website, so the purchasers don't feel deluded and get frustrated. The architects raise the criticalness of this conviction and propose that the electronic business obliging buyers, the way clients encounter the website page, and satisfaction of the buyers' needs to have a fundamental part making trust among the purchasers.

1.7.2 Seven Basic Factors That Influence Trust

The seven basic factors that affect trust impact buyers toward affiliations in diverse ways. The first is bolster, which clarifies that the more a website page is imperative, the more it is trustworthy for the buyers. The originators propose that when a client gets fused with a web page, he or she needs to accomplish his or her goals in the most direct way. That is the reason why a website page ought to be extraordinarily important for meeting the objectives of the clients. The second is straightforwardness in utilization; the less intricate it is to utilize a website page, the more it contributes trust among clients. The planners derive that it ought not be hard for purchasers to utilize the website page, and it ought to be fundamental for buyers to utilize the website page from various perspectives. For instance, it ought to be anything but elusive, the things they need to purchase, to approach, and to effortlessly find the data they require and whatnot. On the off chance, a website page cheats the purchasers it happens as intended into question among the customers [16].

The third fundamental factor that effects trust is called the thought and spread factor, which picks whether the website page acts in a way that matches the best central focus of the client. The fashioners giving a respectable case to this factor is the relentless nature of the data that is on the website page. The architects specify that it is critical that the data on the website page is absolutely significant and is not impartial pronouncements; overall, the website page could lose adequacy among its buyers.

1.7.3 Secure Trading for Electronic Businesses Makes Trust

Agreeing with Tryggehandel.se, every electronic business needs to make a better than average relationship with its customers to have a successful business. This accomplishment can't be possible without creating a trust between the electronic businesses and buyers. It is up to the electronic businesses to exhibit that every client should feel secured and have the trust from the electronic business. To fulfill the solicitation and gain ground, 12 components should be considered, which are indicated as follows [12]:

- *Company's detail:* The electronic business's name and legitimate component should be clearly communicated. The detectable quality of enlistment number of the electronic business, street address, email address, and phone number are key. This makes it easier for the purchasers to find each required unpretentious components successfully, in the period of issue or whatever the case. In case there is any specific opening hours for assisting the customers, the timings should be clearly displayed on the site.
- *The company's support and availability:* The electronic business should reach the customer by email within 48 hours from the minute they get the order. If it is unreasonable to reach in 2 days' time, the electronic business should elucidate the reason for putting off an order to have an average help and availability structure. The electronic business ought to show interests and give the customers a feeling of centrality.
- *The consumer's right to get help:* The buyer always approaches the electronic business for help with regard to criticism, extraction, and other help related to the purchase or demand, paying little respect to the likelihood that the electronic business itself does not offer the thing or organization.
- *Delivery time:* The purchaser must be taught at the time of obtainment about the most extraordinary transport time, not long after the demand has been made. In case the electronic business can't pass on the stock or organization before the agreed time, the client should be instructed as fast as time grants. If it happens twice, the customers have the benefit to scratch off the purchase at no cost.
- *Refunding:* The customer has the benefit to recover the trade before 30 days, i.e. the occasion that he or she scratches off a demand from the date the electronic business got the message.
- *Return policy:* The buyer should be instructed and be made aware of the withdrawal course of action. The name and addresses where purchasers can return to should moreover be outlined. A buyer should have the benefit to reestablish a formally opened package to affirm if the product works. With purchasing

organizations, the organization should be profitable from the minute the assertion happens. In case the organization has begun before the extraction time period (14 days) slips by, the electronic business, with the customer's underwriting, instructs the buyer that the benefit of withdrawal stops and the time advantage begins [16].

■ *Complaints and seller's guarantee:* The customer must be balanced for any conveyance charges. Secure site-based business support electronic businesses ensure to take care of the Consumer Complaints Board's proposition. The terms of confirmation given by the electronic business must be uncovered. The client has the benefit to whimper around a thing or organization if the thing or organization traits deviate from the agreed or given bylaw.

■ *Manuals:* A thing may be close by with the rules in physical or propelled shape that the buyer necessity for usage of the thing, regularly the bearings should be in Swedish.

■ *Secure payment's solution:* In case the electronic business itself or some other social occasion have obligations in regard to card data or other information in the period of direct transmission, they need to fulfill the necessities of Payment Card Industry Data Security Standard (PCI DSS). It is the electronic business's obligation to develop an advancement that enables the recognizing confirmation of cardholders. By saving the individual data of clients by some electronic business, the electronic business is competent to have approval from customers. These individual data must be protected from any external intrusion and should be managed as demonstrated by Personuppgiftslagen (PUL).

1.8 Solutions for Security

As is said in this examination, security issues inside website-based businesses could be dealt with multiple points of view. Innovation is one of the ways, perhaps the most imperative route for fathoming the security issues inside online business. The creators exhibit four stages keeping in mind the end goal to avert or decrease security hazards inside internet business, which are clarified quickly as follows:

■ *Assessment:* The designers infer that each kind of affiliation that is incorporated with the site-based business should constantly put a real focus on their advantages and guarantee that they have a great security structure, which secures their focal points in the best way. In addition, they should know the inadequacies of the structure and what components could cripple the deficiencies. The makers infer that there are various ways of managing such issues, and one of the course is to have a refined and dexterous group of IT individuals inside the affiliation [15].

■ *Planning:* Masterminding could be a persuading variable since nothing ought to be conceivably proper without orchestration. Every strategy, from the astoundingly clear issue to the amazingly obfuscated one, needs a nice masterminding. The designers suggest that the essential purpose behind this stage is to separate which security threats the site-based business associations may go up against, and what will be the costs in dealing with these security risks?

In advance, the makers attest that this stage should clarify for the electronic business which security risks are the most hazardous and which perils should be sorted out, considering the possible damages caused by the threats and the costs to turn them away [13].

- *Implementation:* Right when an affiliation is done with the orchestrating stage, it should put a not too bad push to make sense of what ways and advances are the best to manage these potential threats. Agreeing with the makers, the underlying stage in the stage execution should be to pick essential sorts of advances for the high need perils, and when this errand is done, then the specific programming to deal with these threats should be picked.

- *Monitoring:* In the wake of encountering the three phases stated earlier, an electronic business must continue with stage watching, which never closes. The explanation behind this stage is to evaluate which development is the best to oversee security threats. What ways have been independently productive and unsuccessful? What are the colossal and frightful goals of the progressions being used, and what could be changed if crucial? Are there some new security risks that could happen for the affiliation? Encouraging the makers infers that the checking stage should give a commendable reaction for all these and other practically identical request, and this methodology should reliably be run periodically [13].

The primary part is a man or a social affair, both must be affirmed, and the second segment is both, a man or a get together, where they ought to be isolated from others, for example by something extraordinary, a check. An amazingly careful supervisor is another segment who should care about the system's utilization. The accompanying segment showed by the makers is an approval system or device, which makes careful relationship about the interest of the isolating trademark. Finally, the last part is the use of a chance to control framework, which has the motivation to limit the exercises being done by the affirmed social occasions or individuals.

1.9 Testing e-Commerce Security

The prerequisite for testing the security of san affiliation rises due to two essential components. The first component is the testing of electronic commerce security and the second component is the lack of protection of the present security system to the new risks and enterprises. Starting late, the rate of passage of new sorts of risk and new experiences has been exasperating concerning the information security setting. This prompts the prerequisite for testing of periodical security by which the weakness of the present security establishment to the creation of the number of perils and enterprises can be calculated [12].

The guideline objectives of security testing, hence, fuses as follows:

A. Security Verification needs specific, for instance, territory of the asset(s), the chance to control the instrument for the advantages, operational setting of the affiliation, existing structure organizations and their chance to control frameworks, and the system inside the affiliation and accessibility of the relationship to the outside world.
B. Security Instruments Setup Verification decided in the security establishment, i.e., notwithstanding whether the security gadgets are genuinely acquainted and composed with keeping up the security of the advantage.
C. Hole Verification between the suggested security structure and the completed security establishment.
D. Requirement Verification of the suggested security establishment with respect to the present threats. Thus, there are two sections of testing: consistence checking and entrance testing.
E. Compliance checking: In compliance checking, it is seen whether the security structure, that has been realized, matches the security methodology of the affiliation. A semimechanized mechanical assembly can be used to facilitate the game plans with the present establishment.

The testing stage feedback is use for upgrading the security establishment and security approach of the affiliation. Starting to look into the foreseeable future, the testing is done yet again. Along these lines, security outlining is a dynamic procedure where each one of the dispense that ought to be passed on at standard breaks ensure the security of an affiliation.

1.10 e-Business Threats and Solutions

1.10.1 e-Business Threats

1.10.1.1 Authentication Attacks

These sorts of assaults happen when a client changes framework assets or accesses framework data without approval, by either sharing logins or passwords or utilizing an unattended terminal with an open session. Secret word assault is a habitually used technique for rehashing endeavors on a client record and watchword [12,13].

1.10.1.2 Respectability Attacks

In this kind of assault, information or data is included, adjusted, or evacuated in travel over the system. This requires root access to the switch or a framework. On the off chance that a program does not check as far as possible when perusing or accepting information, this opening can be misused by an aggressor to include self-assertive information into a program or framework. When running, this information gives the gatecrasher root access to the framework. Honesty assaults can make a postponement, making information generally inaccessible for a timeframe. The assailants surge the system with futile activity, making the framework to a great degree ease back to serve the clients, and in the extraordinary case, making the framework crash down. They could likewise make the information be disposed of before the last conveyance. Both postponement and dissent assaults can bring about the disavowal of service to the system clients.

1.10.1.3 Secrecy Attacks

Since organized PCs convey serially (regardless of the possibility that systems impart in parallel) and contain constrained prompt supports, information and data are transmitted in little squares or pieces called bundles. The programmers utilize an assortment of techniques referred to all in all as social designing assaults. With the utilization of many accessible shareware and freeware parcel sniffers, the assailants would catch all system bundles and, subsequently, the clients' login names, passwords, and even records. The aggressors more often than not exploit human propensity, e.g., utilizing a solitary, same watchword for numerous records. All the more regularly, they are fruitful in accessing corporate delicate and private data. Some snooping assaults put the system interface card in wanton mode, while the other bundle sniffers catch the initial 300 bytes of all telnet, document exchange convention (file transfer protocol (FTP)), and login sessions [13,16].

1.10.1.4 Infection

Viruses are PC programs that are composed of malevolent programmers and are intended to duplicate themselves and taint particular computers when activated by a particular occasion. For instance, infections called full-scale infections append themselves to documents that contain large-scale guidelines (schedules that can be rehashed naturally, for example, mail blends) and are then initiated each time when the full scale runs. The impacts of some infections are moderately considerate and cause irritating intrusions, for example, showing the entertaining message when striking a specific letter on the console. Different infections are more damaging and cause issues such as erasing records from a hard circle or backing off a framework. A system can be tainted by an infection just if the infection enters the system through an outside hotspot, for instance, through a contaminated floppy plate or a record downloaded from the Internet. When one PC on the system ends up noticeably tainted, then alternate PCs on the system are exceptionally helpless to the infection [15].

1.10.1.5 Trojan Horse

A trojan horse is a noxious code that expects clients to welcome it in, and is hence masked as something unique. Clueless clients will permit the trojan into their machine through an apparently safe and routine errand, just to have their framework traded off. An average trojan steed will be exhibited as something valuable, for example, an email caution with respect to another security fix. The email may give a connection, welcoming the client to tap on it to download and introduce the fix. At the point where the connection is taken after the trojan accesses the client's PC and, afterward, executes its modified errand. By outline, a trojan stallion is used by programmers to enter a huge system or secure framework to put it to use for its own particular purposes.

1.10.1.6 Worms

PC worms are vindictive projects intended to spread by means of PC systems. PC worms are a type of malware alongside the infections and trojans. A man ordinarily introduces worms by unintentionally opening an email connection or message that contains executable contents. Once introduced on a framework, worms suddenly produce extra email messages containing duplicates of the worm [15]. They may likewise open Transmission Control Protocol (TCP) ports to make systems security gaps for different applications, and they may endeavor to "surge" the system with spurious Denial of Service information transmissions [8].

1.10.2 e-Business Solutions

There is yet one answer for all issues that now and again mark the security of e-commerce administrations: Strict vigil on malignant gatecrashers. Easier said than done? So is each preventive measure. Be that as it may, with online exchanges, advancements in security have been overpowering [15].

The arrangement incorporates two forthcoming: Wireless planned and hard-wired imminent

    A. *Threats Solutions from a Wireless Perspective:*
- A data packet for technical discussion.
- Wireless threats: Man in the middle attacks.
- Way for authentication—Utilization of SSL.
- Way for encryption—Utilization of secure shell.
- Way for tunneling—Utilization of virtual private networks.

B. *Hard-Wired Perspective Solutions to Threats:*
   - Firewall uses.
   - Router uses.
   - Network intrusion devices uses.
C. *Confirmation:* Most prominent are the advances in ID and end of noncertifiable clients. Website-based business benefit planners now utilize multilevel recognizable proof conventions like security questions, encoded passwords (encryption), biometrics, and others to affirm the personality of their clients. These means have discovered wide support all around because of their adequacy in getting rid of unwelcome to get.
D. *Interruption check:* The issue of handling infections and their like has likewise observed fast improvement with hostile to infection merchants discharging solid against infections. These are created by master software engineers those are an indent over the programmers and saltines themselves.

   Firewalls are another normal method for actualizing safety efforts. These projects limit access to and from the framework to prechecked clients/get to focus.
E. *Teaching users:* Online business is run essentially by clients. Along these lines, e-commerce specialist coops have likewise swung to teaching clients about safe practices that raise the whole operation hell free. Earlier issues like phishing have been handled to a decent degree by educating authentic clients of the risks of distributing their private data to unapproved data searchers [13].

1.11 Conclusion and Future Direction

Electronic business is developing quickly. Distinctive movements have joined to enable the augmentation of site-based business. The fast advances in PC improvement joined with smart growing velocity in correspondence systems and the difference in complex programming have changed the way business is finished. In any case, this is not attractive to copy site-based business applications. Certified association of colossal business data security assets is the requirement of unbelievable hugeness. We have, in this chapter, set forward a "security arranging life cycle" way to deal with the data assets of an endeavor so that e-business can be done safely. With good old fashioned comprehension of business needs and association of gigantic business data security assets, web business will develop unlimitedly and will tremendously benefit each person.

All around e-business is growing, yet in any case, it goes with a peril that some bit of the trade is bartered, which may provoke cash-related hardship or unintended shared private information. It is thus the security of site-based business trades that is a fundamental piece of the constant achievement and further advancement of e-exchange. The security risk of e-exchange consolidates diseases, worms, trojan steeds, denial of organization, and mystery key theft. The advances for guaranteeing e-exchange trades fuse together encryption of data, SSL, electronic mark, modernized supports, wise card, and e-cash.

1.11.1 Which Factors Make Questions among the Web Business Customers?

A champion among the most generally perceived components that *make questions among* the buyers is the subject of reality of the website, i.e., in case the Website page is totally genuine and legal. The examination exhibits that phony Website goals are being made remembering the ultimate objective to trap customers, which fundamentally impact antagonistically buyers' trust. Notwithstanding the likelihood that the website is true blue and honest, in spite of all that it could hurt the purchasers trust by not convincing the purchasers. This is the reason why crude look of the website districts is a particularly complete factor on making question among the buyers. Advance examination exhibits another factor that *make questions among* the customers, which is the manhandling of the clients' personal and fragile information. The manhandle ought to be conceivable from numerous perspectives, for example if the information is used for the wrong reason or if someone unapproved gets to it. The examination moreover shows that blackmail done inside different e-portion systems influence serious put to stock in issues among the buyers.

1.11.2 Future Direction

Most site-based business exchanges as of now are secured by the (secure associations layer) SSL custom, which is proposed to scramble information trades over the site. While SSL is for the most part seen as plausible, developing some vulnerabilities and differing issues have poked some site-based business players to consider more secure gauges. SSL's essential disadvantage is its dependence on guaranteeing endorsement at the client end, which envisions that clients will have not much key awareness of the advancement and procedures related with guaranteeing security. A similar insufficiency is responsible for the completion of public key infrastructure (PKI) (open key foundation) security; program vulnerabilities and client deadness routinely result in unsecured exchanges.

The most recent variety of SSL, known as tTransaction level security, has not grabbed hold as all things are considered as its pioneer. Or, on the other hand perhaps, experts foresee that XML will fill in as the clarification behind the going with the time of secure web business exchanges.

XML security, despite the way that it will hold the issue of placing stock in guarantors, will oversee trades just as they were reports, empowering electronic businesses to send purchase demands and checks by way of email. The necessity for complex XML security development will rise later.

The accompanying time of electronic business improvement will be in remote and adaptable exchange. A part of the rising classes of adaptable business applications are recorded. Nonrevocation of organization is a major part of web business security organization to develop the legal introduction of electronic trade.

The dynamic parts of site-based business, for instance, crossing out and reducing portion, or changing portion strategies, can offer to address among individuals. Today, only two or three structures address nondenial of organization; moreover, these frameworks address midway nonrepudiation of organization. Research is in advance to portray new structures of non-renouncement.

References

1. Burns, S. 2002. Unique characteristics of e-commerce technologies and their effects upon payment systems. GSEC (GIAC Security Essentials Certification) – Version 1.3.
2. COBIT. 2000. Control objectives for information and related technology: COBIT, 3rd edn., July 2000. Released by the COBIT Steering Committee and the IT Governance Institute.
3. Duggal, P. 2000. Cyber law in India – An analysis (New Delhi: Saaksharth) ISO/IEC 2000 Information technology – Code of practice for information security management.
4. Kalakota, R. and Whinston, A. B. 1999. *Frontiers of e-commerce.* Reading, MA: Addison-Wesley/Longman.
5. Schneider, G. P. and Perry, J. T. 2001. *Electronic commerce.* Cambridge, MA: Course Technology.
6. Varshney, U., Vetter, R. J. and Kalakota, R. "Mobile commerce: A new frontier", *Computer,* vol. 33, no. 10, (October 2000), 32–38.
7. Leu, F.-Y., Lin, C.-H. and Castiglione, A. "Special issue on cloud, wireless and e-commerce security", *Journal of Ambient Intelligence and Humanized Computing,* vol. 4, no. 2, (2013), 207–208.
8. Mazumdar, C., Barik, M. S., Das, S., Roy, J. and Barkat, M. A. 2003. Final technical report for project development of validated security processes and methodologies for web-based enterprises.
9. Xiangsong, M. and Fengwu, H. "Design on PKI-based anonymous mobile agent security in e-commerce", *Wuhan University Journal of Natural Sciences,* vol. 11, no. 6, (2006), 1907–1910.
10. Antoniou, G. and Battern, L. "E-commerce: Protecting purchaser privacy to enforce trust", *Electronic Commerce Research,* vol. 11, no. 4, (2011), 421.
11. Smith, R. and Shao, J. "Privacy and e-commerce: A consumer-centric perspective", *Electronic Commerce Research,* vol. 7, no. 2, (2007), 89–116.
12. Mazumdar, A., Sengupta, C. and Barik, M. S. "E-commerce security – A life cycle approach", *Sadhana,* vol. 30, no. 2–3, (2005), 119–140.
13. Marchany, R. C. and Wilson, T. A keystroke recorder Attack on a client/server infrastructure. *Proceedings of the Network Security 96 Conference,* SANS Institute, Singapore.
14. Good, D. and Schultz, R. "E-commerce strategies for B2B service firm in the global environment", *American Business Review,* vol. 20, no. 2, (2003), 111–119.
15. Sharma, R., Agarwal, A. K. and Singh, P. K. "Transaction security in RFID credit card by polynomial arithmetic along with Euclidean parameters", *International Journal of Engineering and Technology,* vol. 7, no. 4, (2015), 1194–1199.
16. SSE-CMM. 2003. Systems security engineering capability maturity model. SSE-CMM, Model Description Document Version 3.0, June 15, 2003.

Chapter 2

Understanding the Aspect of Cryptography and Internet Security: A Practical Approach

Anjana Mishra
C.V. Raman College of Engineering

Sukant Kishoro Bisoy
C.V. Raman College of Engineering

Contents

2.1 Introduction

The data frequently travels from one system to another system, leaving the safety of its protected physical surroundings. When the data is traveling through a communication channel, unauthorized people with bad objectives could alter the actual data, either for amusement or for their own profit. Cryptography is a technique that transforms the data and makes it safer throughout the transmission channel. The method is based on the essentials of secret codes, encryption, and decryption operation improved by existing mathematics that protected our private data in most prevailing ways.

2.1.1 Internet Security

Internet security is a subpart of computer security that is mainly related to the Internet. For many of us, Internet technology is embodied in the digital computer, which has is an important tool for our personal needs as well as our work. The Internet represents an insecure medium for exchanging information, which leads to a high risk of fraud, scam, or intrusion, such as viruses, Trojans, phishing, and worms (Forouzan, 2010).

2.1.2 The Aspects of Security Policy

The aspects of security policy are as follows:

Affordability: It defines how much money or finance and effort does the security system need for its implementation or maintenance.

Functionality: It defines the mechanism or method for providing Internet security smoothly.

Culture issues: It simply defines, by the expectation of the end user, what they want, how they want, and when they want.

Legality: It defines all the laws that must be followed; if they are not followed, then some legal action should be taken by the judiciary.

2.1.3 Goals of Internet Security

There are three primary goals of Internet security which are also known as CIA (confidentiality, integrity, and availability) triangle (Figure 2.1).

Confidentiality: Confidentiality is the primary goal of Internet security. The main purpose of this goal is in defending valued business or personal data from an unauthorized person. Confidentiality makes sure that the data is *only* available to authorized and intended persons.

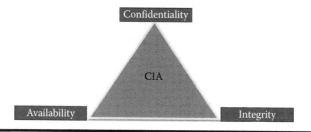

Figure 2.1 CIA triangle.

Integrity: Integrity is the second goal of Internet security. The main purpose of this goal is to maintain consistency and accuracy of data. Integrity assures that the data is exact, trustworthy, and not changed by any unauthorized persons or hackers. The data sent from the sender and received by the authorized recipient must be exactly the same. There will be no change in the data; a single bit of change can be known as loss of data integrity (Forouzan, 2010).

Availability: Availability is the third goal of Internet security. The main purpose of this goal is to make sure that all the network resources or network services and information or data for transmission must be continuously available to the authentic users, whenever they need it (Forouzan, 2010).

Nonrepudiation: Nonrepudiation is defined as a method in which the sender of a message cannot refute in the future having sent the message and that the recipient also cannot repudiate having received the message. It is a legal concept that can only be solved through legal and social processes. Nonrepudiation can be achieved through the use of digital signature, timestamp, or message transfer agent.

Authentication: Authentication involves assurance that the data was generated or sent by the source it appears to be. It usually contains more than one "proof" of identity such as password, pattern, and biometric. A user has to face man-in-the-middle attacks such as spam, website redirection, e-mail phishing, browser hijacking, or other attacks.

Access control: Access control mechanisms will define who will access what. So, simply it can be defined as restricting the availability of network resources to endpoint devices that obey the security policy of an organization. This will not allow any type of access that might be unofficial or illegal. It can be relatively powerful on some devices but with different guidelines for different access protocols (Singh et al., 2014).

2.1.4 Internet Security Attacks

Passive attacks: In this type of attack, the attacker's aim is to obtain the information illegally. They do not damage the system or modify any data, but they can harm the receiver or sender by revealing the message. This is the reason for which it is difficult to detect this type of attack until the sender or receiver finds out any

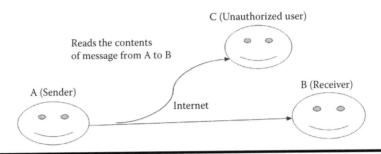

Figure 2.2 Release of message contents.

leakage of secret information. It can be prevented by encipherment of data. So, it is possible to stop the success of these attacks, usually with the help of encryption methods. Thus, in passive attacks, prevention is more important than detection (William, 2011). The two types of passive attacks are as follows:

The release of message content: In this electronic mail, data and transferred file may contain some confidential information, which an unauthorized user can learn from the elements of these communications (Figure 2.2).

Traffic analysis: In this type, an unauthorized user could determine the identity of an interactive host and location, and could observe the occurrence and length of messages being exchanged, which might be useful in predicting the nature of the messaging that was taking place (Figure 2.3).

Active attacks: In this type of attack, the data can be changed or system may get damaged. Active attacks are easier to detect and prevent, because different opponents can use a different method to launch them.

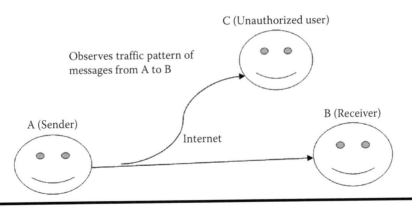

Figure 2.3 Traffic analysis.

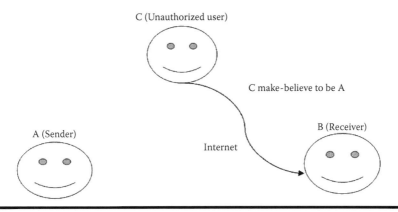

Figure 2.4   Masquerade attack.

The two types of active attacks are as follows:

Masquerade attack: This type of attack takes place when one object pretends (plays) to be another object (Figure 2.4). When transmission takes place between object A and object B, an unauthorized object C can also send a message to B pretending to be object A, which is an illegal activity and known as masquerade attack. For example, a customer of a bank tries to contact a bank, but some other fake site pretends it is a bank and obtains valuable information from the customer (William, 2011).

Replay attack: In this type of attack, the attackers keep track of the authorized user and obtains a copy of a message and keep replaying it later. This kind of subsequent retransmission produces an unauthorized effect on the network (Figure 2.5).

Modification of messages: Modification of messages basically means that some portion of a genuine message is changed, or that messages are illegally reordered by some unofficial user, to yield an illegal effect. For example, an

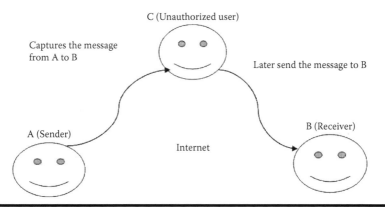

Figure 2.5   Replay attack.

instruction "Transfer of 8,000 from account A to B" is modified to "Transfer of 80,000 from account A to B" (Figure 2.6).

Denial of services: It is considered a very popular attack. It slows down or fully damages the service provided by the system. Different attackers use different techniques to do it. He/she may send various bogus messages to the server, so due to the heavy load, the server may crash or not respond correctly or the attackers intercept the transmission between the server and the client and generate misconception between the server and the client (Figure 2.7).

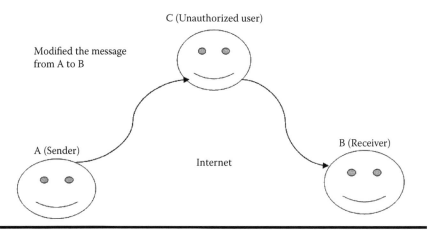

Figure 2.6   Modification of messages.

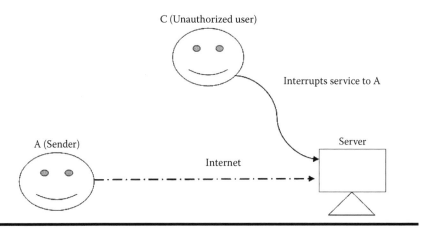

Figure 2.7   Denial of services.

2.1.5 Security Mechanism

The various security mechanisms to provide security are as follows:

Encipherment: In this mechanism, mathematical algorithms are used to alter data into a form that will not be easily understandable, and this is done for the purpose of hiding the data and enhancing confidentiality. Two commonly known techniques for encipherment are cryptography and steganography (Figure 2.8).

Digital signature: Digital signature is a technique that allows senders to electronically sign the data before sending it, and the receiver to electronically verify the signature after receiving it. In this method, the sender encrypts the data to be signed with his/her private key, and for encryption of the result, the receiver's public key is issued (Figure 2.9). After the encryption process is successfully done, the sender sends the encrypted message to the receiver. The receiver decrypts

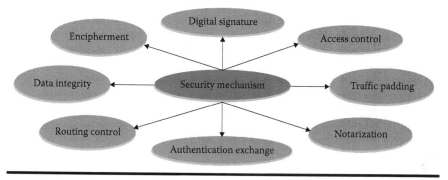

Figure 2.8 Security mechanism.

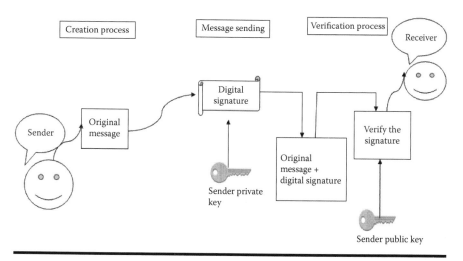

Figure 2.9 Digital signature process.

Table 2.1 Relationship between Security Mechanism and Security Service (Mathur and Alam, 2015)

Security Service	Security Mechanism							
	Encipherment	Digital Signature	Access Control	Data Integrity	Authentication Exchange	Traffic Padding	Routing Control	Notarization
Authentication	Yes	Yes			Yes			
Confidentiality	Yes						Yes	
Data integrity	Yes	Yes		Yes				
Access control			Yes					
Nonrepudiation		Yes		Yes				Yes
Availability				Yes	Yes			

the incoming data with his/her private key and then decrypts the result with the sender's public key. If the actual data is obtained, then this will authenticate and integrate the data and the sender (William, 2011).

Access control: It uses the technique of imposing access rights to resources and the data, for example, pin password, and user ID.

Data integrity: Several techniques are used to guarantee the stream of data units or integrity of a data unit. Therefore, no modification of data is allowed.

Authentication exchange: In this mechanism, the sender and the receiver can exchange some private information, which other people are not supposed to know, to authenticate their own identity to each other.

Traffic padding: In this mechanism, some bogus/false data is inserted into the true data to prevent the traffic analysis of data by an unauthorized user.

Routing control: In this mechanism, secure routes are provided by continuously changing and selecting different routes between the sender and the receiver for data transmission to avert the unauthorized user.

Notarization: It is based on the third-party effect. In this mechanism, a trusted third party is selected to have control over the entire conversation. It assures nonrepudiation, which means that the sender cannot deny later that he/she has sent the data earlier (Table 2.1).

2.2 Techniques to Achieve Security Goals

Cryptography: The word *cryptography* comes from the Greek words *kryptos* meaning "secret writing" and *graphein* meaning "writing." Cryptography mainly concerns the security of digital data and information (Coron, 2006). It includes the techniques based on mathematical algorithms that offer essential Internet security services. According to William Stallings (2011), "Cryptography is defined as the subpart of cryptology dealing with the design of algorithms for encryption and decryption, planned to guarantee the secrecy and/or authenticity of message. So, it is the skill of succeeding in terms of security by encoding the messages to make them in a format that is completely non-readable. Earlier, cryptography meant only the encryption and decryption of messages using secret keys, but nowadays it is well defined as containing three different mechanisms: symmetric key encipherment, asymmetric key encipherment, and hashing (Fiskiran and Lee, 2002; Mandal et al., 2012).

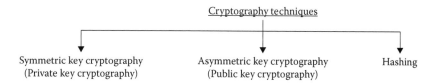

Cryptography techniques

Symmetric key cryptography (Private key cryptography) Asymmetric key cryptography (Public key cryptography) Hashing

1. **Symmetric key encipherment:** In this mechanism, the encryption and decryption procedures can be done using the identical key. Symmetric key is famous for conventional encryption. Sometimes, it is also known as secret key encipherment or secret key cryptography. In this encipherment, a sender, say A, can send information to another object, say B, over an uncertain channel with the hypothesis that an opponent, say C, cannot understand the contents of the sanded information by simply snooping over the channel. A can encrypt the message using the encryption algorithm and B can decrypt the information using the decryption algorithm. It uses a single secret key for both encryption and decryption. A (sender) simply locates the message in a box and, using the shared secret key, locks the box, and at the receiver side, B (receiver) unlocks the box with the same key and receives the information effectively and accurately (Farah, 2012).

2. **Asymmetric key encipherment:** It is also known as public key encipherment or public key cryptography. This encipherment is the same as in the symmetric key encipherment, with some exceptions. There are two keys: one public key and one private key. For sending information securely to receiver B, the sender A first encrypts the information using B's public key, and for decryption operation, B uses his private key.

3. **Hashing:** In this method, form variable or arbitrary length message a fixed-length message digest is found with the help of hash function. This process is known as hashing of data. The size of the message digest is generally smaller than that of the actual message. In this method, the sender A first produces a hash of the message, encrypts it, and then sends it to the receiver with the message itself. The receiver decrypts both the message and the hash, and another hash was generated by the receiver from the received message, and finally compares the two hashes. If they are the same, there is a very high probability that the message was conveyed effectively without any threats. Hashing is used to provide data integrity by checking the values (William, 2011).

2.2.1 Symmetric Key Cipher Model

Previously, cryptographic systems were also referred to as ciphers. A cipher is simply defined as the steps of an algorithm for carrying out both encryption and the resultant decryption operation. The five ingredients of conventional encryption algorithms or symmetric encryption are plaintext, ciphertext, secret key, encryption algorithm, and decryption algorithm (Figure 2.10).

Plaintext: It is the actual understandable data or information that is taken as an input to the encryption algorithm.

Ciphertext: It is the twisted or perverted message generated as an output to the encryption algorithm and also used as an input to the decryption algorithm to regenerate the actual plaintext. So, the ciphertext completely depends on the

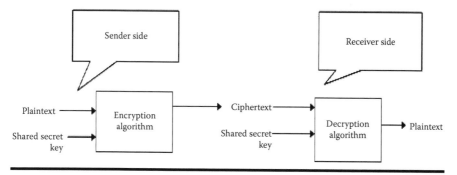

Figure 2.10   A simplified model of a symmetric key cipher.

secret key and plaintext. For a single message, if two different keys are given, then it results in two different ciphertext. It is a random stream of data that is unintelligible (Bali, 2014).

Encryption algorithm: It is used to create the ciphertext from the plaintext by using various operations. It takes plaintext and secret key as inputs and generates ciphertext as an output (Yegireddi and Kumar, 2016).

Decryption algorithm: The opposite process of the encryption algorithm is known as the decryption algorithm. In this algorithm, the ciphertext and secret key are used as inputs to produce the actual plaintext.

Secret key: It is taken as an input to the encryption algorithm. The key does not depend on the encryption algorithm and plaintext (Nadeem and Javed, 2005). The encryption algorithm will generate different outputs depending on the secret key, which means that for the same plaintext, if two different secret keys are used, two different ciphertexts will be produced.

$$C = EK(P)$$

$$P = DK(C)$$

Where
  P is the plaintext
  E is encryption
  D is decryption
  C is the ciphertext
  K is the secret key.

2.2.2 Types of Traditional Ciphers

There are two types of traditional ciphers: substitution and transposition.

2.2.2.1 Substitution Techniques

Substitution technique is a method in which the letters of plain text are substituted by other letters/symbols/numbers. Some of the primary substitution techniques are as follows:

Caesar cipher: In this cipher, each given letter of the alphabet is substituted with the letter standing three places further down the alphabet. After the letter Z, the alphabet is enfolded around so that the letter following Z is A (Kahate, 2007).

Example:

Plaintext: Internet security

Ciphertext: LQWHUQHW VHFXULWB

The transformation is done according to this simple rule:

C = (P+3)

Plaintext: a b c d e f g h i j k l m n o p q r s t u v w x y z

Ciphertext: D E F G H I J K L M N O P Q R S T U V W X Y Z A B C

Monoalphabetic cipher: In this cipher, the plaintext character or symbol and the ciphertext character or symbol always have a one-to-one relationship, which means that the ciphertext character is exactly the same as the plaintext character irrespective of its place in the text. For example, if the letter B is changed to E, then every B in the plaintext will change to E in the ciphertext.

Plaintext: come soon

Ciphertext: FRPH VRRQ

Polyalphabetic cipher: In this cipher, the plaintext character or symbol and the ciphertext character or symbol always have a one-to-many relationship, which means that the ciphertext character is not exactly the same as the plaintext character. Here, each time the character occurs, it has a different substitution. The ciphertext letters depend upon the plaintext letters as well as the location of the plaintext letters. For example, letter can change to D in the beginning, to F in the middle, or N at the end of a text.

Playfair cipher: It is the best-known multiple-letter encryption technique. It uses the two main processes: creation of matrix and encryption (Kahate, 2007).

i. **Creation of matrix:** A key table is created by constructing a 5×5 matrix of letters using keywords of English alphabets that become the key for encryption and decryption. There are some rules by which the alphabets are entered into the matrix.
   a. The keywords are entered row-wise into the matrix, first from left to right and then from top to bottom.
   b. All the duplicate letters should be dropped.
   c. The rest of the vacant places in the matrix are filled by the remaining alphabets between English letters A to Z, which are not the part of the current keyword, while this rule also combines "i" and "j" in the similar cell of a table.

  d. If "i" or "j" is already the part of a keyword, discard both keywords i and
      j while filling the reaming spaces.
ii. **Encryption:**
  a. Before executing these steps, the plaintext message must be broken down
      into groups of two alphabets.
  b. If both the alphabets are equal or only one alphabet is left, then add X
      after the first alphabet.

      AA—AX

      D—DX

  c. If both the alphabets in the pair appear in the same row of the matrix,
      then replace them with the alphabets on their immediate right side,
      respectively. If the pair is on the right side of the row, then wrap it around
      to the left side of the row.
  d. If both the alphabets in the pair appear in the same column of the matrix,
      then exchange them with their alphabets that are immediately below
      them.
  e. If the actual pair letter is on the bottom side of the column, then wrap it
      around to the top side of the column.
  a. If alphabets are not present in the same column or row, then simply change
     them with the alphabets in the same row, respectively, but the other pair of
     the corner of the matrix defines the actual pair.

     MY NAME IS ATUL

M	Y	N	A	E
I	S	T	U	L
B	C	D	F	G
H	K	O	P	Q
R	V	W	X	Z

Encrypted: YNAEYMSTNULI

Another example of substitution cipher is Hill cipher, Vigenere cipher, Vernam
cipher, etc.

2.2.2.2 Transposition Techniques

In this technique, different kinds of mapping are done by executing some sort of
permutation of the plaintext letters.

Rail fence cipher: In this process, characters are written in alternative columns
and rows.

Encryption: Plaintext + key + algorithm

Decryption: Ciphertext + key + algorithm

Algorithm

Step 1: Person A and person B agree on the target prime number n and g.
Step 2: Person A chooses another large random number x, and A is calculated as follows:

$$A = g^x \bmod n$$

Step 3: Person A sends a number A to person B.
Step 4: Person B independently chooses another random number y, and B is calculated as follows:

$$B = g^y \bmod n$$

Step 5: Person B sends a number to A.
Step 6: The secret key K1 is computed by A as follows:

$$K1 = B^x \bmod e \, n$$

Step 7: Now the secret key K2 is computed as follows:

$$K2 = A^y \bmod n$$

Stream cipher: It is a procedure of encrypting the plaintext to generate a ciphertext in which a cryptographic algorithm and key are applied to each binary digit in a data stream, one bit or byte at a time. This technique is not very popular in modern cryptography. For example, RC4, which stands for Rivest Cipher 4, is the most commonly used of all stream ciphers. It is also known as ARCFOUR or ARC4.

Block cipher: It is defined as an encryption or decryption method in which a block of plaintext as a whole produces a block of ciphertext of equal length. A block size of 64 or 128 bits is used typically in this cipher. Many block ciphers have a Feistel structure, which means it involves a number of equal rounds of processing. In each round, a replacement is performed on the one part of the data being processed, followed by a permutation that swaps the two halves so that an altered key is used for each round because a unique key is extended (Forouzan, 2010).

In cryptography, varieties of conventional encryption algorithms exist (Joseph et al., 2015). They are data encryption standard (DES) (Coppersmith, 1994), Triple data encryption standard (William, 2011) Advanced Encryption Standard (Daemen and Rijmen, 1999), Blowfish (Schneier, 1994) Twofish (Schneier et al., 1998), IDEA, and (Arora, 2015).

DES: It is also called data encryption algorithm. DES was developed in the early 1970s, and its implementation was based on the design of Horst Feistel. DES is a symmetric key algorithm, and it is also called a block cipher, whose work is to encrypt the electronic data that is converting a 64-bit plaintext into a 64-bit ciphertext (Ramesh and Umarani, 2012).

DES Technique

1. Initially, a 64-bit plaintext puts down an initial permutation function (Apoorva, 2013).
2. Initial permutation is performed on the plaintext (Coppersmith, 1994).
3. After initial permutation is performed, it creates two halves of the permuted block that is left plaintext (LPT) and right plaintext (RPT).
4. Each LPT and RPT will execute 16 rounds of the encryption procedure.
5. The LPT and RPT will be reunited, and a final permutation will be performed on the combined block in the final steps.
6. The results of final permutation provide a 64-bit ciphertext (Agrawal and Mishra, 2012).

Advantages

1. A simple change in plaintext will drastically change the ciphertext.
2. Each ciphertext bit depends on multiple plaintext bits.
3. The DES instances can be applied various times to a plaintext as it is not considered a group cipher (Shanta, 2012).
4. DES has a 56-bit key. So, there are 2^{56} possibilities of keys that would take a decade using brute force attack to find the correct key.
5. For encryption and decryption operations, the same algorithm is applied. The only thing needed is the function to be reversed and the key must be taken in reverse order. For software and hardware requirements, this will be convenient (Padmavathi and Kumari, 2013).

Disadvantages

1. In today's era of parallel computing, breaking DES with the help of brute force attack is very easy, which was impossible during early years.
2. The key is a problem that is selected in the round. During breaking of keys into two halves and swapping, these might provide a similar result if they have continuous 0s and 1s.
3. The s-boxes on different inputs of permutations may produce the same outputs that are termed as semi-weak keys.
4. The main weakness of DES is its block size, which was very short, and the size of the key (Table 2.2).

Table 2.2   Comparison of Various Cryptographic Algorithms (Anu et al., 2017)

Factor	DES	3DES	AES	Blowfish	IDEA	RSA	ECC
Speed	Slow	Very slow	Fast	Fast	Slow	Fast	Fast
Security	Insecure	Moderate	Secure	Highly secure	Secure	Proven adequate	Highly secure
Flexible	No	Yes	Yes	Yes	No	Yes	Yes
Attack	Brute force attack, linear cryptanalysis	Brute force attack, chosen plaintext, known plaintext	Key attack, side channel attack	Dictionary attack	Linear attack, meet-in-the-middle attack, biclique attack	Brute force attack, timing attack, factoring the public key	Doubling attack

2.3 Advantages and Disadvantages of Cryptography

Advantages

1. Cryptography helps provide accuracy, confidentiality, accountability, fairness, and integrity of data.
2. It can stop the scam in electronic commerce by validating financial transactions.
3. Using the computer system in an extremely effective and secure manner, the cryptography facilitates us to conduct business over the networks.
4. It helps us to prevent spoofing and forgeries of information.
5. It also provides secrecy in storage, which is obtained by storing the data in an encrypted format using the private key (Schneier, 1998).

Disadvantages

1. A strongly encrypted, digitally signed, and authentic message can also create problems for the genuine user at a vital time.
2. Cryptography does not protect against the susceptibilities and warnings that arise from the poor system design, its protocols, and procedures.
3. Selective access control cannot be provided by cryptography.
4. It is very costly, so it is not equally available to people of different economic means
5. It also needs maintenance after some time.
6. It delays information processing.

2.4 Conclusion and Future of Cryptography

The modern era of cryptography depends upon a scientific method and designs the cryptographic algorithms around computational rigidity rules, so that they are unbreakable by an opponent. The elliptic curve cryptography (ECC) has already been developed, but its benefits and drawbacks are not yet known by the users (He and Zeadally, 2015). In ECC, the encryption and decryption operations can be performed in much less time; thus, in this way, more data can be passed with equal security and without time delay. The ECC needs to be confirmed and verified secure before it is widely accepted by private, governmental, business, and commercial sectors. Another new phenomenon is quantum computation. A quantum computer stores data by the use of quantum superposition of multiple states, which is very fast compared with binary format. These numerous valued states of a quantum computer are stored in "qubits" or "quantum bits." The power of the quantum computer is very high; the numbers that would naturally take many years to compute could only take hours or even minutes to solve with a completely established quantum computer.

The fact is that modern cryptography has to look for a more complex problem and plan new technology to achieve the goal of modern cryptography and solve them in less time.

References

Agrawal, M. and Mishra, P. 2012. A comparative survey on symmetric key encryption techniques. *International Journal on Computer Science and Engineering*, vol. 4, no. 5, p. 877.

Anushree, D. and Sindhu, R. 2017. Analysis of cryptography and comparison of its various techniques. *International Journal of Advanced Research in Computer Science*, vol. 8, no. 5, pp. 688–691.

Apoorva, Y. K. 2013. Comparative study of different symmetric key cryptography algorithms. *International Journal of Application or Innovation in Engineering and Management*, vol. 2, no. 7, pp. 204–206.

Arora, S. 2015. Enhancing cryptographic security using novel approach based on enhanced-RSA and Elamal: Analysis and comparison. *International Journal of Computer Applications*, vol. 112, no. 13, pp. 35–39.

Bali, P. 2014. Comparative study of private and public key cryptography algorithms: A survey. *IJRET: International Journal of Research in Engineering and Technology*, eISSN: 2319-1163 | pISSN: 2321-7308, Volume: 03 Issue: 09 | Sep-2014.

Coppersmith, D. 1994. The data encryption standard (DES) and its strength against attacks. *IBM Journal Research Development*, vol. 38, no. 3, pp. 243–250.

Coron, J. S. 2006. What is cryptography? *IEEE Security & Privacy Journal*, vol. 12, no. 8, pp. 70–73.

Daemen, J. and Rijmen, V. 1999. AES Proposal: Rijndael, AES algorithm submission, September 3, 1999.

Farah, S. 2012. An experimental study on performance evaluation of asymmetric encryption algorithms. *Recent Advances Information Science*, vol. 8, pp. 121–124.

Fiskiran, M. and Lee, B. 2002. Workload characterization of elliptic curve cryptography and other network security algorithms for constrained environments. Proceedings of the *IEEE International Workshop on Workload Characterization (WWC-5)*, pp. 127–137, November 2002.

Forouzan, A. B. 2010. *Cryptography and network security.* 2nd edition. Tata McGraw-Hill Publishing Company Limited, 7 west patel nagar, New Delhi.

He, D. and Zeadally, S. 2015. An analysis of RFID authentication schemes for internet of things in healthcare environment using elliptic curve cryptography. *IEEE Internet of Things Journal*, vol. 2, no. 1, pp. 72–83.

Joseph, D. P., Krishna, M. and Arun, K. 2015. Cognitive analytics and comparison of symmetric and asymmetric cryptography algorithms. *International Journal of Advanced Research in Computer Science*, volume. 2, Issue 3, pp. 63–68.

Kahate, A. 2007. *Cryptography and network security.* 2nd edition. Published by Tata McGraw-Hill Education Pvt. Ltd., 2007. ISBN: 0070648239. New Delhi.

Mandal, A. K., Parakash, C. and Tiwari, A. 2012. Performance evaluation of cryptographic algorithms: DES and AES. *IEEE Students' Conference on Electrical, Electronics and Computer Science (SCEECS).*

Mathur, H. and Alam, Z. 2015. Analysis in symmetric and asymmetric cryptology algorithm. *International Journal of Emerging Trends & Technology in Computer Science (IJETTCS)*, vol. 4, no. 1.

Nadeem, A. and Javed, M. Y. 2005. A performance comparison of data encryption algorithms. *IEEE First International Conference on Information and Communication Technologies (ICICT)*. 27–28 Aug. 2005, IEEE, Karachi, Pakistan.

Padmavathi, B. and Kumari, S. R. 2013. A survey on performance analysis of DES, AES and RSA algorithm along with LSB substitution technique. *International Journal Science and Research*, vol. 2, no. 4, pp. 170–174.

Ramesh, G. and Umarani, R. 2012. Performance analysis of most common encryption algorithms on different web browsers. International Journal of Information Technology and Computer Science, vol. 4, no. 12, pp. 60–66.

Schneier, B. 1994. The Blowfish encryption algorithm. *Dr. Dobb's Journal of Software Tools*, vol. 19, no. 4, p. 38, 40, 98, 99.

Schneier, B. et al. 1998, Twofish: A 128 Bit Block Cipher, AES algorithm submission, June 15, 1998.

Schneier, B. 1998. Why Cryptography Is Harder Than It Looks (the magazine No. 34) September 10.

Shanta, J. V. 2012. Evaluating the performance of symmetric key algorithms: AES (advanced encryption standard) and DES (data encryption standard). *IJCEM International Journal of Computational Engineering & Management*, vol. 15, no. 4, pp. 43–49.

Singh, A. et al. 2014. Comparative study of DES, 3DES, AES and RSA. *International Journal of Computers & Technology*, vol. 9, no. 3, pp. 1164–1170.

Stallings, W. 2011. *Cryptography and network security principles and practice*. 5th edition. Pearson Education , United States of America.

Yegireddi, R. and Kumar, R. K. 2016. A survey on conventional encryption algorithms of Cryptography. *International Conference on ICT in Business Industry & Government (ICTBIG)*. 18–19 Nov 2016, Indore, India.

Chapter 3

Attainment of Cybersecurity Using Support Vector Machine Involving Data Mining Techniques

Soobia Saeed and M. Alam

Ilma University

Contents

3.1 Introduction

3.1.1 Overview

Tackling information security issues has become more important with the increasing development of computer networks over the past few years; hence, we have to find an ideal way to protect the information security system and we need a few methods to identify the security ruptures. Information mining has a few security-related applications in national security and cybersecurity. National security threats include attacks on buildings and destruction of critical infrastructure.

Crime is one of the dangerous activities for any country's establishment and reputation. Nowadays, criminals use contemporary technologies to commit any crime. One of the important challenges faced by the enforcement agencies is the difficulty in analyzing a large amount of data involved in committing crimes and terrorist activities. Thus, there is a need to maintain a database containing details of criminals and their activities. Data mining has initiated a potential step to make it easier, convenient, and practical for the user to explore a very large database.

Fortunately, the sort of learning techniques discussed in this book do not present these sensible issues—they are called machine learning. Data mining is a functional subject and incorporates learning in a practical, not a theoretical, sense. The creator is enthused about the techniques for finding and portraying essential cases in information as a gadget for clearing up that data and estimates from it. The data will show up as an arrangement of action of cases—instances of customers who have traded loyalties, for instance, or conditions in which certain sorts of contact convex lens can be suggested. The output shows up as assumptions about new instances of a forecast of whether a particular customer will switch or an expectation of what sort of convex lens will be suggested under given conditions. In any case, since this exploration is about finding and depicting outlines in the data, the output may fuse an honest description of a structure that can be used to arrange obscure cases to clarify the decision. Moreover, this is valuable to supply an express representation of the discovery that is obtained the decision of obscure cases. For the most part, this reflects two implications of learning: getting the information and the ability to use it. Many learning systems look for fundamental depictions of what is discovered; depictions that can end up complex and are commonly communicated as sets of standards, for instance, the ones depicted beforehand or the choices portrayed later in this chapter. Since they can be comprehended by individuals, these depictions serve to clarify what has been realized and the reason for new predictions. Experience demonstrates that in numerous uses of machine learning to data mining as the express learning structures that are obtained, and often described in any event as critical, and frequently especially more important, than the capacity to perform well on new cases. Individuals every now and again utilize data mining to gain knowledge, not simply expectations. Gaining knowledge from information certainly sounds like a good idea in the event that you can do it.

To perform crime analysis, we need to choose an appropriate database mining technique and clustering support vector machine (SVM). Clustering is a procedure of dividing an arrangement of data (or item is an arrangement of significant subclasses called bunches). Clustering is the procedure for coordinating physical objects into communities, as their segment is identical in a few ways.

The numerical and nonnumerical systematic studies on crimes include social demographic crime. The spatial and temporal factors assist the police and law enforcement agencies in anticipating criminal activity. A social demographic crime refers to individual groups and their characteristics such as income, age, education, and analysis of how the particular group or person is related to the crime. Spatial refers to the particular location where the crime occurs, such as any particular organization, business place, school residential area, etc. Cybersecurity aspects are analyzed pertaining to defending web application via harmful file procedures or even in the occurrence regarding fraudulent system types, tools, and criteria, in addition to new assessments, for example. Protection pertaining to web application articles will be shown later by making use of the unit studying method. National security is related to cybersecurity: higher cybersecurity leads to a higher business rate, because when the security of consumer and business assets and information increases, business also increases and it will strengthen our economy. Organizations need to follow cybersecurity standards because it provides a secure side from the cyberattacks.

3.1.2 Problem Statement

- Enhancing cybersecurity by data mining techniques
- Identifying the loophole in cybersecurity, monitoring the traffic crossing through cybersecurity

3.1.3 Background, Objective, and Significance of the Study

"Security" is an unconceivable point that is incorporates the security of nations from military or terrorist assault, the security of PCs from saltines, home security from criminals and different gatecrashers, budgetary security from monetary breakdown, and numerous other related circumstances. Concerning our connection, we must be worried with two unique ideas of security: (1) specialized and (2) those that safeguard the whole country.

As we know that Security as a rule is synonymous with "being protected," yet as a specialized term, so it is secure as well as that things have been secured. For instance, in telecom, the expression security has the accompanying importance: a condition that results from the establishment and support of defensive measures that assure as a state of consecration from threatening acts or impacts. "National security," then again, can be characterized in a target sense as the nonattendance of risk to a general public's center point, and in a subjective sense, as the nonappearance of apprehension that these qualities will be attacked. Likewise, it portrays the measures taken by a state to guarantee its survival and general prosperity [1].

3.1.4 Data Mining and Ethics

The utilization of data—especially data about individuals—for data mining has genuine ethical implications, and specialists of data mining methods must act dependably by making themselves aware of everything that encompasses their specific application. At the point when connected to people, data mining is oftentimes used to separate—who gets the credit, which gets the extraordinary offer, etc. Certain types of segregation—racial, sexual, religious, etc.—are exploitative as well as illegal. However, the circumstance is perplexing: everything relies upon the application. Utilizing sexual and racial data for medical diagnosis is unquestionably ethical; however, utilizing a similar data when mining credit payment conduct is most certainly not. Notwithstanding when sensitive information is disposed of, there is a hazard that models will be constructed based on factors that can appear as substitutes for racial or sexual qualities. For instance, people often live in regions that are related with specific ethnic personalities, so utilizing an area code in a data mining study risks building models that depend on race—despite the fact that racial data has been explicitly excluded from the information [2].

It is widely acknowledged that before people make a decision to give individual data they have to know how it will be utilized and what it will be utilized for, what steps will be taken to ensure its confidentiality and integrity, what the results of providing or withholding the data are, and any rights of change they may have. At whatever point such data is gathered, people ought to be told these things—not in legalistic little print but rather clearly in plain language they can understand. The potential utilization of data mining systems implies that the repository in which a vault of information can be utilized may extend a long way past what was considered when the information was initially gathered. This creates a major issue; it is important to decide the conditions under which the information was gathered and for what purpose it might be utilized [3].

Does the responsibility offer the right to utilize it in ways other than those implied when it was initially recorded? Obviously it does not, because of explicitly gathered personal information. Nevertheless, as a rule, the circumstance is complex. Surprising things rise up out of data mining. For instance, it has been reported that one of the main leading consumer groups has discovered that people with red cars will probably default on their car advances. What is the status of such a "disclosure"? What data is it in view? Under what conditions was that data gathered? In what ways is it ethical to utilize it? Obviously, insurance agencies are in the business of separating people in light of generalizations—youthful people pay intensely for accident protection—yet such generalizations are not constructive exclusively with respect to factual relationships; they additionally include presence of common-sense information on the world. Regardless of whether the previous finding says something concerning the type of person who picks a red car, or whether it ought to be disposed of as an immateriality, is an issue for human judgment in view of information of the world as opposed to a simple measurable criterion. At the point when given information, you have to request who is allowed to approach it, for what reason it was gathered, and what sort of conclusions is real to draw from it [4].

The ethical measurement brings up intense issues for those engaged with practical data mining. It is important to consider the standards of the group that is accustomed to managing the type of data included, gauges that may have advanced over decades or hundreds of years and the ones that may not be known to the data authority. For instance, it is realize that in the library group, it is underestimated that the security of per users is correct that is enviously ensured? This keeps a student from being subjected to weight from a perturbed professor to yield access to a book that the researcher urgently requires for their most recent concede application. It additionally denies enquiry into the questionable recreational perusing tastes of the university ethics panel chairman. The individuals who manufacture, say, digital libraries may not know about these sensitivities and might consolidate data mining systems that investigate and contrast people's reading habits with suggestive new books—may be notwithstanding the pitching outcomes to distributers! Notwithstanding people group guidelines for the utilization of information, legitimate and logical scientific standards must be clung to when making inferences from it. On the off chance that you do think of conclusions (for example, red car owners being more prominent to credit risks), it has to connect caveats to them and back them up with contentions other than statistical ones. The fact of the matter is that data mining is only an apparatus in the entire procedure; it is individuals who take the outcomes, alongside other learning, and choose what activity to apply. Data mining prompts another inquiry, which is truly a political one: as the author discuss the issue of utilize are society's assets being put. The author specified beforehand the use of data mining to wicker container investigation, where store checkout records are examined to identify relationships among things that people buy. On the off chance that information is described as recorded actualities, at that point data is the arrangement of examples, or desires, that underlie the information. You could go ahead to characterize information as the gathering of your arrangement of desires and intelligence as the esteem appended to learning. Despite the fact that we would not seek after it advances here, this issue is worth pondering [5].

3.1.5 Hypothesis of the Study

1. Impact of SVM in enhancing cybersecurity:
   Identifying the framework of Intrusion Detection Systems (IDS) impact of SVM in controlling and monitoring cybersecurity and Close to the security personnel in case of any malicious activity then Analyzing phishing attack of SVM and Analyzing distributed denial-of-service (DDoS) attack

3.2 Literature Review

The term support vector system (SVM) [3] is generally used to describe arrangement with support vector methods, and support vector regression is used to delineate relapse with SVMs. SVM is a useful framework for data characterization. SVM is an imaginative approach which is manage to building learning machines that breaking point speculation mistake. The course of action issue can be bound to think of the two class issues without loss of comprehensive inclusive statement. In this issue, the goal is to separate the two classes by a capacity that is initiated from open outlines. The objective is to convey a classifier that will work decently on concealed cases, i.e., it generalizes well. Here, there are different conceivable straight classifiers that can restrict the information; however, there is an unprecedented case that maximizes the margin (expands the division among it and the closest information inspiration driving each class). These quick classifiers are named as the ideal restricting hyperplane. Instinctually, we would expect that this point of confinement will aggregate up well rather than the other conceivable possible points. An order undertaking for the most part incorporates with getting ready and testing data that contain a couple of data events. Every arrangement set contains one "target regard" (class names) and a couple of "attributes" (features). The goal of SVM is to make a model that predicts target estimation of information events in the testing set, which are recently given the qualities. In the proposed work, straight part is used. This is shown as [6,7]

$$\text{Linear: } k\left(x_i, x_j\right) = x_i^T x_j$$

Kernel with some parameters (C, r)

Moreover, the sigmoid kernel carries on like resting bitch face (RBF) for specific parameters. In a proposed work, one kind of idea deciding IP addresses, IP number, port addresses, and port number is the introduction of utilizing SVM. This group has a unique IP and port number by malicious IP address and port number.

SVM is a successful instrument to order cyber assaults. However, in the meantime it has some disadvantages. The principal disadvantage is that SVM is incredibly unstable for attacks [8]. SVM proposed for the two class issues must be extended to multiclass issues by picking an appropriate kernel function. The execution of the SVM relies upon the kernel function. A few frameworks to enhance the execution of SVM were proposed. SVM [9] is one of the redesigns made on the standard SVM. Few machine-learning superlative models and in addition artificial neural network [10], linear genetic programming, data mining, and what not have been examined for the portrayal of digital assault. Moreover, the machine-learning methodologies are sensitive to noise in the arranging tests. The machine-learning methodologies of mislabeled information, if any information can understand exceedingly for nonlinear decision surface and over fitting of the planning set. This leads to poor theory point of confinement and portrayal exactness. A decision tree-based SVM that consolidates vector machine and choice tree can be a powerful approach to deal with multiclass issues. This strategy can set up the arranging and testing time, broadening the gainfulness of the framework [11]. Improved SVM calculation for characterization of computerized digital cyber data provides 100% recognizable proof precision for normal and DDoS classes and, for all intents and purposes, is indistinguishable to false ready rate, preparing, and testing times [12].

An investigation of drive-by abuse URLs had been performed by Provos, and they use a protected machine-learning algorithm as a pre channel for support vector machine (SVM)-based examination [13]. They remove content-based features from the page including I Frames that are unusual, the closeness of muddled JavaScript, and whether I Frames point to known exploit regions. The particular footings associated with assist vector machines (SVMs) are put together by research-ers. SVMs are gaining more attention because of quite a few advanced, impro-vised characteristics, as well as encouraging empirical performance. This system embodies the structural risk minimization principle, which has been shown to be superior [14].

The manuscript specifies your rating criteria with regard to intrusion prognosis. Sham prognosis can be another division of emphasis while the quantity of net dealings can increase significantly. A variety of frauds, such as computer system fraud, is allowed to happen using their own techniques to overcome the situation. Quite a few approaches tend to be planned with regard to private protection through information mining, e.g., K-anonymity, SVM, clustering, association, etc. [15].

Xiong et al. [6]. proposed a technique for distinguishing an interruption utilizing incremental SVM. SVM is utilized to gain from enormous datasets with extensive measurement information. Registering an SVM is immoderate regarding time and memory utilization. Thus, various SVMs are joined in such a route along these lines, to the point that each incremental SVM in the chain is prepared by the past SVM yield and new cluster of preparing dataset. For two class issues, SVM finds a hyperplane isolated by bolster vector for more than two class information sets, and it is mapped to high-dimensional information utilizing portion capacity. From the test, it has been noted that the model builds location rate and abates false-positive recognition [16].

This chapter proposes another methodology for improving the preparation procedure of SVM when managing expansive preparation of information sets. It depends on the blend of SVM and grouping investigation. The thought is as follows: SVM registers the maximal edge isolating information focuses; thus, just those examples nearest to the edge can influence the calculations of that edge, while different focuses can be disposed of without influencing the last result. Those focuses lying near the edge are called bolster vectors. The author attempts to surmise these focuses by applying grouping investigation [17].

SVM is an efficient and common a single function and against various offered unit finding out methods inside IDA, mainly because SVM strength since the syndication associated with several types of imbalanced violence. The place that the finding out sample dimensions from the low-frequent violence can be also smaller in comparison with the actual high-frequent violence SVM because classifier provides capacity for beneficial generalization against smaller sample dimensions education as well as finding out, which can be often used inside real-world apps associated with category [18].

The leading assumed of SVMs can obtain the optimum splitting hyperplane involving the beneficial as well as damaging biological samples. This can be performed through maximizing the particular perimeter involving a pair of parallel hyperplanes. Acquiring this specific jet, SVM may then predict the particular classification regarding unlabeled small samples by asking what is the best area on the distancing approach the particular small sample is. SVMs can easily deal with a variety of classification troubles including linear as well as nonlinear classification troubles. The two separable as well as no separable troubles are usually handled simply by SVMs from the linear as well as nonlinear circumstance [19].

The SVM methodology changes information into an element space F that as a rule has an immense measurement. It is fascinating to note that SVM speculation relies upon the geometrical qualities of the prepared information, and not on the measurements of the info space. Preparing SVM prompts a quadratic enhancement issue with bound limitations and one direct correspondence constraint. The researcher shows how preparing an SVM for the example acknowledgment issue prompts the after quadratic enhancement issue [20].

This research shows that it would take a long time to coach SVM with a file collection composed of 1 million files. Many proposals are actually presented to reinforce SVM to raise its overall teaching performance possibly by means of arbitrary collection as well as approximation of the marginal classifier. These kinds of solutions are nevertheless impossible with significant file pieces, wherever perhaps, much verification connected with entire file collection usually are too costly to execute, as well as bring about a damage by means of oversimplification connected with any kind of profit to become acquired using SVM.

In 2012, Gaspar et al. gave the audit on systems that are utilized to enhance, boost, and ameliorate the taxonomy execution in terms of exactness or faultless of SVMs and perform some experimentation to examine the impact of components and hyperparameters in the streamlining procedure, utilizing kernel function [20].

There are different reasons why we utilize SVMs for interruption location. The primary is rate of which is "Pattern Accurate Computationally Efficient" as constant execution is of essential significance to interruption discovery frameworks, and any classifier that can conceivably run "quick" merit needs consideration. The second reason is adaptability: SVM is somewhat sensitive to the number of focuses of information, and the multifaceted system of nature does not rely on the most prominent space dimensions, so they can take a larger set of examples and therefore have the ability of neural systems. Once the information is ordered into two classes, a suitable enhancing calculation can be utilized if fundamental for further element-recognizable proof, contingent upon the application [21].

The author proposed a machine-learning model using an adjusted SVM that connects the advantages of directed and unsupervised learning. Besides, a preparatory component choice procedure utilizing Genetic Algorithm is given to choose more proper bundle fields [19].

In the linear SVM, it hunts down a hyperplane with the biggest edge. However, the nonlinear SVM changes its information from its unique direction space into another space, so that a straight choice limit can be utilized to discrete the occasion in changed space. Nevertheless, it drives a serious issue of dimensionality. To take care of this issue, portion trap has been utilized. The portion trap is a strategy for processing the likeness in the change space utilizing the first trait set. Nevertheless, selecting a suitable portion is a major issue. In the SVM, the generally utilized portions are polynomial, sigmoid, and RBF.

The reasons for utilizing SVM for intrusion identification are the information utilized as a part of the IDS model is colossal to handle such information is troublesome; yet, in the SVM, the quantity of operations is not so much relative to the quantity of elements. The bit characterizes a similitude measure between two information focuses, and in this way permits one to join former learning of the issue area [22].

A perfect interruption location framework is one that has a high-assault location rate alongside a 0% false positive rate (FPR). On the other hand, such a low rate of false positives is just accomplished to the detriment of overlooking minor malignant action identification. This provides an assailant a little window of chance to perform subjective practices, making them understand with respect to the kind of interruption discovery framework being used. Building IDS with a small number of false positives is a greatly troublesome undertaking. In this chapter, we show two orthogonal and reciprocal ways to deal with a decrease in the quantity of false usage to encourage points in interruption location ready for post handling. The fundamental thought is to utilize existing IDSs as a ready source and after that apply either disconnected one from the net (utilizing information mining) or online (utilizing machine learning) ready handling to diminish the quantity of false positives [23].

Oddity location is the procedure for discovering the examples in a dataset whose conduct is not typically on. These surprising practices are likewise termed as abnormalities or exceptions. The peculiarities cannot generally be arranged as an assault; yet, it can be an astonishing conduct which is already not known. It could conceivably be hurtful. The peculiarity identification provides exceptionally noteworthy and basic data in different applications, for instance, credit card robberies or character burglaries. At the point when information must be broken down, keeping in mind the end goal to discover relationships or to foresee known or obscure information, mining systems are utilized.

These incorporate bunching, order, and machine-based learning systems. Crossover methodologies are additionally being made, keeping in mind the end goal to accomplish more an elevated amount of precision on recognizing peculiarities.

In this methodology, the creators attempt to join existing information mining calculations to infer better results. In this manner, distinguishing the irregular or unforeseen conduct or oddities will respect ponder and sort it into new kind of assaults or a specific sort of interruption. This review endeavors to provide a superior comprehension among the different sorts of information mining methodologies toward oddity discovery that has been made recently [22,23].

The main objective of the proposed exertion is to recommend another crossbreed interruption discovery framework thought which is join three usefulness, selective of depicting, the preset interruption, and discovery framework utilized as a part of that idea. The proposed hybrid intrusion discovery framework influences the execution performance and investigation of security. The idea of security and the term interruption discovery framework may be threatening and convoluted. To maintain the soaring detection rate and accuracy, and at the same time decrease the false alarm rate, the proposed technique is a combination of three learning approaches [24].

According to the researcher, in context to upgrade execution, the work displays a model of IDS. This enhanced model, named as reduced error pruning (REP) based IDS model, gives yield with more noteworthy exactness alongside the increased number of appropriately characterized cases. It utilizes the two calculations of characterization methodologies, in particular, K2 (BayesNet) and REP (Decision Tree). Here, REP provides a powerful grouping along with the pruning of tree with snappy choice learning capacity [24].

The Malicious clients or programmers utilize the associations inside frameworks to gather and cause vulnerabilities such as software bugs, lapse in organization, and clearing out frameworks to default design. As the web rising into the general public, new stuffs such as infections and worms are foreign made. By threatening in this way, the customers use unmistakable routines like breaking the mystery key and distinguishing decoded substances to make vulnerabilities in the structure. In this manner, security is required for the customers to secure their structure from the impose routine. The firewall system is one of the known security strategies used to ensure your framework of the community system in general. IDSs are used as part of system-related training, repair, and counterfeiting applications for credit card and insurance offices. It is important to clearly point out that secure socket layer (SSL)/Transport Layer Security (TLS) just provides transport-level security and not industrious data insurance. Message-level security requires additional means at a more elevated amount in the convention stack. This infers that the convention suite cannot be utilized for (multibounce) end-to-end security because of the need for persevering encryption and uprightness assurance. Security ensures are accessible for point-to-point associations—correspondence channel security—and not for end-to-end payload security.

SSL/TLS provides various configurable security goals, for example:

■ Testimony—through the utilization of computerized certificates
■ Acquaintance—using encryption

- Integrity—by the utilization of message testimony code media access control (MAC)
- (Nonrepudiation)—by the use of digital certificates
- Replay protection—by the use of implicit sequence numbers

SSL is a convention created by Netscape regarding shifting exclusive information over the World Wide Web. SSL works by utilizing an open key to encode information that is exchanged over the SSL connection. Both Netscape Navigator and Internet Explorer support SSL, and various web areas use the tradition to safely transmit secret data. Different ways to deal with overseeing web security are conceivable. The characteristic philosophies have different views but can differ in relation to their degree of study and the relative region within the transmission control protocol/Internet protocol (TCP/IP) tradition. The situation at the point where the security can be at the level of IP, which is clear to terminate clients and applications. However, another respectable point throughout the useful game plan is that the security performance is basically above the TCP. The prevalent specimen of this system is the SSL [25]. It provides protection to help electronic digital purposes. It works by using a TCP to supply stop-to-end protected products and services. SSL is not a new solo conference but rather a pair of cellular levels associated with conferences. It could be observed that one layer helps in making use of TCP straightforwardly. This specific layer is known as the actual SSL record method and it provides fundamental protection administration to help different higher layer conferences. Three different additionally enhanced total conferences will likewise be produced using this specific layer and tend to be some of the actual SSL layer. They are utilized as part of the administration of SSL trades and are as follows:

1. Handshake protocol
2. Change cipher spec protocol
3. Ready protocol [26]

3.3 Methodology

a. Method of Data Collection

The nature of data is quantitative and secondary, and it is taken from different websites and described in a graphical form. Nature of data is quantitative and secondary. The secondary data was collected through different research projects and published in articles of different years.

b. Sampling Technique

Sampling technique used is SVM, a relatively supervised learning method.

c. Sample Size

The sample size is the current year around 2015-17. Target population for selecting the sample was the published papers.

d. Research Model

A DDoS attack is an assault that looks to impair the objective so that it can never again offer the administrations it typically provides. In the standard web situation, a disavowal of administration assault is where a server is intentionally sent a huge volume of interchanges activity that overpowers it and reasons it to crash. Frequency average attack size increases of 52% from 1 July 2015 to 30 September 2015 observed a rise in the number of DDoS as against our customer continued targeting of specific industries and 54% more attack. Frequency of DDoS attack increases to 34% when compared with the first half of 2015.

As per their study, a quarter of clients admit to succumbing to e-fraudsters, with the normal casualty losing over £285. Counterfeit banking emails and messages are the most well-known technique utilized by criminals, with 55% of those focused on getting apparently real e-correspondence from high street banks.

The total number of phish observed in Q1 was 125,215, a 10.7% expansion over Q4 2013, when a sum of 111,773 was observed. The 125,215 is the second largest number of destinations recognized in a quarter, obscured just by the 164,032 found in the primary quarter of 2012 (Tables 3.1 and 3.2) [26].

The total number of phish observed in Q2 was 128,378, a 3% expansion over Q1 2014, when a sum of 125,215 was observed. The 128,378 is the second highest number of phishing locales recognized in a quarter, obscured just by the 164,032 found in the primary quarter of 2012 (Figures 3.1–3.4).

Table 3.1 Statistical Highlights, 1st Quarter 2016

	April	*May*	*June*
Number of unique phishing websites detected	42,828	38,175	44,212
Number of unique phishing email report (campaigns) received by APWG from consumers	53,984	56,883	60,925
Number of brands targeted by phishing campaigns	384	355	362
Country hosting the most phishing website	USA	USA	USA
Contain some form of target name in URL	56.76%	54.31%	64.47%
Percentage of sites not using port 80	0.85%	0.42%	0.56%

Table 3.2 Statistical Highlights, 2nd Quarter 2016

	April	*May*	*June*
Number of unique phishing websites detected	41,759	44,407	42,212
Number of unique phishing email report (campaigns) received by APWG from consumers	57,733	60,809	53,259
Number of brands targeted by phishing campaigns	332	357	345
Country hosting the most phishing website	USA	USA	USA
Contain some form of target name in URL	56.76%	54.31%	64.47%
Percentage of sites not using port 80	0.85%	0.42%	0.56%

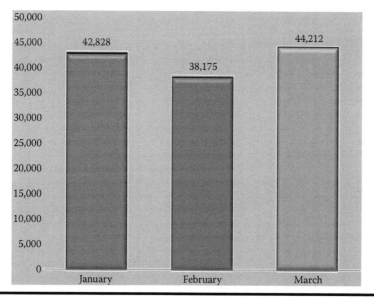

Figure 3.1   Unique phishing sites detected January–March 2016.

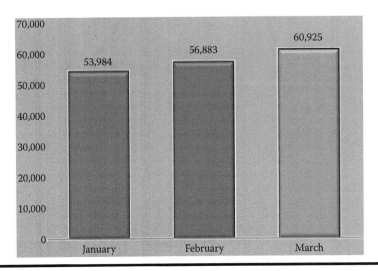

Figure 3.2   Phishing reports received January–March 2016.

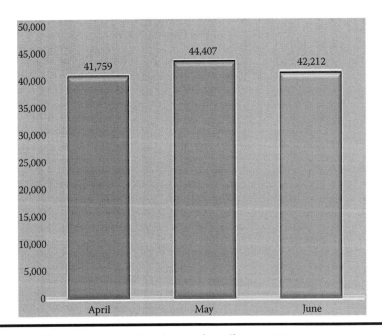

Figure 3.3   Unique phishing sites detected April–June 2016.

The quantity of one of a kind phishing reports submitted to Anti-Phishing Working Group (APWG) amid Q3 was 163,333, a reduction of 5% from the 171,801 got in Q2 of 2014. The quantity of one of a kind phishing report submitted to APWG stayed steady amid the three-month time frame, between a high of 55,282 in July to 53,661 in September (Figures 3.5 and 3.6).

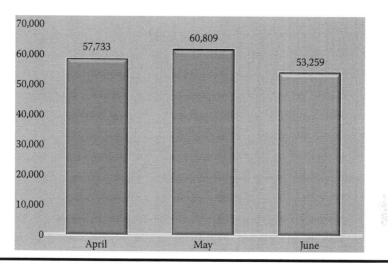

Figure 3.4 Phishing reports received April–June 2016.

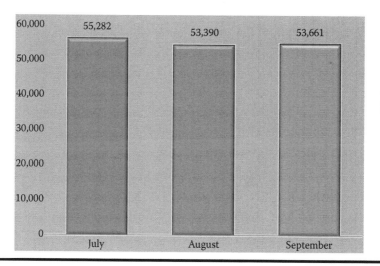

Figure 3.5 Phishing reports received July–September 2016.

The total number of novel phishing destinations observed in Q4 was 46,824. This number is significantly lower than in Q3 by a large portion. A move inferable from methodological refinements in how phishing destinations were checked, and URLs were decopied to recognize really one of a kind phishing site (Tables 3.3 and 3.4).

In the given chart, analysis of security breaches of 2015 are provided, and from this analysis, it is clear that nil accidents in hacking is too high in 2016, so by using the SVM technique of data mining, we can cope up all the breaches of security in future (Figures 3.7–3.9).

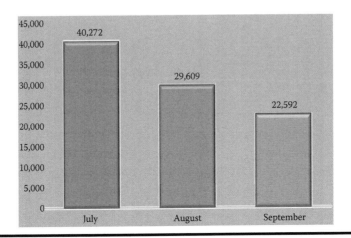

Figure 3.6 Unique phishing sites detected July–September 2016.

Table 3.3 Statistical Highlights, 4th Quarter 2016

	October	*November*	*December*
Number of unique phishing websites detected	15,246	14,528	17,320
Number of unique phishing email report (campaigns) received by APWG from consumers	68,270	66,217	62,765
Number of brands targeted by phishing campaigns	271	273	300
Country hosting the most phishing website	USA	USA	USA
Contain some form of target name in URL	44.88%	50.40%	50.37%
Percentage of sites not using port 80	0.72%	0.35%	1.04%

The given chart is the reflection of the complete year attack ratio monthwise, and data is shown as the largest ratio of hacktivism in the above and below charts (Figure 3.10).

3.4 Implementation

This section tends to explain the issue of finding out queries and evacuating summaries, routinely unidentified beforehand from a lot of data using configuration

Table 3.4 2017 Analysis of Breach Types

Breach Type	No. of Accidents	No. of Record Exposed	Average Record Per Account
Fraud social engineering	152,102	21,999	67,280
Hacking unknown	1,293	529,596,699	458,311
Web	103	138,648,221	1,346,097
Email	69	730,924	10,693
Skimming	34	982	29
Virus	29	2,680,753	92,440

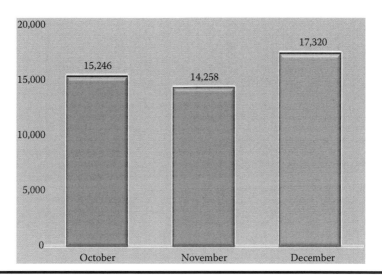

Figure 3.7 Unique phishing sites detected October–December 2016.

planning or other thinking procedures. We have demonstrated the user's profile in view of the most applicable dangers for national security join assaulting structures, destroying fundamental systems, for instance, control lattices and media transmission frameworks. Information mining strategies are being investigated to discover who the suspicious people are and who is prepared for doing dread monger work out. Cybersecurity is incorporated with guaranteeing the computer and network system against corruption, worms, and viruses. Data mining is likewise associated with giving game plans, for instance, interference recognition and assessment. In this work, we discriminate the malicious behavior of clients from the typical conduct by utilizing the SVM. An irregularity is distinguished when

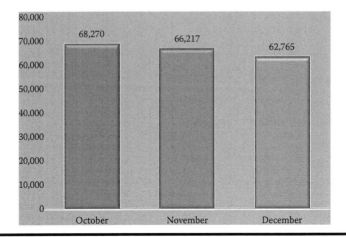

Figure 3.8 Phishing report received October–December 2016.

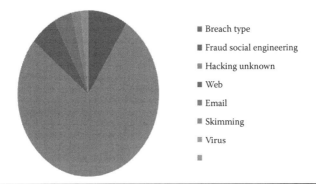

Figure 3.9 2017 analysis of breach types.

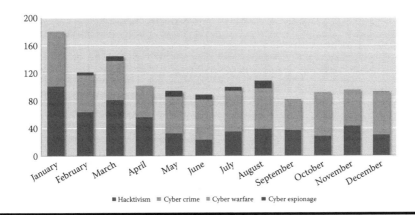

Figure 3.10 2017 attack trend (drill down).

the present example of a client (subject) does not coordinate with any of the person's typical examples. The proposed algorithm depends on the data mining SVM. Input (I): *user_id_user_id_date_time_Customer Relationship Management_Medical Analysis_Diagnostic_Supply Chain Management_Supply Chain Management_Fraud Detection_Detecting Criminal Activities*

*Normalization is performed on the input dataset, D = DDoS dataset representing input data vectors in [0,1] */

where

D = DDoS dataset

D_R = Data Mining dataset

D_t = testing Data Mining dataset

D = DDoS (I)

/*Dimension reduction of D by using principal component analysis, D_R, = reduced dataset */

D = dim_red (**D**)

/* prepare the dataset for giving input in SVM */

D_R = Data Mining dataset (**D_R**) // Data Mining dataset

D_T = testing dataset (**D_R**) // Data Mining dataset /*

/* For training on SVM*/ (C, 6) = crossval_ grid ($D_{R)}$ //Determine best values of C and 6

m = train (D_R, C, 6) //Train the SVM classifier /*

/* Fraud Detection by applying **D** on the model */

For a given record D_R ∈ D

3.5 Comparative Analysis

The effectiveness of our misrepresentation discovery approach is exhibited by testing it with reality mining dataset. We have first standardized (scaled) the information in the range [0,1], as SVM just requires an arrangement of genuine number vectors, i.e., either class 0 or class 1. Subsequent to scaling, dimensionality diminishment is performed to acquire another arrangement of low-dimensional information by utilizing principal component analysis strategy. For the readiness of the DDoS and data mining test dataset, we have utilized part rate (split %) strategy. We have considered 70% part, so the data mining test dataset is made out of 70% of the dataset, and the test dataset contains the remaining 30%. The dataset is utilized to perform the SVM classifier, and test dataset is utilized to gauge the efficacy of the classifier. After the necessary arrangement of dataset is done, a 10-fold cross-validation and network look strategy has been utilized together on the data mining dataset to discover the best regularization parameters C and σ. These two techniques randomly divide the preparation dataset into 10 equal size folds and locate the best combination of C and σ from those folds. These parameters are then used to prepare the entire classifier display. For our approach, the SVM yields the most minimal blunder rate at the mix estimations of C = 8 and σ = 0.5. After the classifier demonstrate is created, the test set is utilized to discover the execution of the proposed D_R and D_T to precision, genuine positive rate (TPR), and FPR.

$$\text{Accuracy} = D_R\left(\text{data mining dataset }(\mathbf{D\_R})\right)$$
$$+ D_T\left(\text{testing dataset }(\mathbf{D\_R})\right)/\text{Total Data Mining Datasets}$$

True positive rate (TPR) + false positive rate (FPR)/Total Data Mining Data Sets

The ratio of accuracy of data mining dataset techniques is calculated and are represented by this section.

3.6 Conclusion

Our idea provides a protected application, in view of the arrangement utilizing SVM. Here is a dataset of various sizes utilized for preparation and characterization. The SVM experiment is conducted on different data such as hacktivism, cybercrime, cyberwarfare, cyberespionage, and these data are taken from the different published researches. SVM classifier is an accurate method for securing cyber from different types of attack. SVM is 98.5556% accurate classifier and nonlinearly it maps the points of data on the high-dimensional features and construction of the hyperplane. The earliest research work provides the review of the IDS, where SVM technique in cybersecurity which is plays a vital role, with the growing ratio of cyberattacks like phishing, DDoS, hacktivism, etc. According to the earliest discussion and analysis of the security breaches in 2016, there is a need to focus and secure the cyberspace from all types of malicious attack with reliable techniques and creating different frameworks of SVM techniques due to its accuracy of the result classifier.

Acknowledgment

The authors are grateful to the Department of Computer Science and Information Technology, Institute of Business and Management (IoBM), Karachi, Pakistan.

References

1. Vipin Das, Vijaya Pathak, Sattvik Sharma, Sreevathsan, M.V.V.N.S. Srikanth, T. Gireesh Kumar. December 2010. Network intrusion detection system based on machine learning algorithms. *International Journal of Computer Science & Information Technology (IJCSIT)*, Vol. 2, No. 6.

2. Stefano Zanero and Sergio M. Savaresi. 2004. Unsupervised learning techniques for an intrusion detection system. In *Proceedings of the 2004 ACM Symposium on Applied Computing*, pp. 412–419. Nicosia, Cyprus: ACM Press.

3. Hilmi Gunes Kayacik, A. Nur Zincir-Heywood, and Malcolm I. Heywood. 2014. On the capability of an SOM based intrusion detection system. In *Proceedings of the International Joint Conference on Neural Networks*. vol. 3, Portland, pp. 1808–1813. IEEE.

4. Snehal A. Mulay, P. R. Devale, and G. v. Garje. June 2010. Intrusion detection system using support vector machine and decision tree. *International Journal of Computer Applications*, Vol. 3, No. 3, pp. 40–43.

5. Shailendra Singh Member, IEEE, IAENG, Sanjay Agrawal, A. Rizvi Murtaza, and Ramjeevan Singh Thakur. October 19–21, 2011. Improved support vector machine for cyber attack detection. In *Proceedings of the World Congress on Engineering and Computer Science (WCECS)*, Vol. 1, San Francisco, CA.

6. Sheng-Wu Xiong, Hong-bing Liu, and Xiao-xiao Niu. August 18–21, 2005. Fuzzy support vector machines based on FCM clustering. In *Proceedings of the Fourth International Conference on Machine Learning and Cybernetics*, pp. 2608–2613. Guangzhou, China. IEEE.

7. Anup K. Ghosh and Aaron Schwartzbard. 2015. A study in using neural networks for anomaly and misuse detection. In *Proceeding of the Eighth USENIX Security Symposium*, pp. 23–36. Washington, DC.

8. Srinivas Mukkamala, Andrew H. Sung, and Ajith Abraham. 2014. Modeling intrusion detection systems using linear genetic programming approach. *The Seventeenth International Conference on Industrial & Engineering Applications of Artificial Intelligence and Expert Systems, Innovation in Applied Artificial Intelligence.*

9. Wenke Lee, Salvatore J. Stolfo, and Kui Mok. 2014. Data mining in work flow environments: Experience in intrusion detection. In *Proceedings of the Conference on Knowledge Discovery and Data Mining (KDD–99).*

10. Motaz M. H. Khorshid and Tarek H.-E.-E. 2015. A Comparison among Support Vector Machine. *Internal Publisher for Advanced Scientific Journals (IPASJ)*. Shanghai, China. pp. 1–11.

11. Preeti Aggarwal, M. M. Chaturvedi. 2013. Application of data mining techniques for information security in a cloud: A survey. *International Journal of Computer Applications*, Vol. 80, No. 13, p. 7.

12. Soobia Saeed, Asaduallah Sheikh, and Syed Mehmood Raza Naqvi. 2018. Impact of data mining techniques to analyze health care data. *Journal of informatics Technology*, Vol. 8, pp. 1–9.

13. Soobia Saeed, Asadullah Sheikh, Muhammad Mansoor Alam, and Muhammad Ali. 2017, *Technique for Tumour Detection Upon Brain MRI Image by Utilizing Support Vector Machine*, Quaid-E-Awam University of Engineering, Science & Technology.

14. Jitendra Kumar Seth. 2014. An optimistic approach for intrusion security in cloud. *International Journal of Computer Applications*, Vol. 97, No. 13, p. 4.

15. Bhavani Thuraisingham and Latifur Khan. 2007. A new intrusion detection system using support vector machines. *The VLDB Journal*, Vol. 16, No. 4, pp. 507–521.

16. Leila Mohammadpour and Mehdi Hussain. 2015. Evaluating performance of intrusion detection system using support vector machines: Review. *International Journal of Security and Its Applications*, Vol. 9, p. 10.

17. Muamer N. Mohammed and Norrozila Sulaiman. 2012. *Intrusion Detection System Based on SVM for WLAN*. Elesvier. Vol. 1, pp. 313–317.
18. Kalyani Waghmare and Vitthal Manekar. 2014. Intrusion detection system using Support Vector Machine (SVM) and Particle Swarm Optimization (PSO). *International Journal of Advanced Computer Research*, Vol. 4, No. 3–16, p. 5.
19. Bhavsar Yogita. 2013. Intrusion Detection system using data mining techniques support vector machine. *International Journal of Emerging Technology and Advanced Engineering*, p. 6.
20. Jayshree Jha and Leena Ragha. 2013. Intrusion detection system using support vector machine. *International Journal of Applied Information Systems (IJAIS)*, p. 6.
21. Ravinder R. Reddy. 2015. Anomaly detection using feature selection and SVM. *International Journal of Computer Applications*, p. 5.
22. Amit Dubey and Bisen Minakshi. 2015. An intrusion detection system based on SVM using hierarichal clustering and genetic algorithm. *The SIJ Transactions on Computer Science Engineering and Its Applications*, p. 5.
23. Jitendra Agrawal and Shikha Agrawal. 2015. *Survey on Anomaly Detection Using Data Mining Techniques*. Elesvier. p. 6.
24. Vasim Iqbal Memon and Gajendra Singh. 2014. A design and implementation of new hybrid system for anomaly intrusion detection system to improve efficiency. *International Journal of Engineering Research and Applications (IJERA)*. Vol. 5, p. 7.
25. R. K. Gupta and Sanjay Sharma. 2015. Intrusion detection system: A review. *International Journal of Security and Its Applications*, Vol. 4, p. 8.
26. Pradeep Kumar Panwar, Devendra Kumar. 2012. Security through SSL. *International Journal of Advanced Research in Computer Science and Software Engineering*. Vol. 2, No. 12. pp. z–184.

Chapter 4

Vision of Internet of Things Framework for Smart Building

Soobia Saeed and M. Alam

Ilma University

Contents

4.1 Introduction

4.1.1 Overview

The Internet of Things (IoT) is an effective and cunning system that interfaces every one of the things in the world through the Internet to empower data trade and correspondence through different gadgets with the arrangement of different conventions. It has the ability to recognize the things brilliantly-IoT, overseeing, and checking them. It is one of the improved forms of Internet-based system, which has the ability to share data not only between humans but also between humans and things. Likewise, it upgrades the collaboration between the physical and virtual world. In an IoT, every one of the things is associated with each other, utilizing Internet, radio frequency identification technology (RFID), and sensor innovation.

4.1.2 Problem Statement

Pakistan is a developing country that faces an electricity crisis. The electricity crisis are getting severe day by day, especially during the summer. Electricity shortfall reaches 6,000 MW this year; currently, Pakistan generated 15,000 MW against a demand of 21,000 MW. The purpose of this research project is to analyze how power consumption can be reduced to provide a possible short-term solution. The author proposes a framework for smart vitality in building through it so that wastage of vitality could be reduced. In this research project, vitality monitoring and the IoT system technique are used. The reason for this choice is its low cost because the connectivity of Internet facility is widely and easily available in all modern sensors and devices. In terms of environmental sustainability, vitality efficient buildings play a vital role globally. In this research work, National Centre for Remote Sensing and Geo-informatics (NCRG) building data is monitored and collected based on data traces, and vitality consumption patterns are identified and various methods for better vitality efficiency are explored. The results led to the conclusion that due to the fixed pattern control the buildings are not vitality efficient, although they are designed as "smart." A smart and automatic vitality control framework is proposed, which uses a smartphone platform that includes organizing, building, and user-level vitality proportionality. Another experimental IoT platform is built which demonstrates a positive outcome of proposed solutions for smart vitality consumption. Economic and social sustainability benefits can clearly be seen from the results.

4.1.3 Internet of Things

The Internet of Things is the Internet effective of bodily widgets, vehicles (moreover alluded to as "linked widgets" and "shrewd gadgets"), formation, and dissimilar belongings surrounded with hardware, encoding, antenna, actuators, and structure accessibility that authorizes these critiques to assemble and deal data. In 2013, the worldwide standards scheme on the Internet of Things-Global Standard Initiative

(IoT-GSI) identifies IoT as "the structure of the information civilization" then it allows staff to be noticed and as well control distantly oblique over vacant system roads, making untie entrance for more uncomplicated merge of the bodily humankind into PC support frameworks, and carrying related to improved efficiency, accuracy, and fiscal advantage. When IoT is enlarged with antenna and actuators, the modernism spins into the incidence of an additional wide group of digital bodily scaffolds, which similarly includes proceed, for illustration, confidence networks, luminous houses, clever shipping, and eager municipal area. All is extraordinarily particular throughout its entrenched dispensation construction so far can interpret indoors the present Internet of Thing. Expert weighs in the IT will contain about 50 billion gripe by 2020.

Regularly, it is relied upon the proffered power accessibility of widgets, structures, and managements that exit history machine-to-machine (M2M) swapping and wrap a mixture of meeting, space, and request. The interconnection of these set-up widgets (counting shrewd items) is required to begin computerization in approximately all pastures, while additionally authorizing pushed appliance similar to a brilliant grid, and expanding to the land, for instance, savvy cities.

4.1.4 Vitality Management

Incorporation of perceiving and commencement scaffolds, linked to the Internet is probably going to streamline vitality consumption as a whole. It is usual that IoT widgets will be synchronized hooked on all kinds of strength-spending widgets and has to be ability to converse with the usefulness contribute association guardian in the brain and the end of objective to sufficiently alter control period and energy use. Such widgets would similarly present the unbolt entrance for customers to distantly manage their widgets, or intermediately run them side to side a cloud-based edge, and authorize pushed capabilities like preparation (e.g., distantly fueling on or off humoring frameworks, scheming broilers, and altering illumination circumstances).

Other than privately arranged imperativeness organization, IoT is especially vital to the style arrangement while it offers structures to assemble and follow up on essentialness and control-associated information in a motorized way with the target to upgrade the viability, constancy, financial issues, and sensibility of the age and course of power. Utilizing advanced metering establishment contraptions related with the Internet spine, electric utilities can accumulate data from end-customer relationships and additionally direct other scattering motorization devices like transformers and loners.

4.1.5 Significance and Background of Study

The IoT is sighted as a modernism and monetary sign in the international information production after the Internet. IoT is an intelligent scheme that envelops all articles to the Internet with the end objective of operating statistics and communicate through the fact perceiving widget as per agreed convention. It achieves the aim of smart distinguishing, judging, pursuing, checking, and watching over things. It is an augmentation and extension of Internet-based schemes, which raises the communication from person and person to person and things or articles and articles. In the IoT globe view, much critique encircling us will be linked into schemes in a few frames. RF familiar evidence (RFID), feeler modernism, and additional keen advancements will be installed into a variety of utility.

As an expanding obsession, there is no typical acknowledged description on IoT. Experts from alternate points of view and associations portray IoT differently. Captivating after modernism advancements, additional outlining power, accumulation, and buttery edge obtain are available at usually negligible attempts and low downhill mass. This prototype is authorizing the advancement of outrageous small-scale electronic widgets with distinguishing proof abilities, which might be entrenched in dissimilar widget, frames, and place of work. IoT has to have the supplementary three features.

4.1.6 Broad Insight

Utilizing RFID, antennas, and two-dimensional scanner tags to acquire the information on question on whatever time and place will be another prospect. Utilizing the information, data and correspondence frameworks can be imperceptibly inserted in the earth. Sensor systems will empower individuals to collaborate remotely with this present reality. Distinguishing proof advances incorporate articles and are a recognizable piece of proof. Recognizable proof and recognition of the corporeal globe is the organization of implementable general observation.

4.1.7 Trustworthy Broadcast

During a collection of reachable broadcasting systems, medium transmission schemes, and the Internet, substance information can be reachable at whatever time. Here, correspondence modernism integrates a collection of restless and distant broadcast advances, swapping advances, systematizing progress, and passage advances. IoT promotes the announcement surrounded by the substantial globe, the implicit planet, the computerized humanity, and the general public. A M2M, moreover, is the input execution and innovation of the system gear, which speaks to the associations and interchanges among M2M and person to mechanism, counting portable mechanism.

4.1.8 Intellectual Dispensation

The Intellectual Dispensation of IoT information into a folder, different insightful processing modernism, including disseminated calculation will have the ability to bolster IoT in sequence appeal. The scheme benefit dealer can handle numerous millions and still disseminate a billion bits of communication in a flash throughout distributed computing. Disseminated figuring modernization along these lines will be the advocate of IoT.

4.1.9 Objective

- To discuss how power consumption can be reduced through vitality monitoring
- To describe and propose an IoT model and framework that influence the consumption of vitality and its impact
- To discuss the impact of IoT framework for smart buildings

4.1.10 Outline of the Study

In this report, building vitality utilization information is assessed and introduced in our discoveries in recognizing the real issues in these structures. In view of that, a savvy area-based arrangement is proposed, which is a vitality control IoT framework configuration to handle the issue and enhance vitality effectiveness. The focal thought is to sum up the cell phone- and area-based vitality control thought and incorporate strategies of various levels of associations. To sum up, the vitality sparing of individual clients permits disseminated and dynamic vitality control, which is the key for vitality proportionality.

4.2 Literature Review

Because of multidisciplinary quintessence of the exploration point, the associated work includes a scope of various territories. We cover a couple of them in a concise manner. Constrained by the space, a more drawn out rundown of the connected work can be found in papers [1,2]. Initially, the linked range is a structured vitality reenactment. Many building recreation programming takes structure measurements as informative and in the wake of preparation yield evaluated vitality use [2]. One of the famous is "Vitality Plus" given by the Department of Vitality (DOV). On examination, checking building vitality utilization with genuine method frameworks and investigating the genuine vitality utilization information are more powerful. Second zone is the atmosphere impact model inquiring about where a lot of current work is done and the association involving vitality utilization and atmosphere or climate variables [3]. The associated work comprises reenacting the warmth exchange procedures and building structures, envelope, and tree protects, etc., and discover how the atmosphere can affect building vitality productivity. The investigation of sun-powered consequences for warmth and mass exchange and their effects. Also the majority of them are in the light of hypothetical warm computations and recreations and not many of them are utilizing the real building vitality information and most of the proficient method to lessen the vitality utilization by fusing tenants' support [4].

Third zone is the utilization of wireless sensor network (WSN) innovations into the building tone and analyses on a particular subsystem like illumination and indoor regulator. For instance, it is utilized to detect and control the lights as per the identification after effects of the daylight for a structure in view of individual exercises that screen the electrical vitality utilization and monitor the person exercises, to modify the working of heating, ventilation, and air conditioning (HVAC) time to give enhanced solace, etc. There are tons of such test examinations. Run of the mill is in [5,6] and others are at random. Notwithstanding, WSN was initially intended for different reasons, yet they can give a decent supplement to further detect and meter innovations in the building environment. For building vitality reenactment devices, large portions of them take building parameters as information and gauge vitality use. A case is "Vitality Plus" by the Department of Vitality (DOE) to anticipate vitality stream in structures [6]. Mostly, recreation programming is moderately a modest path for assessing the building vitality utilization without sending an entire metering framework. There is additionally some exploration to discover the relationship between building vitality utilization and atmospheric or climatic condition through demonstration [7,8]. An entire reference of related endeavors can be found [9]. For the sensor of arrangement applications in the building situation, the examination identifies with electrical observing or lighting checking in a lab or a story level utilizing sensor hubs see the underprivileged.

Previously associated classification is in the data and in software engineering innovations. Apple's iPhone, Android, and Windows set give comparable open stages to create flexible savvy functions with numerous sensors having a global positioning system (GPS). In this way, there are a few broad range of applications for building environmental vitality examination and management. Dispersed computing is an exceptionally hot debated issue identified with our examination [10].

4.2.1 Prospect of IoT

IoT can create a tremendous scheme of millions of "Things" imparting all others. IoT is not a subversive insurgency above the current advancement, and is a complete usage of vacant innovations, and is produced consisting of latest communication modes. IoT combines the imaginary world and the practical world by carrying various ideas and specific segments simultaneously: certain systems, ranging down of gadgets, portable correspondence, and a fresh organic society. Within IoT, functions, administrations, core parts, systems, and last centers can be fundamentally sorted out and consumed being an element of latest ways. IoT presents a way for investigating compound procedures as well as connections. The IoT infers an advantageous cooperation between the genuine/practical and the advanced/imaginary universes. The Practical elements are computerized partners as well as imaginary representation; "things" get to be setting mindful and they can detect, impart, collaborate, and trade information, data, and learning [11].

New open door assembles business prerequisites, and latest administrations are made in view of continuous practical world information. The whole thing within the practice or imaginary world is conceivably associated with IoT. A network connecting the stuff is supposed to be accessible to every part easily and might not be possessed of confidential elements. Within IoT, savvy adapting, quick organization, best data comprehension and deciphering, against extortion and malevolent assault, and security assurance are the basic prerequisites [12].

4.2.2 Position of IoT

As IoT could be viewed as an expansion of existing cooperation among individuals and applications through another measurement of "Things" being used in correspondence as well as mixes. The IoT advancement procedure consists of an intricate, huge range of mechanical development handles. The IoT is advancing from the perpendicular usage to polymeric usage. Initially, IoT arrangement, making of area-specific usage can be the principle advancement technique. Space particular usage might possibly become an assembling control framework with its own particular industry qualities. The application can give different endeavors, administrations being coordinated with the business generation, and business forms [13].

Polymeric usage is usually a cross-industry usage in light of open data benefit stages. Such usages support domestic clients as well as manufacturing clients. The usage has provided and advanced through the correspondence administrators as well as arrangement suppliers consisting of a huge amount. As an example, any automobile having a sensor arrangement, a worldwide situating framework (GPS), as well as broadcasting correspondence innovation might provide far reaching identification, route, diversion, and other data administrations. By keeping up such data through people in general administration staff, shippers, unique hardware makers original equipment manufacturer (OEMs), upkeep suppliers, and vehicle administration offices are supposed to distribute such data by sharing administrations for enhancing the vehicle, the vehicle part plan, as well as creation procedure with the help of vehicle lifecycle administration [14].

4.2.3 Capacity of the IoT

During rundown, the IoT is applied for having the accompanying capacities.

4.2.4 Place Detection and Distribution of Place Information

IoT framework is able to gather any area data belonging to IoT terminals as well as ending hubs, giving administrations in light of the gathered area data. The area data incorporates land position data gathered through GPS, Cell-ID, RFID, and outright or linked location data connected within things. Further, normal IoTs incorporate in any accompanying event [14].

4.2.5 Mobile Resources

IoT is able to detect and screen position of products utilizing the position sensing device as well as corresponding work introduced on the ware [15].

4.2.6 Navy Administration

Trough of armada is able to plan the vehicles including drivers in light of trade necessities as well as the ongoing location data gathered through vehicles [16].

4.2.7 Traffic Data Framework

By using IoT, movement data can be gathered, for example, street activity conditions and congested areas by following the area data of an expansive number of vehicles. The framework in this manner supports the driver to pick the main productive course [16].

4.2.8 Atmosphere Detection

This application gathers and processes a wide range of practical or virtual natural factors through local or generally conveyed ends. Normal atmosphere data incorporates heat, moisture, clamor, conceivability, luminous force, range, radiation, contamination (CO, CO_2, etc.), pictures, and body painters. Average applications incorporate at any accompanying rate [17].

4.2.9 Environment Discovery

IoT frameworks offer natural and biological observation, for example, timberland and ice sheet; catastrophe check, for example, volcanoes and seismic; and observation of the manufacturing plant. All are with programmed caution frameworks utilizing ecological parameters gathered from various sensors [17].

4.2.10 Distant Medicinal Checking

IoT is able to examine repeated marker information gathered from the gadget put on the patients' body and furnish the clients with well-being patterns and well-being counsel [17]. The IoT framework directs its ends by controlling and executing capacities in the light of utilization summons consolidated with data gathered through different sources and administration prerequisites.

4.2.11 Controlling Machines and Devices

Individuals are able to control distant working condition of machines through IoT framework.

4.2.12 Recovery from Calamities

Clients are able to begin calamities healing offices at distances, for decreasing misfortunes brought on through debacles, as indicated by the observation done recently [18].

4.2.13 Ad Hoc Networking

IoT frameworks can quickly self-organize as well as interpreting ability with system/benefit cover for providing linked administrations. In IoT, Explores that within a means of transportation, arrange and with a specific end goal to exchange the information system among vehicles and additionally street frameworks are able to quickly self-constitute [18].

4.2.14 Communicating Safely

IoT framework is able to advance in building up safe information, in communication medium among application or administration stage, and IoT terminals in light of administration necessities. By-and-by, its usage has various sorts of abilities as well as its usage in light of administration requirement [18].

4.2.15 Open and Universal IoT Architecture

4.2.15.1 Motivation and General Description

In the past prologue of the updated IoT, lots of applications would be space particular or need application-specific arrangement. Models including IoT frameworks have been divided and cannot correspond or coordinate information from various storehouses; such segregated IoT arrangements utilize concealed conventions and cause lots of issues in data distribution, innovation multiplexing, organize administrations, as well as upgrading. Such issues can prevent the advancement of IoT. For decreasing aggregate of IoT expenditure and distribute data, it is necessary to coordinate different capacities and assets in a bigger framework. In this way, IoT should be planned to have open plus nonspecific IoT engineering having open boundaries and assets, in view of distinctive trade situations, necessities consisting of applications, as well as existing advances [5]. In this manner, it is also viewed as an inspiration to define an IoT standard coordination, considering the end goal of decreasing the aggregate rate of cash and time from gadgets, improvements, and organizations. An IoT design is a coordinated arrangement having interoperability and would be taking after the attributes [19].

4.2.16 Standard Interfacing and Procedure

Looking at various private IoT frameworks, bland IoT foundation is having a similar equipment as well as programming interfaces and conventions [19].

4.2.17 Public and Working

Generally, the IoT technology is sent for assuming control open applications having an open operating ability. An IoT is a framework of coordinate numerous IoT applications in a single technology framework [20].

4.2.18 Open, Measurable, and Elastic

An open IoT design having open assets, open gauges, as well as open links broadens its usefulness and the size of execution, without much of a stretch. It can consequently adjust to various prerequisites, including specialized adaptable improvements.

4.2.19 Open and Universal IoT Design

China Communications Standards Association suggested an orientation display for IoT, consisting of a detecting coating system, as well as trade and applied coatings. Conforming such orientation display demonstrates the open and universal design, which is coated, open as well as adaptable. This design incorporates three utilitarian stages [20].

4.2.20 Detecting and Opening Platform

Such stage interface detectors, controllers, RFID per users, as well as an area detecting gadget (e.g., GPS) to IoT arranged coating. Modularizing equipment, information arrangement, as well as programming edge has been projected to be used in the IoT terminal, IoT opening, and tip hub. The IoT terminal, IoT entryway, and tip hub incorporate adaptable units connecting control module, normal interface module, and correspondence module. The regular interface unit gathers physical interfaces having different sensors into a typical interface. Regular control module can associate detectors, controllers, GPS, and RFID per users having a typical association convention. Product as well as application factors of IoT end and IoT passage ought to have the capacity to self-design and self-adjust. Modularization, normal interface, clever function, self-adjustment, as well as self-arrangement are the essential qualities [21].

4.2.21 Resource and Management Proposal

System as well as administration coating incorporates spine systems including asset organization stages. The spine organize incorporates 3G, 4G, Internet, optical fiber arrangements, Ethernet arrangements, and satellite systems, as well as concealed systems. Asset and organization stages give normal capacities that lots of IoT applications could utilize, for instance, data, conduct, data storing, security administration, and application support. These abilities may likewise be called through specific IoT application boost capacities, for example, to build further particulars [21].

From the IoT application boost abilities are provides the important directing essentials consisting of system network, i.e., attain and transport asset-directing capabilities, portability administration, verification, or endorsement, as well representing IoT terminals, administrations, applications, clients, and designers [22].

4.2.22 Open Application Proposal

Modularizing outline used in such application stage provides regular capacity as well as open application programming interface. This supplier builds up its application utilizing application programming interfaces. In the meantime, this stage underpins application administrations. Different applications can be distributed to the application stage; furthermore, clients obtain application data as well as utilizing applications through this stage. Helpful plus simple organization, conveyance, and adaptable application environment are the attributes of this stage [22].

Shrewd vitality in structures acts as an essential study region of the IoT. Structures being vital elements of the shrewd frameworks, the vitality effectiveness acts as a key for earth, including worldwide manageability. As indicated by a universal study [19] in the United States, structures play a role responsible for almost 38% aggregate of carbon dioxide emanations, 71% aggregate of electricity vitality utilization, 39% aggregate of vitality use, 12% of water utilization, and 40% of non modern misuse. Meanwhile, the cost of customary vestige powers is increasing including the negative effects of the earth's atmosphere and environment that creates an imperative for people for investigating the current fresh-vitality plus to enhance the vitality proficiency in buyer side shrewd networks having different structures [22].

Be that as it may, structures are intricate frameworks, and many components can influence the aggregate vitality utilization in various structures. Additionally, routine structures are not with an excessive number of smart plans. It is significant to screen the genuine vitality utilization information and locate the main considerations and examples through deliberate display and examination of various sorts of structures. These effects are utilized for more planning as well as executing suitable systems consisting of an IoT administration framework for developing proper techniques and procedures enhancing the vitality proficiency for "building" [22].

4.2.23 Power Scrutinizing

During correspondence organization, the utilization and era of vitality are observed and signed in various granularities together with the entire structure, base, offices, labs, quarters, and tenants [21].

4.2.24 *Power Replication and Assessment*

During disconnected demonstration and assessment, the vitality utilization examples and components that might impact the utilization plus the degree of their effect are recognized [20,21].

4.2.25 *IoT Scheme to Affect Realistic Modification and Policy Alteration*

The demonstration and assessment results are utilized to recognize the key vitality segments of the working, to apply changes, and to devise procedures to decrease vitality utilization. IoT-based system administration framework is outlined and prototyped to understand the methodologies and accomplish the objective [20,22].

Our exploration wraps all the three viewpoints. The author checked and gathered the structure vitality use of information closely. In light of our information, we deliberately recognized the vitality utilization designs and investigated the potential strategies to enhance the vitality productivity. The outcomes demonstrate that because of brought together and altered examples, organizing the authentic in a row of olive structures might not be vitality effective despite the fact that they might be "green" by the plan. Motivated by "vitality corresponding figures" in present-day PCs, we propose a shrewd area-based mechanized vitality control IoT structure utilizing cell phone stage and distributed computing innovations to empower savvy portable organize and comparability. The author promotes assembling an exploratory IoT model framework to exhibit the adequacy of our projected thought. Our outcomes indicate probable monetary and communal supportability advantages [18].

Dissimilar to recreation-based arrangement, our work depends on genuine measured information followed for a present being used on-ground lime construction, and a genuine IoT framework to control the vitality computerization. We utilize the most recent data innovations, for example, versatile cell phones with area benefit, conveyed control, and distributed computing, to effectively include the inhabitants in the vitality sparing procedure. Vitality sparing approaches from various sources, for example, people and associations, are considered in a coordinated strategy system in choosing the last vitality sparing techniques [19].

In this diary form manuscript, we initially compress and filter our past work in two gathering documents. Researchers assessed the structure vitality utilization information and introduced our discoveries in recognizing the significant matters in these structures. In light of that, we proposed a shrewd area-based organized vitality control IoT framework configuration to handle the issue and enhance the vitality proficiency add new commitments to finish the three stages portrayed previously [19]. Especially,

1. The author composes the past independent commitments into the entire IoT structure outline. It is work on the entire procedure of distinguishing the main issues, discovering strategies, and creating a model framework to demonstrate the viability of the proposed technique [20].
2. The author constructs a novel trial model IoT framework that exhibits the ongoing area-based mechanized vitality strategy control over numerous structures. It is considered a fundamental stride in transforming the present incorporated controlling and static vitality utilization modes to suitable and dynamic vitality control on the buyer side keen networks having different normal structures [21].
3. It is proposed to make an eventual fate of multilevel vitality proportionality. The focal thought is to sum up the cell phone-based vitality control thought and incorporate strategies of numerous levels of associations. It totals the vitality sparing of individual clients and permits appropriate control of dynamic vitality, which led to vitality proportionality [22].

4.3 Research Method

4.3.1 Method of Data Collection

The data used for this work was gathered from SUPARCO on campus building name NCRG. This office building is vitality efficient and has sustainability features like ventilation, lighting, air conditioning, cooling, and heating so all features recourses are monitored with a series of sensors and meters deployed on different location of building and centralized plant deployed in building (Table 4.1[23]).

4.3.2 Instrument of Data Collection

The data for the exploration will be accumulated through the sources for data collection, which is given as follows:

- Diaries and magazines
- Web

Table 4.1 Electric Load Estimation (per Hour) by Centralized Plant of Smart Building (NCRG)

Floor	1-Phase (kVA)
Ground	93.85
First	70.55
Total load	164.4

- Books
- Reports provided by different research papers
- NCRG Building

4.3.3 Vitality Efficiency Evaluation and Analysis Methodology

For proposing IoT Framework for smart buildings, data needs to be analyzed using essential parameters that include heating vitality consumption, cooling vitality consumption, total electrical vitality consumption, and environmental factors (indoor and outdoor), e.g., temperature and humidity. The cooling and heating attributes relate to HVAC utilization, whereas the aggregate power utilization relates to different loads in the building. Vitality consumption is based on the following:

1. Environmental factor
2. Occupancy rate

4.3.3.1 Environment Impact Analysis

Two attributes, such as temperature and humidity, have been taken to find the impact of HVAC vitality consumption and total electrical vitality. In summer, more cooling and less heating is required due to season. After analysis of test bed, smart building with sustainability features for heating 8.1 billion British thermal unit (BTU) and for cooling 16.9 billion BTU is required.

4.3.3.2 Occupancy Impact Analysis

Data can be divided into three subsets (Table 4.2):

By taking each data subset, we find the association between electricity and heating vitality average and then compare their results, which show that consumption of heat vitality is 6% higher in afterhours than weekends and 19% above for regular office hours. However, when the average occupancy rate is analyzed, there is very low impact on vitality consumption as shown in Figure 4.1.

Table 4.2 Regular Office Hours

Regular office hours	8:00 am to 8:00 pm of weekdays
After hours	8:00 am to 8:00 pm of weekdays
After hours	8:00 pm to 8:00 am of weekdays
Weekend	Saturday and Sunday whole days

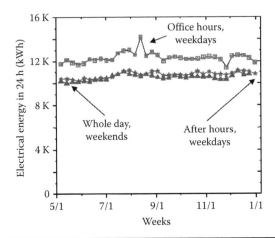

Figure 4.1 Electrical energy.

4.3.4 Smart Location-Based Automated Vitality Control Framework

In this area, the author exhibit the brilliant area-based mechanized vitality control at IoT structure with satisfy these objectives. The author imagine an inhabitant-arranged and included organized system. This key-segments provides cell phone-based appropriate vitality observing and remote control, area application on a cell phone.

4.3.5 IoT Devices Smart Mobile as Remote Controls

Cell phones have numerous system administration interfaces, for example, 3G, WiFi, WiMAX, Bluetooth, and GPS sensors. In view of different network arrangements and worldwide availability to the Internet, they are reasonable for utilizing any framework that needs people's online interaction. The "IoT" incline creates a lower cost, and the sensors are associated with the Internet at record break.

Cell phones are perfect for checking, controlling, and dealing with the vitality control frameworks remotely from any place whenever. After suitable verification and approval, the tenants are permitted to alter and transform their vitality saving approaches online by associating with the arrangement servers of their office and private structures. Such plan permits dynamic changes to the vitality saving strategies and offers better adaptability to the tenants. It can be a decent supplement to the general strategy choice process in view of the displaying events. Such an "application" can be effortlessly created for the cell phone in view of the web innovation (Figure 4.2) [25].

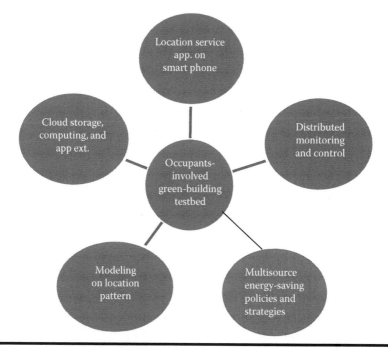

Figure 4.2   Overall structure of our design with components and its interaction.

4.3.6 Cell Phone Location-Based Automatic Control

All telephones can decide their area by alluding to flag qualities from different transmission towers. New eras of cell phone can give limitation to a great deal with more accurately installed GPS chips. We utilize this area data in outlining programmed control arrangements that can turn on/kill vitality devouring gadgets at home or office relying on the area and bearing on the development of the client. Thus, a dynamic and adaptable approach that fulfills the client's inclinations for vitality sparing and comfort can be connected. An application on the widget can naturally authorize these required arrangements.

With the assistance of area of cell phones, these dynamic alteration arrangements could likewise empower the participation and association among various structures. For instance, when the area discovery daemon on the client's cell phone distinguishes that the client has moved out of an edge, remove run from his home building and move into an edge separate scope of his office building, then a message is sent to an incorporated server to trigger the arrangement control handle. In the workplace building, the room possessed by the client will begin prewarming/cooling to set up a client redid or enhanced workplace, while the message likewise triggers the home working to travel into a vitality sparing mode.

Table 4.3 Electrical Records

Electrical Meters	kilowatt	Description
Control device	WeMo	
Servers		Servers in each building which go about as both web daemon server and in-building controller
WiFi routers	N/A	N/A
Location sensors	Global Sat GPS module	Smart devices with region sensors

4.3.7 IoT Prototype Description

The essential limit is to engage the server that is recognize the customer's territory changes and trigger the imperativeness procedure changes by routing the electrical machines in both structures which are identified by the customer. By doing this, the author fundamentally enable the customers to control and realize their own specific essentialness approaches persistently, and enable their imperativeness use to be in respect to their certified utilize.

4.3.8 Hardware and Networking Structure

Hardware and network devices that are used in proposed framework or prototype is shown in (Table 4.3) [26].

The framework's organization structure of the model course of action of the office building is shown in Figure 4.3. The basic limit is that a splendid mobile phone with a territory sensor keeps sending its range data back to the web servers in the home building and the work environment building. The web based servers are the behind of firewall and network address translation (NAT) which are achieved from outside by port of mapping development. Furthermore, it, figures the partition among it and the mobile phones to pick if the detachment passes a specific edge to trigger essentialness approach changes in both the structures. In case it does, then it begins the controller to send rules to turn on/off specific contraptions in its district, as demonstrated by the imperative approaches.

4.3.9 Prototype System Networking Framework

4.3.9.1 Software

Software parts that are used in a proposed framework or prototype are shown in (Table 4.4).

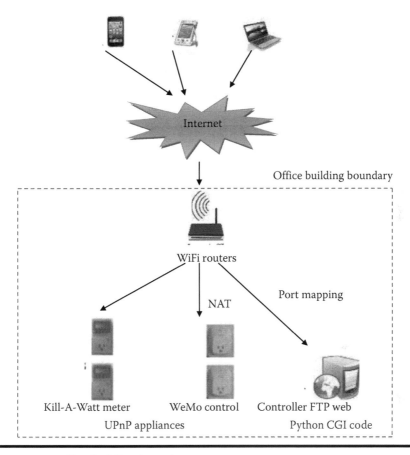

Figure 4.3 Office building boundary.

Table 4.4 Software Framework

NMEA	National Marine Electronics Association – format 0183	For GPS region data recording and sending to the web server
Firewall		
NAT	Network Address Translation	WiFi routers configuration and management software
CGI	Common Gateway Interface	Script to execute Python code
UPnP	Universal Plug and Play	Protocol

The item part consolidates the item for GPS region data recording and sending to the web server in a pleasant course of action, and the WiFi switch's setup and organization programming give a port mapping organization to web access from outside the NAT. The web server is changed with common gateway interface contents to execute Python codes controlling the WeMo (App controls device) contraptions through universal plug and play (UPnP) convention. Other than the zone-based mechanized control, these things taking an interest with the equipment enable the devices in the two structures to be controlled powerfully through marvelous contraptions of the Internet. The load estimation of electrical devices used in office building is presented in (Table 4.5) [27].

Table 4.5 Estimation of Electrical Devices

Appliances with Wattage	Power	Volts	Current	No. of Appliances	Total Current
Photocopier 600 W	600	220	2.727272727	2	5.454545455
Plotter 140 W	140	220	0.636363636	2	1.272727273
Fridge 75 W	48	220	0.218181818	2	0.436363636
Coffee machine 1700 W	1,700	220	7.727272727	1	7.727272727
Laser printers 800 W	800	220	3.636363636	8	29.09090909
Shredder 146 W	146	220	0.663636364	2	1.327272727
Desktop PCs 300 W	300	220	1.363636364	18	24.54545455
Laptops 40 W	40	220	0.181818182	4	0.727272727
Presentation projector 600 W	600	220	2.727272727	1	2.727272727
Fax 150 W	150	220	0.681818182	2	1.363636364
Microwave 1100 W	1,100	220	5	1	5
Scanner 50 W	50	220	0.227272727	2	0.454545455

(Continued)

Table 4.5 (*Continued*) Estimation of Electrical Devices

Appliances with Wattage	Power	Volts	Current	No. of Appliances	Total Current
Tube 120 W	120	220	0.545454545	20	10.90909091
Vitality savor 100 W	100	220	0.454545455	80	36.36363636
Fan 36′ 55 W	55	220	0.25	20	5
Fan 56′ 100 W	100	220	0.454545455	15	6.818181818
17′ LCD 40 W	40	220	0.181818182	6	1.090909091
20–24″ LCD 72 W	72	220	0.327272727	4	1.309090909
17–19″ Cathode ray tube (CRT) 100 W	100	220	0.454545455	8	3.636363636
LED TV 300 W	300	220	1.363636364	1	1.363636364
Exhaust fan 30 W	30	220	0.136363636	10	1.363636364
	6,591		29.95909091	209	147.9818182
	Watts		Amps	Appliances	Amps

4.4 Comparative Analysis

The energy of the benchmark power apparatus related with the client in the two buildings is measured. The real machines in the home working of the model framework and their pattern control estimation are shown in Table 4.6. Note that in this model framework, we fundamentally concentrate on power machines; however, in the genuine case, HVAC can be a noteworthy vitality devouring source worth, applying dynamic control to have any kind of effect in enhancing energy proficiency.

In addition, the appliances in office room and its gauge control estimations are presented in Table 4.7. To look and evaluate the real savings of our model framework, we isolate the clients' energy utilization into three potential modes: luxury mode, moderate mode, and frugal mode. For every mode, we evaluate how much energy will be devoured once a day. The electricity estimation for home and office are shown in Tables 4.8 and 4.9 individually, which likewise clarifies the three modes.

Table 4.6 Home Electricity Appliances' Baseline Power Measurements

Type	Lighting		Refrigerator (GE)	Microwave Stove (Philips)	Laptop (Mac Pro 15")	HVAC
Items	Porch:	54 W	Start: 200W, gradually to 170W Compressor work for 9 min, stop for 9 min	1.3 kW	Normal: 41 W Active or charging: 60W	N/A
	Bedroom:	18*2 = 36 W				
	Living room:	54*2 + 42 = 150W				
	Kitchen:	52*5 = 260W				
	Bathroom:	54 W				
Avg. power		550 W	185/2 W	1.3 kW	50 W	

Table 4.7 Office Room Electricity Appliances' Baseline Power Measurements

Type	Lighting	Desktop	Laptop (Mac Pro 15")	HVAC
Items	32W*6 = 192W	Host: Boot – 110W Normal – 67W Monitor: Normal – 72W, Active – 80~90W	Normal: 41W Active or charging: 60W	N/A
Avg. power	192W	160W	50W	

Table 4.8 Daily Home Electricity Consumption Estimation of Three Modes

	Lighting	Refrigerator	Microwave	Laptop	HVAC
Luxury mode (user is energy insensitive)	Always ON except sleeping 550 W*24*2/3 = 8.8 kWh	Constantly, 185 W/2*24 = 2.22 kWh	Constantly, 1.3 kw*0.05 = 0.065 kWh	Always ON at home 50W*24*2/3 = 0.8 kWh	N/A
Moderate mode	Only ON when at home awake 550 W*24*1/3 = 4.4 kWh			Only ON when at home awake 50 W*24*1/3 = 0.4 kWh	
Frugal mode (user is energy sensitive)	Only 60% ON when at home awake 4.4*0.6 = 2.64 kWh			Only 60% ON when at home awake 0.4*0.6 = 0.24 kWh	
Total	Luxury: 11.90 kWh	Moderate: 7.09 kWh		Frugal: 5.17 kWh	

Table 4.9 Daily Office Electricity Consumption Estimation of Three Modes

	Lighting	Desktop	Laptop	HVAC
Luxury mode (user is energy insensitive)	Always ON when at office 192 W*8 = 1.54 kWh	Always ON 24/7	Always ON when at office	N/A
		160 W*24 = 3.84 kWh	50 W*24*1/3 = 0.4 kWh	
Moderate mode		Only ON when at office	Only 50% ON when at office	
		160 W*24*1/3 = 1.28 kWh	0.4*0.5 = 0.2 kWh	
Frugal mode (user is energy sensitive)		Only 60% ON when at office	OFF when at office, use desktop	
		1.28*0.6 = 0.77 kWh	0 kWh	
Total	Luxury: 5.78 kWh	Moderate: 3.02 kWh	Frugal: 2.31 kWh	

At that point, we apply our location-based arrangement and progressively control the machines in both home and office to decrease the energy squander and amplify the energy proficiency. We track and record the area of the client in 24-h time period and apply dynamic control and strategy changes in both home and office.

The area history appeared in Google scholar for the detailed turning on/off strategy transforms, the author think about some genuine constraints. For instance, in our proving ground, that the author didn't control the on/off status of the cooler. The author apply changes to those gadgets for example, lighting knobs, work area, and workstation, who is on/off status which is not specifically influence the ordinary living of the individual.

In the real activity trace of our examination, it roughly demonstrates that the client burned 14 h at home, in which 8 h for rest, 2 h for lunch and rest, and 4 h for working at home. The aggregate recorded that genuine vitality utilization at home amid this period is 5.285 kWh, which incorporates 2.7 kWh for lighting, 2.22 kWh for fridge, 0.065 kWh for microwave stove, and 0.3 kWh for workstation. The apparatuses in office room are kept in "OFF" status by the control server of the model framework and Location history are additionally demonstrates around 6 hrs are spent in office. The half of the time has working area is utilized and for

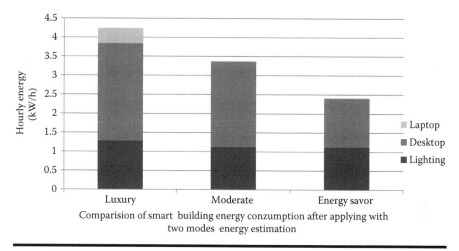

Figure 4.4 **Hourly energy.**

the remaining time are utilized for PC. The total energy utilization of the office is 2.26 kWh, which incorporates 1.15 kWh for lighting, 0.96 kWh for work area, and 0.15 kWh for PC. At the rest of the 4 h, the client are not at home/office, and every one of the gadgets is in "OFF" status, with the exception of the fridge at home. Consequently, for correlation, we put the genuine recorded energy utilization information subsequent to applying our thoughts together with the energy utilization estimation consequences of the three modes, to exhibit how much energy can be spared. The outcomes are shown in Figure 4.4. The basic takeaway message is that the genuine energy utilization of the model framework subsequent to applying our area-based thought is near the thrifty mode's energy utilization. It implies that with our new thought, general clients will appreciate extravagance living style without exceptional care or changes and they will pay what economical mode clients pay.

4.5 Result and Conclusion

4.5.1 Trials and Results

In this chapter, first measure the standard power machines vitality related to the customer in building, and then we apply our territory-based course of action and capably control the devices at office to diminish the imperativeness waste and extend the essentialness adequacy. The author tracks and records the territory of the customer in an 8-h time period and apply dynamic control and technique changes in office (Tables 4.10 and 4.11).

In this chapter, the author applies changes to those contraptions, for instance, lighting handles, desktop, and tablet, belongs to on/off status which do not

Table 4.10 Office Room Electricity Appliances' Baseline Power Measurements

Type	Lighting	Desktop	Laptop
Item	(Tube light = 40W) Qty = 4) 40 W*4	Boot 300W Normal 180	(Mac Pro 15') Normal 40W While charging 60W
		(17–19" LCD) Monitor 40W	
Avg. power	160W	320W	50W

Table 4.11 Estimation of Three Modes (Office Room Electricity Consumption)

	Lighting	Desktop	Laptop
Luxury/static smart building control	ON during office hours 160 W*8 = 1.28 kW/h	ON during office hours 320*8 = 2.56 kW/h	ON during office hours 50 W*8 = 0.4 kW/h
Moderate mode	ON except lunch & Namaz Break		
160 W*7 = 1.12 kW/h	ON except lunch & Namaz Break		
320*7 = 2.24 kW/h	Only 40% ON when Desktop OFF 50W*0.4 = 0.02 kW/h		
Vitality savor mode	ON except lunch & Namaz Break		
160 W*7 = 1.12 kW/h	Only 50% ON when at office 2.56*0.5 = 1.28 kW/h	OFF when at office use desktop 0 kW/h	
Total	Luxury: 4.24 kW/h	Moderate: 3.54 kW/h	Vitality savor: 2.35 kW/h

particularly impact. Eight hours are spent in the office and half of the time the desktop is used, and for the other half of the time the compact workstation is used. The honest total imperativeness utilization of office is 2.35 kWh, which merges 1.12 kWh for lighting, 1.28 kWh for desktop, and 0.15 kWh for adaptable workstation. For whatever remains of the 4 h, the client is not at home/office, and every one of the gadgets is in "OFF" status, with the exception of the refrigerator at home.

Acknowledgment

The authors are grateful to the Department of Computer Science & Information Technology, Institute of Business and Management (IoBM) and Ilma University, Karachi, Pakistan.

References

1. O. Vermesan, P. Friess, G. Woysch, P. Guillemin, S. Gusmeroli, et al. 2012. Europe's IoT Strategic Research Agenda 2012. In: Smith, I. G. (ed.), *The Internet of Things New Horizons*. Halifax, IERC, pp. 22–118, Chapter 2.
2. K. Karimi and G. Atkinson. 2013. What the Internet of Things (IoT) Needs to Become a Reality. White Paper, online at http://www.freescale.com/files/32bit/doc/whitepaper/INTOTHNGSWP.pdf.
3. R. Melfi, B. Rosenblum, B. Nordman, and K. Christensen. July 2011. Measuring building occupancy using existing network infrastructure. In *International Green Computing Conference and Workshops (IGCC)*. pp. 1–8. Orlando, FL, USA.
4. G. Levermore. 2002. *Building Vitality Management System: An Application to Heating. Ventilation. Lighting and Occupant Satisfaction*. Taylor & Francis. Boca Raton, FL.
5. T.-Y. Chen, C.-H. Chen, D.-J. Wang, and Y.-L. Kuo. December 2010. A people counting system based on face-detection. In *Fourth International Conference on Genetic and Evolutionary Computing (ICGEC)*. pp. 699–702. Shenzhen, China.
6. L. J. Lo and A. Novoselac. 2010. Localized air-conditioning with occupancy control in an open office. *Vitality and Buildings*. vol. 42, no. 7, pp. 1120–1128.
7. A. Depaola, M. Ortolani, G. Lo Re, G. Anastasi, and S. K. Das. May 2014. Intelligent management systems for vitality in buildings: Survey. *ACM Computing Surveys*, vol. 47, no. 1, pp. 1–13.
8. D. Bradbury. April 7, 2015. How can privacy survive in the era of the Internet of Things? *The Guardian*, online at www.theguardian.com/technology/2015/apr/07/how-can-privacy-survive-the-internet-of-things
9. M. Zamora-Izquierdo, J. Santa et al., 2010. Integral and networked home automation solution towards indoor ambient intelligence. *IEEE Pervasive Computing*, vol. 99, no. 1, p. 1.
10. D.-M. Han and J.-H. Lim. August 2010. Design and implementation of smart home vitality management systems based on Consumer Electronics. *IEEE Transactions on*, vol. 56, no. 3, pp. 1417–1425.
11. I. Nieto, J. Botía, and A. Gómez-Skarmeta. 2006. Information and hybrid architecture model of the OCP contextual information management system. *Journal of Universal Computer Science*, vol. 12, no. 3, pp. 357–366.
12. Internet of Things in 2020: Roadmap for the Future. May 27, 2008. INFSO D.4 Networked Enterprises & RFID INFSO G.2 Micro and Nano Systems in Co-operation with the Working Group RFID of the ETP EPOSS, Version 1.1.
13. V. L. Erickson, M. Á. Carreira-Perpiñán, and A. E. Cerpa. 2014. Occupancy modeling and prediction for building vitality management. *ACM Transactions on Sensor Networks (TOSN)*, vol. 10, no. 3, p. 42.

14. G. Song, Z. Wei, W. Zhang, and A. Song. November 2007. A hybrid sensor network system for home monitoring applications. *IEEE Transactions on Consumer Electronics*, vol. 53, no. 4, pp. 1434–1439.
15. C. Suh and Y. B. Ko. August 2008. Design and implementation of intelligent home control systems based on active sensor networks. *IEEE Transactions on Consumer Electronics*, vol. 54, no. 3, pp. 1177–1184.
16. R. E. Hall. September 28, 2000. *The Vision of a Smart City*. Presented at the 2nd International Life Extension Technology Workshop. Paris, France, online at www.osti.gov/servlets/purl/773961 PDF.
17. IERC – European Research Cluster on the Internet of Things. October 2011. Internet of Things – Pan European Research and Innovation Vision. vol. 134. Internet of Things Strategic Research and Innovation Agenda, online at www.researchgate.net/publication/260712666_Internet_of_Things_Strategic_Research_and_Innovation_Agenda.
18. D. Evans. April 2011. The Internet of Things – How the Next Evolution of the Internet Is Changing Everything. CISCO White Paper, online at http://www.cisco.com/web/about/ac79/docs/innov/IoTIBSG0411FINAL.pdf
19. D. Clements-Croome and D. J. Croome. 2004. *Intelligent Buildings: Design Management and Operation*. London: Thomas Telford. Chapter 10, pp. 273–288.
20. T. Teixeira and A. Savvides. 2008. Lightweight people counting and localizing for easily deployable indoors. *IEEE Signal Processing Society*, vol. 2, no. 4, pp. 493–502.
21. L. Fretwell and P. Schottmiller. January 2014. Cisco Presentation, online at https://books.google.com.pk/books?
22. O. Puzanov. IoT Protocol Wars: MQTT vs COAP vs XMPP, online at http://www.iotprimer.com/2013/11/iot-protocol-wars-mqttvscoap-vs-xmpp.html.xx.
23. Y. Agarwal, S. Savage, and R. Gupta. 2010. Sleep server: A software-only approach for reducing the energy consumption of PCs within enterprise environments. In *Proceedings of USENIX Annual Technical Symposium (USENIX ATC)*.

Chapter 5

Distributed Denial-of-Service Threats and Defense Mechanisms in Software-Defined Networks: A Layer-Wise Review

Kshira Sagar Sahoo, Ranjan Kumar Behera, and Bibhudatta Sahoo
National Institute of Technology

Mayank Tiwary
SAP Labs

Contents

5.1 Introduction

As remarked by *Arbor Networks*, "DDoS attacks continue to increase in size, frequency, and complexity. Are we equipped to stop them before they affect the availability of our business?" (Arbornetworks, Product and Services, 2017). Safeguarding the security of the network is a rat-race process between attackers and victims for many years. Both academic and industry experts have been working in this area since a decade ago. Technology advancements open up new attack tools to launch various attacks; consequently, the defenders require sophisticated and up-to-date defense mechanism to countermeasure the attack. In contrast to other attacks, distributed denial-of-service (DDoS) attack, can cause a massive interruption in any kind of network infrastructure. There are many intentions behind the DDoS attack, including political advantage, financial advantage, criminal extortion, and personal grudge. At the top list, e-commerce, gaming industry, blogging sites, and finance sectors are the target of the DDoS attack. From a business point of view, while the business is more dependent on the availability of online services, the defense mechanism of DDoS attack must be more innovative and efficient. Otherwise, this attack can defunct the cyber system by exhausting the bandwidth, network devices (such as switches, firewall/Intrusion Prevention System) servers, or storage by launching malicious traffic. It is commonly launched in a coordinated manner by conceding hundreds of systems liberally accessible on the Internet. For detection and mitigation, there are numerous sophisticated techniques adopted by the intrusion detection system (IDS); still, the severity and frequency of this attack are increasing (Yadav, Trivedi, and Mehtre 2016). The increasing number of attacks cause a disastrous impact to the current IT industry (Matthews, DDoS Impact Cost-of DDoS Attack, 2014), (Fayyad and Noll, Security and Safety Composition Methodology, 2014), (Spitznagel, Taylor, and Turner, 2003).

For example, according to a recent survey accomplished by Incapsula, an organization working with various industries across Canada and the USA, stated that an average DDoS attack cost the companies around $40,000 per hour. For quick reestablishment, companies spend nearly half a million dollars for their business. In addition to the financial loss, companies bear the nonfinancial cost, such as loss of intellectual property, customer trust, and malware contaminations (Lafrance, How Much Will Today's Internet Outage Cost? 2016).

In their survey depicted in Figure 5.1, it was concluded that almost all companies of any size in their work force experience the DDoS attack threat. Companies having more than 500 employees face more financial loss, and in turn they require more professionals to fix this risk (Matthews, Incapsula Survey: What DDoS Attacks Really Cost Businesses, 2014). Such incidents clearly indicate that we need more sophisticated efficient tools and methods to combat the severity of this threat.

With the recent advancement and wide acceptance of virtualization-based cloud computing and software-defined network (SDN) paradigm, many organizations and researchers are adopting security solutions using these technologies (Sahoo et al. 2016). The SDN has recently gained a great interest as a new paradigm of networking. The separation of control planes and data planes made SDN a widescale accepted feature in the research community. The control functionalities are removed from the network devices and maintained in an external entity called controller. As a result, the network devices become simple packet-forwarding elements.

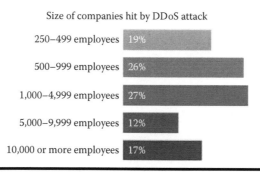

Figure 5.1   DDoS assault to the organizations (Incapsula Survey).

The network infrastructure can be acquired by SDN technology, and it provides networking-as-a-service model in cloud computing environments. Recently, a group of service providers, network operators, and vendors created Open Network Foundation to standardize OpenFlow protocol and promote SDN. The OpenFlow is the most common southbound application program interface (API) that is used in SDN. OpenFlow allows the communication between the control and data planes of SDN architecture. In the traditional network, each switch has its own software that instructs it what to do, whereas in OpenFlow-based SDN, a centralized control handles the packet-moving decisions, which offers a programmed network independent of underlying hardware entities.

SDN provides numerous benefits as well as solves the longstanding ossification problem in networking. Among many, the security solution using SDN is a new research topic. Further, SDN-based solutions to DDoS threat is a point of debate. On the one hand, the programmability and centralized view of the entire network help SDN controllers easily detect the attack, whereas on the other hand, the centralized control architecture is considered more vulnerable. Thus, for instance, the SDN paradigm itself is likely targeted by DDoS threat.

Although few research articles are available, we discuss the SDN-based security issues in networking. In this chapter, we present a layer-wise DDoS threat in an SDN-wired system. After highlighting various threats, we provide a brief discussion on the defense mechanism proposed so far.

The main contributions of this chapter are as follows:

- We present a conceptual view of SDN architecture
- Classification of various attacks along with attacking tools
- We classify the threats existing in different layers of the SDN-wired environment
- Highlight various solutions to these threats proposed by researchers

5.2 Background of SDNs

In the current trend of the network system, the structure of data centers and enterprise networks need to change dynamically with the increasing complexity and additional entities. To address this long standing issue, the SDN was introduced (Alsmadi, AlAzzam, and Akour 2017). It is an emerging network architecture that allows both applications and network elements to interconnect to each other through standard APIs. The routing decisions and packet-forwarding functionalities like network intelligence are moved from the underlying hardware devices to an external centralized controller. The controller simplifies the network management through a programmable interface. SDNs use OpenFlow like southbound protocol to manage the traffic flows incoming to the network. The network administrator can manage the traffic dynamically through northbound applications.

5.2.1 Layers of SDN

According to Open Networking Foundation (ONF), functionally and vertically, SDNs can be divided into three different layers. Figure 5.2 illustrates the basic architecture of SDNs that consist of three layers. It helps abstract lower-level functions and transfers them to a standardized control layer. The classified layers and programming interfaces are open among them in an SDN.

Data forwarding layer: The data forwarding layer comprises network devices such as routers, switches, Open Vswitch, etc. All switches are interconnected to form the physical network. The role of these switches is to forward packets based on the control plane's routing policy. To achieve this role, each switch maintains a forwarding table whose entries are basically forwarding rules that get installed by the control plane. This layer is also known as the infrastructure layer.

Control layer: It represents the network brain and is responsible for monitoring the network, making routing decisions, and programming the physical network how to behave. This layer consists of software-enabled controllers capable of applying custom policies to the underlying infrastructure layer. There are various controllers developed such as POX, NOX, Floodlight, Maestro, OpenDayLight, etc.

Application layer: Primarily, this layer consists of end user business applications that utilize the network service. A few examples are network virtualization and security monitoring. (Stallings 2013).

Service providers achieve many benefits through SDNs. The forwarding information base of SDN can find an optimal path for the incoming traffic without the

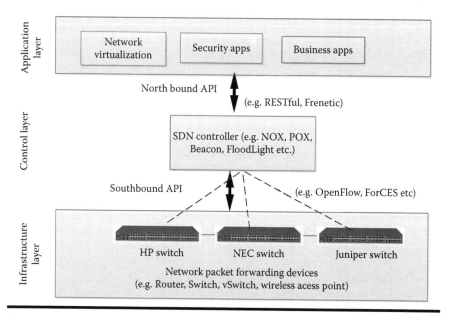

Figure 5.2 The basic architecture of SDNs.

presence of expensive network devices. In addition, the network administrator can experiment many network configurations without changing the actual backplane (Hungyo and Pandey 2016).

5.2.2 Advantages of SDN

An SDN facilitates a global view of the whole network that makes easier for a network administrator to manage the data plane competently. It can implement in the cross-tenant environment such as clouds and data centers. It is possible because of resource virtualization and decoupled architecture. Such an efficient network management is possible by changing the network behavior based on the incoming load in the network. Through the programmable capability, SDN frameworks can control and manage the network. Control layer is responsible for changing the whole network through this programmability characteristic.

SDN brings numerous benefits to the customers who have faced fast changes in their day-to-day network load. With the help of this technology, service operators reduce their Operational Expenditure (OPEX) through low-cost network devices. In addition, SDN filters traffic as it enters the network system. The edge-switches performed as basic firewalls for the entire network. Further, the suspicious traffic can redirect to the higher level IDS/IPS and firewalls by the edge switches.

5.2.3 OpenFlow Protocol

OpenFlow protocol was designed for researchers to implement their works without disturbing the other traffic. However, its applicability increases largely in both industry and academia. Hence, a good number of research activities work on this protocol. Both OpenFlow switches and controller are the two important components for this protocol. Each OpenFlow-enabled device (switch) has one or more flow tables that keep track of the flow entries. All the decisions like addition and deletion modify the flow entries in a flow table are taken by the controller. A flow entry consists of various match fields and action sets for the incoming flow. When a new flow arrives at the switch, its header is extracted and checked for its availability in the flow table. If the flow entry is found, the corresponding action has to execute. If no match is found, then the first packet of the flow moved to the controller. The controller then takes the decision and may install the flow entries into the switch, so that same flows need not be moved to the controller again. The whole process of handling flows by OFDevices is shown in Figure 5.3.

5.3 Various Security Attacks to SDN Layers

There are various security threats as well as possible attacks to various layers of SDN. Akhunzada et al. (2015) have listed various possible attacks disturbing SDN

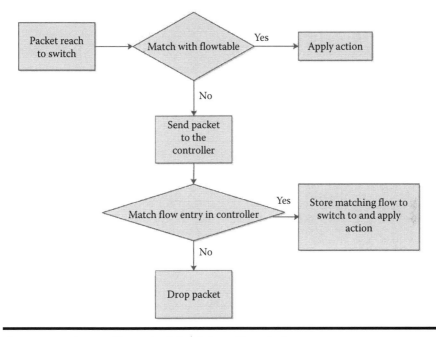

Figure 5.3   The working principle of OpenFlow device.

architecture, presented in Table 5.1. Availability-related attacks generally target the computing resources of the system. Authorization-related attacks can gain the controller access unlawfully. Data alteration related attacks target the forwarding layer. The flow rule alteration is an example of data alteration related attack. Authentication-associated attacks affect application and controller layer of SDN. Side channel attack may persist in the forwarding layer. For example, the flow rules

Table 5.1   Possible Threats to SDN Layers

Possible Attacks	Forwarding Layer	Control Layer	Application Layer
Availability	✓	✓	
Authentication	✓	✓	
Data alteration		✓	✓
Side channel			✓
Policy implementation		✓	✓
Authorization		✓	✓

can be obtained from the input buffer and may help to find the forwarding policy of the flow.

While ensuring the possible availability-related threat, DDoS attack will come into picture. Merely generating a huge number of traffic can make adversary situation to the network. Recently, many incidents clearly signify that the growing nature of DDoS attack can have a devastating impact. The modern cyber infrastructure can be a victim of this attack, which may cause massive disruption to the system.

5.3.1 Intention behind DDoS Attack

DDoS attacks affect many organizations, IT companies, and institutions that are linked to the Internet. Usually, their intention is to interrupt the normal business processes. Practically, such events cause a lot of losses to the organization, and countermeasure to it is a time-consuming and expensive process. There are various reasons behind conducting such attacks. Such motivations can be summarized as follows:

a. For financial gain, the attacker might target the victims' service through his perceived capability. To avoid such disruption, attackers usually demand heavy amount. Such intentions are most dangerous and hard to control.

b. Fighting between two online groups or individuals for disrupting each other's applications and infrastructure. DDoS is a powerful weapon.

c. Sometimes, in reply to a perceived injustice, a frustrated individual becomes an attacker to take revenge through such attack.

d. In some circumstances, a group of people motivated by some ideological belief cause DDoS attack to their opponents (Fultz and Grossklags 2009). For example, the 2010 WikiLeaks event and 2007 Estonia events like sabotages are politically motivated (Greenemeier 2007).

e. For experimental purpose, some young professional hackers try to show-off their caliber by attacking some specific websites or systems through some online tools.

f. Through cyber warfare, a military or a terrorist group of a country may try to attack some sensitive zone of another country and damage and paralyze the economic system of the country. Either these types of attacks are politically or geopolitically motivated. Cyber warfare professionals are well trained and well equipped with high-end resources. Usually, they target the financial institutions, administrative departments, and telecommunication system of a country (Zargar, Joshi, and Tipper 2013).

g. A DDoS attack might target to harm the victim, for declining an extortion demand.

Few methods are proposed that mainly focuses on analyzing the incentives and strategies of the attackers. On this basis, the decision-making models can be built to check the attack (Roy et al. 2010). An attacker targets almost all kind of organizations for several reasons. The organization might be financial institutions, nationalized and private banks, IT infrastructures, etc. Table 5.2 lists some recent DDoS attacks suffered by various organizations across the globe.

Table 5.2   Well-Known DDoS Attacks

Major DDoS Events	Report
Russian Banks 2016 (Bisson 2016)	A massive DDoS attack was conducted for more than two days on five Russian Banks. It was attacked by a bot that consists of around 24,000 systems located around 30 countries. Fortunately, attackers could not affect the bank services provided to their clients.
Rio Olympics- September 2015 (Sullivan 2016)	According to *Arbor Networks*, some public facing websites affiliated to 2016-Rio Olympics suffered from a DDoS attack starting from September 2015. A DDoS for hire service called LizardStresser and several IoT botnets launched the malicious traffic to the victims ranging in size of up to 540 Gbps.
United States election campaign websites	At the time of US election, an anonymous group targeted Doland Trump's websites to crack down his election campaign and his hotel chain business. Later, once again attackers target both Hilary Clinton and Trump to target the campaign website. During the attack, they have used a sophisticated MiraiIoT botnet that continued for 30 seconds.
BBC website cyber- attack 2016 (Baraniuk 2014)	The attack was targeted to BBC website and its ancillary services including iPlayer radio app. Attackers knock the website by injecting overloaded traffic to the websites.
Polish airline hacked June 2015 (Kharpal 2015)	In 2015, June around 1,400 passengers and 10 flights of Polish airliner LOT were stranded after a major hacking attack on the flight plan system. Due to unavailability of the document that carries detail information about the route, weather forecast, and other relevant information, the flights are forced to stop. It was caused due to a DDoS attack that generates a massive request packet that overloads the central server.

(Continued)

Table 5.2 (*Continued*)   Well-Known DDoS Attacks

Major DDoS Events	Report
GitHub attack 2015 (Newland 2015)	The popular programming repository site GitHub experienced an attack that consists of a wide variety of attack vectors. The authority believes that the intention was to remove a specific set of content from the site.
HSBC Internet Banking, 2016 (Schwartz 2016)	HSBC, a leading bank of Britain, faced this kind of attack two days before while taxpayers pay their tax at the deadline. Millions of taxpayers faced three percentage of penalty if they have not paid on time.
Iris public sector websites, 2016 (Weckler 2016)	Several public sector websites including Central Statistics Office and the Department of Justice are forced to stop due to a DDoS attack.

5.3.2 Prerequisites for an Effective DDoS Scheme

Since DDoS attack continues to spread continuously, the detection and mitigation techniques must be efficient. Bawany et al. (2017) have identified some significant prerequisites for an effective DDoS defense mechanism. The requirements are highlighted as follows:

1. The detection mechanism should not affect the normal operation of the forwarding layer. The mechanism should not disrupt the end user's normal operations.
2. The mechanism should prohibit the attack within the network as well as outside the network.
3. Since the controller is the main part of the SDN, the attack performance of the controller should not be degraded.
4. The detection module should not be an overhead for the controller.
5. The deployment cost should be as minimum as possible. The deployment of the module must not require a significant change to the entire network system.
6. Along with the attack detection, the mitigation module must be incorporated in the defense system.
7. False-positive error is minimum, and a high detection rate is desired.
8. The used mechanism should be flexible and robust in nature.
9. An early detection of attack to the control or infrastructure layer is desirable.
10. The designed algorithm must be distributed in nature to prevent multicontroller attack.
11. Defense mechanism must ensure trust between the controllers and application layer.

5.3.3 Strategy to Conduct DDoS Attack

Usually, to conduct an attack there is a plan made by the attacker. These steps might be classified into four stages. The strategy starts with recruiting the agent to the end of the attack.

At the initial phase, attackers hire high-end and state-of-the-art powerful machines as agents. With the help of these agents, attackers start to accomplish their strategy. In the earlier days, attackers manually capture these machines, but later with the advancement of security tools, this can be accomplished automatically.

In the manual attack, the attackers scan the weakness of the remote system, then breach into it, and install the attack code. But in the automated and semiauto-mated attack, the attacker uses an agent called daemon, zombie, or bots. A botnet is a collection of stolen Internet-connected machines used for attacking purpose and operated remotely without the knowledge of the legal owner. In the attacking phase, they use these agents to infect and exploit the victims. These agents send a huge volume of attack traffic to the network.

Again the mode of communication between zombies and the handler machine was divided into direct communication and indirect communication depicted in Figures 5.4 and 5.5. In direct communication, on the one hand, the zombie and the handle machines need to know their identity; On the other hand, an interme-diate layer works between zombies and the victim. This layer makes it difficult to identify or trackback the actual attacker. The inclusion of this layer usually carries out through Code Red like a self-propagating tool. Another fact of this mode is that it is hard for the owner of the machine to be aware that they are part of such activities.

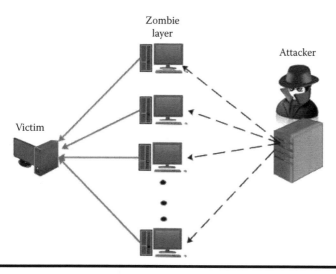

Figure 5.4   Direct DDoS attack.

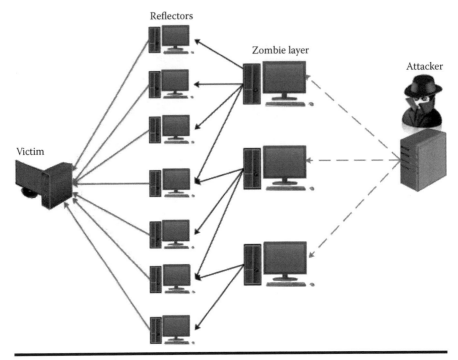

Figure 5.5 Indirect DDoS attack.

The communication between attackers and handlers is carried out through various protocols such as Transmission Control Protocol (TCP), User Datagram Protocol (UDP), and Internet Control Message Protocol (ICMP). The attacker sets the duration of an attack, attack rate, type of attack, port number, etc. In the past few years, the attacker and agent used Internet Relay Chat (IRC) model as an online chatting system. The IRC model replaces the agent-handler DDoS model. The end user machines communicate to the agents via IRC channel. It benefits attackers that it can generate legitimate IRC ports to send commands to agents.

5.3.4 Attack Tools Using Botnets

The tools used for DDoS attack using zombies can be classified into three types (Alomari et al. 2012). These tools are described later.

5.3.4.1 Agent Based Tools

An agent-based model consists of three entities named as agent, client, and handler. During an attack, the attacker communicates with the client. The handler is the software tool positioned on the Internet. These tools are used by clients for making a connection with the agent. The agents actually create the attack and compromise the system. Some of the agent-based tools are Mstram shaft, Tribe Flood Network, and Trin00 (Yarimtepe, Dalkílíç and Özcanhan 2015). Among these tools, Trin00 is a well-known UDP flooding attack tool (Criscuolo 2000). TFN tool is used for various types of attacks such as UDP flooding, ICMP echo, and smurf attack. The Mstram tool is used for TCP ACK flooding attack.

5.3.4.2 IRC Based Tools

The IRC-based tools are the most sophisticated tool and utilize various features of the agent-handler tool. Trinity and Knight tools are the well-known IRC-based attack tool. The TCP Reset (RST), TCP Synchronise (SYN), and TCP Acknowledge (ACK) like attack can perform using Trinity tool (Dietrich, Long, and Dittrich 2000). Knight is an elegant lightweight attack tool for SYN and UDP flood attack.

5.3.4.3 Web Based Tools

Web-based attack tools are specifically designed for application layer attack. These tools usually target the webservers. A combination of IRC tools with Hypertext Transfer Protocol (HTTP) flooding module is used for application layer attack. Examples of some well-known web-based DDoS launching tools are Low Orbit Icon Cannon (LOIC), Blackenergy, Aldi botnet, etc. The LOIC tool was employed during an attack to California Department of Justice (DOJ) and Federal Bureau of Investigation (FBI) webservers in 2012. This tool was employed for generating a large volume of HTTP traffic to the webservers (Sauter 2013). An anonymous hacker group of Russia used BackEnergy tool for attack. Most of the Russian and Malaysian web services were targeted by this tool (Nazario 2007).

5.4 Taxonomy of DDoS Attack

DDoS attacks can be classified based on the protocol layers. According to Zargar et al., DDoS attack can be categorized as depicted in Figure 5.6 (Zargar, Joshi and Tipper 2013).

Usually, DDoS flooding attacks are launched through well-organized botnets or zombies. In Douligeris and Mitrokotsa (2004), DDoS flooding attack has been classified broadly into two categories, which has been shown in Figure 5.7.

5.4.1 Network-Level Flooding Attack

Network- or transport-level attacks are usually made through various control packets such as TCP, UDP, or ICMP. In the network or transport level, an attacker tries

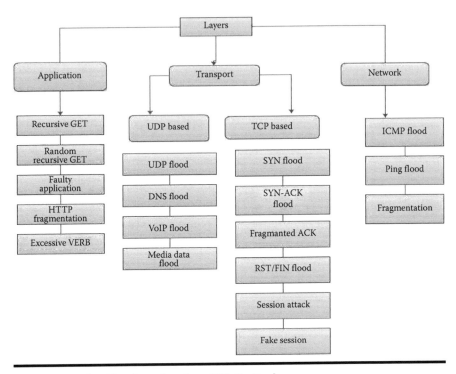

Figure 5.6 Classification of various DDoS attacks.

to disrupt the normal communication channel of the legitimate user through TCP and Voice Over Internet Protocol (VoIP) flood. In reflection-based attack, attackers send some fake requests to the reflectors. In turn, reflectors send the responses to the target and the available resources of the victim get exhausted. Example of the reflection-based attack is smurf attack (Peng, Leckie, and Ramamohanarao 2007).

In amplification-based attack, an attacker tries to exploit the services of the victim by launching a large volume of messages. Upon receiving a message, the traffic becomes amplified toward the victim. Both amplification and reflection were used as carriers to send a large volume of packets during smurf attack.

5.4.2 Application-Level Flooding Attack

This kind of attack was usually made with an intention to disrupt the legitimate user's services by depleting the server resources. This resource might be the Central Processing Unit (CPU) processing speed, the memory being used, input and output bandwidth, bandwidth between main memory and secondary memory, etc. As application-level attack is similar to legitimate traffic, they consume less bandwidth. For disruption, attackers target the specific characteristics of the applications such as Session Initiation Protocol (SIP), HTTP, or Domain Name System (DNS).

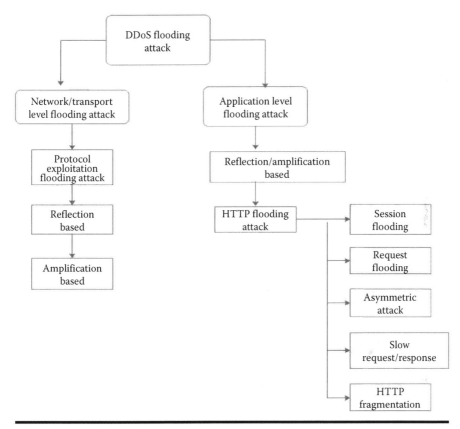

Figure 5.7   Classification of DDoS flooding attack based on protocol level.

SIP and DNS are the most popular amplification flooding attack. Another kind of application-level attack is VoIP attack. In this attack, the attacker sends a large volume of spoofed VoIP packets at a high rate to the victim server. For a proper connection, the victim server utilizes a significant amount of time and resources to identify the fake VoIP packets from the legitimate traffic. If the attacker uses the same source address for a longer time, it will seem like a benign traffic; hence, it is very difficult to identify (Reiher and Mirkovic 2004).

In addition, HTTP flooding is another type of application-level attack. There is a variant of such type of attacks such as session flooding, request flooding, and slow request/response attack. In session flooding attack, the attacker's request rate for session connection is greater than the benign users. Thus, it consumes server resources and causes a DDoS attack in the system. The HTTP get/post is an example of this attack, where a huge volume of legitimate HTTP requests is sent to the server. Usually, these attacks are carried out through botnets. In asymmetric attack, the attacker requests a high volume of workload request to the server. For example, in multiple HTTP get/post attack, an attacker issues multiple requests by creating a single request packet. The single request packet consists of multiple requests, but at the time of issuing, it works as a single one rather than one after another to the server. In this way, it creates an overload situation on the server and hides from deep packet inspection methods. Sometimes, the glitch of the software of an organization creates an opportunity for the attacker to launch the attack. For example, an attacker may generate Structure Query Language (SQL) injection-like requests to seal the database. Slowloris attack is a type of slow request/response attack. It is an HTTP get-message type of attack that can shoot down a server with the help of a few machines or a single system. The attacker sends a part of a HTTP request that continuously grows and is a never-ending process. The attacker continues his operation until all the sockets of the server are acquired by these requests. A slow-reading attack is a kind of slow request/response DDoS attack. The attacker takes advantage of the TCP protocol. The TCP protocol believes in open connection, even though there is no communication. It gradually reads the response rather sending the request. The attacker uses a smaller window size compared with the send buffer of the victim. As a result, it forces the server to open up the connection to a larger extent and eventually creates an attack (Shekyan 2012).

5.5 SDN-Enabled DDoS Attack Detection Technique

DDoS is a popular research field in the SDN research community. Although attack detection becomes easier due to a logically centralized controller and programmability capability, still SDN itself becomes a victim of DDoS attack. But, in this section, we shall discuss how SDN technology will help to detect DDoS attack in an easier way than the traditional network. According to Yan et al. (2016), the defense mechanism using SDN can be classified based on traffic locations. These are as follows:

a. Source based
b. Destination based
c. Network based

In source-based technique, the SDN controller filters out the fake traffic and authenticates the source Internet Protocol (IP) of the traffic before entering into the host network. Mehdi et al. (2011) have shown that a programmable router can provide security to a Small Office Home Office (SOHO) network efficiently. In their work, they have used four important detection techniques like NETAD, rate liming, entropy, and random walk techniques. To create an SDN environment, they have used OpenFlow switches and NOX controller in their work. Experimental results showed that these algorithms can more accurately detect malicious traffic at home network than Internet Service Provider (ISP), without adding any external functionality. Jin and Wang (2013) take advantage of the flexibility characteristics of the SDN. They observed that most of the mobile malware requires Internet connection; hence, they proposed a method in which the incoming traffic can only be allowed if the source addresses are in a permissible IP address range. They have employed both OpenFlow switch and controller in their work. Upon receiving the traffic, the access point sends it to the SDN controller. In turn, controller made a flow rule and desired traffic will enter into the network according to the flow rule. The attack detection module is installed in the controller, and it extracts the necessary traffic information from the incoming traffic sent from access points. For detection purpose, they have used four algorithms such as connection success ratio, IP blacklist, aggregation analysis, etc. The connection success ratio is based on the connection rate probability. A successful connection probability of a legitimate host should be more than an illegitimate host. The IP blacklist algorithm makes a list of the IP address that might harm the network. The IP host list can be found from publicly available resources, historical data, etc. If any traffic comes from the source IP address immediately, those traffic flows will be dropped near the host network. The source address validation implementation, a standardized security architecture, designed specifically for preventing source address spoofing within a network. The Virtual source Address Validation Edge (VAVE) is an improved protocol of source address validation implementation. VAVE has validated it with an OpenFlow device. For each new flow, the first packet will be forwarded to the NOX controller (Yao, Bi, and Xiao 2011).

In destination-based mechanism, the IP tracebacking is mostly used. It is a method that locates the actual source of a given packet that has been sent to the network. Authors have proposed a network debugger called ndb, to recreate the path followed by a packet. It follows the postcard-based method, and the flow table state can be logged through proxy. In another work, Handigol et al. (2012) have proposed NetSight framework that captures the packet histories and uses these histories for network diagnosis.

In network-based DDoS defense mechanism, the tenant's activities are monitored by the SDN controller. A DDoS defense mechanism based on the traffic flow features is proposed (Braga, Mota and Passito 2010). The defense mechanism in this model usually adopts three modules, which are shown in Figure 5.8. These are flow collector, flow extractor, and attack detection.

The flow collector module extracts the flow entries from the flow table periodically. Then, the feature extractor module extracts the relevant features from the collected flows. For example, Braga et al. (2010) have used features such as average byte per flow, average packets per flow, and growth of different ports. Then, the classifier module classifies whether the incoming flows are attacked or not. The mitigation module takes the countermeasure of the attack.

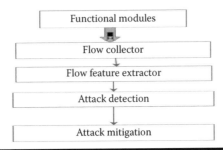

Figure 5.8   The functional modules used by SDN controller for DDoS defense.

In another work, Phan et al. (2016) have used support vector machine (SVM)-based classification technique for attack detection. YuHunag et al. (2010) have proposed a novel framework for DDoS defense mechanism by counting the flow volumes through the controller. To improve Braga's work, Giotis et al. have combined the features of both OpenFlow and sFlow frameworks. The packet sampling property of sFlow is used for fine-grained anomaly detection by the controller. Passito et al. (2014) have proposed AgNOS, an agent-based attack detection architecture that can extend their domain from enterprise network to other SDN network domains. There are some network-based defense solutions adopted by the security services industries. Radware organization (2017) provides an SDN-based DDoS solution with the help of Cisco ONE controllers and SDN-enabled cisco switches. It provides an abstraction of anti-DDoS solution to the OpenFlow-enabled SDN ecosystem. Similarly, Flowmon adopted an SDN-based DDoS attack protection mechanism using Juniper Contrail Networking as a logical network overlay. In contrail networking, each node is having a virtual router instance, and that instance is responsible for directing the traffic flow between VM and itself. During communication, a virtual router collects the flow statistics stored into a Cassandra-based analytical node through Sandesh Protocol (Table 5.3).

5.6 SDN is the Victim of DDoS Threat

In spite of numerous security solutions provided by this new technology, SDN itself might be targeted by DDoS attack. The separation of the two planes causes a real threat to the SDN. A potential malicious attack can be launched either through any layer or north- and southbound APIs. For example, upon receiving a new flow, the switch has to send a *packet_in* control message to controller. The controller responds to it with a *flow_mod* control packet and installs the flow rule in the switches. If an attacker gets this flow rule, accordingly it can launch attack either to control layer, forwarding layer, or data to control channel, as shown

Table 5.3   SDN-Enabled DDoS Detection Techniques

Works	Source Based	Destination Based	Network Based	Report
Mehdi, Khalid, and Khayam (2011)	✓			A programmable router can provide security to a SOHO network efficiently with OpenFlow-enabled switches and NOX controller.
Yao, Bi, and Xiao (2011)	✓			The VAVE is an improved protocol of SAVI. VAVE has validated it with OpenFlow device with the NOX controller.
Handigol et al. (2012)		✓		A network debugger called ndb has introduced to recreate the path followed by a packet. It follows postcard-based technique, and the flow table state can be logged through proxy.
Braga, Mota, and Passito (2010)			✓	Extract the statistical information from SDN flow table, and use these information for classifying the correct traffic through SOM architecture.
Giotis et al. (2014)			✓	For fine-grained anomaly detection, it combines the features of both OpenFlow and sFlow framework. The packet sampling property of sFlow is used by the controller for better anomaly detection.

(Continued)

Table 5.3 (*Continued*)   SDN-Enabled DDoS Detection Techniques

Works	Source Based	Destination Based	Network Based	Report
YuHunag et al. (2010)			✓	A novel framework for DDoS defense mechanism by counting the flow volumes through the controller.
Phan et al. (2016)			✓	OpenFlowSIA: An SVM-based classification framework for attack detection.
Passito et al. (2014)			✓	AgNOS: An agent-based framework designed for outspread of their domain among SDNs.
Chesla and Doron (2015)			✓	Through programmability and dynamic rule updation, each forwarding element forwards packets based on diversion value.
Skoda (2017)			✓	In contrail networking, each node is having a virtual router instance, and that instance is responsible for directing the traffic flow between VM and itself.

in Figure 5.9. Next, we discuss the various threats pertaining to the different layers of SDN.

5.6.1 DDoS Threat to Forwarding Layer

Both the infrastructure layer and southbound API are vulnerable if an attack happens in this layer. The flow-table overflow is a potential issue of this kind. In basic SDN, the principle is that for every new incoming flow, the header information will be sent to the controller, and the entire flow must wait at the switch memory until the flow rule has been returned. This becomes an opportunity for the attacker to

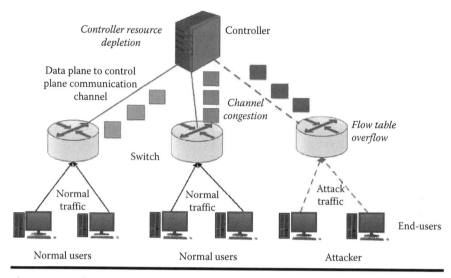

Figure 5.9 Threats of different layers of SDN.

inject new and unknown flows to the victim switch. In the commercial switches, due to high cost, the Ternary Content Addressable Memory (TCAM) is limited in size. The working principle of TCAM is that it compares the incoming traffic with the flow rules present in the flow table in parallel. Moreover, today's commercial switch can accommodate a few thousands of rules at a time. There is always a tradeoff between cost and size of TCAM (Ravikumar and Mahapatra 2004). The cost of TCAM is always more expensive than the normal memory. In addition, updating the rules in TCAM is a slower process, for instance, it can update around 50 rules per second, which is a major constraint for the current network policies (Spitznagel, Taylor and Turner 2003; Jin et al. 2014). On the one hand, by sending a large volume of new flows, TCAM memory becomes overloaded. For instance, Pronto Pica 8 switch can only contain 2,000 flow rules (Katta et al. 2016). On the other hand, for every new flow, the controller will send unnecessary flow rules to the flow table that creates a disruption to the forwarding layer and end user quality of service will degrade. Wang et al. (2014) have shown that a switch can generate not more than 1,000 requests per second to the controller. Hence, flow table and switch overload are two major problems arise due to infrastructure layer attack.

5.6.2 DDoS Threat to Control Layer

The single point of failure is a major risk of a centralized SDN architecture. Once the controller breaks down, the whole system will defunct. Although the distributed controller architecture has proposed to overcome this problem, still the earlier problem is a major threat to DDoS attack (Hussein et al. 2016). If numerous new flow will come to the network, each time a packet_in control message will be sent to the controller. If the overflow request comes to the controller, the computing resources of controller start depleting at a certain threshold. The excessive request packet will consume the CPU time, available memory, and I/O bandwidth of controller. In the ElastiCon framework, Dixit et al. (2013) have experimented the performance of a controller with increasing number of *packet_ins*. To measure the throughput and response time, they send back-to-back 10,000 *packet_in* messages to the controllers installed on a quad-core server. The throughput decreases with the increasing number of control messages. Similarly, for response time, they observed that the response time increases marginally up to a certain threshold value. After that, when the packet rate increases the response time decreases due to queuing delay and overflow of CPU capacity. This finding helps to solve the load balancing problem among controllers of a distributed SDN architecture (Singh et al. 2016; Sahoo et al. 2017). Controller to the forwarding layer communication is carried out via a data-to-control link (Benton, Camp, and Small 2013; Caba and Soler 2015). If the buffer of the victim switch overflows instead of the packet header, the entire flow will transfer to the controller. For which, the new flows will consume the bandwidth of the data-to-control link. As a result, the usual flow request faces a congestion problem (Hussein et al. 2016).

5.6.3 DDoS Threat to Application Layer

An attacker can attack the application layer of SDN by targeting a specific application. Hence, it can affect both the application layer as well as northbound APIs. Since the OpenFlow-based SDN architecture is not standardized, target to one application can affect the other application also (Kamisiński and Fung 2015).

5.7 Potential Countermeasures to DDoS Threats for SDN

An essential task in DDoS is attack detection. In traditional networks, numerous works have been proposed to detect the DDoS attack (Swain and Sahoo 2009; Xiao et al. 2015; Somani et al. 2017). But, in this section, we shall discuss detection methods to this threat for the SDN framework. The traditional approach can also be applied to SDN (XU, YU, and YANG 2017).

Because, a lot of packet_in control messages can exhaust the controller, an easiest technique can be adopted to combat it. The technique can be as follows: when the number of control messages surpasses a certain threshold value, a DDoS attack can be detected. However, these techniques produce a high false detection rate. To improve it, the authors have proposed some more advanced techniques. A Sequential Probability Ratio Test (SPRT), a statistical tool is used to detect low traffic flow coming to the controller (Dong et al. 2016). Because in low-rate traffic, the DDoS attack can effectively work out. Mousavi and St-Hilaire (2015) have used another statistical technique called entropy with limited window size to detect the attack traffic. On the one hand, they assumed that the destination IP address is uniformly distributed, and on the other hand, malicious flows are targeting to a smaller range of IP hosts.

Kloti et al. uses four different modules to detect DDoS (Kloti, Kotronis, and Smith 2013). They have used rate limiting, event filtering, packet dropping, and time-out adjustment techniques to combat the attack. The AVANT-GUARD was proposed by Shin et al. to mitigate the malicious traffic that is sent to the controller (Shin et al. 2013). They have extended the functionalities of OpenFlow switch to implement their work. Two modifications have been made for the extension, such as connection migration and actuating trigger for statistics collection from the switches. Each time, monitoring the network is an overhead task. Hence, Zhang et al. (2013) have proposed an OpenWatch framework that monitors the network periodically. The adaptive counting mechanism detects the attacked traffic more accurately. In another contribution, Shirali-Shahreza and Ganjali (2013) have proposed a FleXam framework that collects the traffic samples deterministically, which is an application-specific task. It can run on a small network and minimize the controller load as well as the controller-to-switch link congestion. The content-oriented networking architecture is a content-centric communication model. Content-oriented networking architecture can efficiently source the attack and can resolve accountability problem. Authors have used NetFPGA and OpenFlow-enabled switches for their experiment (Choi 2010). Onix is an SDN-based distributed controller architecture that helps to overcome the scalability and consistency problem of a single controller model (Berde et al. 2014). Research efforts on SDN-based DDoS threat are listed in Table 5.4.

Table 5.4 Research Effort to the SDN-Based DDoS Solutions

Works	Forwarding Layer Solution	Control Layer Solution	Application Layer Solution	Report
Shin et al. (2013)	✓	✓		DDoS mitigation technique by extending OpenFlow features.
Porras et al. (2012)		✓	✓	A role-based application authentication via digital signature using NOX controller.

(Continued)

Table 5.4 (*Continued*)   Research Effort to the SDN-Based DDoS Solutions

Works	Forwarding Layer Solution	Control Layer Solution	Application Layer Solution	Report
Berde et al. (2014)		✓		A distributed controller architecture overcomes the scalability and consistency problem.
Liyanage, Ylianttila, and Gurtov (2014)		✓		Control channel security architecture uses host identity protocol.
Mousavi and St-Hilaire (2015)		✓		To prevent possible attacks to controller, a statistical technique called entropy with limited window size is used to detect the attack traffic.
Kloti, Kotronis, and Smith (2013)	✓	✓		Both controller and switch become reactive during the attack.
Dridi and Zhani (2016)	✓	✓		Dynamically manage the flow rule and flow routes based on threat probability.
Chen et al. (2016)		✓		During attack to balance and improve the response time of the controller load, it uses a dedicated software tool.

5.8 Techniques Used for DDoS Detection in SDN

Bhuyan et al. (2012) have classified the techniques used for detection of DDoS traffic in a traditional network. Broadly, four types of techniques have been used so far such as statistical, knowledge-based, soft computing, and machine learning (ML). Traditional techniques are also applicable for SDN defense mechanisms. In statistical approach, a model is designed for the normal traffic. Then, an inference test is conducted on the model, if the new incoming traffic is not fit to this model, then the traffic will be classified as attack traffic. In soft computing approach, various classification techniques are used to classify the attack traffic. Radial basis function, neural network, and SVM-like techniques are deployed to classify the traffic intelligently. Usually, to extract the features of the traffic, statistical preprocessing is required, and any soft computing technique is used to classify the traffic. However, in a knowledge-based method, network behavior is compared with the predefined traffic pattern. The common known attacks are formulated to identify the attack traffic from the incoming data.

Each technique is defined based on different characteristics. In the previous section, we had discussed various works proposed by authors for DDoS threats pertaining to different layers of SDN. But, in this section, we present a summary of various techniques used to combat DDoS attack.

5.8.1 Entropy-Based Solutions

Entropy is an effective method to measure the randomness of the attributed in a certain time period. A high entropy value indicates a more randomness of the attribute (dispersed probability distribution). Entropy-based techniques incur a low overhead of calculations. In detection, time entropy checks the randomness of the port address, IP address, number of packets, etc. For example, maximum entropy is achieved when all the packets are sent to a single node, i.e., all the packets have the same destination IP address. This technique is effectively used extensively in a traditional network of IDS (Gu, McCallum and Towsley 2005; Eskin and Stolfo 2007; Nychis et al. 2008).

Mousavi and St-Hilaire (2015) used the entropy-based small window and short-term statistics technique previously proposed by Oshima et al. (2010). The SDN controller cannot process the whole flows; hence, it can only process the initial packets of the flow. As stated earlier, a single host receiving an excess amount of traffic indicates a DDoS attack. They have used two important parameters, one is window size for monitoring the requesting packets *(packet_in)* and another is the threshold value. The entropy value computes for the packets within the window size based on the destination IP address. They have used the window size as 50, because a larger window size may lead to higher false-positive errors. For quicker decision and early notification for the attack, lesser window size will create an unnecessary overhead to the controller. They have taken window size as near equal to the hosts connected to the controller. For each window, the entropy has been calculated and compared with a precomputed threshold value. The new incoming packets are maintained in a hash table. In another work, Wang et al. (2015), used entropy attack detection framework for source filtering of attack traffic. To lessen the burden on the controller, they run the detection module at the edge switch of the network. Once the attack has been detected, the module will send an alert to the controller to take proper action. Mehdi et al. (2011) have conducted an experiment with NOX controller and OpenFlow switch to provide the security solution to SDN. They have utilized the maximum entropy estimation technique to check for normal and attack traffic. The source and destination IP address of the flows are used for entropy variation. A preset threshold is used to compare with the incoming traffic. Giotis et al. (2014) have used this mechanism for DDoS detection and ports can attack in SDN.

Despite its popularity, entropy techniques have some drawbacks. Entropy calculation is based on a single parameter of the incoming flows. By this, other significant information of the distribution become ignored. Further, any anomalies that may not affect the randomness properties remain unnoticed (Javed et al. 2009).

5.8.2 ML-Based Solutions

In the traditional network, Machine Learning (ML)-based algorithms were widely used for anomaly detection (Gelenbe and Loukas 2007; Öke and Loukas 2007; Wu et al. 2011; Sahoo, Sahoo, and Tiwary 2014). Various ML approaches like SVM, fuzzy logic, and decision tree were widely used previously. Generally, these techniques are employed to classify the attack traffic from normal traffic based on certain features. These techniques can also apply for SDN-based IDS (Sahoo, Sahoo, and Panda, A Secured SDN Framework for IoT, 2015).

A practically applicable type of defense mechanism employed a self-organizing map-based neural network technique (Braga, Mota, and Passito 2010). They have taken the Growth of Different Ports (GDP), Average of Duration of flow (ADf), and Average of Bytes per flow (ABf) features of the incoming traffic. For detection purpose, a flow collector module collects the flows for a certain time period, then it transfers to a classifier module for traffic classification. It was considered a low-overhead detection model because for every three seconds the traffic samples are collected from the network. Dotcenko et al. (2014) have used Mamdani algorithm-based fuzzy logic inference for detection purpose. The results show that fuzzy logic-based decision provides better results than usual attack detection algorithm.

Lisa and Bair have proposed a COFFEE: a Concept based on OpenFlow to Filter and Erase Events framework that uses ML algorithms for identifying the botnet activities in a high-speed computer (Lisa Schehlmann and Baier Harald, 2013). Monitoring activities are carried out using NetFlow tool, and for further suspected flows, NetFlow is sent to the controller to extract more features (Schehlmann and Baier 2013). Based on the outcome of the classification controller, high-priority flow rules are installed in the switches. Kokila *et al.* have used SVM classifier for an earlier DDoS detection of the controller (Kokila, Selvi, and Govindarajan 2014). They have compared their work with other well-known classifier techniques. For evaluation purpose, they have used 2000 Defense Advanced Research Projects Agency (DARPA), provided by MIT Lincon lab. They have classified the attack scenario into groups, such as break-in, IPSweep, Probe, and installs. In their study (result section), they showed that SVM provides higher accuracy and less false-positive rate than other ML techniques. ML-based algorithms detect the anomaly based on the abnormal behavior of the traffic.

5.8.3 Scheduling-Based Solutions

The scheduling-based techniques for anomaly detection in SDN are listed in Kalkan et al. (2017). The scheduling-based algorithms run in the central controller of SDN. A hash-based technique was proposed to provide the scalability of the controller (Hsu et al. 2015). Several queues are maintained in the controller to serve the scheduling. The scheduling task performed on the task comes from the switches. A round-robin approach was adopted to provide the service to the incoming request coming from crowded switches. Hence, in a flash crowd event, the controller can work smoothly. Though their work primarily focuses to serve the flash crowd, it ignores the DDoS attack detection. Lim et al. (2015) have proposed an opposite model discussed by Hsu et al. (2015). They try to make the controller live even if a DDoS attack affects the network. For which, they suggest different queues for each ingress switch. In most of the cases, attack traffic at first hit into the ingress switches of the network. The major drawback of this work is that it treats both flash event and DDoS traffic in the same manner; hence, attack traffic can easily affect the controller.

5.8.4 Connection Rate Based Solutions

These solutions are based on the connection rate between controllers to the switches. Connection success rate and the number of connection established are two variants of this type of solutions. Connection success rate states that the probability of connection rate of a legitimate host is greater than the attacked host. One module maintains the list of new connection request such as TCP SYN. If the connection time is out of the bound, the monitoring module increases the attack probability of the host. In SDN, for detection purpose, Threshold Random Walk with Credit Based Rate Limiting (TRW-CB) algorithm has been implemented (Mehdi, Khalid, and Khayam 2011).

5.9 Future Research Direction

There are various security challenges that need to be resolved. In this section, we will discuss some future research directions on the security of SDN.

Introducing SDN in the traditional network is an important open issue. The transformation from the traditional network to SDN requires a lot of challenges, which is an important area of research. The adaption of the controller is a challenging task, because an efficient controller can provide better security solution as well as better reliability. The distributed controller architecture must meet the requirements of availability and scalability through a proper synchronization process. The distributed controller architecture requires a more robust and secure platform to meet the earlier requirement. The application-level DDoS attack has not addressed well. Application-level attack usually targets the specific characteristics of an application such as DNS or HTTP. If an application gets infected, it can infect other applications that are dependent on the target application. It is hard to identify the application-level attack traffic because the characteristics are similar with normal traffic. Current SDN framework provides the security solutions to the lower-level layers of the network. For instance, OpenFlow only offers security visibility to the layer 2 and 3 traffic. Hence, it is a challenging issue to provide security to layers 4–7 as high-level applications are difficult to integrate within it. Mobile attack using SDN is another challenging issue. The rapid usage of mobile device and excess downloading of various apps can be an entry point for the DDoS. Although super proxies are being used by the mobile network, still most of the benign traffic would be blocked by this method.

5.10 Conclusion

In this chapter, we initially highlighted the different threats to the traditional network. Then, we provided a short tutorial on various threats to the SDN architecture. More specifically, we discussed the DDoS threat to SDN, as it has a devastating impact on the entire network. Flexibility, manageability, and programmability properties are the key potential characteristics of SDN. The global view of the entire network by the SDN controller helps to protect the system efficiently through the robust defense mechanism. We have identified various research efforts on defense mechanism adopted with the help of this new technology so far. Then, we have deliberated about the techniques used in the detection mechanism. Although SDN is a good tool to prevent various network threats; however, due to the separation of the control plane from the data plane, SDN itself becomes a victim of SDN. Before we started about SDN-based DDoS threat, we discussed types of DDoS attacks in the traditional network, and then we pointed out the possible threats of SDN layer-wise. Existing works on SDN-based DDoS attack fully focused on a single controller. This might create an overloading situation at the time of attack that might lead to a single point of failure. Although SDN has come up with distributed architecture, still it needs to solve many security issues. In summary, this next-generation network framework has the potential to defend the state-of-the-art attack by the botnet-like attacker. This chapter attempts to give a brief idea about the DDoS threat to SDN, which will help the beginners to start their future research work.

References

Akhunzada, Adnan, Ejaz Ahmed, Abdullah Gani, Muhammad Khurram Khan, Muhammad Imran, and Sghaier Guizani. 2015. "Securing software defined networks: Taxonomy, requirements, and open issues." *IEEE Communications Magazine* (IEEE) 53 (4): 36–44.

Ali, Syed Taha, Vijay Sivaraman, Adam Radford, and Sanjay Jha. 2015. "A survey of securing networks using software defined networking." *IEEE Transactions on Reliability* (IEEE) 64 (3): 1086–1097.

Alomari, Esraa, Selvakumar Manickam, BB Gupta, Shankar Karuppayah, and Rafeef Alfaris. 2012. "Botnet-based distributed denial of service (DDoS) attacks on web servers: Classification and art." *arXiv preprint arXiv:1208.0403.*

Alsmadi, Izzat M, Iyad AlAzzam, and Mohammed Akour. 2017. "A systematic literature review on software-defined networking." In *Information Fusion for Cyber-Security Analytics*, 333–369. Springer.

Arbornetworks. *"Product and services."* https://www.arbornetworks.com/ (accessed October 10, 2017).

Azodolmolky, Siamak, Reza Nejabati, Maryam Pazouki, Philipp Wieder, Ramin Yahyapour, and Dimitra Simeonidou. 2013. "An analytical model for software defined networking: A network calculus-based approach." *2013 IEEE Global Communications Conference (GLOBECOM).* 1397–1402.

Baraniuk, Chris. 2014. "DDoS: Website-crippling cyber-attacks to rise in 2016." http://www.bbc.com/news/technology-35376327 (accessed October 1, 2017).

Bawany, Narmeen Zakaria, Jawwad A Shamsi, and Khaled Salah. 2017. "DDoS attack detection and mitigation using SDN: Methods, practices, and solutions." *Arabian Journal for Science and Engineering* (Springer) 42 (2): 425–441.

Benton, Kevin, L Jean Camp, and Chris Small. 2013. "Openflow vulnerability assessment." *Proceedings of the Second ACM SIGCOMM Workshop on Hot Topics in Software Defined Networking.* 151–152.

Berde, Pankaj, Matteo Gerola, Jonathan Hart, Yuta Higuchi, Masayoshi Kobayashi, Toshio Koide, Bob Lantz et al. 2014. "ONOS: Towards an open, distributed SDN OS." *Proceedings of the Third Workshop on Hot Topics in Software Defined Networking.* 1–6.

Bhuyan, Monowar H, HJ Kashyap, DK Bhattacharyya, and JK Kalita. 2012. "Detecting distributed denial of service attacks: Methods, tools and future directions." (Citeseer).

Bisson, David. The State of Security 2016, https://www.tripwire.com/state-of-security/security-data-protection/cyber-security/5-significant-ddos-attacks-2016/ (accessed October 1, 2017).

Botelho, Fabio, Fernando Manuel Valente Ramos, Diego Kreutz, and Alysson Bessani. 2013. "On the feasibility of a consistent and fault-tolerant data store for SDNs." *2013 Second European Workshop on Software Defined Networks (EWSDN).* 38–43.

Braga, Rodrigo, Edjard Mota, and Alexandre Passito. 2010. "Lightweight DDoS flooding attack detection using NOX/OpenFlow." *2010 IEEE 35th Conference on Local Computer Networks (LCN).* 408–415.

Caba, Cosmin, and Jose Soler. 2015. "Mitigating sdn controller performance bottlenecks." *2015 24th International Conference on Computer Communication and Networks (ICCCN)*. 1–6.

Chen, Kuan-yin, Anudeep Reddy Junuthula, Ishant Kumar Siddhrau, Yang Xu, and H Jonathan Chao. 2016. "SDNShield: Towards more comprehensive defense against DDoS attacks on SDN control plane." *2016 IEEE Conference on Communications and Network Security (CNS)*. 28–36.

Chesla, Avi, and Ehud Doron. 2015. "Techniques for traffic diversion in software defined networks for mitigating denial of service attacks." Google Patents. June 9.

Choi, Yanghee. 2010. "Implementation of content-oriented networking architecture (CONA): A focus on DDoS countermeasure." *Proceedings of 1st European NetFPGA Developers Workshop*.

Criscuolo, Paul J. 2000. "Distributed denial of service: Trin00, tribe flood network, tribe flood network 2000, and stacheldraht ciac-2319." Tech. rep., California University. Livermore Radiation Lab.

Dabbagh, Mehiar, Bechir Hamdaoui, Mohsen Guizani, and Ammar Rayes. 2015. "Software-defined networking security: Pros and cons." *IEEE Communications Magazine* (IEEE) 53 (6): 73–79.

Dietrich, Sven, Neil Long, and David Dittrich. 2000. "Analyzing distributed denial of service tools: The shaft case." *LISA*. 329–339.

Dixit, Advait, Fang Hao, Sarit Mukherjee, TV Lakshman, and Ramana Kompella. 2013. "Towards an elastic distributed SDN controller." *ACM SIGCOMM Computer Communication Review*. 7–12.

Dong, Ping, Xiaojiang Du, Hongke Zhang, and Tong Xu. 2016. "A detection method for a novel DDoS attack against SDN controllers by vast new low-traffic flows." *2016 IEEE International Conference on Communications (ICC)*. 1–6.

Dotcenko, Sergei, Andrei Vladyko, and Ivan Letenko. 2014. "A fuzzy logic-based information security management for software-defined networks." *2014 16th International Conference on Advanced Communication Technology (ICACT)*. 167–171.

Douligeris, Christos, and Aikaterini Mitrokotsa. 2004. "DDoS attacks and defense mechanisms: Classification and state-of-the-art." *Computer Networks* (Elsevier) 44 (5): 643–666.

Dridi, Lobna, and Mohamed Faten Zhani. 2016. "SDN-guard: DoS attacks mitigation in SDN networks." *2016 5th IEEE International Conference on Cloud Networking (Cloudnet)*. 212–217.

Eskin, Eleazar, and Salvatore J Stolfo. 2007. "System and methods for intrusion detection with dynamic window sizes." Google Patents, January 9.

Fayyad, Seraj, and Josef Noll. 2017. "A framework for measurability of security." *2017 8th International Conference on Information and Communication Systems (ICICS)*. 302–309.

Fayyad, Seraj, and Josef Noll. 2014. "Security and safety composition methodology." *International Conference on Advances in Humanoriented and Personalized Mechanisms, Technologies, and Services (CENTRIC)*.

Fultz, Neal, and Jens Grossklags. 2009. "Blue versus Red: Towards a model of distributed security attacks." *Financial Cryptography*. 167–183.

Gelenbe, Erol, and George Loukas. 2007. "A self-aware approach to denial of service defence." *Computer Networks* (Elsevier) 51 (5): 1299–1314.

Giotis, Kostas, Christos Argyropoulos, Georgios Androulidakis, Dimitrios Kalogeras, and Vasilis Maglaris. 2014. "Combining OpenFlow and sFlow for an effective and scalable anomaly detection and mitigation mechanism on SDN environments." *Computer Networks* (Elsevier) 62: 122–136.

Greenemeier, Larry. 2007. "Estonian Attacks Raise Concern over Cyber 'Nuclear Winter.'" *Information Week.* May 24, 2007.

Gu, Yu, Andrew McCallum, and Don Towsley. 2005. "Detecting anomalies in network traffic using maximum entropy estimation." *Proceedings of the 5th ACM SIGCOMM Conference on Internet Measurement.* 32–32.

Hamouda, Sara. 2012. "Security and privacy in cloud computing." *Applications and Management (ICCCTAM), 2012 International Conference on Cloud Computing Technologies.* 241–245.

Handigol, Nikhil, Brandon Heller, Vimalkumar Jeyakumar, David Maziéres, and Nick McKeown. 2012. "Where is the debugger for my software-defined network?" *Proceedings of the First Workshop on Hot Topics in Software Defined Networks.* 55–60.

Hsu, Shih-Wen, Tseng-Yi Chen, Yun-Chun Chang, Shuo-Han Chen, Han-Chieh Chao, Tsen-Yeh Lin, and Wei-Kuan Shih. 2015. "Design a hash-based control mechanism in vSwitch for software-defined networking environment." *2015 IEEE International Conference on Cluster Computing (CLUSTER).* 498–499.

Hungyo, Misha, and Mayank Pandey. 2016. "SDN based implementation of publish/subscribe paradigm using OpenFlow multicast." *2016 IEEE International Conference on Advanced Networks and Telecommunications Systems (ANTS).* 1–6.

Hussein, Ali, Imad H Elhajj, Ali Chehab, and Ayman Kayssi. 2016. "SDN security plane: An architecture for resilient security services." *2016 IEEE International Conference on Cloud Engineering Workshop (IC2EW).* 54–59.

Javed, Mobin, Ayesha Binte Ashfaq, M Zubair Shafiq, and Syed Ali Khayam. 2009. "On the inefficient use of entropy for anomaly detection." *RAID.* 369–370.

Jin, Ruofan, and Bing Wang. 2013. "Malware detection for mobile devices using software-defined networking." *Research and Educational Experiment Workshop (GREE), 2013 Second GENI.* 81–88.

Jin, Xin, Hongqiang Harry Liu, Rohan Gandhi, Srikanth Kandula, Ratul Mahajan, Ming Zhang, Jennifer Rexford, and Roger Wattenhofer. 2014. "Dynamic scheduling of network updates." *ACM SIGCOMM Computer Communication Review.* 539–550.

Kalkan, Kubra, Gurkan Gur, and Fatih Alagoz. 2017. "Defense mechanisms against DDoS attacks in SDN environment." *IEEE Communications Magazine* (IEEE) 55 (9): 175–179.

Kamisiński, Andrzej, and Carol Fung. 2015. "Flowmon: Detecting malicious switches in software-defined networks." *Proceedings of the 2015 Workshop on Automated Decision Making for Active Cyber Defense.* 39–45.

Katta, Naga, Omid Alipourfard, Jennifer Rexford, and David Walker. 2016. "Cacheflow: Dependency-aware rule-caching for software-defined networks." *Proceedings of the Symposium on SDN Research.* 6.

Kharpal, Arjun. 2015. "Hack attack leaves 1,400 airline passengers grounded." https://www.cnbc.com/2015/06/22/hack-attack-leaves-1400-passengers-of-polish-airline-lot-grounded.html (accessed October 13, 2017).

Kloti, Rowan, Vasileios Kotronis, and Paul Smith. 2013. "Openflow: A security analysis." *2013 21st IEEE International Conference on Network Protocols (ICNP).* 1–6.

Kokila, RT, S Thamarai Selvi, and Kannan Govindarajan. 2014. "DDoS detection and analysis in SDN-based environment using support vector machine classifier." *2014 Sixth International Conference on Advanced Computing (ICoAC).* 205–210.

Kreutz, Diego, Fernando Ramos, and Paulo Verissimo. 2013. "Towards secure and dependable software-defined networks." *Proceedings of the second ACM SIGCOMM Workshop on Hot Topics in Software Defined Networking.* 55–60.

Lafrance, Adrienne. 2016. "How much will today's Internet outage cost?." https://www. theatlantic.com/technology/archive/2016/10/a-lot/505025/ (accessed October 10, 2017).

Lim, Sungheon, Seungnam Yang, Younghwa Kim, Sunhee Yang, and Hyogon Kim. 2015. "Controller scheduling for continued SDN operation under DDoS attacks." *Electronics Letters* (IET) 51 (16): 1259–1261.

Liyanage, Madhusanka, Mika Ylianttila, and Andrei Gurtov. 2014. "Securing the control channel of software-defined mobile networks." *2014 IEEE 15th International Symposium on a World of Wireless, Mobile and Multimedia Networks (WoWMoM).* 1–6.

Matthews, Tim. 2014. "ddos impact cost-of ddos attack." Nov.

Matthews, Tim. 2014. "*Incapsula Survey: What DDoS Attacks Really Cost Businesses.*" Incapsula Inc.: Redwood Shores, CA. https://www.incapsula.com/blog/ddos-impact-cost-of-ddos-attack.html (accessed October 13, 2017).

Mehdi, Syed Akbar, Junaid Khalid, and Syed Ali Khayam. 2011. "Revisiting traffic anomaly detection using software defined networking." *International Workshop on Recent Advances in Intrusion Detection.* 161–180.

Mousavi, Seyed Mohammad, and Marc St-Hilaire. 2015. "Early detection of DDoS attacks against SDN controllers." *2015 International Conference on Computing, Networking and Communications (ICNC).* 77–81.

Nazario, Jose. 2007. "Blackenergy ddos bot analysis." *Arbor Networks.*

Newland, Jesse. 2015. "Large scale DDoS attack on github.com." https://github.com/blog/1981-large-scale-ddos-attack-on-github-com (accessed September 20, 2017).

Nychis, George, Vyas Sekar, David G Andersen, Hyong Kim, and Hui Zhang. 2008. "An empirical evaluation of entropy-based traffic anomaly detection." *Proceedings of the 8th ACM SIGCOMM Conference on Internet Measurement.* 151–156.

Öke, Gülay, and Georgios Loukas. 2007. "A denial of service detector based on maximum likelihood detection and the random neural network." *The Computer Journal* (Oxford University Press) 50 (6): 717–727.

Oshima, Shunsuke, Takuo Nakashima, and Toshinori Sueyoshi. 2010. "Early DoS/DDoS detection method using short-term statistics." *2010 International Conference on Complex, Intelligent and Software Intensive Systems (CISIS).* 168–173.

Passito, Alexandre, Edjard Mota, Ricardo Bennesby, and Paulo Fonseca. 2014. "AgNOS: A framework for autonomous control of software-defined networks." *2014 IEEE 28th International Conference on Advanced Information Networking and Applications (AINA).* 405–412.

Peng, Tao, Christopher Leckie, and Kotagiri Ramamohanarao. 2007. "Survey of network-based defense mechanisms countering the DoS and DDoS problems." *ACM Computing Surveys (CSUR)* (ACM) 39 (1): 3.

Phan, Trung V, Truong Van Toan, Dang Van Tuyen, Truong Thu Huong, and Nguyen Huu Thanh. 2016. "OpenFlowSIA: An optimized protection scheme for software-defined networks from flooding attacks." *2016 IEEE Sixth International Conference on Communications and Electronics (ICCE).* 13–18.

Porras, Philip, Seungwon Shin, Vinod Yegneswaran, Martin Fong, Mabry Tyson, and Guofei Gu. 2012. "A security enforcement kernel for OpenFlow networks." *Proceedings of the First Workshop on Hot Topics in Software Defined Networks.* 121–126.

Radware. "DefenceFlow." https://www.radware.com/products/defenseflow/ (accessed September 20, 2017).

Ravikumar, VC, and Rabi N Mahapatra. 2004. "TCAM architecture for IP lookup using prefix properties." *IEEE Micro* (IEEE) 24 (2): 60–69.

Reiher, Peter, and M Mirkovic. 2004. "A taxonomy of DDoS attack and DDoS defense mechanisms." *ACM SIGCOMM Computer Communication Review* (Citeseer) 34 (2): 39–53.

Roy, Sankardas, Charles Ellis, Sajjan Shiva, Dipankar Dasgupta, Vivek Shandilya, and Qishi Wu. 2010. "A survey of game theory as applied to network security." *2010 43rd Hawaii International Conference on System Sciences (HICSS).* 1–10.

Sahoo, Abhaya Kumar, Kshira Sagar Sahoo, and Mayank Tiwary. 2014. "Signature based malware detection for unstructured data in Hadoop." *2014 International Conference on Advances in Electronics, Computers and Communications (ICAECC).* 1–6.

Sahoo, Kshira Sagar, Bibhudatta Sahoo, and Abinas Panda. 2015. "A secured SDN framework for IoT." *2015 International Conference on Man and Machine Interfacing (MAMI).* 1–4.

Sahoo, Kshira Sagar, Bibhudatta Sahoo, Ratnakar Dash, and Brojo Kishore Mishra. 2017. "Improving resiliency in SDN using routing tree algorithms." *International Journal of Knowledge Discovery in Bioinformatics (IJKDB)* (IGI Global) 7 (1): 42–57.

Sahoo, Kshira Sagar, Sagarika Mohanty, Mayank Tiwary, Brojo Kishore Mishra, and Bibhudatta Sahoo. 2016. "A comprehensive tutorial on software defined network: The driving force for the future internet technology." *Proceedings of the International Conference on Advances in Information Communication Technology & Computing.* 114.

Sauter, Molly. 2013. "LOIC will tear us apart: The impact of tool design and media portrayals in the success of activist DDOS attacks." *American Behavioral Scientist* (Sage Publications Sage, Los Angeles: CA) 57 (7): 983–1007.

Schechter, Stuart, Jaeyeon Jung, and Arthur Berger. 2004. "Fast detection of scanning worm infections." *Recent Advances in Intrusion Detection.* 59–81.

Schehlmann, Lisa, and Harald Baier. 2013. "COFFEE: A concept based on OpenFlow to filter and erase events of botnet activity at high-speed nodes." *GI-Jahrestagung.* 2225–2239.

Schwartz, Mathew J. 2016. "DDoS attack slams HSBC." https://www.bankinfosecurity.com/ddos-attack-slams-hsbc-a-8835 (accessed October 10, 2017).

Shekyan, Sergey. 2012. "Are you ready for slow reading?" https://blog.qualys.com/securitylabs/2012/01/05/slow-read (accessed September 5, 2017).

Shin, Seungwon, Vinod Yegneswaran, Phillip Porras, and Guofei Gu. 2013. "Avant-guard: Scalable and vigilant switch flow management in software-defined networks." *Proceedings of the 2013 ACM SIGSAC Conference on Computer & Communications Security.* 413–424.

Shirali-Shahreza, Sajad, and Yashar Ganjali. 2013. "Efficient implementation of security applications in openflow controller with flexam." *2013 IEEE 21st Annual Symposium on High-Performance Interconnects (HOTI).* 49–54.

Singh, Abhishek, Mayank Tiwray, Raj Kumar, and Rachita Misra. 2016. "Load balancing among wide-area SDN controllers." *2016 International Conference on Information Technology (ICIT).* 104–109.

Skoda, Martin. 2017. "DDoS protection in SDN based networking." https://www.flowmon.com/en/blog/ddos-protection-sdn-networking (accessed September 10, 2017).

Somani, Gaurav, Manoj Singh Gaur, Dheeraj Sanghi, Mauro Conti, Muttukrishnan Rajarajan, and Rajkumar Buyya. 2017. "Combating DDoS attacks in the cloud: Requirements, trends, and future directions." *IEEE Cloud Computing* (IEEE) 4 (1): 22–32.

Specification, OpenFlow Switch. 2013. "Version 1.3. 2 (Wire Protocol 0x04)." Open Networking Foundation.

Spitznagel, Ed, David Taylor, and Jonathan Turner. 2003. "Packet classification using extended TCAMs." *Proceedings of the 11th IEEE International Conference on Network Protocols.* 120–131.

Stallings, William. 2013. "Software-defined networks and OpenFlow." *The Internet Protocol Journal* (Citeseer) 16 (1): 2–14.

Sullivan, Ben. 2016. "Rio 2016 Olympics suffered sustained 540Gbps DDoS attacks." http://www.silicon.co.uk/security/rio-olympics-ddos-attacks-196998?inf_by=59d9bf2e681db8054c8b471e (accessed October 1, 2017).

Swain, Biswa Ranjan, and Bibhudatta Sahoo. 2009. "Mitigating DDoS attack and saving computational time using a probabilistic approach and HCF method." *IEEE International Advance Computing Conference, 2009. IACC 2009.* 1170–1172.

Wang, An, Yang Guo, Fang Hao, TV Lakshman, and Songqing Chen. 2014. "Scotch: Elastically scaling up sdn control-plane using vswitch based overlay." *Proceedings of the 10th ACM International on Conference on Emerging Networking Experiments and Technologies.* 403–414.

Wang, Rui, Zhiyong Zhang, Lei Ju, and Zhiping Jia. 2015. "A novel OpenFlow-based DDoS flooding attack detection and response mechanism in software-defined networking." *International Journal of Information Security and Privacy (IJISP)* (IGI Global) 9 (3): 21–40.

Weckler, Adrian. 2016. "Multiple government websites down as servers under 'DDoS attack'." https://www.independent.ie/irish-news/news/multiple-government-websites-down-as-servers-under-ddos-attack-34387566.html (accessed October 10, 2017).

Wu, Yi-Chi, Huei-Ru Tseng, Wuu Yang, and Rong-Hong Jan. 2011. "DDoS detection and traceback with decision tree and grey relational analysis." *International Journal of Ad Hoc and Ubiquitous Computing* (Inderscience Publishers) 7 (2): 121–136.

Xiao, Peng, Wenyu Qu, Heng Qi, and Zhiyang Li. 2015. "Detecting DDoS attacks against data center with correlation analysis." *Computer Communications* (Elsevier) 67: 66–74.

XU, Xiaoqiong, Hongfang YU, and Kun YANG. 2017. "DDoS attack in software defined networks: A survey." *ZTE COMMUNICATIONS* 15 (3).

Yadav, Virendra Kumar, Munesh Chandra Trivedi, and BM Mehtre. 2016. "DDA: An approach to handle DDoS (Ping flood) attack." *Proceedings of International Conference on ICT for Sustainable Development.* 11–23.

Yan, Qiao, F Richard Yu, Qingxiang Gong, and Jianqiang Li. 2016. "Software-defined networking (SDN) and distributed denial of service (DDoS) attacks in cloud computing environments: A survey, some research issues, and challenges." *IEEE Communications Surveys & Tutorials* (IEEE) 18 (1): 602–622.

Yao, Guang, Jun Bi, and Peiyao Xiao. 2011. "Source address validation solution with OpenFlow/NOX architecture." *2011 19th IEEE International Conference on Network Protocols (ICNP).* 7–12.

Yarimtepe, Oğuz, GÖkhan Dalkílíç, and Mehmet Hilal Özcanhan. 2015. "Distributed Denial of Service Prevention Techniques."

YuHunag, Chu, Tseng MinChi, Chen YaoTing, Chou YuChieh, and Chen YanRen. 2010. "A novel design for future on-demand service and security." *2010 12th IEEE International Conference on Communication Technology (ICCT).* 385–388.

Zargar, Saman Taghavi, James Joshi, and David Tipper. 2013. "A survey of defense mechanisms against distributed denial of service (DDoS) flooding attacks." *IEEE Communications Surveys & Tutorials* (IEEE) 15 (4): 2046–2069.

Zhang, Ying. 2013. "An adaptive flow counting method for anomaly detection in SDN." *Proceedings of the Ninth ACM Conference on Emerging Networking Experiments and Technologies.* 25–30.

Chapter 6

Fog Computing in Internet of Things-Based E-Health System—Challenges and Opportunities for Managing Health-Associated Data

Mirjana Maksimovic

University of East Sarajevo, Faculty of Electrical Engineering

Contents

6.1 Introduction

Technological breakthroughs changed the traditional monitoring and delivery of healthcare switching to a new and multifaceted scenario, where the outcome is improved and care is personalized, placing the patient in the center of the treatment process. Instead of the patient going to the care, the increasing number of diverse Internet of Things (IoT)-connected medical devices and sensors placed within or on the human body or located in ambient surroundings enable that the care goes to the patient (Gaddi et al., 2014; MacIntosh et al., 2014). The result of the growing amount of technological solutions put to work helps save lives and enhances the health of the population in an IoT-based e-health solution, whose goal is to provide an effective and efficient healthcare for anyone, anytime, and anywhere. An increasing number of diverse IoT devices [according to Cisco (Evans, 2011), 50 billion IoT devices will be in operation by 2020] produce massive amounts of data. Regarding healthcare data, it is estimated that it will be 25,000 petabytes of healthcare-associated data in 2020 (Feldman et al., 2012). These data have to be processed accurately and on time to enable making the data-driven diagnosis and care faster. Apparently, dealing with and extracting insights from high-dimensional, high-velocity, and high-variety data created by the IoT-driven e-health systems represent a big challenge. Sending these data to the Cloud and transmitting response data back require a larger bandwidth, a considerable amount of time, and can suffer latency issues, which is intolerable in time-sensitive applications, such as healthcare. Instead of posting all these data to the Cloud, which is incapable of handling the escalating volumes of rapidly growing, unstructured health-related data, using miniature data analysis centers that greatly reduce the quantity of data being transmitted to and from Cloud has been presented as a better approach. This approach, which supports decentralized and intelligent processing closer to where the data are produced, refers to Fog computing (Bresnick, n.d.).

In other words, the Fog infrastructure, instead of sending all sensed data to the Cloud, filters out relevant, differentiating information from the large datasets or streams of data and posts only the obtained results to the Cloud for further analysis and storage (Dubey, 2015; Gia et al., 2015). In this way, Fog computing successfully deals with congestion and latency issues. In addition, the Fog layer enables real-time and online analytics even in the case of loss of connectivity or poor connection with the Cloud. Keeping in mind that all information related to a person's health and medical history is considered especially sensitive and in need of protection, it is necessary to pay more attention to the security design and privacy issues in health-related networks than in many other IoT networks. For this reason, the security must be built into each component and the overall system, from the edge device to the Fog and Cloud levels (Maksimovic and Vujovic, 2017). Regarding privacy, implementation of Fog infrastructure leads to easier provided data privacy, since the public and private data are separated while processing and analyzing them at the Fog level, transmitting only valuable data further to the Cloud. Furthermore, properly managed IoT data can improve profits and effectively reduce the cost of healthcare. Hence, the benefits that Fog computing offers [low latency, maximum network bandwidth utilization, heterogeneity, interoperability, better interconnectivity, scalability, optimal operational expense, security and privacy, real-time processing and actions, and enhanced quality of service (QoS)] are of immense importance in health monitoring and delivery of healthcare. However, Fog computing is not a replacement of Cloud computing. They complement each other, and as such become a powerful tool to achieve numerous benefits in various aspects of the healthcare domain. Fog infrastructure immensely contributes to remote and real-time monitoring, and faster data-driven reactions that are considered as the major benefits patients experience in IoT-driven e-health vision. Together with the Cloud, it holds the potential to make IoT-driven e-health systems reliable, simpler, scalable, and with exceptional performance (Maksimovic, 2017).

Successfully dealing with numerous challenges IoT-based healthcare services are faced with, especially IoT-generated data stream management issues, IoT-based healthcare solutions should enable real-time smart decisions, optimize the use of resources, reduce costs, provide higher profits, increase the safety and quality of life, and enrich the experience of both patients and healthcare providers. The significance of accessible, connected, accurate, and actionable data for healthcare, consequently, makes management of IoT-generated health-associated data, in order to turn insight into action, increasingly important.

To get as much possible insights into the problem regarding the management of health-related data generated in IoT-based e-health systems, this chapter examines the current challenges and opportunities of this topic. The chapter is structured as follows. After the Introduction, Section 6.2 represents the essence of IoT-supported healthcare, lists the types and structures of health-related data, and considers and analyzes the present approaches for handling IoT-generated healthcare data. The reasons for improving data management in IoT-driven e-health system, as well as its benefits and challenges, are also presented and discussed. Keeping in mind the potential that IoT has in revolutionizing healthcare delivering and operationalizing, by radically reducing costs and improving the availability and quality of healthcare by focusing on the way people, devices, and applications are connected and interact with each other, Section 6.3 emphasizes the necessity of Fog infrastructure integration in an IoT-based healthcare system. An analysis of the Fog computing paradigm, its implementation, and the objectives that must be fulfilled for achieving significant improvement of IoT-powered e-health approaches is presented. Hence, the performed study includes technological and methodological approaches for the implementation of IoT-based healthcare systems with Fog infrastructure. A particular attention has been paid to the potential of Fog computing to resolve problems regarding latency, bandwidth, heterogeneity, interoperability, scalability, real-time processing and actions, and security and privacy. The analysis of data management in a Fog-assisted and IoT-based healthcare system as well as manners to enable high level of privacy and security, efficient resource utilization, and standardization issues are discussed in Section 6.4. As part of the performed research, this chapter attempts to highlight benefits and expectations, and at the same time point out the challenges, risks, and concerns related to the Fog computing implementation in IoT-driven healthcare. Section 6.5 presents the prototype of a simple, low-cost, Fog-assisted and IoT-based healthcare system aimed to measure vital parameters of the human body. This section emphasizes the directions for future development and implementation of the proposed prototype as well as the course of future research. Finally, Section 6.5 provides the concluding remarks.

6.2 Health-Associated Data

The properties of healthcare data make them unique and difficult to measure. The healthcare data come from various sources and various formats (e.g., text, image, multimedia, videos, paper, numeric). Aggregating different data formats from diverse sources and owners (patients, clinics and doctors, pharma/drug companies, insurance companies) enables data accessible and actionable (LeSueur, n.d.). Hence, to process, manage, analyze, visualize, or share healthcare data, they must be first collected and then aggregated into a single, centralized location. In other words, on-time collection, processing, and analyzing of healthcare data are of crucial importance to make adequate and timely diagnosis, fast reactions, and treatment, consequently leading to enhanced healthcare value and quality alongside significantly decreased costs. Technological progress significantly contributes to overcoming many of the traditional obstacles regarding collecting, sharing, and analyzing data (Groves et al., 2013). Based on the knowledge obtained from gathered and analyzed information, the inclusion of novel information and communication technologies, particularly the IoT, has revolutionized all aspects of healthcare industry. The IoT utilization for healthcare purpose is mainly focused on (Bhatt and Bhatt, 2017)

- A patient's routine medical checkup,
- The high-risk medical treatments,
- The medical treatment performed in standard manners with the assistance of devices, data, and people symbiosis.

The IoT in healthcare significantly contributes to more effective care and patient-personalized care than ever before. Timeliness, efficiency, accessibility, and affordability are additional benefits of IoT-powered healthcare systems. These systems are established utilizing a large number of small devices that are able to monitor various kinds of parameters, being attached to or embedded in the human body or placed in ambient surroundings. The IoT devices used for healthcare purposes can be classified as follows (Glaser, 2014; Maksimovic and Vujovic, 2017):

- Wearable (on/around) devices such as consumer-based devices (e.g., smart watches, fitness-tracking devices, sensor embedded in textile clothing, headbands) and external devices (e.g., insulin pumps, portable Holter monitors),
- Implantable (in) devices (e.g., pacemakers and implantable cardio defibrillator devices, within the body sensors, implantable biomedical devices),
- Stationary surrounding devices (e.g., home-monitoring devices, intravenous pumps, and fetal monitors).

Continuous monitoring with wearable, internally embedded, or stationary devices ensures early detection of emergency conditions and diseases, and their timely diagnosis and treatment (Darwish and Hassanien, 2011). Interoperability among these large number of devices represents a huge challenge. To standardize e-health, which is the most complicated and challenging area of health monitoring, Telecommunication Standardization Sector of the International Telecommunication Union formed IoT Global Standards Initiative. It brings numerous recommendations regarding device identification, data management, and privacy and security issues that are applicable in e-health applications (ITU-T, 2012). Thanks to its highly sensitive nature, standards regarding privacy and security of personal health-related data, data ownership and relevance, confidentiality, data accessibility, processing, storage, reuse, and risks are of high importance in healthcare applications. The devices used in IoT-based e-health produce a large amount of data on a daily basis. These health-associated data generated by IoT technology are usually described with five V's: volume, velocity, variety, value, and veracity:

- *Volume* refers to constantly growing amounts of the health-related data, generated from an increasing plurality of sources, resulting in terabytes and petabytes of data.
- *Velocity* or the data-generating and -processing speed increases nowadays with ever-growing measurements and readings from numerous and diverse medical devices.
- *Variety* represents various types of data. Healthcare records and patient registries encompass electronic healthcare records (EHRs), social media, genomic and pharmaceutical data, telemedicine, mobile health (m-health) applications, clinical trials, home monitoring, and real-time sensors readings as well as environmental, financial and operational data (Figure 6.1) (BDVA, 2016; European Commission, 2014, 2016). These data can be in structured, semistructured, and unstructured formats. Structured data have a well-defined representation and can be easily captured, stored, analyzed, and shared by machine and managed often by Structured Query Language (Papadokostaki et al., 2017). Some examples of structured healthcare data are lab results (e.g., glucose or cholesterol levels), the International Statistical Classification of Diseases and Related Health Problems (ICD9 and ICD10 codes), Current Procedural Terminology,

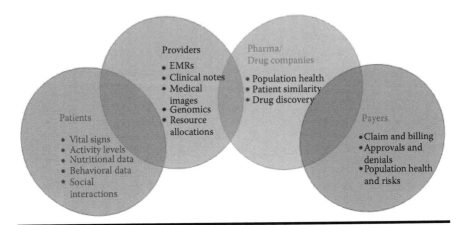

Figure 6.1   The source of health-related data.

IoT-sensed data, etc. Semistructured and unstructured healthcare data are far more difficult to leverage (e.g., clinical notes, photos, paper prescriptions, X-rays, magnetic resonance images, slides, social media data) (Dhamdhere et al., 2016). As 80% of all health-related data are in semistructured and unstructured data formats, their utilization in the Big data system is a challenging task. This implies the need for more effective and automatic conversion formats of data so that it can be efficiently used for healthcare purposes.

■ *Value* means extracting the knowledge or patterns (creating a value) out of the data to gain better insights into new diseases and therapies, and to perform timely diagnosis and treatment.

■ *Veracity* refers to data understandability. In other words, it introduces any noise and abnormalities, and therefore refers to uncertain or imprecise data.

According to Manogaran et al. (2017), there are additional five V's that categorize Big data (Figure 6.2):

■ *Validity* of data refers to precision and accurateness of data.
■ *Variability* refers to consistency and value of data.
■ *Viscosity* represents the latency during transmission of the data from the source to the destination.
■ *Virality* refers to the data transmission speed (sending and receiving data from diverse sources).
■ *Visualization* is realized to symbolize a huge amount of data and discover the hidden values during decision making.

As can be seen, health-related data are uniquely complex, appear in various formats (structured, semistructured, and unstructured), are produced from many diverse

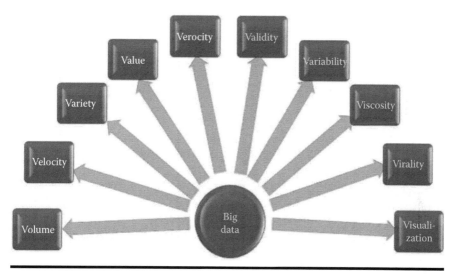

Figure 6.2   Ten V's of Big data.

sources, and their unpredictable and changeable nature makes their management a quite difficult and challenging task (LeSueur, n.d.). The standard database management tools and data-processing applications are not adequate for managing large and complex datasets such as health-associated datasets (Chang, 2015). The Big data analysis demands significant computing power and powerful techniques to extract the knowledge by discovering trends and patterns within and between the existing datasets (European Commission, 2016). Extracting the hidden knowledge from Big healthcare-related data is essential in improving healthcare, particularly in making decisions in emergency situations and complex healthcare problems. The Big data value chain consists of producing and gathering data, data processing, storing, transmitting, visualizing, evaluating, and sharing. Hence, to achieve benefits of modern approaches regarding healthcare, the IoT-driven e-health solution deals with several serious challenges regarding data gathering, analyzing, and interpreting (Maksimovic and Vujovic, 2017):

- Health-related data collection from multiple sources in a remote, secure, and safe manner,
- Analysis of collected data using a wide range of pattern recognition and machine learning techniques,
- Data sharing through wireless connectivity in a private and secure way, with those who can make real-time intelligent feedback.

Big data technologies enable to find answers to what happened (descriptive analytics), why it happened (diagnostic analytics), what will happen (predictive analytics), and how to make it happen (prescriptive analytics), and as such hold the potential to radically improve healthcare quality and accessibility to healthcare systems (Figure 6.3) (BDVA, 2016).

In general, based on the generation source, the knowledge can be (Manogaran et al., 2017)

- Explicit knowledge that is easy to collect, format, and share (e.g., disease diagnosis, hospital and medical procedures),
- Tacit knowledge that is based on personal experience.

Medical personnel have both explicit and tacit knowledge, while patient knowledge is mostly tacit. Hence, Big data analysis enables obtaining insights and the knowledge that can be implemented for retrospective data analysis as well as prospective data monitoring, and may (European Commission, 2014, 2016; Groves et al., 2013)

- Enhance the quality and effectiveness of healthcare (e.g., real-time monitoring of patients, earlier and more accurate disease diagnostic, more effective treatments, reduced medical errors, determination of side effects patterns, cooperation and collaboration of healthcare stakeholders, intensified medical and clinical research),
- Open new possibilities for disease preventions (e.g., identification of risk factors, promoting healthy lifestyle),

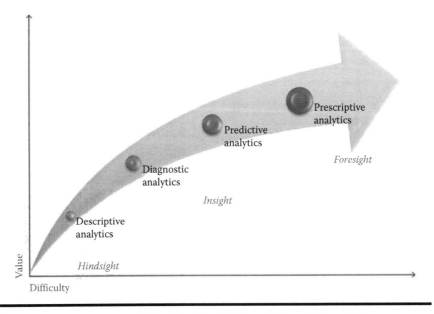

Figure 6.3   Data patterns including hindsight, insight, and foresight.

- Predict outcomes (e.g., predicting diagnosis and right medicine, prediction of infectious diseases and their transmission pathways, disease likelihood and risks determination, as well as predictions of healthcare costs),
- Disseminate the knowledge (e.g., dissemination of information can improve healthcare outcome, help healthcare stakeholders to identify value and opportunities like discovering new pharmaceuticals, and development of more personalized treatments, patients who are more informed become more responsible for their own health),
- Reduce costs, inefficiency, waste, and the risk of fraud and abuse in clinical operations, development, and research (e.g., optimized utilization of resources, reduced avoidable overuse, relevant and cost-effective diagnosis and treatment). According to BDVA (2016), the improvement of the healthcare system productivity realizes the approach of public spending savings to 2% of gross domestic product on average in the Organization for Economic Cooperation and Development countries.

Evidently, data have the potential to revolutionize healthcare by providing the right treatment and care to the right patient at the right time (Chang, 2015). To improve healthcare efficiency, predict and prevent diseases, and reduce costs (Figure 6.4), it is essential to have systematic approaches for data gathering, analyzing, and interpreting.

Therefore, Big data quality, accessibility, and availability are the prerequisites for healthcare systems and processes improvements. The collection and extraction of valuable insights and knowledge from large, diverse, and complex datasets require adequate technologies and techniques. Numerous IoT applications are established on posting data to the Cloud, where powerful processing, analyzing, and storing of sensory data are performed. Despite the numerous benefits of Cloud computing (e.g., scalability, reliability, sustainability, storage options, accessibility, 24/7 support,

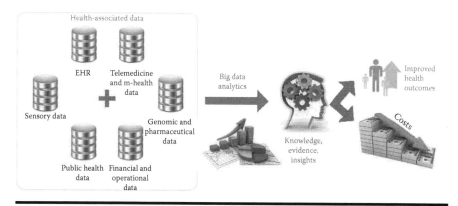

Figure 6.4 Big data analytics role in healthcare applications.

highly automated, device and location independent, environment friendly), it is not the best solution for some applications and services. Issues regarding bandwidth, latency, and lack of mobility support and location of awareness imply that Cloud computing is not adequate for large-scale and geographically distributed applications, fast mobile applications, and latency-sensitive applications such as e-health applications. IoT applications in healthcare demand very low and predictable latency and less congestion, which makes Fog computing more appropriate than Cloud computing. Building a middle layer between end users/devices and Cloud, local processing and storage hold the potential to completely transform IoT-based e-health systems, making it more powerful, accurate, and faster to response.

6.3 Fog Computing and Reasons for Its Integration in IoT-Based Healthcare Systems

Fog computing is a term created by Cisco, and it represents the extension of Cloud computing and services at the edge of the network, where IoT devices generate data. Hence, Fog computing is not a replacement for Cloud computing, but it makes an additional computing layer between sensors and Cloud computing (Figure 6.5), in which huge amount of data are split to subdata and extract key information (Cisco, 2015). In this way, Fog computing enables distribution of storage, computing, communication, control, and decision making, which consequently contribute to improved management of five or ten V's described health-connected data.

The Fog computing architecture is established on Fog nodes. Fog node can be any device with computing, storage, and network connectivity (Cisco, 2015) and can be implemented as a traditional network element (e.g., like routers, servers, gateways, edge devices) or as an intermediate compute node (e.g., stand-alone Fog box) (Byers

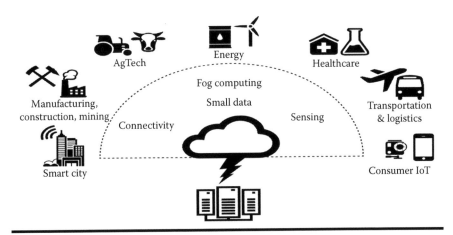

Figure 6.5 Fog computing vision.

and Wetterwald, 2015; Marin-Tordera et al., 2016). However, in most Fog deployments, there are usually several tiers of nodes (OpenFog, 2017). Those in the lower network hierarchy are with simple hardware configurations and modest software performances. The Fog nodes in the upper tiers, closer to the Cloud, are more sophisticated and with better performances. Fog nodes enable a two-way communication—sending data from the end devices to the Cloud and receiving the commands from the Cloud (Farahani et al., 2017). Wired, wireless, and optical networking facilities are used for Fog nodes interconnections. Having in mind the number of IoT devices, Fog-based networks rely on the IPv6 protocol (Byers and Wetterwald, 2015). The architecture of a Fog node is shown in Figure 6.6 (Farahani et al., 2017).

There are several crucial reasons why Fog computing implementation in IoT-based e-health system seems as a far better approach than Cloud. First of all, the sensor devices used in health monitoring are resource constrained and therefore not able to perform complex tasks, such as data processing and analyzing. Another reason for Fog computing implementation is related to communication issues. Numerous applied sensors in IoT vision stream data to IoT networks while the Fog level performs data processing. Only relevant and critical data are transmitted to the best fitting spot for processing incoming tasks (Cloud, Fog, or network resources) depending on application requirements (Dastjerdi and Buyya, 2016). The healthcare applications, in general, require prompt response to the important events as well as a high level of reliability. Hence, in time-sensitive applications, such as healthcare, processing data, decisions, and actions should be made closer to where

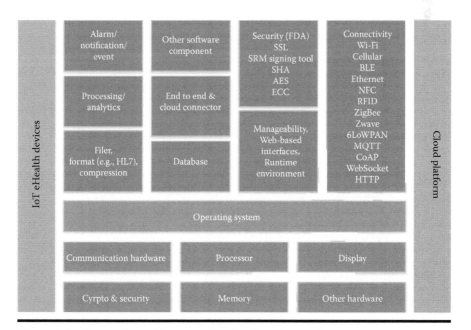

Figure 6.6   Fog node architecture (Farahani et al., 2017).

data are being produced. In other words, Fog level is responsible for receiving sensor data stream from a variety of IoT devices, and it analyzes data using various data-mining techniques (such as artificial intelligence, machine learning, intelligent data mining, computer vision, Big data, and real-time analytics) which are used to discover hidden patterns, detect anomalies, perform predictive modeling, and make actionable decisions. After running IoT-enabled applications, Fog level performs real-time data processing and sends the results back to the user without the use of Cloud (Nandyala and Kim, 2016). Only metadata are uploaded to the Cloud that receives and aggregates information from many Fog devices, does further analyses (e.g., Big data analytics, historical analysis), stores the information for long period of time, and can send new application rules to the Fog devices based on the obtained insights and knowledge (Figure 6.7) (Cisco, 2015; Encash, 2016). Hence, the Cloud performs data processing and storing from a high-level view, making data and the obtained knowledge available and accessible to parties involved in the treatment process (González et al., 2016). The communication between Cloud and resources at the edge of the network is realized with the help of machine-to-machine (M2M) standards and the Constrained Application Protocol (CoAP), while Software-Defined Networking (SDN) contributes to the more efficient management of heterogeneous Fog networks (Dastjerdi and Buyya, 2016). An additional requirement in healthcare is the ability for a patient to move freely while he is under medical supervision through IoT devices (Negash et al., 2017). Obviously, all these demands can be easily met with the help of a Fog computing paradigm.

As Fog computing is the extension of Cloud computing, it retains some of the benefits of Cloud computing. The Fog and Cloud computing paradigms use the same resources and share the same mechanism and attributes (Natraj, 2016). In addition, Fog computing enables easier and faster communication of the data over

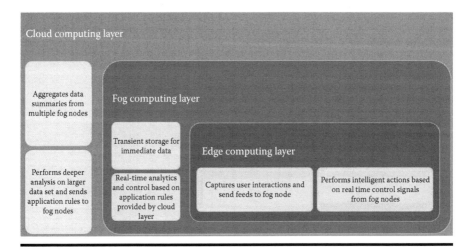

Figure 6.7 The role of computing layers in an IoT ecosystem (Encash, 2016).

IoT devices (Naranjo et al., 2016). The detailed comparison between Fog computing and Cloud computing paradigms is given in Table 6.1.

Based on the Fog computing performances presented in Table 6.1. it is obvious that Fog computing paradigm holds the potential to enhance overall performance of numerous IoT applications. The features of Fog computing that justify its

Table 6.1   Fog Computing vs. Cloud Computing (Augur, 2016; Firdhous et al., 2014; Natraj, 2016)

Requirement	Fog Computing	Cloud Computing
Devices	Heterogeneous	Virtual machines
Hardware	Limited storage/ compute resources	Scalable storage/ compute resources
Data storage	Temporary	Permanent
Computational capability	Normal	Powerful
Latency	Low	High
Delay jitter	Very low	High
Bandwidth	Low	High
Response time	Seconds to minute	Minutes, days, or weeks
Location of server nodes	At the edge of local network	Within the Internet
Distance between client and server	One hop	Multiple hops
Security	Can be defined	Undefined
Attack on data enroute	Very low probability	High probability
Location awareness	Yes	No
Geo-distribution	Distributed	Centralized
Number of server nodes	Very large	Few
Support for mobility	Supported	Limited
Flexibility	High	Limited
Agility	High	Limited
Type of last mile connectivity	Wireless	Leased line

implementation and integration in IoT vision, with reference to healthcare applications, are as follows (Augur, 2016; Firdhous et al., 2014; Natraj, 2016; Peter, 2015):

- Distribution: As Fog computing vision is established for the implementation of a large number of micro centers (small servers) closer to smart objects (edge devices), the computing, communication, storage, and control as well as decision making are distributed. This significantly reduces network load and avoids the existence of one centralized point of failure, which is crucial in healthcare, where safe and fast data management is of immense importance.
- Location awareness: Fog level, as a middle layer between smart edge devices and the Cloud, significantly reduces latency and successfully deals with the bandwidth issues. This is essential for time-sensitive applications such as healthcare applications.
- Mobility support: Fog infrastructure represents the extension of the Cloud at the edge of the network, closer to the smart edge devices, and as such behaves as a "mobile" Cloud. This enables that the patient can move freely without losing medical supervision of his/her health conditions and appropriate level of healthcare.
- Scalability: Capabilities of Fog computing to successfully deal with increased network load contribute to improved scalability. The improved scalability without any degradation in the quality of service is the benefit that Fog computing brings in IoT applications, including healthcare.
- Real time: Low latency and reduced network bandwidth consumption make Fog computing adequate for real-time applications. The ability to make extremely time-sensitive decisions makes Fog computing appropriate for healthcare applications.
- Heterogeneity: Fog computing supports the heterogeneous architecture and configuration of Fog nodes (various manufacturers and model types, different operating systems, and incompatible communication protocols) deployed in diverse environments. The IoT-based healthcare environment is the typical representation of a heterogeneous environment that therefore benefits from Fog computing implementation.
- The density of devices: Fog infrastructure provides strong and reproduced services even in the case when there is ineffective communication with the operation center.
- Standardization: The resources of Fog level can cooperate with different Cloud providers. However, there are still many open research questions regarding standardization of Fog computing paradigm.
- On-the-fly analysis: Fog architecture enables the data aggregation to transmit partially processed data.
- Predominance of wireless access technologies, such as Wireless Local Area Network (WLAN), Worldwide Interoperability for Microwave Access

(WiMAX), as well as cellular access networks (e.g., 4G, 5G), and the radio access network for gaining the access to Fog (Munir et al., 2017).

■ Privacy: Fog computing by analyzing sensitive data at the local level, instead of on the Cloud, and separating public and private data immensely contributes to improved privacy and security. This fact justifies the Fog computing implementation in healthcare applications, since health-associated data are most personal than any other and in need of special protection.

The proven benefits of Fog-assisted and IoT-based healthcare systems can be found in the literature review. Nandyala and Kim (2016) in their work present Cloud to Fog computing in IoT-powered u-healthcare monitoring systems for smart home and hospitals. The idea of Fog computing integration in health-monitoring system is presented by Gia et al. (2015). They have implemented Fog computing in smart gateway, where electrocardiogram signals were analyzed. The results of their case study have shown that Fog computing has led to more than 90% bandwidth efficiency alongside significantly reduced latency, which has contributed to fast real-time response. eWALL system for monitoring chronic obstructive pulmonary disease and mild dementia is presented by Fratu et al. (2015). Based on the Fog computing paradigm, this system significantly reduces the communication overload and keeps the patient's privacy. The shortest amount of processing time and high level of accuracy are the main features of the Fog computing system for e-health applications proposed by Craciunescu et al. (2015). Cao et al. (2015) present a distributed analytics system to monitor fall for stroke mitigation established on Fog computing called FAST. This system has shown high sensitivity alongside minimized response time and energy utilization. Constant et al. (2017) demonstrate wearable IoT device based on Fog computing principles. The presented smart glove can be used as a wearable IoT device applicable in diseases where the hand movement has to be monitored and treated (e.g., Parkinson's disease). The Fog computing-assisted system is also presented by Negash et al. (2017). The authors have proposed a three-layer architecture (sensors, Fog gateway, and Cloud server) to monitor vital parameters of patients, their activities, and situations. HealthFog system architecture, that is, health-related data collected from various sources and processes, has been presented by Ahmad et al. (2016). Rahmani et al. (2017) present Fog-assisted Smart e-Health Gateway called UT-GATE, developed for monitoring patients with acute diseases. The system performance measurements have justified the reasons for Fog computing implementation in IoT-powered healthcare systems. To the same conclusion have contributed the presented works and many others found in literature reviews (Aazam and Huh, 2015; González et al., 2016; Osanaiye et al., 2017; Venkat Narayana Rao et al., 2015) that have shown that Fog computing and IoT-based healthcare connection gather the most attention.

Evidently, in healthcare applications, where processing data and response must be fast, almost immediately, Fog computing is quite useful. A smart healthcare system with implemented Fog infrastructure is able to perform on-site computing, with low-latency data processing and low-bandwidth requirements. Other benefits, such as heterogeneity and interoperability, mobility support, location awareness, real-time and online analytics, instant decision making and fast reaction in case of emergency, decreased energy consumption, enhanced privacy and security, and improved quality of services for streaming and real-time applications, make Fog computing capable to satisfy the requirements proposed by numerous fast-developing IoT applications, including healthcare. Despite the stated benefits, Fog computing is not as powerful as Cloud; therefore, their common coexistence, collaboration, and cooperation in IoT-powered applications can be considered as a precondition for revolutionizing various domains of our lives.

6.4 Data Management in Fog-Assisted and IoT-Based Healthcare Systems

Time-sensitive decision making closer to the devices that generate data, reduced network bandwidth consumption, supported user mobility, resource and interface heterogeneity, and enhanced security and privacy are the characteristics that make architecture with Fog computing layer the most applied approach in IoT-based healthcare applications. In Fog computing architecture, this intermediate layer continuously receives huge quantities of data generated by sensor devices in a short period of time. Successful data management is a precondition for fast and accurate decision making and prompt reaction in emergency cases. In addition, healthcare data are uniquely complex, which implies that the traditional methods for managing data are not applicable in healthcare applications. Hence, completely different and new approaches are required to successfully deal with diverse data that are produced from a wide variety of sources. The lifecycle of data within a Fog-assisted and IoT-powered healthcare system goes from producing data on the sensor devices, while Fog level performs data storing, data processing, data compressing, data fusion, data analysis, and data transfer to the Cloud, where data may be further analyzed, stored, and archived. Based on the additional and detailed analysis, obtained insights and knowledge, and predictive and prescriptive analysis, the Cloud sends back to the Fog level commands and other control actions as well as performs the required updates. Hence, storing collected raw medical data at the local level and local data processing (filtering, compressing, fusion, analysis) to be interoperable and suitable for the other resources are essential tasks performed in a Fog level, which acts as a smart gateway in healthcare applications (Farahani et al., 2017; Negash et al., 2017):

- ◼ The Fog computing architecture enables temporary storage at the edge of the infrastructure environment that can be used to store files in encrypted or compressed format, while data can be further exported in formats according to health-related standards [e.g., Health Level Seven (HL7)]. The short-term database at the edge of the network stores various information such as sensed body/environment/location/time data. After data processing at the local level, only valuable data are being posted to the Cloud center. The advantages of local storage are the ability to save the data when there is poor or no connection with Cloud or using local storage as a local cache memory to enable continual data circulations during misbalance between computation time and transfer time.

■ The IoT-based healthcare architecture with the help of a wide variety of sensor devices deals with a complex, noisy, heterogeneous, and voluminous health-related data. However, the accuracy of sensed health-related data is mandatory, and it may be influenced by environmental effects and hardware problems of sensory devices. After receiving sensory data, the Fog node performs data filtering in order to find anomalies and clean the data by removing any noise or errors.

■ The next step is the data compression that reduces the amount of health-related data needed to be transmitted over the communication network. Data compression can be either lossy or lossless, which is preferred in healthcare applications. At the same time, lossless compression is a complex, resource-intensive task. However, Fog layer, thanks to its features, deals successfully with these challenges.

■ Since data are collected from a multisensory environment, there is a need to perform data fusion to obtain complete and more reliable information regarding an individual's health condition. Data fusion is a challenging task mostly because of data imperfection, conflicting data, outliers and spurious data, data modality, data correlation, data association, data dimensionality, operational timing, processing framework, etc. (Khaleghi et al. 2013). Based on the relationship among sources, data fusion can be complementary (combination of two or more diverse data from various sources), competitive (synthesis of data collected from a single source with two or more sensors), and cooperative (providing new information from one source employing various sensors) (Figure 6.8).

■ As it is already stated, the Fog computing goal is to make a decision close to the data generation place and to transmit only valuable data further. The implementation of machine learning models, data mining, pattern recognition, automated reasoning, etc. locally on a Fog node to make a decision is far better and cheaper than posting and analyzing all the data on the Cloud level. Probabilistic models such as Bayesian reasoning or a Markov decision process, Kalman filtering, and intelligent fusion model (e.g., fuzzy logic, neural network, genetic algorithm) are possible decision-making techniques used in healthcare systems (Lee et al., 2008). More detailed analysis of various data-mining algorithms in classification, clustering, and association and their utilization for the biomedical and healthcare purposes is presented by Yoo et al. (2012). Despite the applied decision-making technique, the data analysis at

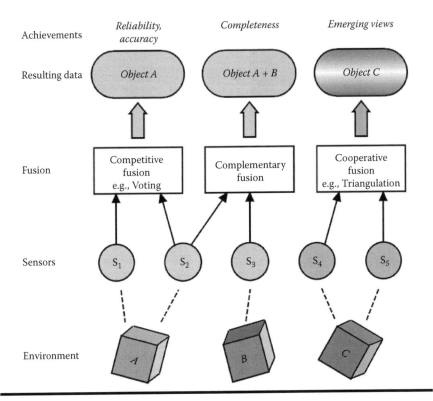

Figure 6.8 Types of data fusion (Elmenreich, 2011).

the edge of the network significantly decreases the amount of data required to be sent to the Cloud and reduce latency. In addition, data analysis at the Fog layer contributes to data reliability and system consistency.

In the realization of the Fog-assisted and IoT-based healthcare system, the security and privacy issues regarding health-related data are essential requirements and at the same time are the greatest challenges. Some of the existing security and privacy challenges connected to the Cloud also remain in the Fog paradigm. As Fog computing poses distinct characteristics (mobility support, location awareness, and low latency), it also brings in novel security and privacy challenges. In other words, enabling security and privacy issues at each level of a Fog architecture and of all the enabling technologies is not enough. To assure overall security, it is necessary to orchestrate diverse security mechanisms at different levels, enabling high level of integrity and interoperability. The threats in Fog computing architecture can be classified according to its hierarchy organization (Roman et al., 2016):

■ End-user devices are exposed to threats such as injection of information and service manipulation. In both cases, denied access to these devices may produce distribution of fake information and service outcome manipulation.

■ At the Fog data center, possible threats are physical damage, privacy leakage, privilege escalation, service manipulation, and rogue data center. Threats to the virtualization infrastructure within the Fog data center include Denial of Service (DoS), misuse of resources, privacy leakage, and privilege escalation.

■ The typical threats to network infrastructure are DoS, man-in-the-middle attack, and rogue gateway.

To reach a high level of defense against these different threats, it is mandatory to implement diverse types of security services and mechanisms. Thanks to its characteristics, Fog computing enables improved security and privacy issues in IoT in the following ways:

■ When data are accumulated by medical devices and transmitted to a Cloud, there is a possible danger of loss of connectivity, and thus information loss. In healthcare applications, this is not tolerable, and in some cases, such situations may lead to fatal consequences. In a Fog computing architecture, privacy preservation is accomplished through processing sensitive health-associated data in the Fog nodes and minimizing data transmission to the Cloud. Hence, local storage implementation at the Fog layer enhances data protection. However, sensitive health-related data from end users have to be encrypted before transfer to the Fog node (Yi et al., 2015). To preserve data privacy, various privacy-preserving techniques (e.g., differential privacy, homomorphic encryption) may be applied between the Fog and the Cloud (Ahmad et al., 2016; Alrawais et al., 2017). Usage privacy and location privacy are also important challenges that must be considered and accomplished in the Fog-assisted and IoT-based healthcare system.

■ Identity and authentication at different levels are of crucial importance in IoT-based healthcare systems. The Fog computing paradigm enables authentication in IoT devices or appliance of lightweight encryption algorithms between Fog nodes and IoT devices to improve authentication (Alrawais et al., 2017; Stojmenovic and Wen, 2014). A lightweight authentication for IoT-enabled devices, proposed by Amin et al. (2016) for the distributed Cloud environment, is applicable in Fog computing paradigm. Another authentication method present in the literature is a user authentication system that allows any end device and Fog node to mutually authenticate each other (Ibrahim, 2016). Nevertheless, the utilization of smart gateway in Fog computing for running secure methods without the need for Cloud enables secure and efficient authentication and authorization.

■ The Fog architecture offers a multilayer security. The overall network security can be achieved by applying SDN techniques in Fog computing like network monitoring and intrusion detection system, traffic isolation and prioritization, network resource access control, and network sharing (Yi et al., 2015). The implementation of Network Function Virtualization (NFV) enables the virtualization of various devices used in Fog computing architecture (e.g., gateways, switches, load balancers, firewalls, intrusion detection devices) and posting these instances on Fog nodes. As virtualization is a key aspect of Fog computing, NFV promises to bring numerous benefits in this paradigm. The NFV in combination with SDN helps to isolate unsecure network devices, reconfigures the systems in real time, directs the traffic toward secure devices, etc. (Ahmad et al., 2015). Despite SDN and NFV benefits, they also pose their own security challenges. Consequently, their implementation in Fog computing paradigm is a challenging task. In addition, required security updates for IoT devices are well managed by Fog computing architecture (Alrawais et al., 2017), which contributes to the overall security of the Fog ecosystem.

◼ Fog computing improves the detection of no typical behavior or malicious attacks, on both the edge of the network and the Cloud sides (Alrawais et al., 2017). Analysis of log files, user login data, and access control policies enables the detection of attacks at the Fog nodes as well as mitigation of attacks before they are passed through the system (OpenFog, 2016). Malicious attacks such as DoS and port scanning can be detected in the Fog network. In other words, Fog architecture has the potential to efficiently observe and control security issues in distributed systems. However, having in mind that Fog computing is mostly applied in large-scale, geographically distributed high-mobile systems, a very challenging task is to implement and enable attack detection mechanism in such systems, satisfying demands for low latency at the same time (Yi et al., 2015).

◼ Regarding access control, it is important to note that the Fog level makes the adoption of numerous standard access control methods easier, enabling at the same time opportunities for the creation of novel access control approaches (Alrawais et al., 2017). Stojmenovic et al. (2016) have proposed attribute-based access control based on the cryptographic usages of primitives such as attribute-based encryption. The policy management framework for Fog computing is presented by Dsouza et al. (2014). The proposed design includes a repository of rules, an attribute database, and a session administrator, and at the same time does not pose specific architectural requirements that make it more applicable to other paradigms. Nevertheless, it is challenging to design access control at all levels of Fog computing architecture and at the same time fulfill designing goals and resource constraints (Yi et al., 2015).

◼ Even trust management is an important security requirement in Fog computing paradigm, and research devoted to this topic is still limited to a few possible approaches (Roman et al., 2016). However, some of the trust management approaches proposed in related areas may be applicable to a Fog computing paradigm, such as self-managed trust management established on the trust metric calculation (Kantert et al., 2015), the quantitative trust management among different trust communities (Figueroa et al., 2015), and a Bayesian network-based trust model for composite Cloud systems (Bennani et al., 2014).

It can be concluded that the security and privacy issues in Fog computing architecture are of crucial importance. The lack of proper security and privacy mechanism puts the benefits of Fog computing paradigms in the shadow. However, despite security and privacy mechanism implementation, the Fog architecture will be attacked. The evidence of these attacks will enable information about the attacker and methods of attacks, and hence contribute to further improvements of security and privacy aspects. Even existing forensic approaches, such as storage forensics, mobile forensics, and virtualization forensics, may be applied in Fog computing paradigm, and there are numerous challenges for the efficient attacker and attack methods identification (Roman et al., 2016).

However, to show its full potential, Fog architecture demands an effective and efficient resource management framework. Therefore, resource management and energy efficiency are the subjects of numerous research (Aazam and Huh, 2015; Dastjerdi and Buyya, 2016; Hong et al., 2013; Ismail et al., 2015; Jayaraman et al., 2014; Ningning et al., 2016; Xiang et al., 2015). For battery-powered devices used in Fog computing architecture, efficient operation is required and efficient resource management frameworks are mandatory. Whenever devices become idle, they should go to sleep mode. When devices are in sleep mode, the communications are performed by the Fog layer (Negash et al., 2017). With the help of efficient communication protocols such as CoAP, effective filtering and sampling techniques, conjoined computing, and optimal network resource utilization, the energy consumption in Fog computing architecture can be drastically reduced (Dastjerdi and Buyya, 2016). Aazam and Huh (2015) have presented a resource management for Fog architecture based on the user characteristic, including service type, service price, and variance of the relinquish probability. They have proved that this approach enables the determination of the right amount of resources demanded, avoiding resource wastage. The Context Aware Real-time Data Analytics Platform (CARDAP) for the Fog computing paradigm is presented by Jayaraman et al. (2014). To reduce data transfer, the proposed platform implements approaches for energy-efficient delivery of data. Regardless of the approach, the optimal usage of resource-constrained devices and environment is of crucial importance in achieving the full potential of a Fog computing paradigm (Ahmed and Rehmani, 2016).

As is already stated, the Fog computing architecture integration into IoT-based healthcare system supports heterogeneity of devices, communication protocols, and data formats. The power of Fog computing paradigm is in enabling services that are able to adapt different platforms, communications protocols, and formats of data (Negash et al., 2017). However, among numerous advantages and challenges for Fog computing implementation, it is important to highlight that the lack of standardization represents one of the main drawbacks. In other words, the success of Fog computing depends on standardization issues. The main standardization challenges encompass bandwidth, latency, and communication challenges (e.g., network connectivity loss, high network latency, endpoint mobility support, bandwidth bottlenecks, and systems and clients' coordination). From the other side, health-related data are under strict regulation mandated by medical standards (Farahani et al., 2017). Therefore, from a standards perspective, the Fog-assisted and IoT-based healthcare system represents a huge challenge. Knowing that the standardization is a long-term and complex process that often lags behind technology development, Dell, Intel, Cisco, ARM Holdings, Microsoft, and Princeton University founded the OpenFog Consortium in 2015 with the aim to standardize Fog computing technology for future use (O'Dowd, 2017). Only with adequate standards and regulation that will enable interoperability, scalability, compatibility, reliability, and effectiveness, Fog computing technology can show its full potential. Therefore, balancing privacy, policy, and innovation is a precondition for Fog computing success. OpenFog Consortium anticipates that Fog architecture is the only paradigm that can deal with the continuously increasing amount of data and enable IoT, 5G, and artificial intelligence.

6.5 Future Research Directions

This chapter presents an attempt to get as much as possible insight and knowledge regarding Fog computing and its significance in managing data in the IoT-powered healthcare system. After performed research, the aim of the future work will be focused on implementing a low-cost and do-it-yourself approach for Fog computing integration into the IoT-based healthcare system. Until now, a prototype of such system exists. It is based on the utilization of three sensors (temperature sensor, pulse sensor module, and blood pressure sensor) attached to the Raspberry Pi (RPi), a small and powerful device that acts as a Fog node (Figure 6.9).

Thanks to its communication, processing, and storage capabilities, the RPi is more than qualified to be implemented as a Fog node. RPi is a small-dimension, low-cost, powerful, and fully programmable computer board that poses a large number of input and output peripherals and network communication (Maksimovic et al., 2015).

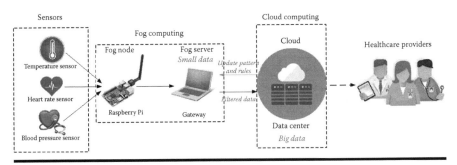

Figure 6.9 Prototype of Fog-assisted and IoT-based healthcare system architecture.

To realize an IoT-based healthcare system, the measurement of the patient's vital parameters, with the help of three sensors, is implemented (Maksimovic et al., 2016):

- Temperature sensor (TTC05)—measuring the temperature of human body and its fluctuations,
- Heart rate sensor (pulse sensor module)—measuring the human body's pulse,
- Blood pressure sensor (US9111)—measuring blood pressure.

Electronic circuit scheme of RPi as a sensing unit for measuring vital parameters and details about delivering measurement information complying IoT ideology is presented in detail in previous works (Maksimovic et al., 2015, 2016).

The next step is to implement some of the data-mining techniques, fuzzy logic approaches, or some other type of artificial intelligence into the Fog server (e.g., laptop or PC) to process intelligently and in real-time raw data and then transmit it to the Cloud. There will be compared two cases, with and without Fog server or data-processing implementation on the RPi and on the PC in the second case. Since the RPi is able to collect data, perform local storage and processing by filtering out relevant, differentiating information from the large datasets, and send the results to the Cloud for further analysis and storage, it is the great candidate for smart gateway realization by implementing Fog computing principles. On the other side, the Fog level will be constantly updated from the Cloud, based on further analysis of medical data and achieved insight and knowledge. The goal is to measure more and more possible performance of such system, response speed, power consumption, and bandwidth utilization mainly.

The special attention will be given to manners of protecting data, where various security and privacy mechanism will be discussed and compared. Based on the results, the most adequate will be implemented in the realization of Fog-assisted and IoT-based healthcare system prototype.

Alongside data management, and security and privacy issues, one particular area where further research will be performed is the analysis of a current situation regarding standardization issues and possibilities for further improvements in this area.

However, there are many open research aspects regarding Fog computing paradigm and its integration in IoT-based healthcare systems (e.g., mobile user equipment and Fog server communication, Fog servers-central Cloud communications, data transmission challenges, 5G as supporting technologies) that will be a subject of future research and work.

6.6 Conclusion

Healthy lifestyle and easy access to the right care and right provider significantly help a nation to be healthy at reduced costs. Technological progress has immensely contributed to the improvement of healthcare in the 21st century, achieving higher and better access and availability of healthcare than ever before. The IoT has a dramatic influence in transforming healthcare. The appliance of numerous medical IoT devices results in immense amounts of diverse health-related data, which are uniquely complex and sensitive. Therefore, successful management of health-related data is a challenging task. Data analysis and decision making closer to the place where medical data are being produced have proven as a mandatory requirement to enable right decisions and prompt responses, which is essential in healthcare applications. With the Fog computing integration in the IoT-based e-health system, further significant improvements in the healthcare sector are evident and far better enhancements are expected. Fog computing benefits—real-time analytics, low latency, reduced network and bandwidth load, improved security and privacy—justify the necessity of its integration in IoT-powered healthcare systems. However, there are still challenges and obstacles that have to be overcome so that Fog computing can show its full potential. Nevertheless, the development of Fog computing architecture has successfully dealt with the numerous challenges, which leads to the widespread omnipresence of Fog computing paradigm. Abilities of Fog computing technology, such as handling huge quantities of diverse data and enabling IoT, 5G, and artificial intelligence, make it a technology of the future. It will revolutionize not just healthcare sector but almost every aspect of our lives where technology is deployed. The better outcome, security and privacy, reduced costs, and effectiveness of Fog-assisted approaches have already become a reality.

References

Aazam, M., & Huh, E.-M. (2015). Dynamic Resource Provisioning through Fog Micro Datacenter. *The 12th IEEE International Workshop on Managing Ubiquitous Communications and Services*, 105–110.

Ahmad, I., Namal, S., Ylianttila, M., & Gurtov, A. (2015). Security in Software Defined Networks: A Survey. *IEEE Communications Surveys Tutorials* 17(4), 2317–2346.

Ahmad, M., Amin, M. B., Hussain, S., Kang, B. H., Cheong, T., & Lee, S. (2016). Health Fog: A Novel Framework for Health and Wellness Applications. *Journal of Supercomputing*. New York: Springer Science+Business Media.

Ahmed, E., & Rehmani, M. H. (2016). Mobile Edge Computing: Opportunities, Solutions, and Challenges. *Future Generation Computer Systems*. doi:10.1016/j.future.2016.09.015

Alrawais, A., Alhothaily, A., Hu, C., & Cheng, X. (2017). Fog Computing for the Internet of Things: Security and Privacy Issues. *IEEE Internet Computing* 21(2), 34–42.

Amin, R., Kumar, N., Biswas, G. P., Iqbal, R., & Chang, V. (2016). A Light Weight Authentication Protocol for IoT-Enabled Devices in Distributed Cloud Computing Environment. *Future Generation Computer Systems*. doi:10.1016/j.future.2016.12.028

Augur, H. (2016). Is Fog Computing the Future of the Cloud? *Dataconomy*. Retrieved from http://dataconomy.com/2016/03/fog-computing-future-cloud/

Bennani, N., Boukadi, K., & Ghedira-Guegan, C. (2014). A Trust Management Solution in the Context of Hybrid Clouds. *Proceedings of the IEEE 23rd International WETICE Conference (WETICE)*, Parma, Italy. 339–344.

Bhatt, Y., & Bhatt, C. (2017). Internet of Things in HealthCare. In C. Bhatt, N. Dey, and A. S. Ashour (Eds.), *Internet of Things and Big Data Technologies for Next Generation Healthcare*, 13–33, Studies in Big Data 23, Basel: Springer International Publishing.

BDVA. (2016). Big Data Technologies in Healthcare – Needs, Opportunities and Challenges. Retrieved from http://www.bdva.eu/sites/default/files/Big%20Data%20 Technologies%20in%20Healthcare.pdf

Bresnick, J. (n.d.). How Fog Computing May Power the Healthcare Internet of Things. *Healthanalytics*. Retrieved from http://healthitanalytics.com/features/ how-fog-computing-may-power-the-healthcare-internet-of-things

Byers, C. C., & Wetterwald, P. (2015). Fog Computing: Distributing Data and Intelligence for Resiliency and Scale Necessary for IoT. *Ubiquity* 2015, 1–12.

Cao, Y., Chen, S., Hou, P., & Brown, D. (2015). FAST: A Fog Computing, Distributed Analytics-Based Fall Monitoring System for Stroke Mitigation. *IEEE International Conference on Networking, Architecture and Storage (NAS)*, Boston, MA.

Chang, H. (2015). Data-Driven Healthcare & Analytics in a Big Data World. Book Review. *Healthcare Informatics Research* 21(1), 61–62.

Cisco. (2015). Fog Computing and the Internet of Things: Extend the Cloud to Where the Things Are. Retrieved from https://www.cisco.com/c/dam/en_us/solutions/trends/ iot/.../computing-overview.pdf

Constant, N., Borthakur, D., Abtahi, M., Dubey, H., & Mankodiya, K. (2017). Fog-Assisted wIoT: A Smart Fog Gateway for End-to-End Analytics in Wearable Internet of Things. *The 23rd IEEE Symposium on High Performance Computer Architecture HPCA*, Austin, TX.

Craciunescu, R., Mihovska, A., Mihaylov, M., Kyriazakos, S., Prasad, R., & Halunga, S. (2015). Implementation of Fog Computing for Reliable E-Health Applications. *49th Asilomar Conference on Signals, Systems and Computers*, Pacific Grove, CA. 459–463.

Darwish, A., & Hassanien, A. E. (2011). Wearable and Implantable Wireless Sensor Network Solutions for Healthcare Monitoring. *Sensors* (Basel, Switzerland), 11(6), 5561–5595.

Dastjerdi, A. V. & Buyya, R. (2016). Fog Computing: Helping the Internet of Things Realize Its Potential, *Computer* 49(8), 40–44.

Dhamdhere, P., Harmsen, J., Hebbar, R., Mandalapu, S., Mehra, A., & Rajan, S. (2016). *ELPP 2016: Big Data for Healthcare*. Berkeley, University of California. Retrieved from http://scet.berkeley.edu/wp-content/uploads/Big-Data-for-Healthcare-Report-ELPP-2016.pdf

Dsouza, C., Ahn, G.-J., & Taguinod, M. (2014). Policy-Driven Security Management for Fog Computing: Preliminary Framework and a Case Study. *Proceedings of the IEEE 15th International Conference on Information Reuse and Integration (IRI)*, Redwood City, CA. 16–23.

Dubey, H. (2015). Fog Data: Enhancing Telehealth Big Data through Fog Computing. *Proceedings of the ASE Big Data & Social Informatics ASE BD&SI '15*, New York.

Elmenreich, W. (2011). The Different Types of Sensor Fusion: Complementary, Competitive, and Cooperative. *Networking Embedded Systems*. Retrieved from https://netwerkt.wordpress. com/2011/03/30/the-different-types-of-sensor-fusion-complementary-competitive-and-cooperative/

Encash. (2016). How Fog Computing Helps Businesses Fully Encash IoT Benefits. Retrieved from http://www.encash.org/2016/08/fog-computing.html

Evans, D. (2011). The Internet of Things – How the Next Evolution of the Internet Is Changing Everything. *Cisco Internet Business Solutions Group (IBSG)*. Retrieved from https://www.cisco.com/c/dam/en_us/about/ac79/docs/innov/IoT_IBSG_0411FINAL.pdf

European Commission. (2014). The Use of Big Data in Public Health Policy and Research. Background information document. Brussels.

European Commission (2016). Study on Big Data in Public Health, Telemedicine and Healthcare. Final Report.

Farahani, B., Firouzi, F., Chang, V., Badaroglu, M., Constant, N., & Mankodiya, K. (2017). Towards Fog-Driven IoT eHealth: Promises and Challenges of IoT in Medicine and Healthcare. *Future Generation Computer Systems*. doi:10.1016/j.future.2017.04.036

Feldman, B., Martin, E.M., & Skotnes, T. (2012) Big Data in Healthcare, Hype and Hope. Dr. Bonnie 360°.

Figueroa, M., Uttecht, K., & Rosenberg, J., (2015). A SOUND Approach to Security in Mobile and Cloud-Oriented Environments. *Proceedings of the IEEE International Symposium on Technologies for Homeland Security (HST)*, Waltham, MA. 1–7.

Firdhous, M., Ghazali, O., & Hassan, S. (2014) Fog Computing: Will It Be the Future of Cloud Computing? *Proceedings of the 3rd International Conference on Informatics & Applications*, Kuala Terengganu. 8–15.

Fratu, O., Pena, C., Craciunescu, R., & Halunga, S. (2015). Fog Computing System for Monitoring Mild Dementia and COPD Patients – Romanian Case Study. *Telsiks*, Serbia. 123–128.

Gaddi, A., Capello, F. & Manca, M. (2014). *eHealth, Care and Quality of Life*. Milan: Springer-Verlag Italia.

Gia, T.N., Jiang, M., Rahmani, A. M., Westerlund, T., Liljeberg, P., & Tenhunen, H. (2015) Fog Computing in Healthcare Internet of Things: A Case Study on ECG Feature Extraction, *IEEE International Conference on Computer and Information Technology; Ubiquitous Computing and Communications; Dependable, Autonomic and Secure Computing; Pervasive Intelligence and Computing*, Liverpool. 356–363.

Glaser, J. (2014). How The Internet of Things Will Affect Health Care. Retrieved from http://www.hhnmag.com/articles/3438-how-the-internet-of-things-will-affect-health-care

González, L. S., Jaedicke, C., Schubert, J., & Stantchev, V. (2016). Fog Computing Architectures for Healthcare: Wireless Performance and Semantic Opportunities. *Journal of Information, Communication and Ethics in Society* 14(4), 334–349.

Groves, P., Kayyali, B., Knott, D., & Van Kuiken, S. (2013). *The 'Big Data' Revolution in Healthcare*. Center for US Health System Reform Business Technology Office. McKinsey and Company.

Hong, K., Lillethun, D., Ramachandran, U., Ottenwälder, B., & Koldehofe, B. (2013). Mobile Fog: A Programming Model for Large-Scale Applications on the Internet of Things. *Proceedings of the Second ACM SIGCOMM Workshop on Mobile Cloud Computing*, New York. 15–20.

Ibrahim, M. H. (2016). Octopus: An Edge-fog Mutual Authentication Scheme. *International Journal of Network Security* 18(6), 1089–1101.

Ismail, B. I., Goortani, E. M., Ab Karim, M. B., Tat, W. M., Setapa, S., Luke, J. Y., & Hoe, O. H. (2015). Evaluation of Docker as Edge Computing Platform. *IEEE Conference on Open Systems (ICOS)*, Bandar Melaka, Malaysia. 130–135.

ITU-T. (2012). E-health Standards and Interoperability. Watch Report.

Jayaraman, P. P., Gomes, J. B., Nguyen, H. L., Abdallah, Z. S., Krishnaswamy, S., & Zaslavsky, A. (2014). CARDAP: A Scalable Energy-Efficient Context Aware Distributed Mobile Data Analytics Platform for the Fog. In Y. Manolopoulos, G. Trajcevski, & M. Kon-Popovska (Eds.), *Advances in Databases and Information Systems*, 192–206. Basel: Springer International Publishing.

Kantert, J., Edenhofer, S., Tomforde, S., & Müller-Schloer, C. (2015). Representation of Trust and Reputation in Self-Managed Computing Systems. *IEEE International Conference on Computer and Information Technology; Ubiquitous Computing and Communications; Dependable, Autonomic and Secure Computing; Pervasive Intelligence and Computing*, Liverpool. 1827–1834.

Khaleghi, B., Khamis, A., Karray, F. O., & Razavi, S. N. (2013).Multisensor Data Fusion: A Review of the state-of-the-art. *Information Fusion* 14, 28–44.

Lee, H., Park, K., Lee, B., Choi, J., & Elmasri, R. (2008). Issues in Data Fusion for Healthcare Monitoring. *Proceedings of the 1st ACM International Conference on Pervasive Technologies Related to Assistive Environments, PETRA 2008*, Athens, Greece.

LeSueur, D. (n.d.). 5 Reasons Healthcare Data Is Unique and Difficult to Measure. *HealthCatalyst*. Retrieved from https://www.healthcatalyst.com/5-reasons-healthcare-data-is-difficult-to-measure

MacIntosh, E., Rajakulendran, N. & Salah, H. (2014). *Transforming Health: Towards Decentralized and Connected Care*. MaRS Market Insights.

Maksimovic, M. (2017). Improving Computing Issues in Internet of Things Driven e-health Systems. *ICYRIME – International Conference for Young Researchers in Informatics, Mathematics and Engineering*, Kaunas, Lithuania. 14–17.

Maksimovic, M., & Vujovic, V. (2017). Internet of Things Based e-health Systems: Ideas, Expectations and Concerns. In S.U. Khan, A.Y. Zomaya, & A. Abbas (Eds.), *Handbook of Large-Scale Distributed Computing in Smart Healthcare*, Scalable Computing and Communications, Cham: Springer. 241-280.

Maksimovic, M., Vujovic, V., & Perisic, B. (2015). A Custom Internet of Things Healthcare System, *10th Iberian Conference on Information Systems and Technologies (CISTI)*, Aveiro, Portugal. 653–658.

Maksimovic, M., Vujovic, V., & Perisic, B. (2016). Do It Yourself Solution of Internet of Things Healthcare System: Measuring Body Parameters and Environmental Parameters Affecting Health. *Journal of Information Systems Engineering & Management*, (Lectito BV, Netherlands), 1(1), 25–39.

Manogaran, G., Thota, C., Lopez, D., Vijayakumar, V., Abbas, K. M., & Sundarsekar, R. (2017). Big Data Knowledge System in Healthcare. In C. Bhatt, N. Dey & A. S. Ashour (Eds.), *Internet of Things and Big Data Technologies for Next Generation Healthcare*, 133–157, Studies in Big Data 23, Cham: Springer International Publishing.

Marin-Tordera, E., Masip-Bruin, X., Garcia-Alminana, J., Jukan, A., Ren, G.-J., Zhu, J., & Farre, J. (2016). What Is a Fog Node? A Tutorial on Current Concepts towards a Common Definition. *Networking and Internet Architecture*. Retrieved from https://arxiv.org/abs/1611.09193

Munir, A., Kansakar, P. & Khan, S. U. (2017). IFCIoT: Integrated Fog Cloud IoT Architectural Paradigm for Future Internet of Things. *IEEE Consumer Electronics Magazine* 6(3), 74–82.

Nandyala, C.S. & Kim, H.-K. (2016). From Cloud to Fog and IoT-Based Real-Time U-Healthcare Monitoring for Smart Homes and Hospitals. *International Journal of Smart Home* 10(2), 187–196.

Naranjo P.G.V., Shojafar, M., Vaca-Cardenas, L., Canali, C., Lancellotti, R., & Baccarelli, E. (2016). Big Data over SmartGrid – A Fog Computing Perspective. *SOFTCOM Workshop*, 1–6.

Natraj, A. V. (2016). "FOG COMPUTING" Focusing on Users at the Edge of Internet of Things. *International Journal of Engineering Research* 5(5), 992–1128.

Negash, B., Gia, T. N., Anzanpour, A., Azimi, I., Jiang, M., Westerlund, T., Rahmani, A. M., Liljeberg, P., & Tenhunen, H. (2017). Leveraging Fog Computing for Healthcare IoT. In A. M. Rahmani, P. Lijeberg, J.-S. Preden & A. Jantsch (Eds.), *Fog Computing in the Internet of Things*, 145–169, Cham: Springer International Publishing.

Ningning, S., Chao, G., Xingshuo, A., & Qiang, Z. (2016). Fog Computing Dynamic Load Balancing Mechanism Based on Graph Repartitioning. *China Communications* 13(3), 156–164.

O'Dowd, E. (2017). Fog Computing Improves Healthcare Cloud for IoT Adoption. Retrieved from https://hitinfrastructure.com/news/fog-computing-improves-healthcare-cloud-for-iot-adoption

OpenFog. (2016). *Top 5 Ways Fog Computing Can Make IoT More Secure*, OpenFog Consortium. Retrieved from https://www.openfogconsortium.org/top-5-ways-fog-computing-can-make-iot-more-secure/

OpenFog. (2017). *OpenFog Reference Architecture for Fog Computing*, OpenFog Consortium. USA.

Osanaiye, O., Chen, S., Yan, Z., Lu, R., Raymond Choo, K.-K., & Dlodlo, M. (2017). From Cloud to Fog Computing: A Review and a Conceptual Live VM Migration Framework. *IEEE Access, Special Section on Recent Advances in Cloud Radio Access Networks* 5, 8284–8300.

Papadokostaki, K., Mastorakis, G., Panagiotakis, S., Mavromoustakis, C. X., Dobre, C., & Batalla, J. M. (2017). Handling Big Data in the Era of Internet of Things (IoT). In C. X. Mavromoustakis, G. Mastorakisand & C. Dobre (Eds.), *Advances in Mobile Cloud Computing and Big Data in the 5G Era*, 3–22. Studies in Big Data 22, Cham: Springer International Publishing.

Peter, N. (2015). FOG Computing and Its Real Time Applications. *International Journal of Emerging Technology and Advanced Engineering* 5(6), 266–269.

Rahmani, A. M., Gia, T. N., Negash, B., Anzanpour, A., Azimi, I., Jiang, M., & Lijeberg, P. (2017). Exploiting Smart E-Health Gateways at the Edge of Healthcare Internet-of-Things: A Fog Computing Approach. *Future Generation Computer Systems*. doi:10.1016/j.future.2017.02.014

Roman, R., Lopez, J., & Mambo, M. (2016). Mobile Edge Computing Fog et al.: A Survey and Analysis of Security Threats and Challenges. *Future Generation Computer Systems*. doi:10.1016/j.future.2016.11.009

Stojmenovic, I., & Wen, S. (2014). The Fog Computing Paradigm: Scenarios and Security Issues. *Federated Conference on Computer Science and Information Systems (FedCSIS)*, Warsaw, Poland. 1–8.

Stojmenovic, I., Wen, S., Huang, X., & Luan, H. (2016). An Overview of Fog Computing and Its Security Issues, *Concurrency and Computation: Practice and Experience* 28(10), 2991–3005.

Venkat Narayana Rao, T., Amer Khan, M. D., Maschendra, M., & Kiran Kumar, M. (2015). A Paradigm Shift from Cloud to Fog Computing. *International Journal of Computer Science & Engineering Technology (IJCSET)* 5(11), 385–389.

Xiang, H., Peng, M., Cheng, Y., & Chen, H.-H. (2015). Joint Mode Selection and Resource Allocation for Downlink Fog Radio Access Networks Supported D2D. *11th International Conference on Heterogeneous Networking for Quality, Reliability, Security and Robustness (QSHINE)*, Taipei, Taiwan. 177–182.

Yi. S., Qin, Z., & Li, Q. (2015). *Security and Privacy Issues of Fog Computing: A Survey.* WASA.

Yoo, I., Alafaireet, P., Marinov, M., Pena-Hernandez, K., Gopidi, R., Chang, J.-F., & Hua, L. (2012). Data Mining in Healthcare and Biomedicine: A Survey of the Literature. *Journal of Medical Systems* 36(4), 2431–2448.

Chapter 7

Security Issues in Distributed Computation for Big Data Analytics

Ranjan Kumar Behera, Kshira Sagar Sahoo,
Sambit Mahapatra, Santanu Kumar Rath,
and Bibudatta Sahoo

National Institute of Technology

Contents

7.1 Introduction

Big data is a term that describes the huge volume of data that are generated from different variety of sources. Approximately, more than quintillion bytes of data are generated every day in the digital world. Data are being exploded at an exponential rate. It is quite difficult to handle huge amounts of data using traditional data processing and analysis tools. Although data have been generated from a vast number of sources, bioinformatics and manufacturing industries are found to be the major contributors of data source for big data applications. All kinds of historical data in the healthcare center allow a data scientist to discover efficient diagnosis for critical health condition. In the same way, industrial data can be analyzed for predicting the future scope of business policies and strategies. Appropriate policies should be enforced for data security. Since cloud computing is a virtual environment that provides resources on demand basis, data have been moving into cloud for faster processing. The virtualization concept in cloud demands strong security measures for protecting user data. Companies are always trying to develop efficient business models for protecting their data from other competitors. A number of data analysis techniques have been adopted for detecting intruder at the cloud data centers. If we consider the security measures at cloud data center as a layered architecture, it can be classified into four levels such as security at data level, network level, authentication level, and application level. As big data handles large amounts of data gathered at one place from various sources, there is the chance of security issues. In big data, it is generally difficult to solve the problems in case of security breach. Big data style analysis techniques can be used to detect and prevent advanced threats and malicious intruders. Along with security issues, data privacy issues are also considered as assets for business organizations and companies. Many organizations are also using big data for fraud detection.

Speed, capacity, and scalability are the most important advantages of big data, especially in cloud. The data are safe as the software packages with a rich set of tools and applications help in mapping the entire dataset across the company. If big data and predictive analytics are used in combination, it will be very useful, but it poses many challenges for many industries. There have been many frameworks that have proved to be effective for the same, such as the map-reduce (MR) technique used in Hadoop (Dean and Ghemawat 2008), Apache Spark (Shoro and Soomro 2015), Storm (Jam, et al. 2014), Samza (Namiot 2015) (Barroso, Dean and Holzle 2003), Flink (Carbon, et al. 2015), etc.

7.2 Characteristics of Big Data

The characteristics of big data can be categorically defined as seven V's such as volume, velocity, variety, veracity, value, valence, and variability.

Volume: The most important characteristic of big data is its huge volume of data that are generated at every moment of time. The quantity of data is exploding at an exponential rate over the years. The volume of generated data in the past two years is more than the data created by the entire human race before. By 2020, it is expected that 2.8 megabytes of data will be created per second for every human being on the planet, which may lead to 44 zettabytes of data. By 2020, one-third of entire data will be processed through the cloud (Khan, et al. 2014; Wu, et al. 2014). The digitized data have been created from a number of resources like social network, sensor data, stock market, healthcare, banking transaction logs, scientific application, and many more. The data collected over the year have been increased exponentially, which accounts for more than hundreds of zettabytes, which is just impractical to handle by traditional computational system. Distributed computing systems that have thousands of computing nodes in cluster might be the best suitable framework for analyzing huge volume of data. Google uses a cluster environment that consists of more than a thousand nodes to process a single query for searching (Barroso, Dean and Holzle 2003).

Velocity: Determination of the rate at which data have been generated may be one of the biggest challenging tasks in data analytics. Velocity refers to the rate at which the volume of data has been increasing in the digital world. As per the survey conducted by the International Data Corporation, the size of data generated will become about 44 times of its current size by 2020 (Ryan and Bernard 2000). The demand on speed of data has always been a major concern for IT organization. A browser that can be opened with the click of a button to read, process, and compile data in a fraction of second is also a challenge in big data analytics. With high-speed data, we need efficient algorithms for big data to be compatible with speed demanded by organizations.

Variety: The beauty of big data lies in its shape and structure. The source data can be completely unstructured like images, audios, videos, documents, and files. Therefore, sorting out these data is of great importance. A variety of generated data come in different forms from various sources of domains. It can be in textual, audio, video, or any unstructured form. Broadly, these data can be classified based on several dimensions such as its structural variety, media variety, semantic variety, etc. According to the structural dimension, data can be classified based on its representation. For example, image data of social network collected from satellites have different types of representations. These different types of representation leads to heterogeneous types of communities in social network (Abrahao, et al. 2012). Representations of tweets collected from Twitter dataset are different from that of stock market data. Sensor data collected from various sensors are different from newspaper articles. In media, variation of data is classified based on the medium through which they are being delivered. For example, audios of any song or a speech are two similar kinds of data, but the ways they get delivered differ. Semantic variety is associated with the meaning of data. Even if two data consist of the same kind of information attributes required for analysis, they may vary based on their meaning.

A variety of models need to be proposed to analyze heterogeneous data. Data can be either structured, unstructured, or semistructured. Structured data are represented in the form of table, chat, or any kind of bar graph. There is always some semantic meaning associated with it, whereas unstructured data have no hidden meaning. Unstructured data may consist of bulk heterogeneous data. These can be call, text, browsing history of different websites, or collection of exchange messages like tweet, chat, or mms. Semistructured data have a decent way of representation, but it cannot be understood by normal people. The meaning associated with semistructured data can be understood only by people who have domain-specific knowledge. Data in xml format, html format, or the data associated with email are few examples of semistructured data (Chen and Zhang 2014).

Variability: The data are not always consistent, they flow in the way it is programmed with its maxima and minima, and hence the system needs to deal with their inconsistent flow. The generated data are typically inconsistent with time. The value of data differs at different points of time.

Veracity: Veracity refers to the qualitative parameters of big data. As the data are received from multiple sources of different domains, biasness and noise involved in big data are extremely high, which make them very difficult to analyze. It also leads to unmeasurable degree of uncertainty or accuracy involved in analysis of these data. Usefulness of generated data depends on the extent to which they are productive and operational. The fruitful result is only possible if proper precaution and care is taken while preprocessing noisy and erroneous data.

Valence: Valence of data refers to the relationships among them. Most of the generated data are directly or indirectly related to each other. For example, data of a Facebook user are related to the data of other people in their friend list. If users are employees, their data are related through their workplaces. If they are authors or scientists, their data are related through a common research field. The ratio between actual connection and the total number of relationships possible among data within a collection of data is known as valence. Less is the valence of collected data more the challenge in analyzing the data (Kaisler, et al. 2013). Density of data depends on the valence of collected data (Figure 7.1).

Complexity: The data are streamed in random directions based on the source and destination, so to shed light on the path followed there are various parameters.

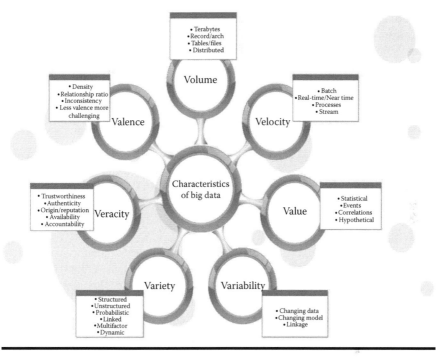

Figure 7.1   Characteristics of big data.

Value: When it comes to data value, people in business and IT field tend to repel each other, because business companies want to analyze large data and gain more insights into them to gain profit, whereas IT companies have a lot of software and hardware technical issues to deal with and hence face problems.

7.3 Big Data Management

The storage of data in the big data ecosystem needs a lot of maintenance, not only in security but also in the way the data flow from one place to another; that is, how we can share the data securely without hampering integrity of data. There are various techniques to manage the data in big data environment. The management of these huge amount of data is a challenge to many big data researchers, from collection to storage of data (Katal, Wazid and Goudar, 2013). The mechanisms proposed for management include having a parameter to detect acceptance level of privacy or dividing the data in a sequenced manner and storing them in a cloud storage service provider.

The data are useless if we do not share them. In big data, to make sense out of many data, we need to share the data in the community for more collaborative results. While sharing again, the problem of secure transmission comes into the picture. There are many approaches used in the past, e.g., keeping a close observation of users taking part in the data transmission. Other approaches include making the transmission itself secure enough so that, even if an intruder attacks, they are unable to decode the data being transmitted.

7.3.1 Data Governance

Data governance deals with management of data in an organization in an efficient and cost effective manner. It involves the following important issues:

1. Accuracy
2. Availability
3. Usability
4. Security

Processes need to be defined for governing data, and hence their efficiency and effectiveness should also be continuously tracked and evaluated. A survey by Rand Worldwide, conducted in 2013, showed that while 82% of companies know they face external regulation, 44% had no formal data governance policy and 22% had no plans to implement (Demchenko, et al. 2013). Though some companies have policies regarding data governance, many were created targeting the relational database-centric world which deals with things like well-defined schemas, structured data, small amount of data, etc. The world of big data is drastically different from these. So, policies also need to be changed accordingly.

7.3.2 Configuration Management

Big data deployments tend to be an infrastructural arrangement comprising emerging open-source tools. By their very nature, single applications are distributed across multiple physical machines, which we call "cluster." This particularly makes the configuration management challenging. Configuration in the production of big data analytics cluster is generally spread across various incompatible file formats like JSON, text files, XML, etc. (Kagal, Finin and Joshi 2001). In addition, when machines are added to the existing cluster, they must be set up in patches so that they should not create a security hole, which makes configuration management further complicated. As organizations start to express concerns about the security of their big data (e.g., Hadoop) deployments, tools like Apache Ranger are appearing in an attempt to address the current vacuum.

7.4 Distributed Computation for Big Data

The growth and availability of data of massive volume with different variety and velocity, termed "Big Data," is accelerated by technically advanced digital devices like mobile phones, scientific instruments, online sensors, etc. Collection, control, and computation of big data are essential for achieving scientific and engineering breakthroughs, cultivating relevant and pertinent information, and decision making (Dwork, et al. 2006). The highly centralized enterprise data center is becoming an outdated thing; hence, organizations must adopt a more distributed model to deal with the huge amount of data being generated (Anglin, 2001).

The argument here is that distributed computing is not essential for all computing solutions. One scenario can be that a business does not have any time constraints in system processing, and an asynchronous remote process can do the job efficiently in the expected time of process. Then, why should the business invest in having either a more competent resource or a distributed environment to bring performance improvements in such a process?

Over the past few years, organizations are looking at reducing costs and are investing in critical and essential business needs. This means that if there is a real need for processing complex data and the organization has a number of additional resources available, it can make use of distributed computing wherein each computing resource, with its own memory, can process a bit of complex data analysis and contribute to its completion. Moreover, instead of having a single huge computing resource, if we utilize multiple commodity hardware to act as a distributed system, this also adds to load-balancing resource optimization with an enormous cluster of nodes (Tanenbaum and Van Steen 2007; Reed and Dongarra 2015).

To summarize all, the need of distributed computation can be understood from the following reasons:

a. Data are growing exponentially
   - Whole-genome sequencing 100–200 GB per Binary Alignment Map (BAM) file
   - New York Stock Exchange (NYSE) 1 TB of trade data per day
   - Large Hadron Collider 15 PB per year (1 PB = 1,000 TB)
b. Storage ≫ access speeds
   - How long does it take to read or write a 1 TB disk?
     • Parallel reads can result in large speedups
c. Most relevant for **big** data
   - 1 billion rows
   - ≫ 128 MB (default block size for Hadoop, a distributed platform)
d. Other solutions may be more suitable
   - Shared memory parallel system
   - Relational databases (seek time is a bottleneck)
   - Grid computing for compute-intensive jobs where network bandwidth is not a bottleneck [High performance Computing (HPC), Message passing interface (MPI)]
   - Volunteer computing (compute time ≫ data transfer time)

7.4.1 How Distributed Computing Helps Big Data?

Distributed computing helps in overcoming the limits of conventional Data Warehouse Technologies like

1. Limiting fault-tolerance capability—not able to scale as required.
2. Complex-type file where huge processing power may not be able to handle properly. For example, video and gaming processing.
3. High level of compression algorithm is required to handle huge volume of data.
4. Limited parallelism was there only when explicitly added.
5. CPU-intensive complex applications are difficult to handle.
6. Big data technology has better price–performance ratio when compared with conventional systems.

Typically, big data analytics in distributed computing tools has the following functionalities:

1. Data are processed using MR programming paradigm.
2. A dedicated distributed file system (DFS) is used [like Hadoop DFS (HDFS) in Hadoop] (Shvachko, et al. 2010).
3. NoSQL database is used for storing and accessing at a faster rate (Han et al. 2011).

7.4.2 MR Paradigm

MR is a programming model typically used in distributed computing model. It is a framework intended for processing huge volume of data in a distributed manner, typically at multiple computing nodes in a cluster (Dean and Ghemawat 2008). The collection of computing node is known as cluster. In the cluster, one node is dedicated for controlling all other nodes, which is known as namenode. All other nodes, except the namenode is known as datanodes. In this type of computing model, huge amounts of data are divided into sets of chunks that are processed at different computing nodes known as datanodes. In MR paradigm, computing nodes are communicated through a message-passing mechanism. The data parallelism and pipeline used are highly abstracted in which the user need not worry about the parallel implementation (Wang, et al. 2012). Typically, programmers are unaware of the task distribution among nodes. MR implicitly handles most of the processing policy in the cluster, for example, the programmer need not worry about the number of processors required for processing. Basically, it is processed in two phases.

Mapper phase: In this phase, the large volume of data are divided into a small number of pieces and then distributed among the worker nodes. Each worker node may further divide its chunk and distribute it to other worker nodes. After the processing on the small chunk that has been assigned before, the results need to be sent back to the respective master node. Master node collects the result from all worker nodes.

Reducer phase: In this phase, the master tries to combine the results that are collected from all the workers to obtain the result to the original problem. Basically, a sorting process is carried out in between the mapper and reducer phases. Master is responsible for routing the data parts to different reducer. There could be multiple map–reduce pair for solving a problem in a distributed manner. This is typically handled by the distributed tool, where MR is employed.

7.4.3 Distributed File System

This is the file system dedicated for a specified distributed computing framework. Hadoop uses a file system known as HDFS (Shvachko, et al. 2010). It is used to store the data in a distributed manner over a cluster of computing nodes. All the interactions between the nodes must be through the dedicated file system, i.e., each of the node must read and write a chunk from or to the file system only.

7.4.4 Nonrelational Data Stores

In recent years, the popularity of NoSQL data stores has surged, MongoDB particularly getting high attention as a database engine (Chodorow 2013). NoSQL databases are commonly being deployed as part of big data installations as they are helpful and effective in managing and analyzing large-scale data (Han et al. 2011). However, some challenges are there with the security of NoSQL databases. Though many NoSQL products have key security features, these are compromised by permissible default options or due to ignorance of configuring them effectively. Relational databases are very mature, and security has long been a critical component of the feature set. There are also auditing tools, checklists, and training courses available for those wishing to harden their SQL Server, Oracle, or MySQL installations. However, NoSQL is at a very young stage in that scenario. The NoSQL security story will also get better quickly, but, currently, care must be taken to ensure that the data they hold are adequately protected.

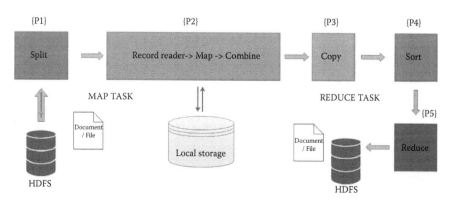

7.4.5 Hadoop Security

Hadoop is one of the suitable distributed platforms, where data are processed at multiple computing nodes to resolve numerous big data challenges. It was initially deployed within the premises of an organization where all the data were stored at the data center of the organization only. Due to lack of computational resources, Hadoop was later designed to work with cloud data centers, where it faces big challenge for security and privacy of data. Hadoop uses a dedicated file system known as HDFS (White 2012). NoSQL is the database that is used in most of the distributed platform for big data analytics. The cluster mode in a Hadoop framework poses a variety of security threats. Some of them are listed as follows:

Replication of more than one copy: Multiple copies are replicated in order to improve fault tolerance in the system. However, it poses a great challenge in maintaining the consistency between the several copies. Developing security mechanism for protecting all the copies simultaneously is quite difficult.

Limited SQL support: As Hadoop is a distributed platform, traditional database software like RDBMS is not supported. Some of the very efficient function like sub-queries and group by are not supported. The security mechanism available for the relational databases are not supported for Hadoop framework.

Ownership and data access: Access permission and role of users are two key attributes to manage the privacy while reading, writing, or updating data from the database (Jam, et al. 2014). For protecting the data, most of the database includes security policy like role, schema, different level of security, and groups for limiting the user access to database at a particular instance of time. NoSQL is no different from it. It integrates both role access facility and identity store, which provides an authentication key to each group of user. Various data access roles are partitioned into certain group, which is further provided to a set of users. It allows the user to have limited access to a database for a specific period of time with a certain role associated with it. There have been many frameworks that have proved to be effective for the same, such as the "MR technique" used in Hadoop, Apache Spark, Apache Kafka (Dunning and Freidman 2016), Apache Storm (Iqbal and Soomro 2015), Storm, Samza, Flink, etc.

7.5 Security Challenges for Distributed Computation

Small- and large-size firms try to improve their business strategies by collecting and analyzing huge volume of data that are collected from different sources of domain. As the size of data is huge, it poses several security and privacy threats, which leads to loss of important information. Infeasible security and privacy policy may incur a great financial loss and economical degradation for any company (Anita 1997). Few of the security challenges for big data deployment are listed in the following.

7.5.1 Privacy and Preserving Analytics

As data are generated from any kind of heterogeneous sources in the internet, it is a challenging task to ensure that the data are not noisy or missing. As the data are related to each other in a number of ways, they cannot be analyzed in an isolated manner. The role of data in "data ecosystem" must be considered for getting a deeper insight (Demchenko, et al. 2013). Data encryption and decryption policy plays a vital role in maintaining data privacy. Data storage mechanism needs to be more secure for avoiding unauthorized access to private data. Data preserving policy must be carefully employed by integrating with different combinations of access control mechanism. Data are prone to more vulnerability while it is moving between the computing nodes in a distributed framework. Data are less secure in a distributed environment when compared with a single computational unit. For example, data process in MR model in a Hadoop framework is more prone to security threats. However, it can be avoided by integrating security policy in mapper and protecting data from unauthorized mapper and reducer.

Big data flows from source to destination through a lot of analyses, processing, and storing, and the road map that big data follows is called "big data ecosystem." This ecosystem is divided into four classifications by Cloud Security Alliance in order to deal with the challenges faced by big data (Inukollu, Arsi and Ravuri 2014). These are infrastructure security, data management, data privacy, integrity and reactive security.

7.5.2 Perimeter-Based Security

It is a security model followed by most at big data installations as big data security tools are lacking specific requirements of security big data systems that network security people are also not familiar with. So, in this model, mission-critical applicants are all kept inside the secure network, while others are kept outside the secure network. The limitation of this perimeter-based security model is that it counts on the perimeter remaining secure, which we cannot always guarantee. The assumption that all bad people are kept outside is also an article of faith.

7.5.3 Granular Auditing and Access Control

Regular analysis of log data could be very much helpful in detecting malicious attack in big data storage. It could provide a certain kind of pattern for cyberattack activity. Granular auditing provides a way of handling such kind of attacks at different levels of storage. As we know, relational database schema is not an efficient way for data storage, as NoSQL database allows the user for efficient access to big data. However, due to its distributed nature, strong granular access and authentication control mechanism is required to maintain data secrecy in the processing. Enterprises must ensure the immunity of the big data infrastructure toward all types of vulnerabilities and security threats. To maintain security from the

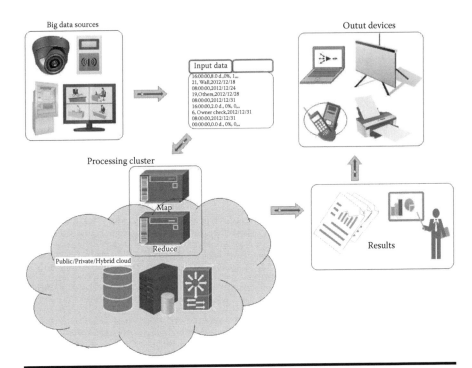

Figure 7.2 Big data ecosystem.

beginning, several security policies must be implemented at the time of data collection step. As the data size is large, protecting data at each step of processing is a challenging task, and it requires extraordinary efforts (Figure 7.2).

7.6 Security Challenges for Big Data Ecosystem

In the present era, an enormous amount of data are generated in the world day by day. The reason behind the growth of data is the extensive use of internet, smartphone, and social network. To handle these data, big data is the solution, which is complex and very large in size. Big data continues to grow with structured, semistructured, and unstructured data, as the use of internet increases. It provides different ways for the business and government to analyze these various categories of data (Demchenko, et al. 2013) (Inukollu, Arsi and Ravuri 2014) (Kaufman 2009). Big data is an emerging topic in IT industry as its application domain is very large, such as banking, retail, traffic management, and healthcare (Tankard 2012). But use of big data brings a variety of challenges as well. The continuous and enormous growth in the volume and importance of data has generated challenging problems. These cannot be solved by traditional tools and techniques. Hence, these problems can be solved through the evolution of a new technique called big data. However, this technique generated new issues related to the volume, variety, security, quality, privacy, and acquisition of data. Introduction of large-scale cloud infrastructure with a variety of software platforms also increases the new level of attacks to the entire system. Therefore, big data becomes the main hindrance that could slow down the pace of technology without advent security solutions. So, the need of hour is to obtain effective, efficient, and secure solutions to overcome these burning problems (Moreno, Serrano and Fernandez-Medina 2016; Moura and Serrao 2016).

The current trend of technology such as cloud computing provides a suitable platform to collect, store, process, and manage data. This enables the rapid growth and spread of big data techniques. Basically, the challenges are categorized into four aspects of big data ecosystem as per the research done by the big data working group at the cloud security alliance organization (Chen, Chiang and Storey 2012) (Prakash and Darbari 2012).

1. Infrastructure Security
   a. Security for Hadoop
   b. Availability
   c. Architecture Security
   d. Authentication
   e. Communication Security
2. Data Privacy
   a. Cryptography
   b. Access Control
   c. Confidentiality
   d. Privacy-Preserving Queries
   e. Anonymization
   f. Privacy in Social Networks
   g. Differential Privacy
3. Data Management
   a. Security at Collection or Storage
   b. Policies, Laws, or Government
   c. Sharing Algorithms
4. Integrity and Reactive Security
   a. Integrity
   b. Attack Detection
   c. Recovery

7.6.1 Infrastructure-Based Security

As the name suggests, it is the infrastructure where the data are stored, and if we talk about data security, it is necessary to build the infrastructure strong enough to keep the data safe (Figure 7.3). Most of the time, Hadoop technology is the infrastructure for data storage, and so there are a couple of issues need to be discussed

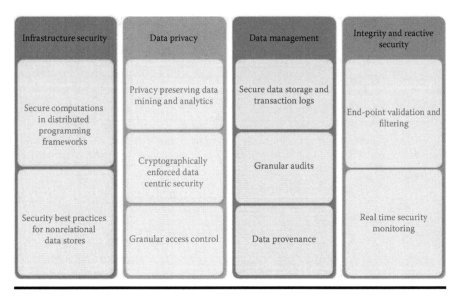

Figure 7.3 Challenges in security with regard to big data computation.

regarding security of data, i.e., communication security in big data and availability of that data. Hadoop technology is the main and basic technology most frequently used in the big data system. To achieve the infrastructure security, it is necessary to secure the Hadoop technology. Apart from these, the other security-related issues are discussed in the following.

Security for Hadoop: Hadoop can be considered as the most widely used standard technique for implementing a big data environment in an organization. MR scripts may produce unwanted results by untrusted mappers as they may produce inconsistent data by accessing private tuples. As the mappers and reducers are distributed over several computing nodes, it is often difficult to detect the faulty mapper or reducer that may degrade the performance of the distributed system (Vavilapalli, et al. 2013). It leads to a huge damage of financial and scientific calculations that is intolerable for any company. Cryptography and authenticity are two widely accepted mechanisms for protecting data while present in DFS. Wang et al. have proposed an elegant solution to protect Hadoop known as G-Hadoop. It provides user authentication and security mechanism in distributed environments (Wang, Tao and Ranjan, et al. 2013) (Zhao, et al. 2014).

Availability: Researchers have also addressed the availability issues related to big data systems. System must be available when required. An efficient architecture needs to be developed to support clustering framework with multiple nodes, where data are distributed and stored. The primary objective of the solution is to provide processing resources by making it available in a fault-tolerant manner.

Architecture Security: To improve the security, we could also modify the architecture according to our needs. Hybridization of accessing data from multiple node and code sharing between the mapper may be the appropriate solution or creating protocols for group communication in large networks dealt by big data system.

Authentication: Authenticity measures the consistency of data items before and after the big data processing. Few authors have developed solutions related to authentication problem. This can be achieved by incorporating a signcryption approach in big data analytics (Cheng, et al. 2015).

Communication Security: Security issues related to communication between gateway parts are often ignored, but communication security is vitally important. It comes under network protocols and security for data transfer techniques.

Therefore, we can conclude that in infrastructure security, main problem lies in the security management of Hadoop system because that is the place where all data are processed and stored. The remaining problems can be resolved by altering the old scheme of the system and adding new security protocols and security layers to achieve our infrastructure security. Infrastructure arrangement for big data installations is also arranged with the help of cloud computing. Thus, infrastructural security issues also turn from complex at in-house premises to more complicated at cloud-based arrangements.

7.6.1.1 In-House Big Data Infrastructure Security

Hadoop is one of the most commonly used big data platforms. If we take the example of Hadoop, it is an open-source distributed framework that consists of several components which are periodically communicating each other. Because of continuous interaction, the system is vulnerable to security threats. The main issue with this arrangement at a practical scenario is that sometimes inner premise securities are neglected due to more focus on perimeter security. Sometimes, nonstandard authorization policy is implemented over the distributed components, which may lead to inefficient configuration for data processing that results in a structural hazard in the system. It is necessary to customize few critical security policies on the layer above the default setting in Hadoop ecosystem. Authorization, authentication, data encryption, and data encryption are the four major phases need to be carefully designed to provide a secure Hadoop framework (Kagal, Finin and Joshi 2001) (Nunan and Di Domenico 2013).

7.6.1.1.1 Authentication

At first when Hadoop was developed, it was meant to process data in a confined and secure environment. With the increase in popularity, it was widely adopted in a multiple heterogeneous environment that demands strong authentication policies. Few of the scenarios are explained in the following:

1. As the Hadoop works in a multistep process, it requires file from HDFS at several points of time. Security measures must be implemented at each point.

2. Security constraint must allow a component to run a job seamlessly while maintaining accounting and program trace information.

7.6.1.1.2 Authorization

Security of Hadoop infrastructure largely relies on the authorization aspect. Authorization is highly important from privacy point of view as it defines the action users are able to perform after authentication. Some major hurdles can be

1. Right configuration of authorization to prohibit unnecessary access between different entities.
2. Authorization configuration at multilevels with queue management techniques.
3. Managing the uniqueness of each component from configuration point of view because of the variety in services that the component provides.

7.6.1.1.3 Auditing

Auditing measures have been highly effective in prevention of security breaches as it provides the past record of all issues that happened within a security model. So, it needs to be treated as an important and necessary step to make a security model complete rather than a satisfying regulatory. Some scenarios depicting the usefulness of auditing are as follows:

1. Active auditing can be utilized to issue an alert on the need to identify security breaches at an instant.
2. Passive auditing can be used to find out the loopholes in the security model, making the security breaching possible if any.

7.6.1.1.4 Data Encryption

In a security model, data-level controls are essential to reinforce the security setup. In the case of Hadoop framework, two types of data need to be secured, i.e.,

1. Data that have been uploaded to HDFS for analysis. These are generally business- and customer-related data, hence sensitive.
2. Data after analysis, which contains technical information. These are highly important as their disclosure can lead to a great loss.

7.6.1.2 Cloud-Based Big Data Infrastructure Security

Most enterprises do not have a proper infrastructure or storage capacity to handle huge amount of data in-house. So, they count on cloud data storage and cloud computing that are more complicated to secure. The main problem comes down to the ownership of data and the responsibility for security. For example, most companies are storing petabytes of data from clickstreams, web logs, social media conversations, and other sources as fodder for big data analysis (Dikaiakos, et al. 2009) (Dillon, Wu and Chang 2010) (Ji, et al. 2012). These data can be used not only to provide deeper customer insight but also to introduce malware into the system. Ownership and classification of Information become more difficult. Just because the data are stored in the cloud does not mean you do not have responsibility for securing the data or meeting the regulatory requirements.

Unlike enterprise data, you cannot dig a moat to protect data in the cloud. If you cannot secure the data repository, then you have to secure the data itself. It may be necessary to adopt new security strategies such as attribute-based encryption to manage access control, where attributes of the data are protected rather than the storage environment; these strategies are still foreign to most data centers (Subashini and Kavitha 2011). Authentication is another security solution. Hadoop is still one of the most popular development platforms for big data applications. When Hadoop was developed, security was not a priority, since the objective was to share large datasets and data processing. As it became clear that Hadoop needed security controls, developers started using authentication patterned after Kerberos. Today, the data used in biggest data initiatives are protected by data encryption and token-based authentication (Takabi, Joshi and Ahn 2010).

Even with authentication and encryption in place, the sheer volume of data transactions is creating a security challenge for big data users. Conventional security information and event management technologies cannot handle the volume of data, so in many environments, big data is being deployed to protect large amount of data (Miller et al. 2010).

7.6.2 Data Privacy

Data privacy is probably one of the major topics in security aspects of big data techniques. Big data can potentially enable invasions of privacy, invasive marketing, decreased civil liberties, and increased state and corporate control. Generally, in big data system, user's data are collected by organizations, which are accessed by system analysts and other people like business partners and outside contractors. A malicious attacker or untrusted partner can exploit these data. However, most data are naive in nature and cannot be retained, thereby preserving the anonymity. Privacy-preserving mining algorithms that are robust and scalable must be used to increase everyone's safety. Following are the main ways in which data privacy problem is dealt with.

Cryptography: This the widely adopted approach to protect user's data in big data computing environment. Malicious attacks can be prevented by embedding efficient encryption and decryption algorithm. Bitmap encryption scheme is an example that guarantees users' privacy.

Access Control: Its main aim is to restrict outsiders from accessing the system. It is a traditional method to achieve the security of a system. It is achieved by separating different combinations of access right for different-level users.

Confidentiality: Confidentiality is the subset of privacy. In big data system, data must be kept confidential to protect it from intruder's attack. Keeping a tremendous impact of privacy on big data system, confidentiality is represented in a different order of privacy. Some authors proposed a new technique called "computing on masked data" to gain the confidentiality in big data system (Kepner et al. 2014). Similarly, trusted scheme for Hadoop cluster (Quan et al. 2013) is another architectural framework technique used to improve the aforesaid issues.

Queries to Protect Privacy: The primary objective of big data ecosystem is to extract meaningful information from large dataset by analyzing it. However, while processing data, data privacy should not be ignored. Some authors addressed this issue and elaborated the ideas of making queries without violating the meaning and privacy of data.

Anonymization: It is the most extended way in which protection of data can be achieved. It mainly removes or hides the sensitive information by applying some useful techniques. It is a very useful way in big data systems. There are mainly two hybrid anonymization techniques that are widely used in big data system: one is top-down specialization, and the other is bottom-up generalization.

Privacy in Social Networks: There are a large variety of social networks used by the people. At the present scenario, popularity of social network is at its highest level. Unaware of its bad consequences, people share a large volume of structured and unstructured data with each other. As the data are made available publicly through social network, it is the greatest challenging task to protect user's private data.

Differential Privacy: It provides methods by which value of analysis on the datasets can be maximized without affecting the user's identity. One popular method is distorting the data by adding noise.

The main purpose of building the system and having security protocols and studying how to process data is for working with data. Hence, it is natural that data privacy is one of the greatest concerns for the organizations that use big data techniques. These organizations depend greatly on data of personal and market information to gain their benefits; so to what extent it can use the information is an argument. There is a need for techniques that restrict complete access of any organization to these data but give access only to sufficient data to gain their benefits. When we deal with data privacy, cryptography definitely comes to our minds. Cryptography is the study of techniques used for secure communication; it is about building protocols that prevent an outsider from accessing the data. This is a common solution used for a long period of time in big data as well (Zikopoulos, et al. 2011).

In recent years, growth of data that are generated and stored has been exponential, which is due to the increase of information the public shares in social networks. The private data shared are also a great concern because these data are carelessly uploaded without the knowledge of who might view them. Many cryptographic techniques are proposed with slight modifications to meet the security demands.

7.6.3 Data Management

An enormous amount of personal data are present in the big data system. Multitiered storage media are used to store data and transaction logs. Manually moving data between different tiers permits the IT manager to track which data are moved and when. However, as the volume of dataset grows exponentially, auto-tiering is the method used by big data storage management for scalability and availability of data. This section mainly focuses on the management techniques after capturing the data in a big data system. Apart from data storage, it also describes on how to share the data. Following are the different policies and legislation suggested by some authors to achieve data management security in big data system (Chen, Chiang and Storey 2012) (Cheng, et al. 2015).

7.6.3.1 Security at Collection or Storage

It is essential to protect data when they are stored in a big data environment. It is also important to know about the data collection. Some methods are employed to protect privacy of data owner by imposing some parameters. These parameters measure the acceptable range of privacy. Another approach suggests the secured storage. This can be achieved by dividing the storage system into sequenced parts and storing them in different cloud storage service providers.

7.6.3.2 Policies, Laws, or Government

Problems associated with big data are mostly related to the use of the technique to extract information from the large dataset. This is possible because of its powerful analytical characteristics. This may result in a threat of leakage of people's private information. To reduce this risk, new legislation and laws need to be implemented, which will confront these new problems in an effective manner.

7.6.3.3 Sharing Algorithms

Sharing data among nodes in a cluster environment is one of the most suitable methods to gain maximum possible information from the data in a big data environment. However, sharing data among the nodes may result in leakage of private information and insecurity of data because of nonguarantee issues. So, few authors proposed some useful approaches to overcome these problems, such as implementing the inspection techniques so that the user takes part in data sharing and securing the transmission itself by adopting nested sparse sampling and coprime sampling techniques.

7.6.3.4 Data Integrity

The whole purpose of securing the data is to protect the data and not let the intruder modify the content of the data. Data integrity means to maintain the data as they are, and it is the responsibility of the system to take care of the data's life cycle and protect its integrity while they are being stored, processed, or retrieved. Data integrity is a very important aspect for any security protocol, and in big data, since data are in large amounts and altering data could be an easy task for any intruder, reliable techniques need to be proposed to preserve the data. One way of validating data integrity is using MR process. It protects data from alteration by any unauthorized user. As we know, MR function first divides the data into many parts, and a mapper for every part computes the data and gives outputs. The outputs are in the form of keys and values. The reducer now combines all the outputs and maps to the key and generates the result. Since we are dealing with big data, securing the data from a false mapper is a concern because we may get incorrect results with a large amount of data, and it is hard to detect them, causing damage to the data and hence failing to secure data integrity. Some of the threats to data integrity are replay attack, man-in-the-middle attack, etc.

7.6.4 Integrity and Reactive Security

Big data system collects data from a variety of sources, which also include endpoint devices. It receives a stream of data in different formats, structured, semistructured, and unstructured, from different origins. The main challenge in the collection phase is validation of input: how can trusted data be collected? How can the user be sure about the data source that it is not a malicious one? And how can filtering be done on malicious inputs?

Integrity: Integrity can be summarized as the maintenance of accuracy, trustworthiness, and consistency of data. Integrity is considered as the basic dimension of security along with availability and confidentiality. Achieving integrity is a complex and tedious task in a big data environment. Integrity can be achieved in a big data system by employing a framework or external integrity verification of the data during MR phase.

Attack Detection: Malicious users may attack on big data system. This can be prevented by introducing certain indicator (sign) in big data system. Computational systems are developed to capture the provenance data. An intrusion detection system especially intended for the attack detection is useful for monitoring the attack in the big data system.

Recovery: Recovery mechanisms are used by the system to recover as soon as the system encounters a disaster. When a disaster occurs, many organizations are opting different policies to store their data in cloud environment.

7.7 Conclusion

Big data is the demand of the second and is a hot topic for IT industries due to the ample opportunity it provides to enhance the business. In today's scenario, it is literally impossible to imagine an effective application without containing data-driven algorithms. The popularity and application of big data are increasing exponentially due to cheaply available compute machines, powerful cloud technology, and reliable networking infrastructure. But with enhancement in big data technology, security issues have become a major concern for businesses. As big data applications are becoming more important and more diverse day by day, an awareness needs to be developed about the adversity of big data if misused. In this chapter, we have highlighted several possible security issues in big data and how to deal with them. Distribution framework is an important part of the discussion which implies less operation in any one system, but it also indicates multiple systems where security issues can arise. Database systems like NoSQL usually lack security. Authenticity of endpoints needs to be validated before acquiring data from them. Available real-time security tools generate many false-positive cases which need to be ignored. It is critically important to validate and verify the users and the extent of authentications they have. Auditing of data and metadata can be handy in dealing actively with security concerns.

Furthermore, as more data are aggregated, privacy concerns will strengthen in parallel, and government regulations will be created as a result. More and more, the question "What is happening to my data, and where does it go?" will be asked not just by business and government organizations but also by every citizens worldwide. We hope this chapter will prompt the research and development community to focus on the discussed issues, thus leading to a more secure and trustworthy big data platform. With the increasing adoption of big data technologies, there will be an increase in expertise on big data security issues in the market.

References

Abrahao, Bruno, Sucheta Soundarajan, John Hopcroft, and Robert Kleinberg. 2012. "On the separability of structural classes of communities." *Proceedings of the 18th ACM SIGKDD international conference on Knowledge discovery and data mining.* 624–632.

Anglin, Matthew Joseph. 2001. "Direct data retrieval in a distributed computing system." *Direct data retrieval in a distributed computing system.* Google Patents, US Patent 6,260,069.

Anita, Sebastian. 1997. "Security in distributed computing: Did you lock the door?" *IEEE Concurrency* (IEEE) 5 (3): 76–77.

Barroso, Luiz Andr, Jeffrey Dean, and Urs Holzle. 2003. Web search for a planet: The Google cluster architecture. *IEEE Micro* 23 (2): 22–28.

Carbone, Paris and Katsifodimos, Asterios and Ewen, Stephan and Markl, Volker and Haridi, Seif and Tzoumas, Kostas. 2015. "Apache flink: Stream and batch processing in a single engine." *Bulletin of the IEEE Computer Society Technical Committee on Data Engineering* 36(4): 28–38.

Crdova, Patricio. 2015. "Analysis of real time stream processing systems considering latency." *University of Toronto patricio@ cs. toronto. edu.*

Chen, CL Philip, and Chun-Yang Zhang. 2014. "Data-intensive applications, challenges, techniques and technologies: A survey on big data." *Information Sciences* (Elsevier) 275: 314–347.

Chen, Hsinchun, Roger HL Chiang, and Veda C Storey. 2012. "Business intelligence and analytics: From big data to big impact." *MIS Quarterly* 36 (4): 1165–1188.

Cheng, Bin, Salvatore Longo, Flavio Cirillo, Martin Bauer, and Ernoe Kovacs. 2015. "Building a big data platform for smart cities: Experience and lessons from santander." *Big Data (BigData Congress),* 2015 IEEE International Congress on. 592–599.

Chodorow, Kristina. 2013. *MongoDB: The Definitive Guide: Powerful and Scalable Data Storage.* Sabastopol, CA: O'Reilly Media.

Dean, Jeffrey, and Sanjay Ghemawat. 2008. "MapReduce: simplified data processing on large clusters." *Communications of the ACM* (ACM) 51 (1): 107–113.

Demchenko, Yuri, Paola Grosso, Cees De Laat, and Peter Membrey. 2013. "Addressing big data issues in scientific data infrastructure." *Collaboration Technologies and Systems (CTS), 2013 International Conference on.* 48–55.

Dikaiakos, Marios D, Dimitrios Katsaros, Pankaj Mehra, George Pallis, and Athena Vakali. 2009. "Cloud computing: Distributed internet computing for IT and scientific research." *IEEE Internet computing* (IEEE) 13 (5).

Dillon, Tharam, Chen Wu, and Elizabeth Chang. 2010. "Cloud computing: Issues and challenges." *Advanced Information Networking and Applications (AINA), 2010 24th IEEE International Conference on.* 27–33.

Dunning, Ted, and Ellen Friedman. 2016. *Streaming Architecture: New Designs Using Apache Kafka and MapR Streams.* Sabastopol, CA: O'Reilly Media.

Dwork, Cynthia, Krishnaram Kenthapadi, Frank McSherry, Ilya Mironov, and Moni Naor. 2006. "Our data, ourselves: Privacy via distributed noise generation." *Eurocrypt* 486–503.

Han, Jing, E Haihong, Guan Le, and Jian Du. 2011. "Survey on NoSQL database." *Pervasive computing and applications (ICPCA), 2011 6th international conference.* IEEE. 363–366.

Inukollu, Venkata Narasimha, Sailaja Arsi, and Srinivasa Rao Ravuri. 2014. "Security issues associated with big data in cloud computing." *International Journal of Network Security & Its Applications* (Academy & Industry Research Collaboration Center (AIRCC)) 6 (3): 45.

Iqbal, Muhammad Hussain, and Tariq Rahim Soomro. 2015. "Big data analysis: Apache storm perspective." *International Journal of Computer Trends and Technology* 19: 9–14.

Jam, Masoumeh Rezaei, Leili Mohammad Khanli, Morteza Sargolzaei Javan, and Mohammad Kazem Akbari. 2014. "A survey on security of Hadoop." *Computer and Knowledge Engineering (ICCKE), 2014 4th International eConference on.* 716–721.

Ji, Changqing, Yu Li, Wenming Qiu, Uchechukwu Awada, and Keqiu Li. 2012. "Big data processing in cloud computing environments." *Pervasive Systems, Algorithms and Networks (ISPAN), 2012 12th International Symposium on.* 17–23.

Kagal, Lalana, Tim Finin, and Anupam Joshi. 2001. "Moving from security to distributed trust in ubiquitous computing environments." *IEEE Computer* 34 (12): 154–157.

Kaisler, Stephen, Frank Armour, J Alberto Espinosa, and William Money. 2013. "Big data: Issues and challenges moving forward." *System Sciences (HICSS), 2013 46th Hawaii International Conference on.* 995–1004.

Katal, Avita, Mohammad Wazid, and RH Goudar. 2013. "Big data: Issues, challenges, tools and good practices." *Contemporary Computing (IC3), 2013 Sixth International Conference on.* 404–409.

Kaufman, Lori M. 2009. "Data security in the world of cloud computing." *IEEE Security & Privacy* (IEEE) 7 (4): 61–64.

Kepner, Jeremy, Vijay Gadepally, Pete Michaleas, Nabil Schear, Mayank Varia, and Arkady Yerukhimovich, and Robert K Cunningham. 2014. "Computing on masked data: A high performance method for improving big data veracity." *High Performance Extreme Computing Conference (HPEC), 2014 IEEE.* IEEE. 1–6.

Khan, Nawsher, Ibrar Yaqoob, Ibrahim Abaker Targio Hashem, Zakira Inayat, Waleed Kamaleldin, Mahmoud Ali, Muhammad Alam, Muhammad Shiraz, and Abdullah Gani. 2014. "Big data: Survey, technologies, opportunities, and challenges." *The Scientific World Journal* 2014: 1–18.

Miller, David, Shon Harris, Allen Harper, Stephen VanDyke, and Chris Blask. 2010. *Security Information and Event Management (SIEM) Implementation.* New York, NY: McGraw-Hill Professional.

Moreno, Julio, Manuel A Serrano, and Eduardo Fernández-Medina. 2016. "Main issues in big data security." *Future Internet* (Multidisciplinary Digital Publishing Institute) 8 (3): 44.

Moura, Jose, and Carlos Serrão. 2016. "Security and privacy issues of big data." *arXiv preprint arXiv:1601.06206.*

Namiot, Dmitry. 2015. "On big data stream processing." *International Journal of Open Information Technologies* 3 (8): 48–51.

Nunan, Daniel, and Maria Di Domenico. 2013. "Market research & the ethics of big data." *International Journal of Market Research* (Warc) 55 (4): 505–520.

Prakash, Vijay, and Manuj Darbari. 2012. "A review on security issues in distributed systems." *International Journal of Scientific and Engineering Research* 3 (9): 1–15.

Quan, Zhou, Deqin Xiao, Chunming Tang, and Chunming Rong. 2013. "TSHC: trusted scheme for Hadoop cluster." *Emerging Intelligent Data and Web Technologies (EIDWT), 2013 Fourth International Conference.* IEEE. 344–349.

Reed, Daniel A, and Jack Dongarra. 2015. "Exascale computing and big data." *Communications of the ACM* (ACM) 58 (7): 56–68.

Ryan, Gery W, and H Russell Bernard. 2000. "Data management and analysis methods." *Handbook of Qualitative Research.* Thousand Oaks, CA: Sage Publications. 769–802.

Shoro, Abdul Ghaffar, and Tariq Rahim Soomro. 2015. "Big data analysis: Apache spark perspective." *Global Journal of Computer Science and Technology* 15 (1): 1–9.

Shvachko, Konstantin, Hairong Kuang, Sanjay Radia, and Robert Chansler. 2010. "The hadoop distributed file system." *Mass storage systems and technologies (MSST), 2010 IEEE 26th symposium on.* 1–10.

Singh, Hardeep, and Gurpreet Singh. 2016. "Big data-a review." *i-Manager's Journal on Information Technology* (iManager Publications) 6 (1): 25.

Subashini, Subashini, and Veeraruna Kavitha. 2011. "A survey on security issues in service delivery models of cloud computing." *Journal of Network and Computer Applications* (Elsevier) 34 (1): 1–11.

Takabi, Hassan, James BD Joshi, and Gail-Joon Ahn. 2010. "Security and privacy challenges in cloud computing environments." *IEEE Security & Privacy* (IEEE) 8 (6): 24–31.

Tanenbaum, Andrew S, and Maarten Van Steen. 2007. *Distributed Systems: Principles and Paradigms.* Prentice-Hall.

Tankard, Colin. 2012. "Big data security." *Network Security* (Elsevier) 2012 (7): 5–8.

Vavilapalli, Vinod Kumar, Arun C Murthy, Chris Douglas, Sharad Agarwal, Mahadev Konar, Robert Evans, Thomas Graves, et al. 2013. "Apache hadoop yarn: Yet another resource negotiator." *Proceedings of the 4th annual Symposium on Cloud Computing.* 5.

Wang, Lizhe, Jie Tao, Holger Marten, Achim Streit, Samee U Khan, Joanna Kolodziej, and Dan Chen. 2012. "MapReduce across distributed clusters for data-intensive applications." *Parallel and Distributed Processing Symposium Workshops & PhD Forum (IPDPSW), 2012 IEEE 26th International.* 2004–2011.

Wang, Lizhe, Jie Tao, Rajiv Ranjan, Holger Marten, Achim Streit, Jingying Chen, and Dan Chen. 2013. "G-Hadoop: MapReduce across distributed data centers for data-intensive computing." *Future Generation Computer Systems* (Elsevier) 29 (3): 739–750.

White, Tom. 2012. *Hadoop: The definitive guide.* "O'Reilly Media, Inc.".

Wu, Xindong, Xingquan Zhu, Gong-Qing Wu, and Wei Ding. 2014. "Data mining with big data." *IEEE Transactions on Knowledge and Data Engineering* (IEEE) 26 (1): 97–107.

Zhao, Jiaqi, Lizhe Wang, Jie Tao, Jinjun Chen, Weiye Sun, Rajiv Ranjan, Joanna Kołodziej, Achim Streit, and Dimitrios Georgakopoulos. 2014. "A security framework in G-Hadoop for big data computing across distributed Cloud data centres." *Journal of Computer and System Sciences* (Elsevier) 80 (5): 994–1007.

Zikopoulos, Paul, Chris Eaton, and others. 2011. *Understanding Big Data: Analytics for Enterprise Class Hadoop and Streaming Data.* New York, NY: McGraw-Hill Osborne Media.

Chapter 8

Internet of Things (IoT) Security Challenges

Ramesh C. Poonia

Amity University Rajasthan

Contents

8.1 Introduction

The Internet of Things (IoT) is a machine-to-machine technology empowered by secure network connectivity and cloud infrastructure to reliably transform data into useful information for people, business, and institutions [1]. The IoT is based upon known technologies like sensors, networking, and cloud computing, but its capability of transformation is incredible [2]. All around the world, billions of people are actively using the Internet for almost every kind of purpose on a regular basis. Nowadays, the Internet is vastly used, mostly to send emails, use social networks, share voice and image files, transfer money, watch events, and perform different kinds of actions using it. In an estimate, by 2020 there will be 50–100 billion devices connected to the Internet [3]. It is estimated by 2025 that best-in-class organizations that will extensively use IoT technologies in their products and operations will be up to 10% more profitable. Also by 2020, there will be 5.4 billion connections across the globe, including cellular, fixed line, satellite, and short-range wireless connections, up from 1.2 billion devices till date.

8.2 Understanding Wireless Communication Technologies

Wireless communication technologies are the backbone of any communication system. To connect different devices as well as applications, communication protocols allow interaction of devices on network with different machines. Following is the analysis of available wireless technologies [4]:

8.3 Generic Architecture

Generally, IoT has four levels, as shown in Figure 8.1, described as follows [5]:

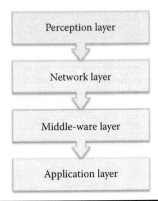

Figure 8.1   Generic architecture of IoT.

8.3.1 Perception Layer

It includes various types of data sensors like radio-frequency identification (RFID), barcodes, and other sensor networks [6]. The main objective behind this layer is to recognize the unique objects and handle the gathered data acquired from the real world with the assistance of various sensors.

8.3.2 Network Layer

The objective of this layer is to transfer the collected information acquired from the perception layer to a system that processes information using the already existing reliable kind of communication networks like Internet Mobile Network [7].

8.3.3 Middleware Layer

This layer manages information-processing systems that perform automated actions based upon the results of processed data and is responsible for linking them with the database that stores the processed data results. This layer provides a similar service type between the connected devices [8].

8.3.4 Application Layer

This layer is responsible for demonstrating the implementation of applications based on IoT as per the requirement of the users. It includes different IoT-based industries and applications like smart cities, smart home, smart hospitals, etc. [9].

8.4 Security Goals

The security goals of IoT are to provide confidentiality regarding the data and ensure proper identity authentication mechanisms. The security triad or Confidentiality, Integrity, and Availability (CIA) triad implements security mechanisms using three important areas, i.e., data confidentiality, integrity, and availability, as represented in Figure 8.2. Any intrusion caused into the system is accountable. It can be represented as follows [10]:

8.4.1 Data Confidentiality

Data confidentiality can be understood as ensuring no external intrusion. Preventing access of any user information is considered a privacy breach. Various security mechanisms are thus are in place to keep this privacy breach in check. Methods such as data encryption or two-step verifications like biometric identification ensure that every person is uniquely identified. In case of IoT-based applications and devices, it is ensured that the sensors do not reveal data to the unauthorized neighboring nodes and the tags do not transmit data to unauthorized readers [11].

8.4.2 Data Integrity

Data can be affected during communication through various known and unknown methods. Data integrity means preventing user information from any such kind of alteration during the transmission. Methods such as checksum and cyclic redundancy check are employed to detect errors for a major part of data. Backing up data regularly and features such as version control can also help in maintaining integrity of the user data on IoT-based devices by keeping it in its original form always [12].

Figure 8.2   The CIA triad.

8.4.3 Data Availability

As the name suggests, data is made available to its users 24/7. It means ensuring access to the authorized users in any condition. Since many enterprises and organizations depend on it, firewalls are required to prevent denial-of-service (DoS) attacks that can prohibit an authorized user from accessing it. Data must be available in such a way that there should be no issue faced by the user during access, such as lagging, slow access, etc. Flow of information must be smooth in nature. One of the most important way to ensure the availability of data is to have redundant copies of data, and thus, backup of the system components is essential in case of system failure [10].

8.5 Security Features

8.5.1 Secure Communication

In the IoT, communication should be protected by providing the security services discussed in previous section. By using standardized security mechanisms, we can provide communication security at different layers. Table 8.1 represents the standard security solution at different layers.

Link Layer: IEEE 802.15.4 Security: 802.15.4 link-layer security is the current state-of-the-art security solution for the IoT. It looks after each node on a per-hop base, protects the communication path, and ensures it is a trusted path [13], for which a single preshared key is required throughout to protect all communication systems. In a normal case, if an attacker compromised one device and access to one key, it means that the whole network will be compromised; but, in this link layer, as its per-hop security, only one hop/device will be compromised and can be detected at an initial state. Still, the link layer security is limited; but it is quite flexible and operates with multiple protocols on different layers.

6LoWPAN Networks: Internet protocol version 6 (IPv6) is used on sensor node to simplify the connecting task, and it is quite successful, especially in all

Table 8.1 Stack with Standardized Security Solution

IoT Layer	IoT Protocol	Security Protocol
Application	CoAP	User-defined
Transport	UDP	DTLS
Network	IPv6, KPL	IP sec, RPL security
6LoWPAN	GLoWPAN	None
Data-link	IEEE S02.15.4	802.15.4 security

Low-Power Wireless Personal Area Networks (LoWPAN) devices [14–17]. IPv6 can be used in IoT as it also supports development for commissioning, managing, configuring, and debugging networks [14]. The Internet Engineering Task Force introduced an additional adaptation layer between data link and network layers and made the IPv6LoWPAN working group to represent the IPv6 support over IEEE 802.15.4 LoWPAN networks, as specified in Fig.1. There are three different kinds of LoWPAN architecture types: (a) Ad-hoc LoWPAN, with no infrastructure; (b) LoWPAN, with a one-edge router; and (c) LoWPAN with multiple-edge routers. Figure 8.3 illustrates a security framework for 6LoWPAN, which aims at bootstrapping security associations between a newly authenticated device and those that want to connect to the same domain, without letting intermediary foreign entities gain any knowledge of the exchanged key material.

As illustrated in Figure 8.4, the joining device discovers the identities of its neighbors, which then undergoes a procedure of authentication and generation of key and distribution.

Network Layer: IP security: As IoT is basically implemented on the Internet, it uses network IP security (IPsec) provided by network layer. IPsec provides end-to-end security with authentication as well as confidentiality and integrity. Any transport layer protocol can operate IPsec, i.e., Transmission Control Protocol (TCP), User Datagram Protocol (UDP), Hypertext Transfer Protocol (HTTP), Constrained Application Protocol (CoAP) [18]. It maintains confidentiality and integrity of the IP payload with the assistance of encapsulated security payload (ESP) protocol [19], whereas the authentication header protocol [20] helps in IP header plus payload. Thus, IPsec is required in all IPv6 protocols and is by default compatible with the IPv6 devices as well [21].

1905.1 Abstraction Layer: With the increase of home care solution, every device is connected with Internet-made wired and wireless home networking a hot topic. To address a wide variety of application, regions, environments, and

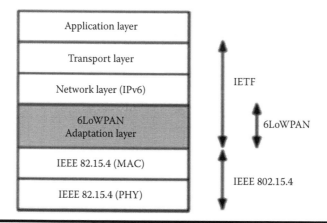

Figure 8.3 6LoWPAN adaptation layer.

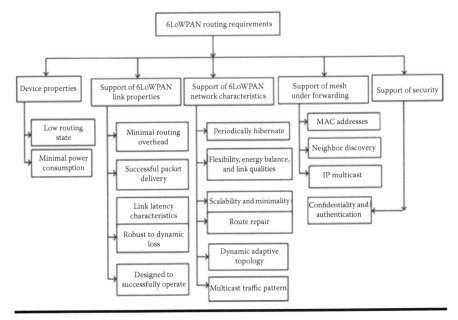

Figure 8.4   Security framework of 6LoWPAN.

topologies, multiple connectivity technologies should be used. A typical home network is shown in Figure 8.5. As with any network deployment, many problems need to be addressed for the network.

The design of IEEE 1905.1 is flexible and scalable to accommodate future home networking technologies. This layer is compatible with interface selection for packet transmission between any interface and application. It also requires no changes for the given home network technologies, i.e., no effect to the behavior and implementation too. Here, the control message data unit is transmitted using an abstraction layer among 1905.1-compliant devices.

8.5.2 Securing Data

Securing communication is important in IoT, but most of the application developer forgets about securing data that is generated from all IoT devices. Most of the devices in IoT are small and does not have enough constraints due to limited size to secure them from security threats related with hardware. Several solutions exist but due to different communication technology, only one solution may not be enough to secure everything.

A number of articles proposed a secure storage solution [22–25]. Codo [22] is a security extension for the Coffee [26] file system in the Contiki OS [27]. Bagci [28] developed a communication framework for secure storage and communication based on IPv6/6LoWPAN protocols. In IPv6/6LoWPAN, IPsec/ESP facilitates

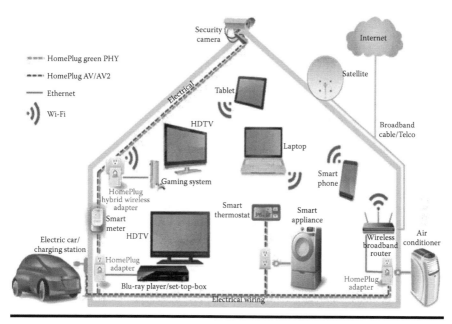

Figure 8.5   Hybrid home network.

encryption and authentication mechanism of data packets being transmitted. The author uses cryptographic methods and data formats that are defined by ESP for data processing before storage. In this architecture, they also need to store header information along with data, which also need cryptographic processing. This encrypted data must be stored in ESP compatible over network, which they achieve by using IPsec as a base for communication and storage, and the existing key exchange mechanisms defined for IPsec can be reused for the storage element of the framework.

8.5.3 Supporting Technologies

Development of technologies such as communication capabilities, sensors, smart phones, cloud computing, network virtualization, and software empowers items to connect with each other [29]. IoT is used to interconnect electronic devices capable of sharing data within the digital world. Following are some of the technologies that support the concept of IoT:

1. **Identification Technologies:** The two major players for identifying devices in IoT are RFID and wireless sensor networks (WSNs) [30–33].
2. **Network and Communication Technologies:** Technologies (wired and wireless) such as Global System for Mobile communications (GSM), Bluetooth, WiFi, and ZigBee will be used to connect billions of devices and services

[34–36]. IoT network communication requires properly secured and scalable architectures for reliable transmission between devices and services [37].

3. **Software and Hardware Technologies:** Small, low-cost, and highly functional designed electronic devices are being developed for better communication [32]. Better interdevice communication will depend upon the smart devices that will lead to setting up of smart systems that have high intelligence quotient and are autonomous in nature. Use of such devices will facilitate a rapid growth in creation of new services and deployment of IoT-based applications [38].

8.6 Security at Each Layer

Researchers are being carried out to facilitate a well-defined and reliable secured architecture, which can provide data confidentiality along with data security and privacy. The architecture was proposed by Zhang et al. [39] to secure it against the possible threats, as represented in Figure 8.3.

8.6.1 Perception Layer

It is the bottommost layer of the IoT architecture that is responsible for providing various security features to the hardware. It is mainly responsible for four basic purposes: authentication, data privacy, privacy of sensitive information, and risk assessment, which are discussed later.

8.6.1.1 Authentication

It requires cryptographic hash algorithms to provide digital signatures to the terminals so that it could hold possible known attacks such as brute force attack, side-channel attack, and collision attack.

8.6.1.2 Data Privacy

Privacy is ensured using encryption algorithms (symmetric and asymmetric encryption algorithms) like RSA, DSA, DES, etc. that are responsible for preventing any kind of unauthorized access during data transmission to the next layer. Sensors consume very less power so that they are easily implemented into the sensors.

8.6.1.3 Privacy of Sensitive Information

Certain methods are required sometimes to hide sensitive and highly confidential information, which even requires hiding the location and identity. K-approach is used to ensure that the location and identity of the user remains anonymous of the user [40].

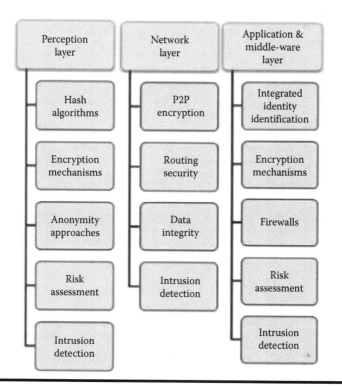

Figure 8.6   Security architecture of IoT.

8.6.1.4 Risk Assessment

It is obvious that with each passing day new threats to the system are discovered. It helps in with holding the intrusion attempts and forging new security strategies. One such method employed in case of IoT is dynamical risk assessment [41].

However, if we still find some security breach in the system, a kill command is initiated automatically by the RFID reader to the RFID tag to prevent any intrusion attempt to access the RFID tag data [42].

8.6.2 Network Layer

Wired and wireless networks are both susceptible to various attacks. Wireless channels are more prone to attacks due to their openness. Security is, therefore, further categorized into three types that have been discussed later:

8.6.2.1 Authentication

A strong authentication mechanism in place can prevent unauthorized access to sensor nodes and prevent them from spreading false information [43]. DoS attack is the most common type of attack. It can result in flooding of unnecessary traffic that may affect the network.

8.6.2.2 Routing Security

Routing algorithms are held responsible to facilitate privacy during data exchange between the sensor nodes and the processing systems once authentication process is completed [43]. Researchers have been carried out to find out the routing procedures, such as source routing [45], in which data to be transferred is stored in packets to the processing systems. Nodes act as the intermediate point that analyze the packets and transmit them to the known destination hop-by-hop. Multiple paths are used for routing data to the destination to avoid any error detection by the system. It is also adopted to keep the system up and running in case of failure in the system [46].

8.6.2.3 Data Privacy

Intrusion is monitored using safety control mechanisms in place, and then data integrity methods ensure that the data received on the receiving end is similar to the original one.

8.6.3 Middleware and Application Layer

This layer merges the middleware and application layer to make a combined security mechanism that is categorized as follows:

8.6.3.1 Authentication

Authentication is implemented to avoid access to an intruder by regular identity mechanisms. It is similar to the authentication process in earlier layers, but this layer shares information between the services in both the layers. Major technologies that are part of this layer include cloud computing and virtualization, and both are vulnerable to attacks. Cloud is vulnerable toward inside threat, whereas virtualization is more vulnerable to attacks such as DoS and data theft. Research is required to plug up this issue to make the environment more secure.

8.6.3.2 Intrusion Detection

Intrusion detection techniques are responsible for detecting threats and generating alarms if any such activity is detected after continuous monitoring. Logs are maintained in order to trace the intruder. Various intrusion detection techniques exist [47] such as data mining [48] and anomaly detection.

8.6.3.3 Risk Assessment

Risk assessment provides proper assessment of the existing security mechanisms and architecture to provide effective solutions to plug the loopholes found.

8.6.3.4 Data Security

Encryption mechanisms are used to prevent any kind of data stealing threats. Other than this, anti-DoS firewalls and antivirus software or antispyware or malware are used to eliminate such kind of malicious threats.

8.7 Security Requirements

8.7.1 Requirements Related to IoT Technology

The technical architecture of the IoT definitely poses threats for security and privacy of the users to which the users are rightly entitled [12,13]. End users are unaware of most of the technicalities related with the user. Thus, it may lead to traces of data left unattended in cyberspace due to some reasons. In addition, in today's world, it is not limited to states, and private players are now one of the major actors in collecting the respective data.

Business processes require high reliability. Following are the security and privacy requirements during a business process [16]:

- **Resilience toward attacks:** Systems must avoid any kind of node or single point of failure.
- **Data authentication:** Every retrieved information must be authenticated [17].
- **Access control:** Data provided must be access controlled by those who provide the information [18].
- **Client privacy:** Privacy must be ensured. It must be inferred that only the user or a customer is responsible for its data and no external interference is possible in the system.

The earlier listed requirements must be fulfilled by any enterprise using IoT technology to avoid any risk, especially the business activities in general.

8.7.2 Privacy-Enhancing Technologies (PETs)

Fulfilling each requirement of the customer regarding his privacy concern is very difficult. Here, privacy-enhancing technologies (PETs) come into play to achieve privacy goals outlined by the users. These PETs are listed as follows [19]:

Virtual Private Networks are created by a group of business partners to keep their business activities in check. Only partners can have access, so it looks to be confidential and have integrity. But in case of exchanging information with global or third-party services, its relevance seems to be shattering and beyond its capability.

Transport Layer Security also improves confidentiality and integrity in a global structure of IoT. A new transport layer security connection is required for each delegation step, which would badly affect other layers as well.

DNS Security Extension uses a digital signature to ensure originality, authenticity, and integrity of the received information. However, DNS security extension can only ensure global ONS information authenticity unless the whole Internet adopts it.

Onion Routing Technique is used to encrypt and amalgamate Internet traffic from various sources, using the public keys of the onion router that are being transmitted. In this process, it would obstruct matching IP packets with the source. However, it does results in increase of waiting time that leads to performance issues.

Private Information Retrieval systems hide a customer's detail, after locating Electronic Product Code Information Services (EPCIS). However, issues such as scalability, performance, and key management exist in globally accessed systems like ONS, thus making it infeasible.

Peer-to-Peer Systems can be used to step-up security and privacy. Peer-to-peer systems usually are scalable and are performance-wise efficient in applications. These are based upon distributed hash tables. However, access control's implementation is required at the EPCIS first rather than on the data that is stored in the distributed hash table. It is carried out due to the absence of an encryption mechanism in both the designs. [20] As per our assumption, encryption and authentication can be successfully implemented using the Internet and available web security services [21]. Public-key cryptography mechanism can be used to authenticate the customer.

RFID tag can also be disabled in future to let the customers decide whether they want to make use of it or not. They can be destroyed using a protective mesh of foil aka "Faraday Cage" that makes it impenetrable for radio signals or one can simply destroy them. Though both these options are not recommended, putting multiple tags in a single cage or destroying each one of them can cause overlooking of certain tags and can still be traced. Even a "kill" command is of no use as it leaves the possibility of reusing the tag again, which makes it vulnerable and a cause of concern for everybody. Even small businesses may purchase used tags to reuse them again or whatever they want to do. What it means is that rather than killing or restricting access to them, it leaves the device vulnerable. The best solution is to destroy or delete the information on ONS to prevent any breach in privacy of the owner of the tagged object. This step ensures that while the tag can still be used and read, the previous information about the concerned person is inaccessible.

Another issue is transparency in the information accessed by RFID. A running RFID tag can help in locating users in real time, making everyone out there vulnerable. Therefore, there is a need to review our laws, and we must understand quickly whether much-valued information should be covered under the existing privacy laws, or new specific laws or amendments are required.

8.7.3 Legal Course of Action

The world in recent times has risen and has acknowledged the threat to the security and privacy related to the RFID and IoT. In an instance, in May 12, 2009, the European commission has recommended implementing proper measures to protect data that supports RFID. They have emphasized upon ethical and lawful operation of such applications to honor the right to privacy and protection of personal data [27]. Similar steps are necessary and must be taken by every state that employs the use of RFID and IoT-based applications to maintain the new world order.

8.8 Security Challenges and Issues

"Internet is the first thing that humanity has built that humanity doesn't understand, the largest experiment in anarchy that we ever had." —Eric Schmidt

Undoubtedly, in the past few years, there has been an uprise in the use of IoT-based applications. We all know how much cybersecurity threats prevail in the current world of the Internet. Hence, it is quite evident that similar threats or challenges exist and have been experienced in the past few years. Regardless of the fact that whether such threat looms over the world of IoT or not, one thing is sure that it cannot be denied in this world of uncertainty. Our past experiences have rightly taught us to never underestimate any kind of cyberthreat posed by anyone. Certain researchers have worked a lot in this field over the past few years, and based upon their research, the common security threats, challenges, vulnerabilities, and its effect on IoT are listed out [49].

8.8.1 Challenges in IoT

8.8.1.1 Sensors

Sensors are the tools used to connect different tools via the Internet. Therefore, it is of utmost importance that sensors must be ready to send and receive data 24/7. Energy and power management is an important issue within the IoT research area. Hence, low-power wireless sensors that do not need battery replacement over their lifetimes are needed.

8.8.1.2 Identification

IoT includes a variety of hybrid devices that are connected on the same network but may not have the same role and specifications. Therefore, identifying them becomes a big challenge in IoT. Miorandi has suggested two ways of identifying objects in IoT: "The first one is to physically tag one object by means of RFIDs, QR code, or similarly returning an identifier that can be looked up in a database for retrieving the set of features associated to it. The second possibility is to provide one object with its own description: if equipped with wireless communication means, it could communicate directly its own identity and relevant features. These two approaches are not mutually exclusive and can complement each other."

8.8.1.3 Scalability

With the increasing number of objects connected in an IoT network, network and frequency have to anticipate the enormous flow coming in soon by scaling the network at different levels. One of the issues that arise during scalability is addressing. The most common standard used to address a device on the Internet is IP. Since IoT implies that infinite number of devices can be connected in IoT, it is something that IPv4 addressing scheme does not allow, which even Ipv6 may find difficult in future to adjust.

8.8.1.4 Heterogeneity

IoT has devices that may range from small chips to big airplanes and a building, which means that a set of protocols and formats used by them may vary with their different capacities and size. Standards are required to implement communication among objects. Addressing is an issue where standardization does not apply. IEEE is one of the institutions that is working in regard to solving this problem. Packets that are routed on the network must follow the same norms and specifications in order to be synchronized. Standards in IoT include different area of concerns such as security, privacy, architecture, and communication.

8.8.1.5 Governance

Since we are talking of making every device autonomous, more governance is needed. Questions arise, such as which organization will regulate and care about the legal enforcements in IoT or how the users and their data will be protected. The issues such as privacy and data theft by third-party apps arise.

8.8.1.6 Security

Security is a major issue in IoT, and it will be discussed in detail later [50].

8.8.2 Design Challenges in IoT

8.8.2.1 Heterogeneity and Interoperability

Interoperability among heterogeneous devices causes major issues in IoT. Backend logic of many IoT devices is custom designed for each device. Application Programming Interface (API) translator is used for multiversion or multivendor deployment of IoT devices. However, API translation and message formats can expose a set of APIs while using subcomponents of adapter to interoperate among heterogeneous kind of devices. Such components expose a public IP, as they are accessible from the field area. Hence, flooding this component with false requests could occupy some valuable bandwidth that may lead to DoS attacks. Spoofing is also a cause of concern, since alternate false routes may be created to get unauthorized access to sensor data.

8.8.2.2 Connectivity

Two kinds of connectivity are required for IoT applications, and each have their own set of challenges. The first kind of connectivity is required at physical level, where the sender and receiver need to communicate using physical or Media Access Control (MAC) addresses. IoT device preferably communicates using low-power radio standards such as ZigBee and Bluetooth, and traditional Ethernet networks are used for bridging information among IoT-supported devices.

The second type of connectivity involves service connectivity. It ensures whether packets reaching to the backend from any device needs to be registered to ensure proper delivery of messages to the desired services. In this case, any change is notified to the respective devices to avoid unnecessary flooding requests that can lead to DoS attacks.

8.8.2.3 Mobility and Scalability

Due to the constant increase in the number of IoT devices, there could be disruption in connectivity. Even in case of mobilization of IoT, devices to new location-uninterrupted service still has to be provided through certain mechanisms. The isolated nodes remaining after the disruption in service have to be reverified to resume services. In most of the scenarios, only on field device have to be reverified, but in some sensitive situations, backend system has to be verified as well. Here, an adversary node can pose threat of repudiation attacks by hiding itself in the roaming network. However, duplicate nodes may also exist and exploit in the last network.

Scalability in case of field deployments can occur either vertically or horizontally. To lower the burden and improve service availability, hardware load balancers are used, thus allowing only verified devices to pass through. Otherwise, the isolated nodes can become a launching pad for DoS attacks. In case of vertical scalability, network can be extended to multiple hops. Therefore, having faith in the intermediate nodes becomes important or rather, it will end up initiating sinkhole or wormhole attacks.

8.8.2.4 Addressing and Identification

IoT applications usually use low-power radios to connect device located at the end. The connecting nodes have the authority to allocate addresses to the device that are connected to it and these addresses do not follow any common standard. Also, the addressing scheme always remains unknown. To avoid this, a common addressing scheme like 6LoWPAN is used to obtain a unique IPv6 address each time [51,52].

8.8.2.5 Spatiotemporal Services

Spatiotemporal impulse is used to identify an event in the world of IoT. Thus, time synchronization of the deployed nodes becomes important, and hence they are able to tag data with a spatial geolocation. Location services such as GPS are used to apply it. However, proper attention must be paid toward the user data so that it may not be susceptible to unauthorized user access. Additionally, backend systems are also required to understand the change in location available from the end nodes to avoid the inaccuracy in results that may lead to false information and incorrect decisions.

8.8.2.6 Resource Constraints

There are a variety of constraints related with the peripheral IoT devices, such as HDD and Hard Disk Drive (HDD), Random Access Memory (RAM) availability, network bandwidth, and energy utilization and availability. Since these nodes are easily accessible, there is a possibility of their manipulation in a bad way. These nodes are basically the entry points to upload data into the cloud for storage. That is where user data privacy issues really come in. Therefore, strong encryption mechanisms are needed.

8.8.2.7 Data Interchange

Since different IoT devices may possess different data unpacking mechanisms as per the hardware specifications, a packet has to be encrypted and decrypted at multiple points, which may prove to be vulnerable and can be a cause of information leakage. Since keys will be shared on such a vast scale in case of a long route, the intermediate nodes become prone to DoS attacks. That is why end-to-end encryptions are better preferred [51,52].

8.8.2.8 Resource and Service Discovery

Any IoT application involves a large number of devices deployed in the actual field that are autonomous in nature and can discover services they require. Thus, coordination is required to maintain service directories that can be queried over a public interface. Two-way authentication is carried out so that duplicate or redundant services may lead to spoofing that can also cause DoS-like attacks. Data is distributed in the clouds due to the distributed nature of IoT architecture. Hence, to avoid leakage and privacy issues, such security measures are required [51,52].

8.8.3 Architectural Issues in IoT

8.8.3.1 Security Issues in Application Layer

Security issues in the application layer can cause applications to shut down and work inappropriately. Due to this, inappropriate authentication can be carried out. Malicious attacks in this layer can cause malfunctioning of the application due to bugs. Since many devices are divided under the category of application-level entities, it becomes a cause of grave concern. Following are some of the common threats to application layer:

- Malicious Code Attacks: Malicious code attacks such as "worm" attacks can prove fatal for a range of small Internet-enabled devices like home routers. For example, a worm may spread into a car's Wi-Fi and can result in fatal injuries to the car and the person.
- Tampering with Node-Based Applications: Hackers can intrude into the device nodes by exploiting the application vulnerabilities and can install malicious root kits. That is why it becomes important that the security design should be at least tamper-resistant. Hence, protecting some parts will always prove insufficient. Such threats can result in malfunctioning of the node that may result in tampered or incorrect data.
- Inability to Receive Security Patches: Security patches are necessary to update or upgrade the existing software packages already in use. In critical fields such as nuclear energy sector, if the security patches of the moving node are not updated, it may result in catastrophic consequences.
- Hacking into the Smart Meter/Grid: Smart meter is responsible for sending the usage data to the operators for automatic billing to make it secure. If somehow such illegal access of data transmission occurs, one can gain access that may prove ideal for burglary or even worse. Such attacks on smart grid can prove catastrophic and can prove financially unviable for the economy.

8.8.3.2 Security Issues in the Perception Layer

Generally, security threats in perception layer exist at node level. Since nodes are made up of sensors and are a prime target for hackers, they can intrude into the device who wishes to replace it with their own dummy device. Mostly, the threats are from outside entities. Commonly existing threats in the perception layer are as follows:

- Eavesdropping: The mode of communication among devices is generally wireless and through the Internet. Thus, making them vulnerable to eavesdropping attacks, since they will be unattended for most of the time. In such scenarios, for example, sensors in smart homes or health domains can act as a way to compromise with a user's privacy.

■ Sniffing Attacks: In such kind of attacks, intruders or hackers can put malicious sensors or devices in such a way that information being transferred through those nodes is being acquired by them. The smarter the environment in which the IoT devices are being employed, the bigger the risk is, especially, areas where human–human and human–device interactions are more.
■ Noise in Data: Transmitting data over a long distance through a wireless medium may possess some kind of noise, i.e., incorrect or damaged information. Sometimes, this misrepresentation of data can lead to scenarios where accurate information is required [53].

8.8.3.3 Security Issues in the Network Layer

Network layer is quite prone to attacks because it carries a large amount of data that causes "network congestion." Integrity and authentication are the two major issues in this layer. Any attack from hacker through the affected nodes on the devices located in the network is a serious issue. Common threats to network layer are as follows:

■ DoS Attack: It involves an overflow of information that is sent over a network on a device to shut down its process. This results in a blockade that causes the device or server unable to access the service. For example, in a lower bandwidth IoT network such as health information system, such seizure of services can prove fatal.
■ Gateway Attacks: Such attacks halt the connection between the sensors and the Internet by cutting the existing route of communication. These attacks could include DoS attacks that may interrupt flow of information from the Internet to sensors or devices, therefore, compromising with the functioning of the subdomains like vehicular networks or smart cities.
■ Unauthorized Access: Open devices that are to be used by anyone are quite unsecure. Such devices are meant to transmit and receive data, and some malicious nodes may try to show themselves as "authenticated" and access these devices without having the required authority that may result in compromising with the security of the device.
■ Storage Attacks: Each bit of information is usually saved on a traditional storage device or maybe on cloud, both of which are vulnerable to attacks. It can result in compromising and changing it to incorrect details. This replication and duplication of data with access to different types of people can result in an increased surface area of attacks.
■ Injecting Fake Information: False data is injected sometimes by the intruders, to which the system can react very dangerously. That is why it can become a cause of physical attacks in future, and it can be used to hide such threats.

8.8.3.4 Security Issues in the Physical Layer

There are many issues at the physical layer as well. Existing security methods are surely not enough. Therefore, there is a need to protect our power devices and physical security mechanisms, both from the physical attacks and individuals. They need to be efficient and capable of withstanding situations where regular power sources are not available. Batteries need to hold charge for a sufficient amount of time to keep the devices running. Some commonly found issues in physical layer are as follows:

- Physical Damage: Physical devices in an IoT system like sensors, nodes, and actuators can be physically damaged by malicious entities. This can lead to the disruption of functionalities being provided by the particular device and can become vulnerable to other risks too.
- Environmental Attacks: The best examples of environmental parameters are quite known to all of us like rain, snowfall, various forms of storms, etc. This can cause the IoT devices to lose their functionality and become vulnerable for other risks.
- Loss of Power: Devices that run out of power due to no backup or any other cause can result in DoS, even in cases where devices operate.
- Hardware Failure: These devices in an IoT network are the lifelines to the users associated with these devices located in a network. Therefore, it becomes important to avoid any kind of hardware failure under any circumstance. Such cyberattacks can lead to chaos in smart cities.
- Physical Tampering: Ensuring safety of the existing security controls in the existing IT infrastructure is very important. Especially, in cases where deeply embedded programmable logic controllers are deployed to operate, the robotic systems are integrated into the enterprise IT infrastructure. Thus, protecting those programmable logic controllers from humans is also one of the important priorities [53].

8.8.4 Security Issues in IoT

8.8.4.1 Applications/Services Security Issues

Attacks on the Cloud: Clouds are mobile in nature and data backed up in clouds can be accessed anywhere and anytime. However, clouds are susceptible to a variety of attacks, and accessing information can have negative consequences sometimes, especially in terms of sharing of sensitive information.

Service Interruption: Distributed DoS (DDoS) attacks are one of the most common threats faced on the Internet. This attack can result in interruption of services being provided by the cloud server as it becomes unable to respond due to the lack of service quality.

Third-Party Attacks: Positioning is an issue in IoT, and third-party malicious attacks can, therefore, access valuable information such as location to use it for illegal activities. As IoT chips are dependent upon RFID, they are also vulnerable to attacks getting private information.

8.8.4.2 Gateway-Related Issues

Gateway is an important aspect of network security as it deals with the fact how the data is transported. IoT and the Internet use a similar kind of standards. Following are some of the security issues related to it:

Wi-Fi Security: The most common wireless standard used to connect devices is Wi-Fi. It also faces many threats such as phishing, hacking, etc. Accessing is an important asset of a Wi-Fi connection. Not everyone should possess the authorization to connect to a Wi-Fi network, except the ones having the security key. In IoT, not every device has a user interface or keyboard. Therefore, a Wi-Fi network is at constant risk that a connected object in a network can access the unauthorized object in the same network. It is quite an important issue for IoT security.

Other Standards: Other present standards such as 3G and 4G also are vulnerable to DDoS, phishing, and identity attacks.

8.8.4.3 Device's Security Issues

Heterogeneity in Technologies: IoT allows all types of objects to connect with it. With heterogeneity, security issues are also raised. For example, there is no uniform encoding standard for RFID tag due to which access problems or errors can occur while reading. Tags and data also vary. Sometimes, data can also be incompatible and in different formats. This can lead to data destruction and privacy loss. Hence, all formats and protocols must be standardized to ensure better security in IoT.

Encryption: In the world of modern Internet security, sending information directly is like making a fool of yourself and the system. That is where encryption mechanisms come in place. Here, the information to be transferred is converted into a code with the help of a key. Many encryption mechanisms are present. With the advent of time, many safe and advanced encryption mechanisms have been developed to ensure data's safety, which is being transferred over the network. However, these classical algorithms are not suitable for IoT. The "things" were not designed to be connected in IoT but rather to do their natural function. This does not mean they do not need to be protected. That is why the term "lightweight" cryptography is coined, and algorithms with small footprints, low power consumption, and low computational power needs will resolve security and energy issues as well.

Trust Management: Trust is always an important criterion in all transactions. IoT is not an exception too. Exchanges in IoT also should come from trusted sources. However, IoT does not adhere to complex cryptic techniques. Therefore, the trust system should be simple yet efficient. Authentication must be present, and the user must easily login while having a secure mechanism present. The four-pin authentication system is easy to break and presents a weak security model. Therefore, the research challenge is to find a new authentication mechanism that is simple and secure at the same time.

Secure Routing Protocols: New protocols are required for WSNs in case of IoT due to its limited power and computing abilities where classical routing protocols cannot be used. It is important part of IoT as it is an important part of networking and attacks toward a weak routing protocol can result in the collapsing of network.

8.8.5 Exploits and Attacks

The main threats of IoT are listed later:

8.8.5.1 Attacks to the Physical Layer

1. **Jamming:** Radio signals are generated with the purpose of disrupting the communication signals. Wireless interference such as jamming is intended to harm and focus on a specific target. An attacker that possesses a powerful jamming source can disrupt the whole communication of attacked network. Batteries are also drained out to refrain from communication and transmission, which may also lead to DoS attacks.

2. **Tampering:**
   - **Injection attacks:** Injecting malicious software into the debugging interface of device causes network disruption and instability by spreading the malicious code across the entire network is a typical example of injection attacks. Thus, attackers may obtain private information by using such method of attacks in a smart home or city.
   - **Extracting security information:** There are kinds of information such as preinstalled encryption keys that can be stolen by tampering with the actual device drivers or the firmware.
   - **Duplication of a device:** Creating an exact replica of the existing device and using it to affect the actual working of the device to steal or destroy information is an issue. There are certain cases reported when duplicate chargers are used to charge an iPhone was developed to install a Trojan into the device software.

8.8.5.2 Attacks to the Data Link Layer

The most vulnerable algorithms in the communication stack are present in the data link layer.

1. **Killer Bee:** It is an exploiting tool specifically made for exploiting vulnerabilities of ZigBee and IEEE 802.15.4, which has made it easy to exploit using techniques like injecting traffic, sniffing, packet decoding, and manipulation. Attacks such as PAN Id conflict, replay attack, packet capturing, and network key sniffing can be carried out using killer bee.
2. **Guaranteed Time Slot Attack:** Guaranteed time slot attack is aimed upon the IEEE 802.15.4 superframe organization in beacon-enabled operational mode. These slots can result in the creation of weak points that can lead to holding of the frames by the attackers and using it later to initiate an attack against the network by disrupting the communication between a device and its gateway.
3. **Back-off Manipulation:** These attacks are specifically based on networks such as IEEE 802.11 and IEEE 802.15.4 networks. In this attack, a malicious device tries to interrupt access to an authorized device using the distributed coordination function.
4. **ACK Attack:** During the occurrence of eavesdropping in a communication channel, ACK attack can be launched by some intruder. It involves blocking genuine devices from receiving the dropped packet and then can mislead the sender device by transmitting a fake ACK from the receiver device.

8.8.5.3 Attacks to Network layer

Attacks such as flooding, spoofing, network sniffing, data capturing, and modification of DoS are common when so many protocols are in use. Attacks on the network layer of IoT networks are described:

1. **Black Hole Attack on RPL:** In this kind of attack, the RPL implementation of Contiki OS is challenged. Here, all packets that are routed through the network are dropped in a black hole, which may result in network disruptions. This attack is hard to detect as it is well disguised in nature and behaves almost similar to a healthy network.

8.8.5.4 Attacks to the Transport Layer

Flooding and desynchronization are the two most common attacks yet detected on the transport layer in an IoT network.

8.8.5.5 Attacks to the Application Layer

In this particular layer, the most common threats are faced by the client and server side running XMPP protocol. XMPPloit, a command-line exploit tool is used to exploit this vulnerability. This attack disables encryption mechanism during communication, Hence, the data transmitted can be successfully read and modified by during its transmission [54].

8.8.6 Classification of IoT Attacks

8.8.6.1 Physical Attacks

These attacks are basically focused upon the hardware components of the IoT system in which the attacker is directly involved. Attacks that affect the working of the hardware components are included in this category. Some of the main physical attacks such as node tampering, node jamming in WSNs, malicious node injection, malicious node injection, and physical damage have been discussed earlier [53,54]. Some of the other attacks that have not been discussed earlier are covered in the following:

1. **Social Engineering:** It is based upon attacker manipulating users of an IoT system to extract private information of the user. This attack is classified under the physical attack category, since it requires physical interaction with the IoT network user to achieve his goals.
2. **Sleep Deprivation Attack:** Sensor nodes in the IoT system are mostly powered by replaceable batteries and are programmed to shut down when are not being used. In this attack, the nodes are kept awake till they get shut down due the full consumption of battery.

8.8.6.2 Network Attacks

These attacks do not require any physical interaction with the attacker.

1. **Traffic Analysis Attacks**

    Attackers that can identify the information being transmitted from the RFID technologies. Attackers always first try to gain information about the host network before initiating any kind of attack. Third-party applications such as port scanners and packet sniffers are employed to gain such information.
2. **RFID Spoofing**

    Here, attacker spoofs the RFID signals to read and record the data being transmitted via RFID tag. Then, the captured original ID of the tag is sent along with his own data, appearing to be valid now to gain full access of the system pretending to be the original source.

3. **RFID Cloning and Unauthorized Access**

An attacker can create a replica of the RFID tag captured. Since the original ID cannot be duplicated, unlike spoofing the original and duplicate, RFID tag can be identified. In addition, absence of proper authentication mechanism can make the tags to be vulnerable, allowing them to be accessed by anyone. Thus, it is nothing but an open invitation to the attackers to read, modify, or delete data on the RFID nodes.

4. **Sinkhole Attack**

In this attack, the attacker creates a virtual sinkhole allowing all traffic to pass through WSN nodes. Such attack affects the credibility of network by being a threat to the confidential data and also drops all packets to deny them from reaching the destination.

5. **Man-in-the-Middle Attack**

In this attack, an attacker manages to control the communication between any two sensor nodes in a network, thereby getting access to confidential information, violating privacy, eavesdropping, etc. In such an attack, the attacker does not need to be physically present to perform this attack, whereas it is totally dependent upon the network protocols of the IoT network.

6. **Routing Information Attacks**

These attacks are just the part of the spoofing attacks resulting in loop creations, traffic problems, spreading false messages, etc. Examples of such attacks are Hello and Black hole attack.

7. **Sybil Attack**

An affected node known as Sybil node that acts an image of other nodes can lead to transmission of false information to the nearby nodes.

8.8.6.3 Software Attacks

These are the main security threats to any computerized system and network. Software attacks exploit systems using Trojans, viruses, worms, malicious software, malicious scripts, etc.

8.8.6.4 Encryption Attacks

These attacks are solely based on cracking the encryption mechanisms being used in an IoT system.

1. **Side Channel Attacks**

Specific techniques such as timing, power, fault, and electromagnetic analysis on the devices in an IoT system can help in cracking and retrieving the key being used.

2. **Cryptanalysis Attacks**

This attack's purpose is to find the encryption key being used by the encryption mechanism in use. Common cryptanalysis attacks known are Known-plaintext attack, Chosen-plaintext attack, Chosen Cipher text attack, Cipher text-only attack, etc.

8.9 Future Directions

An IoT system consists of three different layers, each having its own security vulnerabilities and attacks. To address this issue and protect the IoT system, a multilayered approach is followed to provide protection at each layer in an IoT system, as shown in Table 8.2 [55].

8.9.1 Scientific and Technical Challenges

It is predicted that by 2020, 6 exabytes of data will be transmitted every second on the global Internet, assuming that the number of IoT devices continue to increase at the current projected rate. Providing 24×7 access and high bandwidth will be one of the challenges that come with it. From adding encryption mechanism to the protocol redevelopments to adjusting low power and real-time automotive control networks will require extensive and expensive reengineering of existing systems. Detecting and providing services coming from heterogeneous devices will be an uphill challenge in the future. An area of study that has been deemed as one of the solution is a biologically inspired approach to tackle the upcoming problems in the field of IoT. Animal brains are well suited for solving the real-world problems, such as self-healing ability for networking applications, like cloud-based elasticity, virtualization, and multiple-zone data center availability. Models such as Simple Public Key Infrastructure (SPKI) have also been deemed as good for IoT. Common criteria defined a set of privacy qualities for privacy-preserving identity management. They are as follows [56]:

■ Anonymity
■ Pseudonymity
■ Unlinkability
■ Unobservability

The aforesaid challenges clearly state the importance of anonymous and pseudoanonymous identities to evolve with spatiotemporal variables. A single authority should not be responsible to allocate identities to the heterogeneous entities in an IoT network. In addition, safeguarding measures such as biometrics alone are not an answer, whereas the adoption of cryptographic mechanisms seems to be a much better prospect. Standards must be developed for protocols to ensure interoperability.

Table 8.2 Security Countermeasures

IoT Layer	Counterattacks for the Specific Layers	Counterattacks for All Layers

Physical layer	1. Secure booting for all IoT devices
	  a. Low-power cryptographic hash functions
		1. Risk assessment
		  a. Finding new threats
		  b. Applying updates
		  c. Applying patches
		  d. Providing improvements
		  e. Upgrading systems

	2. Device authentication using low-power techniques
	  a. Data integrity
	  b. CRC—Cyclic redundancy check
	  c. cheesum
	  d. Parity bit
	  e. WH cryptographic hash function	

	3. Data confidentiality a. Encryption algorithms like Blowfish and RSA	
	4. Data anonymity a. K-anonymity	

Network layer	1. Secure communication between the devices
	  a. Network authentication—challenge-response mechanisms
	  b. Point-to-point encryption for the confidentiality of transmitted data
	  c. Cryptographic hash functions for the integrity of the transmitted data
		2. Intrusion detection mechanisms specific to IoT systems

	2. Implementation of routing security
	  a. Use of multiple paths
	  b. Encrypting routing tables
	  c. Hashing routing tables
		3. Securing the IoT premises
		  a. Physical barriers
		  b. Intrusion detection alarms
		  c. Monitoring devices
		  d. Access control devices
		  e. Security personnel

	3. Secure user data on the devices
	  a. Data authentication
	  b. Data confidentiality; Encryption schemes for encrypting the data
	  c. Data integrity; Cryptographic hash functions	

(Continued)

Table 8.2 (*Continued*) Security Countermeasures

IoT Layer	Counterattacks for the Specific Layers	Counterattacks for All Layers

Application layer	1. Data security
	    a. Authentication; biometrics, passwords, etc.
	    b. Confidentiality; Strong encryption schemes (AES)
	    c. Integrity; Cryptographic hash functions
		4. Trust management
		    a. Trust relation between layers
		    b. Trust of security and privacy at each layer
		    c. Trust between IoT and user

	2. Access control lists (ACLs)	
	3. Firewalls	

	4. Protective software
	    a. Antivirus
	    b. Antiadware	

Securing IoT from a technical point of view should be our goal, which must include end-to-end solutions. Another grand challenge to IoT is creating a standard security stack similar to a network stack having standard interfaces and degree of assurance. IoT devices in a local network must be integrated with a higher-level web-of-things without any problem. A Web of Things (WOT) is where an IoT network meets the Internet and cloud.

8.9.2 Social and Regulatory Challenges

Data from different applications can pose a big social challenge of IoT. Data is so much that it might never be erased and people may lose their control over a time period. Therefore, it becomes important to store that data from different nationalities within their physical borders, so that the data is geographically near, their rights are not violated, and their right to privacy is not hindered anyway.

8.10 Conclusion

Currently, IoT is one of the hottest aspects in the field of technology. It is also one of the most rapidly developing and researched field right now. It has been a decade now, and it is a sense of great achievement that IoT has come so far in terms of reengineering and developing new and efficient methods to interconnect billions of devices by the end of this decade. This chapter has tried to discuss the breakthroughs made in the field of IoT, especially in terms of security. Using the researches that have been carried out in this field, security challenges of IoT have been classified to explain the security threats in a better way. Countermeasures and future directions that can be used to minimize threats and guide future-based researches connect billions of heterogeneous devices in a much efficient way than ever. While understanding the impacts of the security of IoT devices in future and ensuring their security, developing new technologies and standards helps to make this place a better world.

References

1. L. Da Xu, W. He, and S. Li. "Internet of things in industries: A survey." *IEEE Transactions on Industrial Informatics* 10.4 (2014): pp. 2233–2243.
2. R. H. Weber. "Internet of Things–New security and privacy challenges." *Computer Law & Security Review* 26.1 (2010): pp. 23–30.
3. C. Perera, et al. "Context aware computing for the internet of things: A survey." *IEEE Communications Surveys & Tutorials* 16.1 (2014): pp. 414–454.
4. M. Sain, Y. J. Kang, and H. J. Lee. "Survey on security in internet of things: state of the art and challenges." *Advanced Communication Technology (ICACT), 2017 19th International Conference on*. IEEE, 2017.
5. H. Suo, J. Wan, C. Zou, and J. Liu. "Security in the Internet of Things: A review." *Computer Science and Electronics Engineering (ICCSEE)*, 2012, pp. 648–651.
6. Y. Zhang. "Technology framework of the internet of things and its application." *Electrical and Control Engineering (ICECE)*, pp. 4109–4112.
7. X. Yang, Z. Li, Z. Geng, and H. Zhang. "A multilayer security model for internet of things." *Communications in Computer and Information Science* 312, (2012), pp. 388–393.
8. R. Khan, S. U. Khan, R. Zaheer, and S. Khan. "Future internet: The internet of things architecture, possible applications and key challenges." *10th International Conference on Frontiers of Information Technology (FIT 2012)*, 2012, pp. 257–260.
9. S. Yan-rong, and H. Tao. "Internet of things key technologies and architectures research in information processing." *Proceedings of the 2nd International Conference on Computer Science and Electronics Engineering (ICCSEE)*, 2013.
10. M. U. Farooq, et al. "A critical analysis on the security concerns of internet of things (IoT)." *International Journal of Computer Applications* 111.7 (2015).
11. D. Miorandi, et al. "Internet of things: Vision, applications and research challenges." *Ad hoc Networks* 10.7 (2012), pp. 1497–1516.
12. L. Atzori, A. Iera, and G. Morabito. "The internet of things: A survey." *Computer Networks* 54.15 (2010), pp. 2787–2805.
13. A. Cui, and S. J. Stolfo. "A quantitative analysis of the insecurity of embedded network devices: Results of a wide-area scan." *Proceedings of the 26th Annual Computer Security Applications Conference*. ACM: Austin, TX, 2010, pp. 97–106.
14. N. Sastry, and D. Wagner. "Security considerations for IEEE 802.15.4 networks." *Proceedings of the 3rd ACM workshop on Wireless security*. ACM, 2004, pp. 32–42.
15. G. Mulligan. "The 6LoWPAN architecture." *Proceedings of the 4th Workshop on Embedded Networked Sensors (EmNets'07)*. ACM: New York, 2007, pp. 78–82.
16. J. W. Hui, and D. E. Culler. "IP is dead, long live IP for wireless sensor networks." *Proceedings of the 6th ACM conference on Embedded network sensor systems*. ACM, 2008.

17. M. Durvy, J. Abeillé, P. Wetterwald, C. O'Flynn, B. Leverett, E. Gnoske, M. Vidales, G. Mulligan, N. Tsiftes, N. Finne, and A. Dunkels. "Making sensor networks IPv6 ready." *Proceedings of the 6th ACM Conference on Embedded Network Sensor Systems.* ACM: New York, 2008, pp. 421–422.

18. S. Kent, and R. Atkinson. Security architecture for the internet protocol, 1998. www.ietf.org/rfc/rfc2401.txt.

19. S. Kent. IP authentication header. RFC 4302, 2005. http://tools.ietf.org/html/rfc4302.

20. S. Kent. IP Encapsulating security payload. RFC 4303, 2005. http://tools.ietf.org/html/rfc4303.

21. R. Atkinson. Security architecture for the internet protocol. RFC 1825 (Proposed Standard), August 1995. Obsoleted by RFC 2401.

22. I. E. Bagci, M. R. Pourmirza, S. Raza, U. Roedig, and T. Voigt. "Codo: Confidential data storage for wireless sensor networks." *8th IEEE International Workshop on Wireless and Sensor Networks Security (WSNS 2012)*, October 2012.

23. N. Bhatnagar, and E. L. Miller. "Designing a secure reliable file system for sensor networks." *Proceedings of the 2007 ACM workshop on Storage security and survivability*, 2007, pp. 19–24.

24. J. Girao, D. Westhoff, E. Mykletun, and T. Araki. Tinypeds: Tiny persistent encrypted data storage in asynchronous wireless sensor networks. *Ad Hoc Networks* 5 (September 2007), pp. 1073–1089.

25. W. Ren, Y. Ren, and H. Zhang. "Hybrids: A scheme for secure distributed data storage in wsns." *Proceedings of the 2008 IEEE/IFIP International Conference on Embedded and Ubiquitous Computing*, vol. 02, pp. 318–323, 2008.

26. N. Tsiftes, A. Dunkels, H. Zhitao, and T. Voigt. "Enabling large-scale storage in sensor networks with the coffee file system." *Proceedings of the 2009 International Conference on Information Processing in Sensor Networks.* IEEE Computer Society, 2009, pp. 349–360.

27. A. Dunkels, B. Gronvall, and T. Voigt. "Contiki: A lightweight and flexible operating system for tiny networked sensors." *Proceedings of the 29th Annual IEEE International Conference on Local Computer Networks*, 2004, pp. 455–462.

28. I. E. Bagci, S. Raza, T. Chung, U. Roedig and T. Voigt. "Combined secure storage and communication for the internet of things." *2013 IEEE International Conference on Sensing, Communications and Networking (SECON)*, New Orleans, LA, 2013, pp. 523–531.

29. O. Vermesan, and P. Friess. *Internet of Things: Converging Technologies for Smart Environments and Integrated Ecosystems.* River Publishers, Denmark, 2013.

30. L. Atzori, A. Iera, and G. Morabito. "The internet of things: A survey." *Computer Networks* 54.15, pp. 2787–2805, Oct. 2010. [Online]. Available: http://dx.doi.org/10.1016/j.comnet.2010.05.010

31. H. Sundmaeker, P. Guillemin, P. Friess, and S. Woelfflé. "Vision and challenges for realising the internet of things." *Cluster of European Research Projects on the Internet of Things*, European Commision, 2010.

32. O. Vermesan, P. Friess, P. Guillemin, S. Gusmeroli, H. Sundmaeker, A. Bassi, and P. Doody. "Internet of things strategic research roadmap." *Internet of Things-Global Technological and Societal Trends* 1 (2011), pp. 9–52.

33. A. M. Riad. "A survey of internet of things." 2013. [Online]. Available: www.researchgate.net/publication/257957332 A Survey of Internet of Things.

34. L. Tan and N. Wang. "Future internet: The internet of things." *Advanced Computer Theory and Engineering (ICACTE), 2010 3rd International Conference on*, vol. 5. IEEE, 2010, pp. V5–376.

35. F. Mattern, and C. Floerkemeier. "From the internet of computers to the internet of things." In *From Active Data Management to Event-based Systems and More.* Springer, Berlin, Heidelberg, 2010, pp. 242–259.

36. P. N. Mahalle, B. Anggorojati, N. R. Prasad, and R. Prasad. "Identity authentication and capability based access control (iacac) for the internet of things." *Journal of Cyber Security and Mobility* 1.4 (2013), pp. 309–348.

37. D. Bandyopadhyay and J. Sen. "Internet of things: Applications and challenges in technology and standardization." *Wireless Personal Communications* 58.1 (2011), pp. 49–69.

38. O. Vermesan, et al. "Internet of things strategic research roadmap." *Internet of Things-Global Technological and Societal Trends* 1, (2011), pp. 9–52.

39. W. Zhang, and B. Qu. "Security architecture of the internet of things oriented to perceptual layer." *International Journal on Computer, Consumer and Control (IJ3C)* 2.2, (2013), pp. 37–45.

40. K. El Emam, and F. K. Dankar. "Protecting privacy using k-anonymity." *Journal of the American Medical Informatics Association* 15.5 (2008), pp. 627–637.

41. C. Liu, et al. "Research on dynamical security risk assessment for the Internet of Things inspired by immunology." *Natural Computation (ICNC), 2012 Eighth International Conference on.* IEEE, 2012.

42. T. Karygiannis, et al. "Guidelines for securing radio frequency identification (RFID) systems." *NIST Special Publication* 80 (2007), pp. 1–154.

43. Y. Maleh, and A. Ezzat. "A review of security attacks and intrusion detection schemes in wireless sensor networks." *International Journal of Wireless & Mobile Networks (IJWMN)* 5.6 (2013).

44. Z. Xu, Y. Yin, and J. Wang. "A density-based energy-efficient clustering algorithm for wireless sensor networks." *International Journal of Future Generation Communication and Networking* 6.1 (2013), pp. 75–86.

45. S. Agrawal, and D. Vieira. "A survey on internet of things." *Abakós* 1.2 (2013), pp. 78–95. DOI:10.5752/P. 2316-9451.2013 v1n2p78.

46. C. Qiang, G.-R. Quan, B. Yu, and L. Yang. "Research on security issues of the internet of things." *International Journal of Future Generation Communication and Networking* 6.6 (2013), pp. 1–10.

47. A. Patcha, and J.-M. Park. "An overview of anomaly detection techniques: Existing solutions and latest technological trends." *Computer Networks* 51.12, (2007), pp. 3448–3470.

48. J. Gubbi, et al. "Internet of things (IoT): A vision, architectural elements, and future directions." *Future generation computer systems* 29.7 (2013), pp. 1645–1660.

49. H. Rolf. "Internet of things–New security and privacy challenges." *Computer Law & Security Review* 26.1 (2010), pp. 23–30.

50. A. Sedrati, and A. Mezrioui. "Internet of things challenges: A focus on security aspects." *Information and Communication Systems (ICICS), 2017 8th International Conference on.* IEEE, 2017.

51. S. S. Basu, S. Tripathy, and A. R. Chowdhury. "Design challenges and security issues in the internet of things." *Region 10 Symposiums (TENSYMP), 2015 IEEE.* IEEE, 2015.

52. S. Suhail, et al. "Introducing secure provenance in IoT: Requirements and Challenges." *Secure Internet of Things (SIoT), 2016 International Workshop on.* IEEE, 2016.
53. S. A. Kumar, T. Vealey, and H. Srivastava. "Security in internet of things: Challenges, solutions and future directions." *System Sciences (HICSS), 2016 49th Hawaii International Conference on.* IEEE, 2016.
54. R. Billure, V. M. Tayur, and V. Mahesh. "Internet of things—A study on the security challenges." *Advance Computing Conference (IACC), 2015 IEEE International.* IEEE, 2015.
55. I. Andrea, C. Chrysostomou, and G. Hadjichristofi. "Internet of things: Security vulnerabilities and challenges." *Computers and Communication (ISCC), 2015 IEEE Symposium on.* IEEE, 2015.
56. G. A. Fink, et al. "Security and privacy grand challenges for the Internet of Things." *Collaboration Technologies and Systems (CTS), 2015 International Conference on.* IEEE, 2015.

Chapter 9

Big Data and Behavior Analytics in Marketing

Archana Singh
Amity University Uttar Pradesh

Jayanthi Ranjan
IMT Ghaziabad

Mamta Mittal
G.B. Pant Govt. Engineering College Okhla, New Delhi

Contents

9.1 Introduction to Behavioral Analytics

Behavioral analytics (BA) is an upcoming research area in marketing and business that exposes perceptions of consumer behavior on online shopping and social websites. It enables the marketers to learn the underlying pattern of user activities, interaction, negotiations, navigations, and dynamics (Even, 2014). The study is to map this data to the underlying user behavior, which is called . Business analytics not only answers the questions such as what, who, when, and where, but answers the questions pertaining to why and how. BA is a subset of business analytics that determines the how and why of the users using ecommerce platforms, web applications, and online gaming. BA uses the data captured from various sources, which is used by Google analytics (Habermann, 2013) platforms, etc. Traffic data from such platforms is recorded, analyzed, and compiled either by looking at the products the user booked or bought before or by time progression, i.e., the time when the user first entered the website and when he or she actually made its first purchase. Traffic data used for this purpose includes social media interactions, clicks, purchasing decisions, navigation paths, and marketing responses. The specific metrics used are the advertising metrics that include how much time was spent on site and the money spent on a particular order or click to conversion time.

BA has entered the commercial environment in a big way (Loller, 2014). Amazon is a world leader in using BA in terms of recommending additional products to the customer that he or she is likely to buy based on previous purchases from other sites. In commercial space, it is used to recommend products to customers based on their preference, and in political campaigns, it is used to determine the way in which a voter should be approached. Apart from political and retail applications, it is also used in banking and manufacturing sectors to help prioritize leads.

This chapter is divided into the following sections: In Section 9.2, literature review and research methodology used to prepare the chapter are discussed. In Section 9.3, behaviors to track at various stages and tools used to analyze BA are explained. In Section 9.4, applications of BA and the companies that are using the concept of BA are presented. In Section 9.5, analysis of various tools used by analytics is described, and then in Section 9.6 the future scope and conclusion of BA are enlightened.

9.2 Literature Review

Hsinchun, Chiang and Storey (2012) examined how companies such as Amazon, Google, and Starbucks in the U.S. have been using big data analytics and how the U.S. government has used big data. In the end, they have done a thorough comparison of how big data has been used by big companies and by the U.S. government. The main objective of this research was to signify how big data can be used effectively by the government besides their regular usage in other sectors. The author's understanding of the proposed seven challenges of big data and how overcoming these challenges can help in extracting valuable insights is presented.

Shahriar and Wamba (2016) presented an interpretive framework that explores the definitional aspects, different characteristics, types, business values, and challenges of big data analytics in the e-commerce landscape. Lekhwar and Singh (2018) discussed the opportunities and possibilities arising from the big data in retailing, particularly along with five major data dimensions data pertaining to customers, products, time, location, and channel. It explored the role of big data and predictive analytics in retailing and was set to rise in importance, aided by newer sources of data and large-scale techniques-Ilieva et al (2015)analyzed the capabilities of big data technology to solve the important problems in retail and e-commerce and proposed a new model for automation of key business processes in e-commerce through new technology. Uyoyo Edosio (2014) resented an overview of the unique features that differentiate big data from traditional datasets and the various technologies that make analytics of consumer data possible. Nam and Pardo (2011) discussed the requirements for a smart city and the important factors that can result in the success of a smart city initiative. They proposed a model based on tactical principles such as learning for human factors, integration of technology factors, and governance of institutional factors that can help in making a smart city. Chourabi et al. (2012) attempted to bridge the gap in the literature about smart cities. They proposed a framework that can help in understanding the fundamental concepts related with smart cities. The authors have reviewed different literary works and have identified eight critical factors and how the local governments play a major role in the rise of smart city initiatives. Zuboff (2015) described the concept of surveillance capitalism and its effect on information technology adaptation. For the analytics, the authors have taken into consideration the operations and procedures of Google Inc. as described in the articles by a Google chief economist. They introduced the concept of "big other" that offers plenty of opportunities and challenges in the markets through behavioral prediction and amendment. Accenture (2015) signified the importance of business analytics as a new means of capturing consumer behavior trends for marketing. The article pointed out how the consumer behavior is changing with the help of a few examples and has given three common elements—an analytical toolkit, an adaptive mind-set, and an agile organization—behind the successful growth in the industry. These three elements have been discussed along with examples of their application by various companies for understanding consumer preferences. In 2002, the U.S. Government collaborated with IBM, IBM Info Sphere Stream, and IBM Big Data for infrastructural support in an effort to develop massively scalable and clustered infrastructure to manage real-time data analysis. In the year 2010, Australia launched data.gov.au for public access (IBM, 2012, 2013). In 2012, Obama administration announced a $200 million "big data" research and development initiative. This was one of the most significant steps taken by any government to promote big data, which clearly set an example for other nations to show more concern towards using big data analytics as an asset for the public sector. During the Obama election campaign, a total of over $1.5 billion was spent and more than 1000 paid staff was employed with the objective of measuring everything that happened during the election campaign using big data analytics. This was regarded as one of the many factors that led to Obama's win. The German government announced a big data research initiative named "production intelligence," with the mission of performing real-time analytics on all manufacturing data.

The related work done earlier mentioned the usage of big data in all major international and national projects. The exponential increase of volume in data and its analysis leaves a challenge for the analytics. In big industries, such as retail, e-commerce, and government organizations huge data is produced and added on an hourly basis. It has been realized that the customer or user-related data is increasing the volume or size of the database rapidly. In forming marketing and business strategies online or offline, studying the mind-set or behavior of the customers is a significant factor in generating revenues. This chapter explored the big data behavior analytics.

9.2.1 Research Methodology

A state of the art considers BA as the central component in formalizing various marketing strategies. The data and information cited in this chapter were taken from various IT journals, experts, and white chapters. Few significant questions were prepared regarding BA, marketing strategies, various tools used, and BA applications practiced by the industry people. These questions were sent to experts and professionals through various emails and online discussion forums. The feedback and reference to reputed journals enabled to gather the relevant information in the context of big data BA.

9.3 Proposed Metrics to Track Behaviors

The foundation of BA lies in tracking the requisite behavior to produce desired results. The fundamental set of behaviors tracked by every analyst firm to complete the cycle of behavior analysis can be broadly divided into five groups: demographics, email behavior, relational information, web behavior, and offline behavior The authors have proposed the metrics to track the behaviors of consumers.

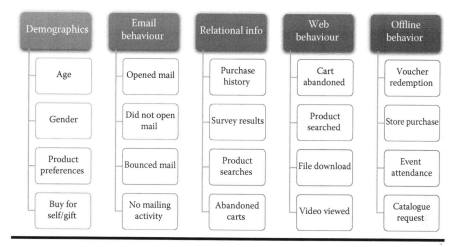

Figure 9.1   Kinds of behaviors to track (proposed by authors).

The metrics to evaluate BA of consumers purchasing products online or offline can be classified into the following stages:

Stage 1: Site Analysis
- This stage answers some of the key insights
- Number of visitors at the site
- The approach of using the site
- Website experience

Stage 2: Site and ad Optimization

This stage is fueled by web analytics to identify and solve the bottlenecks in optimized performance of site. The output helps in improving the structure and content of the website to fuel the conversion rates. Second, the advertisement allocation can be reallocated so as to attract the money-making customers.

Stage 3: Segment Targeting

This is the stage where behavioral analysis comes into play and remains an effective tool for stages 4 and 5. The optimization in stage 2 helps in converting the customers, but it needs more rectification as different groups of visitors have different goals when they visit the site. The behavioral analysis helps in identifying the important customer segments and the content required to convert these segments. Thus, this stage gives the following key insights.

- The customer segments that are most valuable, and grouping them is based upon the information gathered from their behaviors such as clicks. Content that is suitable for the target segment
- Leveraging the insights of this stage in optimizing other communications

Stage 4: Personalized Marketing (Online Channel)

To fuel Return on Investment this stage goes beyond group-level customization to personal-level customization. The BA is used to get information from the customers' past and current behavior. The information is helpful in the following ways:

— It gives the most preferred channel of communication with the customer and also gives the contents liked by the customer.

— The timing of messages that has to be sent for onboarding, cross-selling, or retention.

Stage 5: Personalized Marketing (Cross-Channel)

The behavioral analysis of cross-channel customers helps in devising strategies to engage with them across channels. The stage 4 output helps in this purpose to give the following insights:

— The best channel to continue the sales dialog with the customer

— The communication and its content required through a particular channel

— The timing to give offers

Some of the ways in which the visual in-app analytics can fetch useful information are as follows:

■ **Touch heatmaps:** The visual in-app analytics equip the developers with an ability to monitor the usage of apps. These are shown by touch heatmaps that are aggregated copies of the interactions made by all users. The touch heatmap includes tap, swipe, and pinch. The touch heatmap can be used to solve some of the complex issues such as "low conversion rate reason". For example, sometimes the user is not able to find the buy button and can tap elsewhere, which can lead to no conversion.

If you give users what they want, they will remain loyal to your app. Touch heat maps can be used to find such problems, and by rectifying them, user experience can be enhanced.

■ **User recording:** The companies can use user recordings for getting answers to some of the key questions in the app world. The questions spread from why customers stop using an app and how a loyal user interacts with the app to when and where the users were when the app crashed. These questions can help developers in enhancing the customer experience by rectifying and modifying the app.

User recording works on a very simple principle of recording the usage pattern of the app. This particularly helps in visualizing the app usage through the user's eyes. This allows monitoring the experience of app and problems faced by the app user, and ultimately enhances their experience by acting on the solution to the questions discussed earlier.

The example of user recording usage is that one of the developers found out that the users faced some technical error and hence abandoned the app. The developer rectified that error and the user started using it again.

■ **Real-time in-app analytics:** The mobile analytics tool does possess a great ability to process and generate lot of information, but apart from this app, the publisher depends upon the way in which information is presented.

Presently, the organizations have massive amounts of data, but they need strategies and techniques to collect, manage, analyze, and visualize in an optimal manner. The significant parameters or analysis that helps in tracking BA for data analysis and optimal visualization of data are listed in Section 9.3.1.

9.3.1 Key Drivers Used to Track BA

The following are the key drivers used to track BA:

1. **Key performance indicators:** These are used to predict the trends and factors contributing to success of each business event. These indicators could be financial or related to lead generation, customer satisfaction index, market share, or customer retention. These key performance indicators are collected and analyzed through some visual widget.
2. **Path analysis:** In this analysis, the company analyzes the complete path traversed by the user whenever the user enters or leaves the website. This can be logging in, adding products to cart, amount of time spent on jumping from product to product, etc. These events are tracked down through a single path and depict the progress the user makes as the time progresses.
3. **Cohort analysis:** In this analysis, user data is segmented into cohorts based on parameters such as gender, age, and geographic location and also on the behavioral aspects such as group of people who are on the same level in a game. Analyzing the segmented user data may form more meaningful inferences. This analysis is carried out for user retention and measures the trend that enables a company to improve the conversion rate and user experience.
4. **Funnel analysis:** It is used to find out the problematic event in the flow of events. It could be used for online gaming, e-commerce website or mobile app. It tracks where the user is exiting the system that has the effect of ongoing improvements.
5. **Predictive analytics:** It predicts the user's behavior in future using various statistical and analytical models. Basically, models are built and scores are developed for many business variables to assess the higher and lower effects on a particular attribute.

Broadly, there are two kinds of insights that can be mined from web analytics: aggregate-level insights and individual-level insights. Traditionally, digital marketers have mainly focused on aggregate-level analytics to improve the performance and effectiveness of advertisements over the Internet. Analytics is an incredible concept that can surprisingly increase the return on investment of online marketing expenditure.

It is crucial to understand that a lot of useful insights are still lying unexplored in the vast ocean of online customer and visitor data. One such source is behavioral insights derived after application of web analytics on online customer and visitors. If marketers are not leveraging this powerful set of BA, then they forgo a huge opportunity to improve upon their return on investment.

Web-enabled BA can transform online marketing by directly engaging customers, improving customer experiences, and increasing sales and custom and personal communication. There are firms that use web BA to improve their effectiveness on the Internet (e.g., increasing the click rate in online marketplace).

Many online marketplaces use web-enabled BA to provide custom recommendations of the products listed on their website to the traders based on their interests. Web-enabled BA monitors all recent searches, purchases, etc., to provide instant recommendations. This kind of analytics substantially increases the click-through rate on the website (e.g., engaging customers who were disinterested in a particular vertical).

Most banks use web-enabled BA not only to identify customers who left their processes midway but also to devise a multimodal communication campaign around such customers to reengage them and eventually convert them. Such a campaign not only makes the communication effective by removing information overlap and contact fatigue but also improves the loyalty of the customer.

9.4 Applications of BA

The table in Figure 9.2 lists the various application areas of BA

The analysts or people of companies investigate the behavior of consumers by understanding the methods of consumption, sentiments, and motivations driving a customer to purchase a product, not just who their customers are and their location. The companies attempt to answer "where and when" of consumers to "who and why" of consumers with the help of BA. Executives of the companies tried to answer a few questions about customers, such as "Why customers are buying this product?," "From where customers are buying?" "What can be offered to customers?" and "How can we add physical and mental welfare to consumers along with the product?" Companies tried to understand the needs of consumers, before it is developed. All these led to the growth of BA.

These companies always keep consumers in their radar to observe their shopping pattern, whether it is online or from stores. This answered the question "how" of consumers. To answer "why" of consumers buying and consumption, consumers were monitored deeply almost at all instances. These companies not only wanted

	Retail	Finance	Telecom	Publishing	B2B
Onsite behavioural targeting	Product categories or features studied, example: clothes colours, styles, and price levels selected on a fashion retailer's site	Products and educational content studied, example: IRA calculators	Service details studied, example: regional coverage maps	Content categories preferred, example: type of sports	Products and educational content studied, example: web pages covering technical details versus business benefits
Remarketing	Contents of abandoned shopping carts	Abandoned online forms for quotes or opening accounts	Cross-sell offers received by email or on the site, yet not clicked	Subscription options studied but not purchased	When online lead form is abandoned, capture company name through IP address, and target by mail, phone sales, or both
On-boarding	Bad review rating given after completed product purchase; or failed site searches for accessories performed	Missing or failed events, example: no or unsuccessful online registration, or failed site searches	Same as Finance. Also, missing click-through from marketing emails	After registration, visitors don't return to site, or read few content categories	Unsuccessful searches in the self help knowledge base or keywords used that indicate issues with using the purchased product
Cross-and up-sell	Products viewed frequently together	Account options studied but not yet owned	Available service features studied on the site, example: email access	Articles read in a category that the reader doesn't normally use	Products studied that customer does not yet own
Retention marketing	Fewer product categories viewed, less frequent visits, or both	Repeated reviews of loan payoff amounts	Review of contract duration period, or click-through from sites that compare competitors	Fewer content categories read, and/or less frequent visits	Reduced frequency of self-service logins to the customer support area, or searches performed in knowledge base with no results found

Figure 9.2   Application of BA in some key areas (proposed by authors).

to provide and improve the product experience of these consumers but also wanted customers to feel mentally and physically better.

Further growth in the BA is led by understanding different behaviors that drive consumer sentiments to purchase a particular product. This is evident from a recent survey conducted by Accenture, in which they tried to understand different consumer behaviors and sentiments from a sample of 10,000 online consumers collected from ten different countries. With this survey, they categorized behaviors that drive online consumers into ten different dimensions: experimental, resourceful, conscientious, minimalist, social, connected, disconnected, communal, individual, and coproductive.

Gaming industry has also seen a rapid growth in behavior analytics to improve the customer experience and their entertainment. The organization in gaming activation captured data of 250 million daily consumers and data on 190,000 with the help of an analytics firm. With this data, Activision tried to understand the in-game behavior of consumers. So, Activision developed an in-game BA platform, which helped them to enhance real-time gaming experience of consumers. BA adaptive real-time changes as per consumer preferences and compatibility in the game were applied. As a result, they were successfully able to improve consumer experience. This was possible with the development of BA.

Educational institutions have also seen a rapid growth in BA. Universities collected data through feedback and monitored the behavior of students at classrooms and in campus. With the growth of BA, these universities were able to improve instructions for students and match students to programs, and to employment and efficient system administration.

Universities collected data by monitoring online academic activities of students, quizzes, response times, sessions, questionnaires, interviews, and demographics to develop educational BA.

Few examples of the companies using BA are discussed in Sections 9.4.1–9.4.5.

9.4.1 CoolaData

CoolaData is one of the fastest emerging companies in the field of BA Alpher (2013). It was founded by Guy Greenberg and Tomer Ben Mosche, and has never turned back from them. CoolaData has always tried to do something different that reflects from their name. Coola as a word in Hebrew has a double meaning, which relates to the opposite side of the coin, i.e., "nothing" and "everything." That is, they could say that CoolaData deals with "no data" and "all the data." Functioning of CoolaData involves providing BA solution to the companies. CoolaData helps people to actually embed analytics in their system to resolve their queries. It is majorly in the areas of e-commerce and gaming companies. CoolaData offers to bring external data and customer's data together for the purpose of querying using CoolaSql (an SQL language extension developed by the company). The company also quotes that CoolaSql is free from coding problems and offers widgets that help to solve the issues by asking questions in English language. Screenshots of some of the widgets are given later.

9.4.2 Infinite Analytics

Like opportunity waits for no one, opportunity does not even inform anybody before it comes (Chaudhary, 2014). The same happened with Akash Bhatia and Purushotham Botla when opportunity knocked their door one day, and it was the cofounder of Taipei Angels. Change was about to come as was evident by the interest shown by the cofounder in their project. As asked by the cofounder, they sent him a project proposal pitch just to receive an amount of $90,000 after 45 days. Infinite Analytics got a financial boost to ramp up their activities. From then on, Infinite Analytics took on an elevator path and has captured nine investors in the past 1 year. The objective of Infinite Analytics is to analyze the information shared by people in their social networking sites and predict their behavior. Proper care is taken to follow the privacy law and give the information that is lawful. A tool, SocialGenomix, developed by them helps to create a profile with the information put on social sites. It can create a profile that involves age, interests, spending power, frequently visited places, etc. It works with a mix of social networking sites and online retail sites. As social networking sites are used to enter the online retail site, the information regarding the consumer is available, and it helps to suggest a product according to the liking. Infinite Analytics relies on the speed with which it produces results in 24 ms, and the suggestion is made to customers depending on his/her liking. From a hopeless situation, few years back to processing the information of 95 million users, 5.9 billion attributes have been processed for customer's engagement. From investor's satisfaction to customer's interest and finally landing to client's engagement, Infinite Analytics has excelled in all. At a place where small firms die soon, it has shown the skills to stand up and fight and actually succeed in giving others a piece of competition. It has shown it might be a small company but has big goals and bigger ambitions.

9.4.3 Fractal Analytics

Fractal Analytics can proudly say that it has become India's second largest analytics company as it helped P&G in their analytics approach towards the always increasing data problem (Bhat, 2013). It is proud to be called a strategic partner of P&G in handling their data. Currently, the company stands at the revenue of 120 crores and spans across 50 offices of P&G. TA Associates has recently invested 150 crores for the company, reasoning the benefits earned by data-driven decision-making environment the companies are working in. This data-driven ability will help to make strategic decisions. AIG is also approaching Fractal Analytics to work with them, but the story was not always the same. Fractal Analytics started its journey of big projects with ICICI in 2001, which required them to design a credit risk scorecard for the bank as a pilot project. But the time wasn't right for data analytics, and the story was to be rewritten with P&G in picture. They first approached them in 2006 with no results and were finally successful in convincing them in 2008 for a project worth $2000. The first project started in 2008 for which P&G sent 10 employees to work with Fractal Analytics, and now the strength has risen to 200, showing the 1900% increase in employee strength over 6 years. Other projects done by Fractal Analytics include developing a system to recover money from bad loans for an automotive company. Their story shows only one thing that it's not the big hotshots that could work with the big firms. If you have talent and trust in your ability, you can very well land among the best firms and beat them to reach the top.

9.4.4 ISD Analytics

ISD Analytics focuses on using Gartner's model to observe, predict, and influence the behavior of customer. They use the process of simulation to predict the trends. BA is based on three pillars of questions to be answered through a huge amount of unstructured data lying unlocked for value decision-making.

1. **Observe:** This forms the basis for valuable decision-making. It helps to understand the historical background of actually what has happened over time as well as the reason for such happening.

   Some of the tools existing for such data analytics are ad hoc database queries, OLAP processing, Solver, dashboards, etc.
2. **Predict:** The next step in BA is the prediction part called predictive analytics. It answers to the part of what is likely to happen based on the past observation. It is the forecasting phase in which techniques such as regression, predictive data mining, forecasting, and trend analysis are used.
3. **Influence:** It is the last and most crucial phase of the BA model. It answers beyond short-term future results to predict what more should be done to extract the maximum value of data. It is likely to find out the factors focusing the future and predicting what more in the future apart from simple forecasting in a unidirectional way.

These three steps together form the basis of how and what needs to be done in BA to extract value-based information from a huge amount of unstructured data present in the landscape.

ISD Analytics goes in a different manner and says that simulation projection's study is based more on what people are doing and not why are they doing it. This approach of ISD Analytics is known as Simulait. Simulait uses real scenarios to predict what people are doing, why, and where. The decisions are based on the external factors such as weather, marketing, product features, changing demographic information, environment, policies, and prices. ISD Analytics promises that without all these factors also, Simulait can guess the past consumers' behaviors easily. Simulait can be used in different industries to predict the behaviors of different customers based on the templates used for that particular industry. It can also help to prepare personalized data models based on the data about an individual customer, and all this could be done using a single template. Events could be predicted even before the customer could think of the same. It helps in managing the profit factors based on the study developed by analyzing the behavior.

9.4.5 Absolut Data

Absolut data is one of the biggest and well-known companies in India Phandis (2013). The company began its operation in 2001 and involves around 65 clients, with many of them being Fortune 500 companies. Currently, it stands at a revenue of $20 million. With offices spanning across the globe from San Francisco, Dallas, Singapore to Dubai, it has around 300 employees with an aim to take it to 500 by the end of the year. The journey began with the failures, with the first one being Globedecor.com, an online portal for home decor. The data-driven company began only after a hard work of data collection for 6 years and did not have any growth. The company then grew into a marketing analytics firm with only one aim in mind: to serve customers to the fullest. Side by side, they also developed conjoint analytics for determining newly developed product features, for example, identifying the credit card features after update to identify what needs to be incorporated according to the spending pattern of the customer.

9.5 Analysis of Various BA Tools in Marketing

9.5.1 Predictive Marketing Analytics

Predictive marketing analytics takes inputs such as historical data (sales, customer, market segments) and applies some statistical calculations and machine learning methods to make out the prediction. The following are the various popular tools used in predictive marketing analytics.

Tool Name	Functions
EverString	Figures out identical customer segments with detailed information about them and puts them together to convert into active customers. Useful in building account-based marketing
INFER	Scoring matrix and predictive models take inputs from various e-data, public data, previous rules, and keys. This data enables to identify potential customers.
Radius	Focuses on cloud-based predictive B2B marketing. Radius Customer Exchange ties the company profile with other similar businesses. Radius Connect provides insights about the sales team. Sharing of data among team members.

9.5.2 Industry-Specific Analyst

The customized solutions are prepared for the specific industry by an expert or an analyst known to be industry-specific analyst. IBM provides various industry-based solutions to the decision architects.

Tool Name	Functions
HALO	Supply chain management for business intelligence platform. It uses "what-if" modeling. Cloud-based, a complete risk assessment tool. It works in the real-time environment.
BOARD	Rule-based predictive modeling, plugging in cloud, OLAP, ERP, flat files to produce results without remodeling. It's a realtime updating dashboard. Best used in retail, logistics, banking, manufacturing sectors, etc.
Statistica	Provides parallel BI, Business Intelligence tools and learning patterns, applies contextual rules, predicts customer behavior, and explores new business openings. Most popular in detecting fraud and risk in financial sectors.

9.5.3 Data Scientist/Analytics

Data analytics deals with unstructured, semi structured-, and structured data. The process involves the preprocessing of data to extract information. The analytics have been used in the industry to enable the organization for efficient decision-making.

Tool's Name	Functions
SAS Advanced Analytics	It has 33% market usage. Its visual feature is quite prominent. Code-based analytics. It has visualization, mapping automatic process, and time-based rules. Most useful in large datasets and online help available in the software.
Rapid Miner Studio	It associates data preparation and analysis with custom business deployment. It has the flexibility in terms of extension. Best used for automated reporting system and for visualization.
SPSS	Predictive models and visual dashboard. Based on linguistic and NLP (Natural language Processing) technology to include social media. Majorly used for CRM, clusters, and regression models.
SAP HANA	It featured big dataset visualization, It is cloud based. It has Predictive Analytics Libraries. Majorly used in customer-centric industries to learn and predict BA. Popular in social media analytics. An R code compatible software.

9.6 Future of BA and Conclusion

We have seen a shift from a brick-and-mortar mode of business to a digital mode of doing business. It has fundamentally transformed the way business is done. In the old brick-and-mortar model, the sellers were able to observe the buyers directly, but the same is just not possible in the digital model. These direct interactions made it possible to identify minor changes in the customer behavior and intentions, which was used to make instant changes in the selling strategy. This facility just doesn't exist in the online world, because the binary world seemed to be flat and featureless to identify such subtle changes.

It is this gap that web-enabled BA fills. In the future, it will be used to achieve the following marketing-related objectives.

- To learn the decision-making process of an individual
- Customize the marketing campaigns
- To predict the difference between the want and demand of a person
- To distinguish between an online visitor and a potential customer
- To predict the switching behavior (between product and services) of customers

The concept of web-enabled BA is broadly restricted to online or digital marketing at present. In the future, the scope will be widened to address a whole lot of other issues.

9.7 Conclusion

The field of web-enabled BA is in the nascent stage. Gradually, it will come out from its closet of marketing and spread into other sectors such as retail, finance, fraud, and security. The chapter discussed about BA and various metrics to track BA of consumers purchasing products online and offline. Companies such as Amazon, Google, CoolaData, and ISD Analytics are rigorously using BA to develop effective marketing strategies. The applications of BA in some key areas help in promoting business. Thus, the growth of BA could bring breakthroughs into Internet marketing and advertising. Companies could apply different marketing strategies to consumers who possess different behaviors and pitch them differently. However, as has been the case with such advances in technology; it has to go through more stringent information and data security rules and regulations that will soon be transformed in a drastic way to protect the privacy of Internet users (e.g., manipulation of behavior of Facebook users), which has become a concern specially after the invasion of mobile Internet devices.

References

Accenture. (2013, June). A new path to growth stay ahead of changing consumer behavior-marketing. www.accenture.com/in-en/insight-outlook-new-path-to-growth-stay-ahead-of-changing-consumer-behavior-marketing.

Alpher, D. (2013, Oct 22). CoolaData closes $7.5m series a round for big data analytics as a service. Retrieved Aug 26, 2014, from Yahoo Finance! http://finance.yahoo.com/news/cooladata-closes-7-5m-series-120000655.html.

Akter, S. & Wamba, S.F. (2016). *Electron Markets* 26: 173. DOI: https://doi.org/10.1007/s12525-016-0219-0.

Bhat, S. (2013, Nov 15). Fractal analytics: India's second-largest analytics firm. *Forbes, India* www.forbesindia.com/article/work-in-progress/fractal-analytics-indias-secondlargest-analytics-firm/36445/1.

Chaudhary, D. (2014, Jun 13). Infinite Analytics: Small company, big data, bigger ambition. *Forbes, India.* www.forbesindia.com/article/work-in-progress/infinite-analytics-small-company-big-data-bigger-ambition/37918/1.

Chourabi, H., Nam, T., Walker, S., Gil-Garcia, J. R., Mellouli, S., Nahon, K., & Scholl, H. J. (2012, Jan). Understanding smart cities: An integrative framework. In System Science (HICSS), 2012 45th Hawaii International Conference on (pp. 2289–2297). IEEE.

Even, A. (2014, Jan). Understanding user behavior via visual in-app analytics. Retrieved Aug 20, 2014, from Online Behavior: http://online-behavior.com/analytics/in-app-analytics.

Experfy. (2014, June 21). Big data and the transformation of the gaming industry. Retrieved Aug 22, 2014, from www.experfy.com/blog/big-data-transformation-gaming-industry/.

Fiorletta, A. (2015, Sep 18) *Analytics Optimization: Spotlighting Trends and Success Stories.* New Jersey: Retail Touchpoints.

Forbes. (2014). Big data analytics and the future of marketing sales. Retrieved from www.forbes.com/sites/mckinsey/2013/07/22/big-data-analytics-and-the-future-of-marketing-sales/#1b169295587d.

Ha, A. (2014, Feb 6). CoolaData takes its behavior-focused analytics platform out of beta. Retrieved Aug 26, 2014, from Tech Crunch: http://techcrunch.com/2014/02/06/cooladata-general-availability/.

Habermann, G. (2013, June 27). My top 5 most used custom reports in Google analytics. Search Engine Watch.

Hsinchun, C., Chiang, R. H. L., & Storey, V. C. (2012, December). Business Intelligence and Analytics: From Big Data to Big Impact, *MIS Quarterly*, 36 (4): 1165–1188.

IBM. (2012, Aug). Big data analytics for video, mobile, and social game monetization. Retrieved Aug 22, 2014, from www.ibm.com/developerworks/library/ba-big-data-gaming/.

IBM Corporation Software Group. (2013, Feb). Oh behave! How behavioral analytics fuels more personalized marketing from Thoughts Leadership white paper, IBM, http://hosteddocs.ittoolbox.com/OhBehave.PDF.

ISDAnalytics. (n.d.). Simulation's role in analytics and big data. Retrieved from www.isdanalytics.com/index.php?option=com_content&task=view&id=70&Itemid=69.

Ilieva, G., Yankova, T., & Klisarova, S. (2015). Big Data Based System Model of Electronic Commerce, *Trakia Journal of Sciences*, 13(Suppl. 1).

Lekhwar, S. & Singh, A. (2018). Big Data Analytics in Retail. In *International Conference on Information and Communication Technology for Intelligent Systems*, April 06–07, 2018, Hotel Pride Plaza, Ahmedabad, India, Springer.

Loller, B. (2014, May 29). Five tips for using behavioural analytics to combat fraud. Retrieved Aug 20, 2014, from Econsultancy: https://econsultancy.com/blog/64919-five-tips-for-using-behavioural-analytics-to-combat-fraud#i.ubbfz6476degtu

Nam, T. & Pardo, T. A. (2011, June). Conceptualizing smart city with dimensions of technology, people, and institutions. In *Proceedings of the 12th Annual International Digital Government Research Conference: Digital Government Innovation in Challenging Times* (pp. 282–291), ACM.

Phadnis, S. (2013, Feb 13). How data analytics company absolutData grew despite setbacks. *The Times of India*.

Predictive Analytics 101. (n.d.). Predictive Analytics. Retrieved Aug 26, 2014, from http://practicalanalytics.wordpress.com/predictive-analytics-101/.

The P&C customer rediscovered through analytics. (2012, Sep 13). Bain & Company. Retrieved Aug 26, 2014, from www.bain.com/publications/articles/the-p-and-c-customer-rediscovered-through-analytics.aspx.

Uyoyo Zino Edosio (2014, April) *Big Data Analytics and its Application in E-Commerce, E-Commerce Technologies*, University of Bradford, Volume: 1.

Zuboff, S. (2015). Big Other: Surveillance Capitalism and the Prospects of an Information Civilization, *Journal of Information Technology*, 30(1), 75–78.

Websites

http://technologyadvice.com/blog/information-technology/top-predictive-analytics-tools/
www.starpoint.com/index.php/analytics/analytics-by-industry
www.guardiananalytics.com/products/behavioral-analytics.php
http://mckinseyonmarketingandsales.com/nuggets

Chapter 10

Recent Trends in the Era of Cybercrime and the Measures to Control Them

---

Pooja Kamat and Apurv Singh Gautam
Symbiosis Institute of Technology
Symbiosis International (Deemed University)

Contents

10.1 Introduction

The recent advancements in technology have made mankind dependent on the Internet to a large extent. The Internet has found a place in our everyday lives in terms of communication, online shopping, storing data, online reservation, gaming, etc. However, this overdependency on the Internet has given rise to a number of cybercrimes. Cybercrimes is a general term wherein the computer is either a tool or a target or a medium of communication for carrying out criminal activity. This might include crimes such as phishing, credit card fraud, electronic hacking, distribution of viruses, and other such wrongdoings. It also covers the traditional crimes in which computers or networks are used to enable the illicit activity. Figure 10.1 illustrates the cybercrime cloud.

Figure 10.1   Cybercrimes.

10.2 Recent Trends in Cybercrimes

10.2.1 Steganography

Steganography is the art of hiding and transmitting data, including photo, video, and audio, through apparently innocuous carriers. Steganography hides the message, so there is no knowledge of the existence of the message in the first place [1]. If a person views the object, then he or she will have no idea if there is any hidden information; therefore, the person will not attempt to decrypt the information. Steganography is not really a new method, as it has been in use since the times of ancient Rome. It can be used in both positive and negative ways. Nowadays, steganography is being used in advanced ways for illegitimate purposes. The steganography process is depicted in Figure 10.2.

In today's digitally connected world, sensitive private information is transferred through various digital platforms for everyday tasks such as financial transactions [2]. It is therefore imperative for the users to be aware of steganography used for malicious purposes. The attacker may hide the malicious code within a legitimate looking file which, when executed, takes control of the target machine. The digital steganography application is used to steal sensitive information by sending the information to fraudsters outside the organization without anyone's knowledge [3].

Cyber criminals use steganography techniques to encode malicious scripts into pictures or crafted webpages to smuggle malware through firewalls into the system under attack [4]. On successful running of the malicious script, the control commands order a victim's machine to obtain executable code from remote servers, which allows an outsider to gain access to local files within the compromised network.

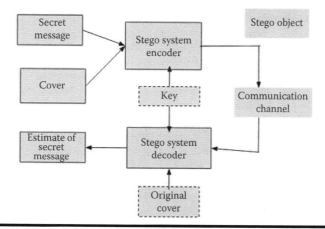

Figure 10.2   Steganography process.

The advantage of steganography is being taken by more and more malware authors in a number of ways, hiding encrypted information inside JPEG images and sending out of an infected network easily bypassing content filtering [5].

Recently, an exploit kit known as Stegano was discovered, which hid malicious code in pixels of banner advertisements that were put up on high-profile websites. In this malvertising campaign, malware authors hid malicious code inside transparent PNG images' Alpha channel (defining transparency of each channel) by altering the transparency value of several pixels [6]. It is then displayed as an advertisement on several high-profile websites.

Malicious steganography is not limited to geographical boundaries. The motive of this is to hide the malicious code to help it to access the system and break the security. Given the rise of digital usage, one has to be aware and careful of this trend.

10.2.2 Next-Generation Malware

Malware, or malicious software, remains one of the most pressing problems our society is facing today. As technology advances and there is an onset of new devices, new vulnerabilities and challenges in the security of information technology (IT) come along. The number of malware-related attacks keeps increasing day by day.

As the malware industry grows, more people are trying to find out the vulnerabilities in software and system configurations. Software vendors neglect security and validation of software for rapid development of software. They push security patches, but the upgrades are applied slowly because of the manner in which upgrades are handled at corporate level. The struggle between attackers and vendors is destined to be never-ending.

It is clear that cyber criminals have evolved adaptive next-generation malware that is capable of bypassing the defense systems used in many organizations. It is capable of sensing sandboxing environments and is mutating like a biological virus. The next-gen malware is becoming more aware and adaptive to evade behavior detection.

Malware as a Service (MaaS) is creating market for malicious software [7]. This service provides customers with access to exploits, botnets, and creation and distribution of malware. In a way, attackers are outsourcing malware service for a price. The market for malware is growing rapidly. There are many new ways in which next-gen malware is evolving to avoid detection. Figure 10.3 illustrates the MaaS.

First level: The elite individuals or groups are a set of general researchers who write malware and develop exploits.

Second level: These are spammers, botnet owners, distributors, and hosted system providers. These people are skilled but not always elite. Here, the distribution is handled.

Third level: These are fraudsters, middlemen, and financial data providers.

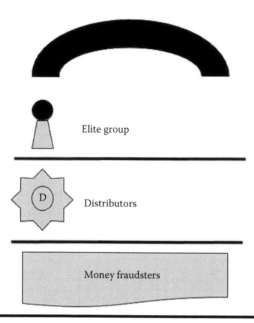

Figure 10.3 Malware as a service.

Source: Webroot Threat Blog.

These three levels fall under the umbrella of MaaS which can be sold and pur-chased as an entire package or individual services by a vendor.

10.2.2.1 Virtual Machine Awareness

Previously, malware could be discovered by sandboxing or isolating it in a virtual environment that would mimic a company's desktop systems. While they are in the sandbox, the suspect files are examined. If the file shows malicious behavior, then the file is marked as malicious. But an increasing number of attackers are creating malware that can detect when they are being opened in a virtual environment. If the malware senses that it is being opened in a sandbox, then it will disguise itself by getting into dormant state.

The malware does this in one of the two ways. One way is to look for any human interaction with the malware; if there is no human interaction, then it will presume that it is a sandbox and go into dormant state. The other way is checking for drivers like virtual drivers and entries in registry.

10.2.2.2 Polymorphic Malwares

Malware files are being morphed and mutated like a virus to escape signature-based antiviruses. The process is used by hackers to change some letters, inserting few extra bits, and recompiling the code to generate lots of variants. In this way, every time a file is presented, it looks different.

10.2.2.3 Encrypted Malwares

Malwares are being encrypted using suitable encryption like SSL (Secure Socket Layer), as it is not decoded or detected by network security systems, and thus hackers find it easy and effective to build communication tunnels between embedded malware and remote C&C (Command & Control) servers.

10.2.2.4 Sleeping Malwares

Malwares are also programmed to be inactive until activated on a specific date. It may be analyzed but is not considered malicious as it is in a dormant state.

There are many new ways of distributing malwares, and among those malvertising is widely used [8]. It is the prime target for malware distribution as most of the websites on the Internet are supported through advertisements. The attackers utilize this and spread malicious advertisements into large mainstream webpages such as of Forbes, Daily Motion, and MSN.

Each platform faces its own challenges, and it is really difficult to respond to any particular platform in the same way as for other platforms. Each platform is vulnerable to every malware category that is found on any other platform [9].

10.2.3 Next-Generation Ransomware

Ransomware is a type of malware that encrypts your file until you pay a ransom. The criminals provide step-by-step instructions on how to pay and sometimes also offer a helpline for victims who are unsure of how to pay in bitcoins. They design cheap-enough prices so that people pay instead of giving up. Figure 10.4 depicts the next-gen ransomware technique.

Ransomware is at the forefront of any discussion about security today, and we are sure to encounter even more advanced ransomware in the future. The basic process of ransomware is that it generally revokes access to the victim's endpoint or encrypts data before prompting the victim to pay a ransom to regain control. These ransomware attacks have grown drastically more frequently in recent years. It exploded into a billion-dollar industry since 2016. This high amount of money is creating a gold-rush atmosphere for cyber criminals who are releasing new ransomware variants into the market. Ransomware targets both consumers and businesses, but the number of attacks directed at organizations is growing at a more rapid pace. Every 10 seconds, a consumer gets hit with ransomware, and every 40 seconds, a company gets hit with ransomware. There are more number of attacks on a company as it represents a much bigger potential payday.

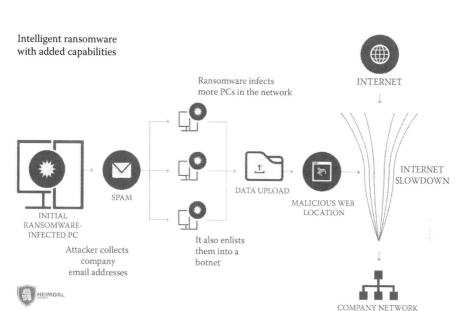

Intelligent ransomware with added capabilities

Ransomware infects more PCs in the network

INTERNET

SPAM

DATA UPLOAD

INTERNET SLOWDOWN

MALICIOUS WEB LOCATION

INITIAL RANSOMWARE-INFECTED PC

Attacker collects company email addresses

It also enlists them into a botnet

HEIMDAL

COMPANY NETWORK

Figure 10.4   Next-generation ransomware.

The fifth generation of ransomware is knocking our doors [15]. These future ransomwares may have the ability to detect any encryption protection tools installed on the targeted system. They may also try to disable the specific protection layer so that they can advance toward their malicious objective. We also expect ransomware attacks to be individually targeted in the near future.

According to security experts, ransomware cyber criminals tool in about $1 billion last year includes more than $50 million each for the three wallets associated with Locky ransomware, Cryptowall close to $100 million, and CryptXXX gathered $73 billion. Furthermore, it is getting difficult to track the amount of money flowing into criminals [21].

Everything is becoming a computer in this era, including microwave, refrigerator, car, television, national power grids, etc. All these devices are connected to the Internet and becoming vulnerable to ransomware and any other computer threats [16]. It will be only a matter of time before people get messages on their car screens saying that the engine has been disabled and pay some amount in bitcoins to turn it back on or pay some amount to get into your house tonight.

Intelligent ransomware are being created with added capabilities [17]. It allows the cryptoware to flood the outgoing network bandwidth both before and after encryption. This would enhance the threat. This attack technique could be especially impactful in large organizations.

10.2.4 Social Engineering Attacks

Social engineering is an art of manipulating people so that they give their confidential information. The types of information the criminals seek can vary, but when an individual is targeted, the criminals usually try to trick him or her into giving them his or her passwords or bank information, or access his or her computer to secretly install malicious software [22]. A newer method of social engineering has been in the market. The focus of the newer attacks is to penetrate a hoax that will cause recipients to respond in ways in which they inflict self-damage on their computer systems and then spread this hoax to different recipients. This type of virus hoax is often called "email worm."

Figure 10.5 depicts a typical social engineering lifecycle. It begins with identifying the victim and investigating his/her background. Research is then undertaken to identify a suitable attack method. During the hook period, the victim is further engaged and the attacker tries to gain full control of the interaction. During play, the attacker executes the attack and disrupts the business. Finally at exit, the attacker closes the interaction ideally without arousing suspicion and removes all traces of malware. The attacker then begins the cycle to identify the next victim.

Sulfnbk.exe hoax was a mistake made by a computer user. The investigation of this virus started when someone's PC was attacked by Magistr worm. This worm spreads itself through email attachments with executable files.

These types of hoaxes work because the information in it is really sounding enough to guarantee faith and that the sender is a known person. Those vulnerable to such attacks are individuals who have less knowledge of a computer and its applications. Most people with a desire to be helpful pass on the information without considering its safety.

Only such people, those suffering from what is classified as "false authority syndrome," fall prey to such attacks. The people suffering from false authority syndrome are those who think that they know about computer virus and spread false information about it but have no genuine experience.

Social engineering continues to be an increasing attack vector for the propagation of malicious programs. The attack vector is a combination of psychological

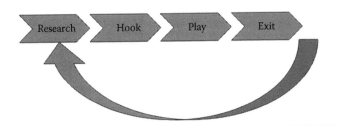

Figure 10.5   Social engineering attack lifecycle.

and technical ploys that includes luring a computer to execute a malware and also combining any existing technical countermeasures [24].

The attackers have moved their bases to countries that have less stringent laws that govern the mass mailings, i.e., spam. They infect computers in these countries and then use it to send out spam and malware to millions of machines worldwide [25]. As there is lack of detection and remedy tools, the computers remain infected for long periods of time and are used to spread the malware. Once the malware is spread, they perform two major activities in the infected computers: (1) they combat existing protection mechanisms, and (2) they continue to execute by opening backdoors or installing key loggers.

Social engineering malware have also succeeded in disabling antivirus software and blocking attempts to go to the Microsoft's website for patches of Windows systems. Social engineering is majorly used today to spread ransomwares. These ransomwares are intelligent next-gen-type ransomwares.

There are different types of social engineering attacks like baiting, scareware, pretexting, and phishing. Table 10.1 shows the difference between the social engineering attacks.

Even though computer systems are becoming more and more secure through better software development and testing, they are easily subverted by hackers using social engineering techniques. Technology and security policies alone cannot evade social engineering attacks, and they are useful only if adopted and accepted by people in the organization.

10.2.5 IoT and Artificial Intelligence in Cybercrime

In today's world, not only our computers and smartphones provide potential access points for an attacker but also other connected infrastructure projects in our homes and streets, which just takes a weak link to compromise an entire network. The number of IoT devices is set to hit 15 million by 2021, predicted by a security research firm Juniper [26].

Consumers and businesses are already reaping the benefits of these IoT devices, ranging from wearable healthcare devices that monitor vitals to intelligent heating systems. This wave in connected devices has created an opportunity for cyber criminals. Generally, IoT devices are built with affordability in mind rather than with security in mind. This in turn provokes cyber criminals to penetrate into IoT devices and thus increases the population of legacy devices that remain unpatched and forever vulnerable to attacks.

Automated vehicles are hackable as your smartphone can be used as a weapon. An estimated 1.3 million people die every year in road accidents, but after utilizing this attack, it could be used by black hat hackers for political assassinations. Major damage in the case of IoT devices is related to healthcare. Security flaws have been found in cardiac defibrillators, which could be accessed by hackers. Even hospitals are good targets for ransomwares, and these types of attacks will increase

Table 10.1 Comparative Analysis of Social Engineering Attacks

	Baiting	Scareware	Pretexting	Phishing
Definition	It uses false promises to pique victims greed or curiosity and steals their personal information or infect their system with malware	It involves victim being bombarded with false alarms and fictitious threats. They are deceived to think their system is infected with malware, promising them to install software that is malware itself.	Attackers obtain information through a series of cleverly crafted lies. Attacker starts by establishing trust with the victim. They ask the victim questions to gain important personal information.	These are emails and text messages aimed at creating a sense of urgency, curiosity, or fear in victims. It then prods into revealing sensitive information by clicking on links to malicious websites.
Attack vector	Physical media such as pen drive.	Browser of mobile or desktop.	People that are being lied to.	Email or SMS containing malicious links.
Examples	Attackers leave the bait typically malware-infected flash drives to be picked up by someone.	Legitimate-looking popup banners in the browser that will redirect to malicious site.	Getting personal information such as social security number and phone records by lying to the victim.	Email sent to the user of an online service alerts them of a policy violation requiring immediate action.

in the future. Cases have been seen in which hackers hold patient data hostage, directly endangering the lives of patients. One can only imagine what will happen if a hacker gains access to life-sustaining devices like pacemakers. This is a real scenario for which cybersecurity professionals must prepare for.

Machine learning and artificial intelligence (AI) have also seen a vast increase of cyber threats recently. Machine learning is used as a support for cyberattacks. There have been instances where the attacks have coincided with the travel dates of businessmen, which increases the odds of cyberattacks. Malicious machine learning algorithms could be made by cyber criminals to pick targets more precisely and with greater levels of success.

Cyber criminals are working on new techniques for getting through the security of established organizations, having access to everything from IP addresses to individual customer information. They can cause damage, disrupt sensitive data, and steal intellectual property. Hackers are executing their attacks in more sophisticated ways which are harder to defeat. It is really difficult for anyone to tell which type of attacks will emerge after 5 or 10 years.

Although organizations pay a hefty amount of money on cybersecurity software and services, the incidence of attacks keeps increasing. With increasing IoT, more entry points are being made, which in turn will increase the potential for damage. Hackers will use innovative techniques including IoT hacks, ransomware, and AI to launch even more attacks.

10.3 Preventive Measures to Curb Cybercrimes

Protective measures are necessary when these types of security trends keep on increasing. Different trends of cybercrime require different approaches to be taken, which needs to be discussed here.

10.3.1 General Measures

Protection against malicious digital files can be done by scanning PCs regularly for questionable software. One should not open emails or download attachments from unknown senders or sources. OS updates and patch downloads should be enabled regularly to keep the OS protected against latest vulnerabilities and exploits.

10.3.2 Defense against Steganography Crimes

The best defense against steganography is to prevent infection in the first place. A strong security practice would be active monitoring of system and strong access control to your data. Also, updated software, apps, and antiviruses should always be used.

10.3.3 Curbing Malware

Security researchers have designed next-generation analysis techniques that identify and neutralize malware. They block new and unknown threats and also grade the risk of each thread. New malware pieces are dissected constantly to understand how they operate. After dissecting malwares, security researchers create an algorithm that can analyze and recognize malicious behavior when it occurs. Every company and individual should know which hardware they are using and whether it comes from trusted sources. Education of users is necessary in preventing malware attacks, as many users do not understand the risks associated with the technology. It is necessary for IT administrators to vet carefully all applications on the network before installing on trusted devices.

10.3.4 Firewall

A complete network separation should be established between trusted and untrusted devices. Trusted devices should be behind a firewall IT policy should be kept in mind before performing any major changes in the system. A next-generation firewall software has been released by Forcepoint which adds support for the new cloud-based malware detection service. The entire department on an enterprise level should keep their system up to date with patches without compromising the functionality of a proprietary system. Figure 10.6 depicts next-generation firewalls.

10.3.5 Measures against Ransomware

With ransomware attacks becoming more prevalent, we should urge everyone to separate levels of access accurately and use different logins to manage your network's security. Everyone should know that ransomware only needs one administrator's credential to spread across the entire network. Network admins should

NEXT-GENERATION FIREWALL

Application based filtering
Lower administrative cost
Better QoS
Easier to identify threats
Identifying network traffic by user
Groups
Inspection of SSL/SSH traffic

Figure 10.6   Next-generation firewall.

focus on patching as a key proactive security layer. Traffic filtering should be used as an extra security measure against ransomware. More importantly, every user should be educated and be familiar with baseline cybersecurity measures.

A backup policy should be kept in place, and backups should be conducted on a regular basis. Backups are critical in ransomware recovery and response. Ransomware detection should be integrated in the data-backup technology of every company.

10.3.6 Guard against Social Engineering Attacks

Social engineering attacks are going hand in hand with ransomware attacks. The key is to recognize the threat. We should always compare the communication received with past experiences and industry standards before giving out any valuable information. Emails should be checked for online social scams. Every company should secure third-party services holding critical parts of your business. Consultation should be taken from IT administrators and security experts about countermeasures and monitoring process. Organizations should protect themselves by blocking suspicious communications with spam filters and by educating end users about security practices. Always keep an eye for typos, redirected links, and other tricks to lure innocent and unaware people.

10.3.7 Guard against AI and IoT Attacks

AI is used to perform cybersecurity tasks to stop cybercrime. AI identifies potential threats using machine learning by reviewing data from millions of lines of code every day. AI cybersecurity system will become a valuable tool for protecting against attacks using machine learning. More and more people should be educated on the IoT and AI security perspective.

10.4 Conclusion

The cybercrime landscape has grown in parallel with software and emerging technologies like AI and IoT. It adapts new techniques and strategies for targeting industries. The inherent cat-and-mouse game between cyber criminals and security researchers has existed for years with no sign of stopping.

Administrators all across the industries need to protect their devices from cybercrimes. They should focus on keeping OSs and security up to date and harden their infrastructure against open vectors of attack. Infrastructure security solutions are evolving with an increase in the threat of data breaches. Network defenders should stay aware of the new patches, security advancements, and state of cybercrimes to help them face any new challenges against security.

References

1. Kumar, Pramendra, and Vijay Kumar Sharma. Information Security Based on Steganography & Cryptography Techniques: A Review. *International Journal* 4, no. 10 pp. 246–250 (2014).
2. Navhind Times. Keeping Cyber Crime in Check: Beware of Steganography. June 28, 2015 www.navhindtimes.in/keeping-cyber-crime-in-check-beware-of-steg-anography/.
3. Kevin Lonergan. How Cyber Criminals Are Using Hidden Messages in Image Files to Infect Your Computer, Information Age. June 27, 2015 www.information-age.com/how-cyber-criminals-are-using-hidden-messages-image-files-infect-your-computer-123459881/.
4. John Leyden. Intruder Alert: Cyber Thugs Are Using Steganography to Slip in Malware Badness, The Register. August 8, 2014 www.theregister.co.uk/2014/08/08/malware_steganography/.
5. Pierluigi Paganini. Hackers Used Data Exfiltration Based on Video Steganography, Security Affairs. November 29, 2014 www.securityaffairs.co/wordpress/30624/cyber-crime/hackers-used-data-exfiltration-based-video-steganography.html.
6. Mohit Kumar. Hacking Millions with Just an Image, The Hacker News. December 6, 2016 https://thehackernews.com/2016/12/image-exploit-hacking.html.
7. Blue Coat Systems. Defeating Next-Generation Malware with Next-Generation Analysis. 2014 www.symantec.com/content/dam/symantec/docs/white-papers/next-gen-malware-analysis-en.pdf.
8. SentinelOne. Critical Features of Next-Generation Endpoint Protection, Part Two: Dynamic Malware Detection. July 13, 2016 www.sentinelone.com/blog/critical-features-next-generation-endpoint-protection-part-two-dynamic-malware-detection/.
9. Ralf Benzmuller. Malware Trends, GDataSoftware. October 4, 2010 www.gdatasoftware.com/blog/2017/04/29666-malware-trends-2017.
10. JP Buntix. Top 5 Malware Trends for Q1, The Merkle. April 1, 2017 https://themerkle.com/top-5-malware-trends-for-q1–2017.
11. Homeland Security. Malware Trends, ICS-CERT, NCCIC. 2016 https://ics-cert.us-cert.gov/sites/default/files/documents/NCCIC_ICS-CERT_AAL_Malware_Trends_Paper_S508C.pdf.
12. WeLiveSecurity. The Year in Security: Trends 2017. January 4, 2017 www.welivesecurity.com/2017/01/04/year-security-trends-2017/.
13. Kate Cohen, Michael Viscuso. Customer Case Study: Stonewall Kitchen Prevents a New Trend in Malware with Carbon Black, Carbon Black. July 10, 2017 www.carbonblack.com/2017/07/10/customer-case-study-stonewall-kitchen-prevents-new-trend-malware-carbon-black/.
14. Virginia Satrom. Forcepoint Advanced Malware Detection to Next Generation Firewall, Force Point. April 4, 2017 www.forcepoint.com/newsroom/2017/forcepoint-adds-advanced-malware-detection-next-generation-firewalls-0.
15. Morten Kjaersgaard. Prediction: the Next Generation of Cyber Attacks as Shaped by the Top 3 Evolutionary Trends, Heimdal Security. August 10, 2016 https://heimdalsecurity.com/blog/prediction-next-generation-cyber-attacks-shaped-top-3-evolutionary-trends/.

16. Larry Loeb. An Evolving Threat: Ransomware in 2017, Security Intelligence. 2017 https://securityintelligence.com/an-evolving-threat-ransomware-in–2017/.
17. Jonathan Crowe. Ransomware Trends and Forecasts, Barkly. February, 2017 https://blog.barkly.com/new-ransomware-trends–2017.
18. Tracy Rock. Ransomware Statistics 2016–2017: A Scary Trend in Cyberattacks, Invenio IT. February 27, 2017 http://invenioit.com/security/ransomware-statistics-2016/.
19. Jonathan Barkly. 2017 Trends in Ransomware: 5 Disturbing Predictions, Spiceworks. February 21, 2017 https://community.spiceworks.com/topic/1967355-2017-trends-in-ransomware-5-disturbing-predictions.
20. Bruce Schneier. The Next Ransomware Attack Will be Worse than WannaCry, Schneier on Security. May 16, 2017 www.schneier.com/essays/archives/2017/05/the_next_ransomware_.html.
21. Maria Korolov. Ransomware Took in $1 billion in 2016—Improved Defences May Not Be Enough to Stem the Tide, CSO Online. January 5, 2017 www.csoonline.com/article/3154714/security/ransomware-took-in-1-billion-in-2016-improved-defenses-may-not-be-enough-to-stem-the-tide.html.
22. Shelly A. Waltz. Recent Trends in Social Engineering and Hoaxes—Destroy Yourself, GIAC. 2002 www.giac.org/paper/gsec/2056/trends-social-engineering-hoaxes-destroy/103545.
23. Trend Micro. Ethereum Classic Wallet a Victim of Social Engineering. July 4, 2017 www.trendmicro.com/vinfo/us/security/news/cybercrime-and-digital-threats/ethereum-classic-wallet-a-victim-of-social-engineering.
24. Abraham, Sherly, and InduShobha Chengalur-Smith. An Overview of Social Engineering Malware: Trends, Tactics, and Implications. *Technology in Society* 32, no. 3 (2010): 183–196.
25. Tamlin Magee. Cybersecurity Trends 2017: Malicious Machine Learning, State-Sponsored Attacks, Ransomware and Malware, Computer World UK. January 2, 2017 www.computerworlduk.com/security/cybersecurity-trends-2017-malicious-machine-learning-state-sponsored-attacks-ransomware-3652298/.
26. Charles McLellan. Cybersecurity in an IoT and Mobile World: The Key Trends. June 1, 2017 www.zdnet.com/article/cybersecurity-in-an-iot-and-mobile-world-the-key-trends/.
27. EY. Cybersecurity and the Internet of Things. 2015 www.ey.com/Publication/vwLUAssets/EY-cybersecurity-and-the-internet-of-things/$FILE/EY-cybersecurity-and-the-internet-of-things.pdf.
28. Ulf Mattsson, David Morris, Mandeep Khera. Trends in IoT Cyber Attacks, Bright Talk. September 13, 2017 www.brighttalk.com/webcast/14723/260163/2017-trends-in-iot-cyber-attacks.
29. Private Tunnel. 6 Malware and Hacking Trends to Watch Out for in 2017. 2017 www.privatetunnel.com/home/6-malware-and-hacking-trends-2017/.
30. AT Kearney. VR, IoT, AI and Hacks: Digital Trends and Themes of 2017. January, 2017 www.atkearney.in/paper/-/asset_publisher/dVxv4Hz2h8bS/content/id/10960083.

Chapter 11

Electronic Wastage: Prospects and Challenges for the Next Generation

Sudan Jha
Kalinga Institute of Industrial Technology

Le Hoang Son
Vietnam National University

Raghvendra Kumar
LNCT College

Manju Khari
AIACT&R

Jyotirmoy Chatterjee
GD-RCET

Contents

11.1 Introduction

11.1.1 Background of Study

There is a huge increase of e-waste generation in the developing, underdeveloped, and developed countries and their surrounding nations too. Advancement and rapid increase in the technology and the increased economic activity lead to an increase in the production of electrical and electronic waste (e-waste). Since 1990, the growth in electrical and electronic equipment (EEE) production and consumption ratio has increased exponentially. As the technology is changing rapidly, innovation in technology takes place day by day, and hence the use of the technology is also rapidly changing in nature. All the discarded, obsolete, or broken electric or electronic devices are considered as e-waste. As per current estimates, e-waste is growing almost three times the rate of municipal solid waste (MSW) globally (Status Report, Sri Lanka 2014 cited in Samarakoon, 2014). Both white and brown goods are included in e-waste. Refrigerators, washing machines, and microwave-enabled devices are considered as white goods, while television (TV), computers, and radios are considered as brown goods. There is a constant replacement of old goods by new ones (Baldé et al., 2015; Borthakur, 2013; Carisma, 2009; Cherutich, 2013; Fleischmann, 2001; Ideho, 2014; Joseph, 2007; Kacheong, 2012; Kahhat, 2008; Liu et al., 2014; Mak, 2012; Naidu, 2015; OECD, 2014; Ongondo et al., 2011; Osibanjo and Nnornm, 2007; Pradhan, 2010; Queiruga et al., 2012; Shah et al., 2014; Sije and Ochieng, 2013; Sinha, 2013; Târţiu, 2009; Taye and Kanda, 2011; *The Himalayan Times*, 2015; Widmer and Pucket, 2005).

Technological advancement is not a boon all the time, and they have some adverse effects on the environment. They are hazardous in nature or in some stage of their recycled life cycle. The use of electronic products is ever increasing in all domains of life. Hence, the electronic and electric industry is the world's largest and fastest growing industry. None can think the life without EEE, but handling electronic device after their end of life is not an easy task. The production rate of e-waste is continually increased at a rapid pace due to the increased rate of use in all types of device, and on the other hand, higher rate of production of better product results in the product obsolete at a faster rate. e-Waste management (EWM) itself is a major challenge in a developing nation. Different initiative and methods are accepted by the national government of Developing Nations and the local municipal community. Private organizations are also appointed as stakeholders for management of solid waste (Fleischmann, 2001; Ideho, 2014; Joseph, 2007; Kacheong, 2012).

The study was responsible for the identification and quantification of the related products being imported and/or manufactured/assembled in the countries with the potential to contribute to e-waste. The consulting report was concluded with the statement: imports of electronic products are rising fast in Developing Nations as well, and the defectives are repaired until they are repairable due to lower purchasing power. The summary of recommendation is "Due to hazardous nature, e-waste should not be dumped together as MSW. Before it is too late, initiatives for proper management of e-waste must be commenced in the countries" (Kahhat, 2008; Liu et al., 2014; Mak, 2012; Naidu, 2015; OECD, 2014).

11.1.2 Problem Statement

As various literature stated, most of the electronic and electric devices contain high levels of toxic material such as mercury, barium, and cadmium that renders them hazardous when not properly disposed. e-Waste may not be such hazardous as the chemical waste, but they may be hazardous in some stage of the recycle process. There are no formal agencies formed in developing nation, which are working for the proper disposal of e-waste. Accumulation in the production of e-waste may lead to an environmental disaster if measures are not taken to manage e-waste in a proper manner. There are no such researches being carried out in the field of EWM in Developing Nations. According to the UN report on e-Waste Monitoring published in 2014, Developing Nations are lacking government policies to trace and handle e-waste and related matters. The following are the statement of the problem of present research:

1. What is the overall situation of EWM in the context of a developing nation?
2. What are the causes of e-waste generation in a developing nation?
3. What could be the major barriers of EWM in a developing nation?

11.1.3 Research Objectives

The major objective of this research is to investigate the current situation and practices in EWM in a developing nation. The focus is on computers and IT equipment, including laptops, PCs, TV, printers, mobile phones, and other major home appliances. The specific objectives are as follows:

■ To identify the current situation of EWM in a developing nation
■ To find out the sources of e-waste generation in a developing nation
■ To assess the barriers of EWM in a developing nation

11.1.4 Research Significance

This study focuses on the study of EWM based on the causes and barriers of EWM in the context of a developing nation. The reasons for this research are many, and some of them are as follows:

Very low amount of research is carried out in EWM in Developing Nations. This research will help to understand the current situation of EWM in Developing Nations. This will also help to understand the effect of different demographic variables associated with EWM.

On the other hand, this research will also help to determine the causes of e-waste generation from different sectors and barriers of EWM in developing nation. Management of e-waste is not an easy task in the context of developing nation. How to manage e-waste is the major significance of the study. To answer this question, four dimensions of EWM need to be assessed (Kahhat, 2008; Liu et al., 2014; Mak, 2012; Naidu, 2015; OECD, 2014).

Majority of the studies in EWM are being carried out in electronic manufacturing sector. The employees who work in IT sector and some agents who work under EWM projects identify the current situation of EWM in Developing Nations. It will also help to study EWM practices in developing countries and identify their barriers and challenges (Ongondo et al., 2011; Osibanjo and Nnornm, 2007; Pradhan, 2010; Queiruga et al., 2012; Shah et al., 2014).

11.1.5 Definitions of Terms

11.1.5.1 e-Waste Management

EWM can be viewed as the process of collection, transportation, processing, recycling or disposal, and monitoring of e-waste. EWM can involve specialized expertise and different methods of waste management to make it more effective. Management of e-waste is becoming more and more challenging as rapid evolution takes place in the electronic and electric technology. There is a lot of choice in choosing the electronic equipment, gadget, home appliances, etc. and the want for more sophisticated devices can facilitate more desirable functionalities. For the sake of easy handling and for new technology, customers frequently change their devices, which result in a high rate of e-waste generation. As the generation of e-waste increases day by day, the management of e-waste is becoming a tedious job.

11.1.5.2 Political/Regulatory Factors

Under the political–legal constraints of EWM, it includes some political and legal dimensions related to EWM. It consists of existing rules and regulation of EWM, government instability, tax system, and labor unions.

Similarly, private sector involvement procedure, performance-related pay, and incentives also come under these factors.

11.1.5.3 Socioeconomic Factors

Specific socioeconomic conditions prevail in many economically developing countries, including developing nation, which also include rapid population growth, migration to urban areas, lack of sufficient funds and affordable services, and a generally low-skilled labor force. In such circumstances, all economically valuable resources become a trade even if they are wastes of primary or other levels. Although somewhat old but highly relevant, according to the United Nations Development Program survey of 151 mayors of cities from around the world, the second most serious problem those city dwellers face (after unemployment) is insufficient solid waste disposal.

11.1.5.4 Technical/Institutional Factors

It includes lack of human resources at both national and local levels with technical expertise necessary for EWM planning. Another technical constraint is the lack of overall plans for EWM at the local and national levels. Research and development activities in solid waste management are often a low priority (Sije and Ochieng, 2013; Sinha, 2013; Târţiu, 2009; Taye and Kanda, 2011; The Himalayan Times, 2015; Widmer and Pucket, 2005).

11.1.5.5 e-Waste Production/Disposal

Under this topic, most of the ways of e-waste generation are considered. The main concern is to identify the source of e-waste generation. Consumers are considered as the main source of e-waste generator, as they discard the electronic and electrical equipment, and as a consequence, the volume of e-waste increases. Besides consumers, manufacturer, importer, and retailer are also considered as the generator of e-waste. They have their share in generating e-waste. Either they may generate e-waste by manufacturing the e-material or they may turn the electronic device to an unusable condition. Both of them contribute in e-waste generation. On the other hand, most of the entities that take action toward the management and disposal of e-waste are considered. They have a share in the management, recycle, and disposal of e-waste. All e-waste collectors fall under this group.

Thus, to manage e-waste, one should develop and impose proper rules and regulations over socioeconomic factors, e-waste producing factors, and e-waste disposal factors.

11.2 Components and Hazardous Substances of e-Waste

11.2.1 Printed Circuit Boards

The manufacturing process of the printed circuit board is so difficult. Due to the complexity of the process, various wastes are generated during printed circuit board manufacturing. Solid wastes include edge trim, copper clad, protection film, drill dust, drill pad, cover clad, waste board, and tin/lead dross. Liquid wastes include high-concentration inorganic/organic spent solutions, low-concentration washing solutions, resistor, and ink. Nevertheless, some of the spent solutions contain high concentrations of copper with high recycling potential. These solutions have been subjected to recycling by several recycling plants with a great economic benefit for many years (Taiwan, October 2012).

11.2.2 Mercury-Containing Components

Mercury-containing equipment means a device or part of a device (including thermostats, but excluding batteries and lamps) that contains elemental mercury integral to its function (EPA, 2015). Under the New York State Department of Environmental Conservation regulations, a hazardous waste is a waste specifically listed because it contains certain chemicals that are harmful to human health or environment, or it exhibits hazardous properties, such as being ignitable, corrosive, reactive, and toxic in nature. Hazardous wastes from schools are most often generated in science laboratories, shop and art rooms, photography studios, and maintenance operations. Some of the hazardous wastes are solvents, alcohols, paint thinners, paints and stains, acids, bases, photographic chemicals, batteries, toxic metals, automobile fluids, pesticides, and lamps.

Universal wastes are hazardous wastes meeting certain criteria, which make them eligible for reduced, streamlined regulatory requirements. The following materials for disposal are hazardous wastes commonly found in daily life.

- Batteries such as nickel–cadmium, lead-acid, lithium, and mercury-containing button type
- Lamps such as fluorescent, mercury vapor, metal halide, and high-pressure sodium
- Thermostats containing a metallic mercury ampule
- Pesticides meeting certain conditions for being unwanted, recalled, suspended, or cancelled

11.2.3 Liquid Crystal Display

The Health and Safety Executive website notes that liquid crystal display (LCD) screens contain mercury within the Compact Fluorescent Light (CFL) backlights. Mercury is a heavy metal, and its properties are a health concern to humans as it has toxic properties. When a lamp (contained within the LCD screen unit) is damaged, it is possible for direct exposure to mercury vapor and mercury dust, which poses a high risk. The metal can vaporize at room temperature, and employees who come into contact routinely are not always aware of the risks. It is easily absorbed through the lungs and can lead to severe respiratory tract damage with the symptoms of shortness of breath, muscle weakness, headache, and fever.

Ingestion can cause burning of the mouth, abdominal pain, vomiting, and bloody diarrhea (Wikipedia).

Skin contact with mercury may cause irritation and burning with symptoms of redness and pain. Contact with mercury may also result in skin sensitization. Mercury eye contact may cause symptoms of redness, pain, and blurred vision, and in some cases, permanent eye damage. It is for this reason that LCD screens have been classed as hazardous waste and why the Environment Agency has issued a regulatory statement setting out the storage and treatment requirements for these appliances. LCD screens must be treated by licensed operators who have adequate mercury abatement systems in place, which are inspected and regulated by the EA or the Scottish Environmental Protection Agency or Northern Ireland Environment Agency (Google).

11.2.4 Batteries

Batteries in the modern-day world have become ubiquitous, in the sense that they provide energy for a wide range of products that are used across all segments, spanning from households to large industrial enterprises. They are also a major source of backup power for activities that require an uninterruptible supply of power.

For humans, both lead and cadmium can be accidently ingested or inhaled. Mercury, another harmful metal, can even be absorbed through the skin, although this metal's use in batteries has declined greatly due to laws and regulations that are in place (US Battery Act, 1996) to reduce its content.

These harmful substances permeate into the soil, groundwater, and surface water through landfills and also release toxins into the air when they are burnt in municipal waste combustors. Moreover, cadmium is easily taken up by plant roots and accumulates in fruits, vegetables, and grass. The impure water and plants in turn are consumed by animals and human beings, who then fall prey to a host of ill effects. Studies indicate that nausea, excessive salivation, abdominal pain, liver and kidney damage, skin irritation, headaches, asthma, nervousness, decreased IQ in children, and sometimes even cancer can result from exposure to such metals for a sufficient period of time.

11.2.5 Cathode Ray Tube

Under federal regulations, most cathode ray tubes (CRTs) from computers and color TVs are considered hazardous waste when disposed (unless they come from households). They are classified in this manner because of the presence of lead.

As stated by United Nation Environment Protection Agency in their site, CRTs sent for recycling, however, are not considered wastes as long as certain conditions are met. Used intact CRTs stored by collectors or recyclers are subject only to speculative accumulation requirements (i.e., 75% must be recycled within a year). Used broken CRTs sent for recycling within the United States must be stored in a building or packaged and labeled, and they must be packaged and labeled during transport. They must also comply with speculative accumulation limits. In addition, CRT glass processors may not use temperatures high enough to volatilize lead (Wikipedia).

Besides the aforementioned requirements, exporters of CRTs for recycling must also file a notice with Environment Protection Agency and obtain consent from the receiving countries before shipping the CRTs. However, exporters of fully processed CRT glass-to-glass manufacturers or lead smelters are not subject to the notice and consent requirements.

11.2.6 Health and Environment Hazard

The main environmental concerns related to the management of e-waste are the uncontrolled release of hazardous substances into the environment and the suboptimal use of recyclable materials. Incorrect disposal can be extremely hazardous for the environment and health. Documented health hazards include various kinds of ailments from coming in contact with toxins such as cadmium, mercury, lead, and dioxins and furans among others, emitted during landfilling or incineration. Recycling e-waste is also dangerous, and care needs to be taken to prevent emissions and effluents from processing.

Electronic equipment contains a combination of highly toxic substances, and improper handling of e-waste raises many issues related to human health and environment. Lead and cadmium contained in CRT monitors may leach to groundwater after dumping, while brominated flame retardants used in the plastic protection casing and printed boards could spread in the environment if ignited. In context of developing nation and, especially, in Kathmandu, where landfilling is the only measure being implemented for solid waste management, it is of more concern because of the possible percolation of leachate of such toxins with degradable organic material in the landfills through soil to ground and surface water. Researchers have found that toxic metals and organic compounds can be released from e-waste, causing irreversible damages such as contamination of the food chain with its toxic substances, which eventually transfers to humans causing respiratory and reproductive problems and even cancer.

More direct route for such toxins to enter human body is during the primitive recycling processes, creating both chronic and acute health issues. Primitive processing, haphazard disposal, and burning of such waste release the toxins to the environment, affecting the quality of air, water, and soil. The presence of recyclables in waste from EEE (WEEE) makes it an attractive business opportunity for the informal sectors while the improper practice of recycling poses great risks to human health and environment. If WEEE is disposed of or recycled without scientific measures, there cause predictable negative impacts on the environment and human health.

11.2.7 e-Waste Management

EWM can be viewed as a process of collection, transportation, processing, recycling, or disposal and monitoring of e-waste. EWM can involve the specialized expertise and different methods of waste management to make it more effective. Managing e-waste is becoming more and more challenging as rapid evolvement takes place in the electronic and electric technology. There is lot of choice in the electronic equipment, gadget, home appliances, etc. and the want for more sophisticated devices can facilitate more desirable functionalities. For the sake of easy handling and for new technology customer frequently changes the devices, which results in a high rate of e-waste generation. As the generation of e-waste increases day by day, the management of e-waste is becoming a tedious job.

Apart from recycling e-waste, reduction of e-waste should also be a priority because the manufacture of these products is extremely resource intensive. A recent study showed that the manufacturer of one desktop computer required 240 kg of fossil fuels, 22 kg of chemicals, and at least 1500 L of water.

11.2.8 e-Waste Handling and Separation, Storage, and Processing at the Source

To make the management of e-waste easy, we can introduce the methods that assist the consumer in identification of e-waste, separate them, store them, and process them if that is applicable at the source of waste generation.

Management of e-waste is not as straightforward as other waste streams (organic waste, for example) because of the compositional complexity in terms of materials used in the electronic products and toxic substances they contain. Due to the lack of capacity for handling and recycling the heterogeneous and hazardous materials, e-waste is growing as the "next" environmental threat, especially in countries like ours, where there is no infrastructure in place even for MSW management or recycling of common materials like plastic, paper, and glass. This leads to disposal of WEEE with municipal waste in dumpsites, thereby polluting the environment and creating health risks to the nearby community and the population at large.

11.2.9 Collection of e-Waste

This is another component of EWM. It states how e-waste is generated in a certain territory. Local government or the local community may introduce certain methods of collection of e-waste. They may introduce certain places for the collection of waste or they may introduce the body to collect e-waste and give the task of collecting and management of e-waste.

11.2.10 Storage

e-Waste destined for recycling may be consolidated and stored by the waste generator or another person before it is de-manufactured. The following management practices apply to storage and consolidation of e-waste:

- Store e-waste in a way that protects it from the weather and from breakage
- Store e-waste in an area that is inaccessible to the public
- Label waste containers to identify the contents
- Store e-waste on-site for no longer than one year
- Train employees who handle e-waste to prevent breakage and how to safely clean up any breakage that occurs

11.2.11 Reuse

Though e-waste is a huge problem, it begins with each one of us. So think twice before discarding your old PC or mobile phone. There are many uses for your PC. For starters, if your PC or laptop is in a reasonably good condition, you can give it to those in need. You can even donate it to local municipal schools or non-government organizations (NGO). Alternatively, you can also use the hard drive from your old PC as a server to back up your data. If peripherals like keyboard, mouse, speakers, printers, scanners, etc. are in fairly good condition, you can sell them on online sites like sastobazar.com. You can sell your old mobile phone, MP3 player, DVD player, digital camera, TV, etc. using another online shop or give them away. Your discarded devices may the fulfill requirements of others.

11.2.12 Transportation of e-Waste

Once e-waste is collected, it should be transported to the place where it can be recycled or disposed. This function may be carried out either by the government agencies or private agencies that are working for the management of e-waste.

11.2.13 Export

Leading brands like HCL, HP, Nokia, Samsung, Sony Ericsson, Wipro, Dell, and IBM have taken up recycling initiatives. You can contact them or drop off your computers/handsets at their authorized collection centers from where they will be transported to be recycled. For instance, you can walk into any Nokia Gallery and drop off your Nokia mobile, charger, or even battery in the dedicated collection box, and rest assured that it will be taken care off. To encourage people to opt for recycling, many of these brands also offer discounts on their next purchase.

11.2.14 Recycle/Disposal

This involves the actions that are carried for the recycle of e-waste and the final disposal of e-waste. Landfill, reduction, reuse, incineration, and recycling are the examples of disposal of e-waste. The use of electronic products has grown substantially over the past two decades, changing the way and the speed in which we communicate and how we get information and entertainment. According to the Consumer Electronics Association, Americans now own approximately 24 electronic products per household (EPA, 2015). Recycling electronics prevents valuable materials from going into the waste stream. Consumers now have many options to recycle or donate for reusing their used electronics. Many computers, TVs, and cell phone manufacturers as well as electronic retailers offer some kind of take back programs or sponsor recycling events.

11.2.14.1 Characteristics of WEEE

There are various types of solid waste, which may have their unique characteristics. Electric and e-wastes are the wastes with some unique characteristics, which require some special mechanism of management. They may have functional and material value. An electronic or electric appliance that is a waste for its current owner or user can be in various conditions, as in the following image that depicts an example of a laptop (Figure 11.1).

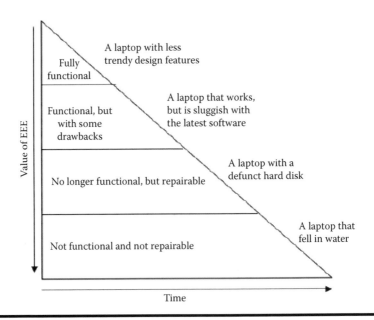

Figure 11.1 Stages of EEE.

The products from the first three categories have positive functional values and can be reused, for example, for lower applications or by upgrading a small component of the product. However, increasingly, owners of EEE are disposing products from the first three categories due to rapidly changing technologies and higher costs of repair.

e-Waste is considered highly poisonous, especially parts and musters containing proscribed substances. Therefore, it requires special management and handling methods. Most of the chemical wastes are toxic in nature, unlike it, e-wastes are not toxic themselves, but they become toxic during treatment and recycling. For example, an old battery, which is lying unused is not so much poisonous in itself. However, when it is broken and burnt for recycling, it emits acids, furans, and dioxins.

It is a very difficult task to predict the estimated quantity of waste flows because most of the e-product lasts for so many years. As Mathew (1998) suggests, the difficulty in estimating e-waste flows arises because it does not follow a straight path to disposal. There can be several stages between use of the various types of products that are been either reused or simply stored in basements.

11.2.14.2 What Is Being Done to Manage e-Waste?

As the technology rapidly develops, the rate of e-waste generation is increased day by day. With the increasing rate in the generation of e-waste, the task of managing e-waste becomes more difficult and challenging. National and international communities have realized the importance and urgency to adopt frameworks to regulate, monitor, and control the disposal of e-waste. Hence, several efforts on national as well as international levels are on the move to manage e-waste.

11.3 Theoretical Framework

Based on the review of recent relevant literature on EWM, a schematic image showing the theoretic framework has been developed (Figure 11.2).

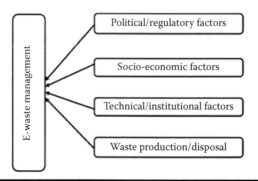

Figure 11.2   Theoretical framework of e-waste management.

Some of the unorganized sectors are active in EWM in the developing nation. There are wide variations in the opinions and solutions about the informal sector regarding EWM. Since there is no authentic information available on how many organizations and how much e-waste is actually recycled in developing nation by both the formal and informal sector, it is difficult to estimate the real economic benefits.

11.3.1 Governmental Regulatory Factors

Under the political–legal constraints of EWM, it includes some political and legal dimensions related to EWM. It consists of existing rules and regulation of EWM, government instability, tax system, and labor unions.

Similarly, private sector involvement procedure, performance-related pay, and incentives also come under these factors.

11.4 Research Design and Methodology

This chapter deals with the research methods that were used to collect the desired data to attain the objectives of the study. It discusses the subjects, data collection instruments, data collection procedures, and the method of data analysis used in carrying out the research.

In this section of research methodology of this graduate research project, the overall research plan and research design are explained. It also explains the instrumentation that is used to collect data from respondents. A detail of methodology also clarifies how data is collected and the time frame required accomplishing the data collection is defined. Identifying the important measures to check validity and reliability of data are also included under this section. Finally, analysis plan of undergoing study is another imperative element specified here.

11.4.1 Research Design

The research design refers to the conceptual structure within which the research is conducted. This study was undertaken with the objective of examining the existing situation of EWM in developing nation and its barriers. This survey research design was used in this study as it seeks responses directly from the respondents. The methods of collecting data from the respondents were through questionnaire and interviews. The respondents were requested to fill up a questionnaire.

Data are collected through surveys by means of physical forms. The designed questionnaire will follow the prepared theoretical framework given in Chapter 11.3, which was also adopted in other research studies related to similar topics in different countries.

The respondents were asked to answer on their own for the questions provided. The research work studies the casual relationship among the variables, which is exploratory in the context of Developing Nations' environment and quantitative in terms of data collection and analysis.

11.4.2 Populations and Sample

11.4.2.1 Population

The target population for this study is all those who are working in electronic sectors and some agencies that are working for EWM and the people who are using electronic items.

11.4.2.2 Sample Size

Basically, for the study of existing situation of EWM in developing nation, the study involved the collection of information from the different agencies of waste management. For the study of existing situation in terms of constraints they are facing, personnel associated with EWM of private and public agencies were considered.

The sample size in this study is not based on any kind of scientific formula suggested by different scholars. Sample size was estimated to be 180 based on researcher's comfort and required minimum level of respondents for a better research work. Among 180 questionnaires distributed, only 151 respondents responded. Among the total 151 respondents, few responses were collected from people who work in an IT company. Similarly, few responses are collected from the people who work in electronic shops, and some responses were collected from the manpower that is handling EWM in Sankhamul area, Kathmandu.

11.4.3 Nature and Source of Data

The initial parts of the study (background, problem identification, literature review, theoretical framework) are outcomes of secondary data such as previous reports, journal articles, websites, books, periodicals, and graduate research projects or theses. In this study, particularly to achieve the study objectives, primary data will be collected to address the issues identified. As explained in the sampling section, the respondents will be asked to fill the questionnaire to collect the primary data.

11.4.4 Variables of the Study

EWM is considered to be the main independent variable of the study. Dependent variables are political and regulatory factors, socioeconomic factors, technical and institutional factors, and e-waste production and disposal.

11.4.5 Instrumentation

For the study of factors of EWM in developing nation, the main instruments of the study were structured questionnaire and informal interviews. A questionnaire is a formal list of questions designed to gather responses from the respondents on a given topic. The structured questionnaire has been designed to secure the attitude and opinions from the respondents toward e-waste, EWM, and its barriers and challenges in the Developing Nations' context.

Measurement scales have been adapted to find the effect of independent variables on the dependent variable as shown in theoretical framework. The first section consists of demographics of the respondents like age, gender, qualification, and profession. The second section consists of questionnaire related to research variables to be answered using a four-point Likert scale. The questionnaire was kept short and concise for respondents. All the involved questions were measured using a four-point Likert Spectrum consisting of four comments spectrum (1 = Strongly Agree, 2 = Agree, 3 = Disagree, and 4 = Strongly Disagree).

11.4.6 Data Collection Procedure and Time Frame

There are many ways to collect information in a research activity. This research is based on primary data, and primary data has been used obtained through various sources. The researcher personally visited the leaders of EWM and gathered the information by physically asking them with all the queries regarding EVM in the context of a developing nation. Accordingly, the data collected through those queries, the researcher analyzed those data to test the hypothesis developed from theoretical framework.

11.4.7 Validity and Reliability

To measure the reliability of this study, Cronbach's alpha was used once the data were collected. This measures the internal consistency of data to reflect the reliability. Though the cut-off level of Cronbach's alpha has to be at least 0.7, which can keep an item in an adequate scale; in addition, a higher cut-off level 0.8 is expected to be achieved. Respondents were asked to confirm that all the information they provide is true and that they clearly understand the structured questionnaire. On the other hand, the outcomes can be compared with the previous studies to identify the validity of the model proposed. In addition, construct validity is used to measure the validity of the model, whereas variance inflation factor (VIF) and test–pretest is used to measure the validity of the questionnaire.

The overall Cronbach's alpha was found to be 0.71 (No. of items = 20) in the pilot test (Table 11.1).

Table 11.1 Overall Cronbach's Alpha of Pilot Test and Final Test

Number of Items	Cronbach's Alpha
20	0.71

Regarding the validity of the test and the questionnaire proposed, the model used is similar to several previous research studies as explained in literature review on the same topic. In addition, during the collection of information, feedbacks were also obtained from respondents. As per their suggestion, questions were framed in a concise and understandable manner.

11.4.8 Data Analysis Plan

Once the questionnaire was collected from respondents, only valid responses were considered for the study. The responses collected were summarized using Microsoft Excel 2013 and SPSS PASW Statistics 18, and all the responses were recorded in an easy-to-use format. The next step of analysis includes the use of different kinds of descriptive statistics of the study to explain the general background of the respondents with reference to study objectives. The major analysis part of this research is to establish the causal relationship among the variables used in hypotheses, either to accept the statement undertaken or to reject the same. Inferential statistical tools will be used to test the stated hypotheses that best match with nature of the data, basically, responses collected from Likert Spectrum Measurement. These four levels of agreement in Likert scale is a psychometric response of the respondents. For the easy analysis of data, being less than two shows agreement and more than two shows disagreement.

In case of hypotheses test under inferential study, mean of all the corresponding items of all the individual research variables was calculated and taken under the consideration. In addition, the statistical tools like Pearson correlation was used depending on the nature of the data collected.

11.5 Descriptive Analysis of Research Variables

Descriptive analysis of this research includes the basic explanation of central tendency, particularly, mean and variation of variables of the study. These variables were further divided into 24 measurable questions while collecting responses. In addition, the descriptive central tendency and variation of the 4-subscale was calculated to find out EWM in developing nation. Thus, this section consists of descriptive analysis performed to analyze measurable questions as well as study variables.

11.5.1 Political/Regulatory Factors

The effect of political and regulatory factors on EWM has been analyzed based on four different questionnaires. Out of these four items, Political/Regulatory factors 1 (PRF1) denotes that government initiation is highly present in EWM in the developing nation. PRF2 denotes that there is proper policy for EWM in the developing nation. PRF3 denotes that the developing nation has full support of foreign countries in EWM in developing nation, and finally PRF4 represents that the developing nation is following the international practices to handle e-waste (Figure 11.3).

It can be concluded that respondents feel that there must be a proper policy for EWM in the developing nation. Proper policy helps to manage e-waste in effective ways that is generated every year.

11.5.2 Socioeconomic Factors

The effect of socioeconomic factors on EWM has been analyzed based on four different questionnaires. Out of these four items, Socioeconomic Factors 1 (SEF1) denotes e-waste is environmentally hazardous. SEF2 denotes electronics parts may be profitably recycled. SEF3 denotes everyone should be ready to pay for e-waste collection, and finally SEF4 represents a promotional activity necessary for EWM (Figure 11.4).

It can be concluded that respondents feel that promotional activity is very necessary for EWM in a developing nation. Many of the people are unaware about how to manage e-waste. We can find many small groups of people who are working for EWM, but many people do not know about such kind of efforts and activities. So, promotional activity is necessary to make it successful.

11.5.3 Technical/Institutional Factors

The effect of technical and institutional factors on EWM has been analyzed based on four different questionnaires. Out of these four items, Technical/Institutional

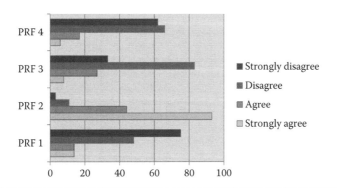

Figure 11.3 Political/regulatory factors.

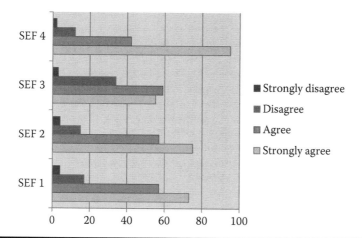

Figure 11.4 Socioeconomic factors.

Factors 1 (TIF1) denotes there is proper technology for EWM in the developing nation. TIF2 denotes every organization needs a procedure of handling e-waste. TIF3 denotes training facilities is easily available to reuse and recycle e-waste, and finally TIF4 represents there is a separate government agency to manage e-waste in a developing nation (Figure 11.5).

It can be concluded that the respondents feel that every organization needs a procedure for handling e-waste in a developing nation. If every organization makes the procedure to handle e-waste in their own way, the generation of e-waste could be minimized, and there will not be problems for the countries to handle a large volume of e-waste.

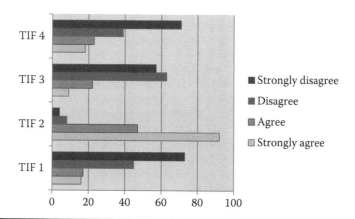

Figure 11.5 Technical/institutional factors.

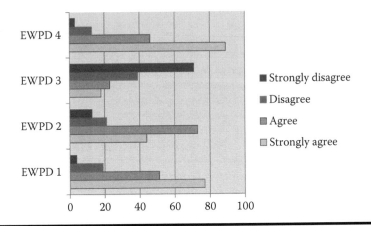

Figure 11.6   e-Waste production and disposal.

11.5.4 Waste Production/Disposal

The effect of waste production and disposal on EWM has been analyzed based on four different questionnaires. Out of these four items, Waste Production/Disposal 1 (WPD1) denotes that the volume of e-waste generation is increasing day by day. WPD2 denotes that discarded e-equipment must be sold or donated to others. WPD3 denotes that discarded e-equipment must be thrown away with other waste, and finally WPD4 represents that the hazardous parts in e-waste need special methods for safety disposal (Figure 11.6).

Due to continuous technological advancements, many electronic items are produced, and simultaneously, the items are damaged; thus, e-waste is generated. In a developing nation, there is no accessibility to advanced technology to manage this e-waste, and only items are generated, but damaged items are not disposed properly. Therefore, respondents feel that the volume of e-waste generation is increasing day by day, and so there is a need for a special method for its disposal.

11.5.5 Analysis of e-Waste Management

EWM has been analyzed based on four different questionnaires. Out of these four items, EWM1 denotes that I am aware about e-waste and its management. EWM2 denotes that there is a need of an e-waste collector in each area. EWM3 denotes that the current method of e-waste collection is convenient, and finally EWM4 represents information that EWM is easily accessible in a developing nation (Figure 11.7).

It can be concluded that respondents feel that there is a need for an e-waste collector in each area for effective EWM in a developing nation. If there is an e-waste collector in each area, it could be very easy to collect e-waste for the disposal, and

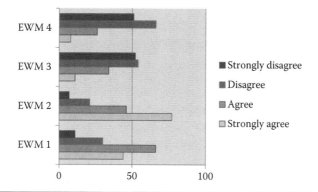

Figure 11.7 e-Waste management.

people will have no confusion on what to do with e-waste and simply they will go and dump e-waste in the collecting area.

11.5.6 e-Waste Generation

e-Waste generation has been analyzed based on five different causes. Out of these five causes, new products are cheap, malfunction during operations, outdated technology, the completed lifespan, and finally high repairing cost. From this study, it can be concluded that respondent feels that e-equipment is discarded due to the outdated technology.

11.5.7 Barriers of EWM

The barriers of EWM have been analyzed based on eight different factors. Lack of infrastructure, lack of organizational policy, absence of technology recycling possibilities, lack of legislation, lack of sufficient budget, lack of public awareness, lack of human resources, and finally, lack of political support. It can be concluded that respondents feel that lack of infrastructure is the main barrier to a developing nation for EWM. It is 100% true that a developing nation is lacking the infrastructure to handle e-waste in an effective way. Many of the institutions are eager to work under EWM, but due to the lack of infrastructure, they are not being able to carry out their projects in a proper way.

11.5.8 Inferential Analysis

Under the inferential analysis, hypothesis testing has been accomplished using the mean of all the items of each corresponding variables. The research hypotheses listed in Chapter 1 are thoroughly tested using the bivariate Pearson analysis. The study was based on a sample size of 151.

11.6 Summary and Conclusion

In the previous chapter, the data analysis and hypotheses testing have been done according to the objective of the study. This chapter gives a brief overview of findings and conclusion of the study. It also draws the inferences from the findings, which lead to generalization. Based on the study, some recommendations and suggestions for the further study have been mentioned. There are three sections in this chapter, consisting of a summary of the findings in the first section, conclusion of the study in the second section, and suggestions for further study in the third section.

11.6.1 Summary of the Findings

This study has been conducted to find the factors responsible for EWM in the Developing Nations' context. Based on the literature review, several factors affecting EWM have been recognized. Therefore, researchers recognized some of the relevant variables such as political and regulatory factors, socioeconomic factors, technical and institutional factors, and waste production and disposal. There are no such researches carried out in the field of EWM in a developing nation. According to the UN report on e-Waste Monitoring published in 2014, developing nation is lacking the government policy to trace and handle e-waste and related matters. During this survey, Civic Engagement Project was initiated by the members of United States Embassy Youth Council and supported by U.S. Embassy and Youth for Unity and Voluntary Action. It has been initiated with the aim to manage e-wastes from household and workplaces so as to make them reusable and provide those reusable items to remote communities, women groups, and the needy. The major objective of this study is to investigate the current situation and practices in EWM in a developing nation. The main objective of this study is to identify the current situation of EWM, to find out the sources of e-waste generation, and to assess the barriers of EWM in a developing nation.

The study is based on the sample size of 151, where the responses were collected in physical form. To measure the reliability of this study, Cronbach's alpha will be used after the collection of data. This measures the internal consistency of the data to reflect the reliability. Among the total 151 respondents, few responses are collected from people who work in an IT company. Similarly, few responses are collected from the people who work in electronic shops, and some responses were collected from the manpower that is handling EWM in Sankhamul area, Kathmandu.

Regarding the demographic profile, out of 151 respondents, there are 61 females and 90 males comprising 40.4% and 59.6%, respectively.

Concerning age of the respondents, 37.7% were aged below 25 years, 56.3% were aged 26–35 years, 2.6% were aged 36–45 years, and 3.4% were aged 46–55 years.

Similarly, regarding the qualification, the respondents are categorized under four categories as School Leaving Certificate (SLC) or below, intermediate (+2), undergraduate, and postgraduate and above: 1.3% of the respondents were SLC or below, 10.6% were intermediate (+2), 51.0% were undergraduates, and 37.1% were postgraduates and above.

Similarly, out of 151 respondents, 33.1% of respondents were students, 53% of respondents were service holders, 9.9% of respondent were self-employed (business), and 4% of respondents were engaged in other professions.

The major findings of the study are summarized as follows:

- There is no proper policy for EWM in a developing nation. Proper policy helps to manage e-waste in effective ways that is generating every year.
- Many of the people are unaware about how to manage e-waste. We can find many small groups of people working for EWM, but people do not know about such kind of efforts and activities, which shows there is a lack of awareness among government as well as public about EWM. Therefore, promotional activity is necessary to make it successful.
- Every organization needs a procedure for handling e-waste in a developing nation. If every organization makes the procedure to handle e-waste in their own way, the generation of e-waste could be minimized, and there will be no problem for a countries to handle the large volume of e-waste.
- The volume of e-waste generation is increasing day by day, so there is a need for a special method for its disposal. Due to continuous technological advancements, many electronic items are produced, and simultaneously, the items are damaged; thus, e-waste is generated. In developing nation, there is no accessibility to advanced technology to manage e-waste, and only items are being generated, but damaged items are not disposed properly. Therefore, respondents feel that the volume of e-waste generation is increasing day by day, so there is a need for a special method for its disposal.
- Proper implementation of technical and institutional factors creates a positive impact on EWM. There is lack of human resources at both national and local levels for EWM. Staff members have little or no technical background in EWM. Research and development activities are low in EWM. If the emphasis was given priority in such factors, there would be a positive impact on EWM.
- The generation of e-waste and its proper disposal brings a positive impact on EWM. Proper disposal method of e-waste helps to reduce the problems of e-waste in a developing nation and also helps in managing e-waste.

11.6.2 Conclusion

The rapid advancement in information and communication technology has resulted in improved capacity in computing devices, but simultaneously decreases the lifetime of the product, causing the rapid generation of wasted electronic and electrical components. As the generation of e-waste is increasing day by day in large volume, there seems to be major problem in its management. As a result, large volume of e-waste is generated due to outdated technology. This study aimed at finding the causes of e-waste generation and the barriers of EWM in a developing nation's context. In these researches, several factors affecting EWM were examined. Data for this study was collected using an online questionnaire from different people of Kathmandu Valley. The study findings demonstrate that the problem of EWM is experienced by everyone at their place. With regard to the objectives as mentioned for this research, the following conclusions can be drawn.

EWM is a critical and subjective issue. All the stakeholders have to be concerned before imposing rules and regulations. The law should not be imposed on a hit-and-trial basis. Before making any policies for the management of e-waste, it would be wise to learn from the failure of banning plastics in a developing nation. EWM is a new topic for a developing nation; but it is the one that requires immediate attention. We do not have the means and resources for managing e-waste and it is being sent to India. But what will Nepal do if India restricts the transnational movement of scraps of e-waste from a developing nation.

There is a problem of policy and budget in EWM due to lack of awareness in government and public about e-waste and its potential hazardousness. As a result, e-waste generation in the developing nation is increasing due to outdated technology. The challenges faced by developing countries like developing nation in EWM include lack of infrastructure for appropriate waste management, lack of legislation dealing specifically with e-waste and its management, lack of public awareness, lack of human resources, lack of organizational policy, and lack of political support.

In the context of developing nation, lack of budget is also a major barrier to carry out the activities related to EWM. Recycling and treatment facilities require a high initial investment, particularly those fitted with technologically advanced equipment and processes. Lack of regulation dealing specifically with e-waste is a major problem in managing e-waste. Without proper implementation of regulation, no individual or private agency can work efficiently for EWM. For the effective management of e-waste in a developing nation, it demands the establishment of effective product reuse through the remanufacturing and use of efficient recycling methods. For proper handling of e-waste, every organization needs a procedure to deal with EWM by which large generation of e-waste could be minimized, and as a result, there could be a better management of e-waste.

Thus, EWM in a developing nation is based on the ground idea of generating and executing a fugal plan about turning unwanted e-wastes into productive and useful reusable goods, which can be of use to remote communities, create employment and training opportunities, and reduce such waste generation and their hazardous effects to health.

References

Baldé, C., Wang, F., Kuehr, R., & Huisman, J. (2015). The Global E-Waste Monitor 2014. Bonn, Germany: United Nation University.

Borthakur, A. (2013, September). Generation of electronic waste in India: Current scenario, Dillemmas and stake holders. *African Journal of Environmental Science and Technology, 7*(9), 899–910. doi:10.5897/AJEST2013

Carisma, B. (2009). Drivers of and barriers to E-waste management in the Philippines. Lund University – University of Manchester – University of the Aegean – Central European University.

Cherutich, E. J. (2013). E-*Waste Management* in *Kenya*: *A Case Study* of *Mobile Phone Waste* in *Nairobi*. Retrieved from: http://erepository.uonbi.ac.ke/bitstream/handle/11295/57912/Cherutich_E-waste%20management%20in%20Kenya%3A%20a%20case%20study%20of%20mobile%20phone%20waste%20in%20Nairobi.pdf?sequence=1&isAllowed=y

EPA. (2015). E-Waste. Retrieved 2015, from www.epa.sa.gov.au/environmental_info/waste_management/disposal/e_waste

Fleischmann, M. (2001). Reverse Logistics Network Structures and Design. Rotterdam School of Management/Faculteit Bedrijfskunde Erasmus University Rotterdam.

Ideho, B. (2014). E-*Waste Management: A Case Study* of *Lagos* state, *Nigeria*. University of Jyväskylä.

Joseph, K. (2007). *Electronic* Waste Management *in* India–Issues *and* Strategies. Centre for Environmental Studies, Anna University, Chennai, India.

Ka-cheong, M. (2012). Electronic Waste: An Evaluation on Its Environmental Impacts and Management Practices. Hong Kong: The University of Hong Kong (Pokfulam, Hong Kong). Retrieved from http://hub.hku.hk/handle/10722/180095;jsessionid=FD917041A7E339C34C20C000544A3B83

Kahhat, R. (2008, May). Exploring e-waste management systems in the United States. Resources, Conservation and Recycling, 52(7), 955–964. Retrieved 2015, from www.sciencedirect.com/science/article/pii/S0921344908000360

Liu, X., Tanaka, M., & Matsui, Y. (2014). *Electrical and Electronic Waste Management in China: Progress and the Barriers to Overcome.* UK: ISWA: Waste Management & Research; University College London, UK.

Mak, K.-C. (2012). Electronic waste: An evaluation on its environmental impacts and management practices. Retrieved from http://hdl.handle.net/10722/180095

Mathew, G. (1998). Methanogenic Population Dynamics during Start-Up of Anaerobic Digesters Treating Municipal Solid Waste and Biosolids. University of Illinois at Urbana-Champaign, Urbana, IL.

Naidu, N. (2015). Electronic Waste Management Services in India. India: Frost & Sullivan. Retrieved from www.frost.com/sublib/display-report.do?Id=9AAF-00-0F-00-00

OECD. (2014). The state of play on Extended Producer Responsibility (EPR): opportunities and challenges. Issues paper, Global *Forum* on Environment: Promoting Sustainable Materials Management through Extended Producer Responsibility. Retrieved June 17–19, from https://www.oecd.org/environment/waste/Global%20Forum%20Tokyo%20Issues%20Paper%2030-5-2014.pdf

Ongondo, F., Williams, I., & Cherrett, T. (2011, April). How are WEEE doing? A global review of the management of electrical and electronic wastes. Waste Management, 31(4), 714–730. Retrieved 2015, from www.sciencedirect.com/science/article/pii/S0956053X10005659

Osibanjo, O., & Nnornm, I. C. (2007). *The Challenge of Electronic Waste (E-Waste) Management in Developing Countries.* Los Angeles, CA, London, New Delhi and Singapore: Waste Management & Research.

Pradhan, K. (2010). Http://www.panossouthasia.org/. Retrieved from pannossouthasia: www.giswatch.org/country-report/2010-icts-and-environmental-sustainability/developing nation

Queiruga, D., González Benito, J., & Lannelongue, G. (2012, March). Evolution of the electronic waste management system in Spain. *Journal of Cleaner Production,* 24, 56–65. Retrieved 2015, from www.sciencedirect.com/science/article/pii/S0959652611004781

Samarakoon, M. (2014). *A Review of Electrical and Electronic Waste Management in Sri Lanka.* Singapore: International Conference on Chemical, Civil and Environmental Engineering (CCEE' 2014).

Shah, A., Dhakal, T., Pandey, T., & Shah, D. K. (2014). *An Assessment of Public Awareness Regarding E-Waste Hazards and Management Strategies.* India: SIT World Learning – India: Sustainable Development and Social Change.

Shumon, R. H., et al. (2014). Electronic waste: Present status and future perspectives of sustainable management practices in Malaysia. *E-Waste Management System.* doi:10.1007/s12665-014-3129-5

Sije, A., & Ochieng, P. A. (2013, December 8). Cell phone disposal and strategic evaluation of electronic waste management in kenya, a case of mobile phone dealers in kisumu county. *European Journal of Business and Innovation Research,* 1(4), 1–8. Retrieved 2015, from www.ea-journals.org

Sinha, D. (2013). The *Management* of *Electronic Waste*: *A Comparative S*tudy on *India* and *Switzerland. Environmental Impact Assessment Review,* 25(5), 492–504. July 2005.

Taiwan. (2012). Recycling Regulations in Taiwan and the 4-in-1 Recycling Program. Taiwan: EPA. Retrieved from www.epa.gov/sites/production/files/2014-05/documents/handout-1a-regulations.pdf

Târțiu, V. (2009). The management of waste from electrical and Electronic equipment (WEEE) in the European Union. *The Ninth International Conference* (pp. 218–223). Romania: The Bucharest Academy of Economic Studies, Romania.

Taye, M., & Kanda, W. (2011). E-Waste Management in Botswana. Linkoping University.

The Himalayan Times. (2015, August 20). Retrieved from http://thehimalayantimes.com/opinion/letters-e-waste-management/

US Battery Act. (1996). Public Law 104-142—May 13, 1996. Retrieved 2015, from www3.epa.gov/epawaste/laws-regs/state/policy/p1104.pdf

Widmer, R., & Pucket, S. (2005). Global perspectives on E-waste. Environmental Impact Assessment Review, 436–458. Retrieved 2015, from www.elsevier.com/locate/eiar

Chapter 12

Strategies for Improving Cyber Resilience of Data-Intensive Business Information Systems

Balakrishnan Unny R
Institute of Management, Nirma University (IMNU)

Gaurav Mishra
Development Management Institute (DMI)

Nityesh Bhatt
Institute of Management, Nirma University (IMNU)

Contents

12.1 Need for Cyber Resilience

Contemporary organizations have been investing heavily in information technology (IT) to gain strategic advantage, to bring in operational excellence, or just to survive in the changing business ecosystem (O'Brien and Marakas 2008). This mad rush to procure, upgrade, and maintain IT at its optimal level is evident in the global IT spending figure. Latest industry studies suggest that the global IT spending is close to 3.5 trillion dollars and is expected to grow over the next 5 years (Stamford 2017). Organizations are also becoming more dependent on IT for their functioning, and any disruption to these IT assets has a significant disruptive impact. The IT infrastructure has thus become a vital asset that needs to be safeguarded.

The role of cybersecurity in safeguarding of IT assets from unexpected disruptions is enormous. The organizations have spent billions of dollars to protect their information and IT assets (Pathak 2005). Organizations spend a majority of the cybersecurity budget on the methods that primarily aim to "bulletproof" their IT assets, i.e., make their infrastructure impenetrable. Yet, we have seen many organizations falling prey to some form of cybercrime (Clark and Harrell 2013; S′a, Carmo, and Machado 2017). Forbes contributor Morgan (2016) predicted that the global cost of cybercrime will reach the two trillion mark by 2019. The cost of cybercrime study published by Accenture has thrown up the following interesting statistics (Accenture and Ponemon Institute LLC 2017):

1. 27.4 percentage increase in average annual number of security breaches
2. 22.7 percentage increase in the cost of cybersecurity in a year
3. 50 days is the average time to resolve a malicious insider attack
4. 23 days is the average time to resolve a ransomware attack

These findings depict a dire picture with regard to the cybersecurity levels of contemporary organizations. Even with increased spending, there is an increase in cyberattacks, and organizations are spending a significant amount of resources to fight these attacks. Additionally, the evolution of IT has been mirrored by the evolution of what the Information Security Forum has coined "Malspace," i.e., the infrastructure that supports cybercrime (De Crespigny 2012). From IP spoofers to artificial intelligence (AI)-controlled bots, there is a whole array of tools that are available to a cyber criminal (Hoque, Bhattacharyya, and Kalita 2015; Lemieux 2015).

Disruption to the IT infrastructure is not limited to those caused by cybercrime alone. Disruptions caused by factors such as natural disasters, internal disturbance, or component failure must also be considered. Organizations are starting to understand that there is not much they can do to stop these cyber disruptions. A recently conducted study by Ernst and Young has found that 87% of the senior management believe that their organizations may be attacked at any time (Ernst and Young 2017). In this study, the authors also point out that the industry experts are now looking to augment the IT infrastructure in a way such that it may not be immune to attacks but is designed to recover once attacked. This change in thinking is the core premise of this chapter.

This chapter introduces the readers to the idea of cyber resilience as a natural progression to the cybersecurity mechanisms that the majority of organizations use. Section 12.2 deliberates on the evolution of cyber resilience. Section 12.3 is dedicated to the discussion on components of cyber resilience. Section 12.4 provides a suggestive list metrics for measuring the cyber resilience.

12.2 Evolution of Cyber Resilience

Before we start the discussion on the evolution of cyber resilience, let us consider two recent events that have hit the news. In December 2016, Yahoo reported that, in August 2013, they were hit and a billion of their user accounts were compromised. In September 2017, the company changed its position to state that three billion was the actual count, i.e., every single account at that time (Newman 2017a). The second news story was even more bizarre. The US credit reporting agency Equifax was hacked in mid-May 2017, exposing 145 million of their customers (i.e., half of the US population) to potential identity fraud (Newman 2017b). In both the cases, the hacks were detected much later and caught the companies off guard. Additionally, there are three reasons why these cases are of particular interest:

1. Even well-established organizations are potential targets that could be hit.
2. Ramifications of any attack extend beyond the boundaries of the organization.
3. Companies have a hard time figuring out the right response to any attack.

The aforementioned incidents show us the importance of having a resilient IT infrastructure that is able to detect, manage, and respond to a security incident (Clark and Harrell 2013; Kuru and Bayraktar 2017). Before deliberating on the evolution of cyber resilience, it is important to have a discussion regarding the fundamentals of security.

The ISO 27001 standard defines the term "information security" as the preservation of confidentiality, integrity, and availability (CIA) (International Organization for Standardization 2016). Confidentiality is the property that ensures the information is not made available or disclosed to unauthorized individuals, entities, or processes. Integrity is the property of accuracy and completeness of data. Availability is the property of being accessible and usable upon demand by an authorized entity. The typical information security management system (ISMS) in an organization revolves around identifying and managing the risks that may influence CIA of the information processing facilities. Thus, information security has its roots in risk management. Even the ISO 27001 standard that outlines the implementation of ISMS has a formal, quantified risk assessment stage (Eling and Schnell 2016).

The starting point of the implementation of ISMS is conducting a risk assessment wherein the assets are defined, threats and vulnerabilities are identified, and risk levels are determined. Based on the risk levels, a risk treatment plan is created, and therefore, additional corrective and preventive controls are implemented. This process is incorporated into the plan–do–check–act cycle to continuously improve the information security level (Atoum, Otoom, and Abu Ali 2014; Collier et al. 2014; Katsumata, Hemenway, and Gavins 2010; Pathak 2005). These risk management activities are incorporated in almost all of the information security standards.

12.2.1 Rationale for Investing in Data-Intensive Information Systems

While understanding the influence of risk management in security, it is important to recognize the paradigm shift in modern organizations. Organizations have understood that for an effective information system to exist, procurement of technology components is not the only prerequisite. The components of the modern-day information system extend beyond the technology into people and process as well (O'Brien and Marakas 2008). Contemporary organizations have established data-intensive information processing systems that collect a multitude of information (Laudon and Laudon 2016).

Let us take an example of two companies that have established a reputation for using IT systems effectively. First, Walmart, the global retailing giant, has established a collaborative supply chain system with their suppliers that is mostly automated. Walmart depends on its IT system to collect data from its over 11,000 stores so as to ensure smooth operations on a daily basis (O'Brien and Marakas 2008). With this collaborative supply chain, Walmart has established a mechanism to keep its stores well stocked for the next shopping cycle.

Second, Netflix, the entertainment company, has established itself as the global leader for generation and distribution of paid digital content. One of Netflix's many success stories is the hit series House of Cards, which came about as a result of the data analytics infrastructure at Netflix (David 2013). Both these examples show that organizations are becoming data driven, and this dependence is not only at the operational level but has also extended to tactical and strategic levels.

The creation of data-intensive systems has been propelled by two major factors: the explosive growth in the methods and tools for data collection and the infrastructure for data collection and processing which is becoming much more affordable. Be it Netflix using the online behavior of its viewers to determine what will be the next big hit, or be it Amazon using algorithms to determine its dynamic pricing, the avenues for data collection and processing are endless in the digital market place.

Additionally, the growing investment into Internet of things is opening up the opportunity of digitizing the real world that will provide the data scientists access to an enormous dataset (Ernst and Young 2017). There is also a rise in companies that are willing to invest their IT infrastructure to tap the potential gold mine of big data (Ning, Liu, and Yang 2013). The combination of the aforementioned factors clearly shows why contemporary organizations are looking at data-intensive systems for their continued strategic advantage.

However, this data-intensive IT infrastructure is a security nightmare (Choo 2011) and raises the following questions:

1. How to keep the IT systems protected when there are external players who require access to the same?
2. Has the interplay between these technology components been explored to ensure that there are no gaps in the security infrastructure?
3. Have we considered about the protection of data in transit as well as data at rest?

12.2.2 Interplay between Threat, Vulnerability, and Risk Management

The aforementioned questions are compounded by the fact that the cyber threat matrix is mutating at a rapid pace (Brewer 2015; Schnell 2016). For most of the general public, the security threat is limited to hacking and other malicious acts that are aimed at stealing information. This view is far too limited while considering the potential threats and vulnerabilities of the contemporary data-intensive systems.

Threat is an external event or entity that has the potential to influence security of an organization, and vulnerability is the weakness that can be exploited by the threat to harm the organization (International Organization for Standardization 2016; Wolden, Valverde, and Talla 2015). So even natural disasters, employee strikes, pandemic outbreaks, and power outages have the potential to disrupt the normal functioning of an organization (Agarwal et al. 2010; Goldman and Smith 2016; Greenberg 2017a, 2017b; Martins et al. 2015; Matthews 2015; Pidd 2012). The existence of threats doesn't necessarily lead to a disruption, as there must be an internal weakness that the threat could exploit (Renaud 2016).

The vulnerabilities may exist in three domains: people, process, or technology, and these vulnerabilities could be utilized to create disruption. Hence, a risk only exists when threat is able to exploit a vulnerability to cause disruption. Once the risk has been identified, the next logical stage is to deal with the risk.

The risk management literature divides the risk management approaches into four categories that are commonly referred to as the 4Ts of risk management: treat, transfer, terminate, and tolerate (Borum et al. 2015; Meland, Tondel, and Solhaug 2015; Vlacheas et al. 2013). Treat approach is the most popular and most common approach. It revolves around dealing with risk, either by limiting its chance of occurrence or by reducing the impact or combination of both. This approach can be further subdivided into 4Ds, namely, deny, delay, deter, and detect.

This interplay between threat, vulnerability, and risk is evident from the Equifax breach that was discussed in Section 12.2. In the case of Equifax, the hackers gained access to the customer information through the vulnerability in a web application software. There was a bug that was discovered in the software during March 2017, and the company that supplied the software had requested its customers to apply a patch to prevent any exploitation. Equifax later admitted that there was a delay in applying the patch, and many security experts felt that this delay was the reason for the data breach (Newman 2017b).

The treat in this case is clear; the external malicious act of hacking is the threat. The vulnerability is not that clear from the information that is available in the public domain; however, we can make some educated assumptions. We can notice that the vulnerability is spread across the three domains: people, process, and pechnology. First, the security gap was in the technology domain. However, the solution was updated with a patch to plug the security gap. Later, the relevant partners were apprised about the security gap and the importance of updating the patch. Second, it is safe to assume that like any organization that uses commercial of-the-shelf software, Equifax also would have established a process of updating patches on their critical IT assets. However, the delay in updating the patch shows that that there was a failure in the process. Third, the people were also to blame since there was a process that was not followed.

Thus, it is evident that the combination of hacking threat and the vulnerability spread across the three domains has caused a failure at Equifax. In the Equifax example, the best possible tactic was to use the treat approach specifically using the deny approach and plug the security gap by applying the patch at an appropriate time (Figure 12.1).

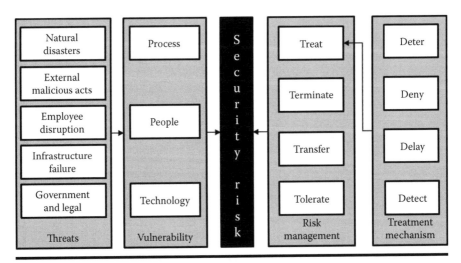

Figure 12.1   Relationship between threat, vulnerability, risk, and risk management.

In the earlier discussion, Equifax dealt with only one risk caused by one threat. However, if we consider the entire gamut of threats and their associated vulnerabilities, the level of risk may be completely different. The earlier depicted relationship is explained in detail in Table 12.1.

Hence, organizations use this interplay between threat, vulnerability, and risk management as a guiding principle behind their ISMS implementation. Organizations routinely conduct risk assessments and therefore identify the best way

Table 12.1 Risk Management Methodology

Threats	Natural disasters	Natural events such as earthquake, hurricane, flood, solar flares, and pandemic outbreaks
	External malicious acts	Attacks instigated by actors outside the organization such as malware, vandalism, sabotage, and dumpster diving
	Employee disruption	Disruptions caused by employees such as union strikes, labor actions, fraud, theft, and human error
	Infrastructure failure	Failure of supporting infrastructure components such as network failure, air conditioning failure, and power failure
	Government and legal	Events such as cyberwarfare, terrorism, change in regulations, and espionage
Vulnerability	Process	Gaps in the processes of the organization such as lack of access control policy, nonsegregation of duties, and inadequate or irregular backup
	People	Gaps created by people such as inadequate supervision of vendors and inadequate training of employees
	Technology	Issues that create security gaps such as default passwords not changed, equipment sensitivity to changes in voltage, equipment sensitivity to moisture and contaminants, and equipment sensitivity to temperature

(*Continued*)

Table 12.1 (*Continued*)   Risk Management Methodology

Risk Management	Treat		Reduce the impact and/or chance of occurrence of risk	
		Deter	Create a deterrence to reduce the chance of occurrence of risk	
		Deny	Deny the chance of occurrence of risk to create an impact	
		Delay	Create a mechanism to delay the impact	
		Detect	Create a mechanism that will detect the risk providing you the ability to launch countermeasures	
	Terminate		Eliminate the risk	
	Transfer		Transfer the impact of the risk to a third party, e.g., insurance	
	Tolerate		Do nothing	

to manage the identified risk. In certain conditions, additional preventive and corrective measures are taken to reduce the threshold risk levels (Dwivedi, Tebben, and Harshavardhana 2010). This method of information security management has been practiced in many organizations (Atoum, Otoom, and Abu Ali 2014; Collier et al. 2014; Katsumata, Hemenway, and Gavins 2010; Martins et al. 2015; Pathak 2005).

12.2.3 Shifting from Security to Resilience

Previously discussed risk-based ISMS methodology has its definite advantages, but there are two fundamental assumptions that have always caused it to be less effective in the modern dynamic security environment. The first assumption is that there is a perfect knowledge of all threats and associated vulnerabilities that impact IT assets (Rezvani et al. 2015). In the real world, this assumption fails because the level unknown-unknowns far exceeds the known-knowns, known-unknowns, or unknown-knowns, in the case of information security (Sharkov 2016). A brief overview of these types of risks is depicted in Figure 12.2.

Second, the methodology also assumes that a threat–vulnerability combination acts independently; however, it is known from experience that this is not the case. When one threat exploits a vulnerability, chances are that there are other

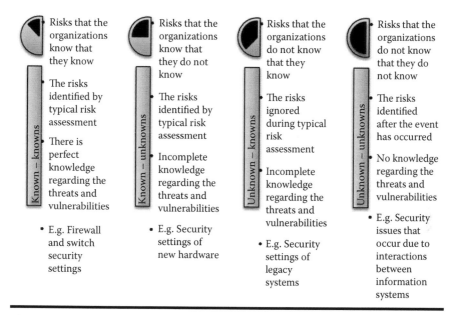

Figure 12.2 Types of cyber risk.

threat–vulnerability combinations that may impact an organization. These broad threat–vulnerability matrix events are more likely to happen, and many organizations are not prepared for it (Dowdy et al. 2010; Florio 2017; Goldman, McQuaid, and Picciotto 2011; Herrington and Aldrich 2013; Masys et al. 2014; Yan, He, and Sun 2014). The lessons that we see from cyber warfare suggest that any organization or country will be hit by multiple simultaneous attacks (Greenberg 2017c; Hsu 2017; Karabacak, Yildirim, and Baykal 2016; Simonite 2017; Symantec Corporation 2016; Waters, Ball, and Dudgeon 2008; Wilson 2014).

The two assumptions stated earlier have a far-reaching impact on the method and tools used to protect the organization's IT assets. Even though the risk-based approach is essential to ensure that the IT assets are appropriately protected, there is a need to look at the security problem from a different perspective (Collier et al. 2014). Information security deals with the known-knowns, whereas cyber resilience provides the organization the ability to deal with unknown-unknowns (Figure 12.3).

The perspective depicted in Figure 12.3 is simple, since we can't identify all the threats and their corresponding vulnerabilities. The best approach will be to protect ourselves with appropriate methods and additionally create an environment that will enable the IT infrastructure to detect, manage, and recover from an attack without too much of an impact (Acheson and Dagli 2016; Cheese 2016; Dacus and Yannakogeorgos 2016; Ferdinand 2015; Khaitan and McCalley 2015; Khan, Al-shaer, and Rauf 2015).

This is essentially the focus of cyber resilience, i.e., prepare for the unknown and recover when you are hit (Goldman, McQuaid, and Picciotto 2011). Cyber

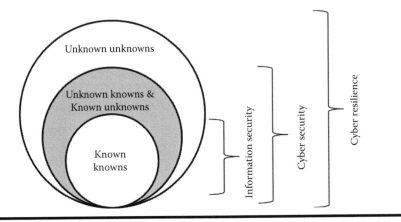

Figure 12.3 Information security to cyber resilience.

resilience builds on the existing infrastructure of cybersecurity to develop a set of tools and processes that are aimed at creating an IT infrastructure that is resilient. Key differences between cybersecurity and cyber resilience are the flexibility of the tools and the level of involvement of external parties (Herrington and Aldrich 2013; Tran et al. 2016; Vlacheas et al. 2013).

12.3 Components of Cyber Resilience

In this section, we will be exploring the various components of cyber resilience (Figure 12.4). Based on the literature, the components have been categorized into the following categories:

1. **Sense:** The ability of the organization to predict and detect disruptions
2. **Resist:** The ability of the organization to defend against disruptions
3. **Recover:** The ability of the organization to recuperate from disruptions

12.3.1 Sense

As pointed out earlier, the "sense" deals with the ability to predict and detect potential attacks. Sense is the first line of defense when it comes to cyber resilience as it provides the organization with the ability to identify potential disruptions before they occur. The ability of sense can be subdivided into two parts:

1. **Monitoring and detection:** The tools that enable the organization to scan their IT assets for any anomalies
2. **Collaboration:** The mechanisms that allow the organization to remain vigilant about the potential threats and vulnerabilities

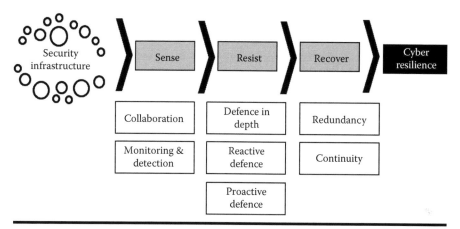

Figure 12.4   Components of cyber resilience.

Monitoring and detection tools can be further classified as active tools and passive tools. Active tools are the methods that keep track of anomalies as they happen and are often embedded in the IT infrastructure. Supervisory control and data acquisition (SCADA) system (Huawei Technologies Co. Ltd. 2012) and intrusion detection system (IDS) are good examples of such active monitoring methods (Alcaraz, Lopez, and Choo 2017; Brewer 2015; Kosek 2016; Nazir, Patel, and Patel 2017; Vollmer, Manic, and Linda 2014). Passive tools are as important as active tools as they are able to provide insights into the potential vulnerabilities that may not occur during routine operations. Threat hunting and use of ethical hackers are some of the passive tools (Anguluri, Gupta, and Pasqualetti 2016; Mansfield-Devine 2017). Collaboration may sound weird as a tool for cyber resilience; however, in a contemporary cyber risk environment, it is important to learn from our mistakes as well as learn from others' mistakes. Hence, it is imperative that the organizations learn the best security practices and share their best practices with their partners so that there is no weak link in the chain (Comizio, Dayanim, and Bain 2016; Kshetri and Murugesan 2013; Nykänen and Kärkkäinen 2016; Shackelford 2016; Sharkov 2016; World Economic Forum 2014). A representative set of "sense" tools according to the literature is provided in Table 12.2.

12.3.2 Resist

As discussed in the Section 12.3, "resist" deals with the organization's ability to defend itself from an attack. The majority of organizations spend their entire security budget on procuring and maintaining these security apparatus. The "resist" strategies can be further classified into three categories:

1. **Defense in depth:** The multilayered security techniques that provide protection from disruptions

Table 12.2 Sense Tools

"Sense" Category	*Tools*	*Description*
Monitoring and detection	SCADA	Monitors the critical infrastructure
	IDS	Helps to detect network penetrations
	AI-based anomaly detection	Detects anomalies in the IT infrastructure parameters, such as power consumption, network traffic, number of active connections and CPU utilization
	Staged attacks	Perform routine drills under simulated circumstances to determine potential disruptions in an IT infrastructure
	Threat hunting	Also referred to as vulnerability assessment; deals with conducting routine security checks to seek out the weaknesses in the security apparatus
	Desktop simulations	Review the response strategies of key personnel under simulated situations
	White hat hacking	Allows ethical hackers to penetrate the infrastructure so that they can point out the gaps
Collaboration	Knowledge management	Creates an internal knowledge repositories for security-related issues
	Institutionalize security	Involves security in the day-to-day activities
	Emergency response team	To be set up with relevant stakeholders
	Training	Develops internal skill set to meet the global standards
	Industry partnerships	Develops industry partnerships to share information and best practices

2. **Proactive defense:** The architectural and inherent strategies that exist before an attack
3. **Reactive defense:** The techniques that are invoked during the time of attack.

The defense in depth strategy is the founding principle behind the information security. The core idea is to maintain CIA by implementing multiple complementary and supplementary controls. For example, the access of information can be restricted by implementing a complex password requirement. Additionally, we could also have a policy of access based on the need-to-know principle, thereby adding another layer of protection. This methodology is based on the fundamental idea that the multiple layers will plug the gaps of the proceeding layer. Figure 12.5 depicts the various layers in defense in depth from data (lowest level) to policy (highest level).

Proactive and reactive strategies are extensions to the defense in depth strategies. The aim of these strategies is to effectively counter the attacks by deceiving the attackers. The strategies include methods such as deception, moving target, and segmentation (Carvalho et al. 2013; Lam, Skiles, and Grisham 2013; Pradhan et al. 2016; Thebeau et al. 2014). There may be some overlaps across the three strategies; however, an organization requires all three to effectively resist attacks (Chaves et al. 2017; Cook et al. 2017; Goldman, McQuaid, and Picciotto 2011; Miraglia and Casenove 2016; Ning, Liu, and Yang 2013). A representative list of strategies for "resist" tools from the literature is provided in Table 12.3.

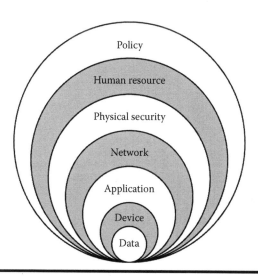

Figure 12.5   Defense in depth layers.

Table 12.3 Resist Strategies

"Resist" category	Strategy	Description
Defense in depth	Policy	Provides management direction and support for information security in accordance with business requirements and relevant laws and regulations
	Human resource security	Ensures that employees understand their responsibilities and are suitable for the roles for which they are considered
		Ensures that employees are aware of and fulfil their information security responsibilities
	Physical and environmental security	Prevents unauthorized physical access, damage, and interference to the organization's information and information processing facilities
	Network access security	Ensures authorized user access and prevents unauthorized access to systems and services
		Ensures the protection of information in networks and its supporting information processing facilities
	Device-level security	Ensures correct and secure operations of information processing facilities
Proactive techniques	Segmentation	Segregates the IT assets based on their exposure and criticality
	Unpredictability	Makes changes in the IT infrastructure frequently and randomly
	Diversity	Use of varied set of technologies including hardware, software, firmware, and protocols
	Moving target	Moves a service from server to server
	Nonpersistence	Disallows continuous access to data, applications, and connectivity
	Substantiated integrity	Maintains integrity across data stores

(Continued)

Table 12.3 (*Continued*)   Resist Strategies

"Resist" category	Strategy	Description
Reactive techniques	Deception	Uses obfuscation and misdirection to confuse the attackers
	Dynamic positioning	Dynamic relocation of IT assets
	Dynamic composition	Dynamically changes the composition via virtual machines, cloud computing services, etc.
	Adaptive response	Takes actions in response to indications that an attack is under way based on attack characteristics

12.3.3 Recover

Now let us consider the third part of the cyber resilience triad. Recover strategies focus on the organization's ability to resume its operations post an incident. To understand the recovery methodology, we need to understand the anatomy of a disaster. In Figure 12.6, an incident and recovery metrics such as recovery time objective (RTO), recovery point objective (RPO), and maximum tolerable period of disruption are portrayed. The core premise of any recovery methodology is that there will always be some impact due to disruption. The faster RTO and RPO will mean that the organization will recover with minimum impact on its business operations. Additionally, there is also another metric that is relevant with regard to complex distributed systems, which is recovery consistency objective (RCO). RCO is expressed as a percentage of data lost during disaster. This is important to maintain synchronous data across various systems (Figure 12.6).

Based on the literature, the recovery strategies can be classified into two major categories:

1. **Redundancy:** The maintenance of redundant technology and infrastructure to enable smooth recovery
2. **Continuity:** The procedures and plans that help an organization to manage its recovery effort

Redundancy in the organizations can be implemented at many levels such as location, device, component, people, and process levels (Benameur, Evans, and Elder 2013; Sano et al. 2016). Redundancy also removes the single point for failure from the IT infrastructure. Redundancies allow the organizations to switch over in case

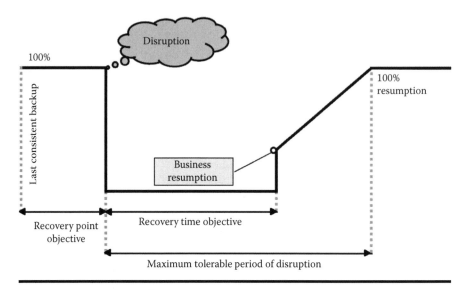

Figure 12.6 Anatomy of recovery.

of failure and therefore reduce their RTO. Additionally, with improved connectivity, it is also possible to have redundancy at the data level by using cloud computing and mirroring sites. This strategy, when implemented, will also improve the RPO and RCO levels. The continuity strategy is basically the extension of the ISO 22301 standard for business continuity. In the standard, the organizations are recommended to create a recover plan that is based on the risks identified. The continuity plan is a simple, executable set of instructions that are independent of the people, process, or technology limitations (St-Germain et al. 2016). A representative list of tools that are part of the recover strategy identified from literature is provided in Table 12.4.

The Sections 12.3.1, 12.3.2 and12.3.3 have detailed the tools available for any organization that is planning to achieve cyber resilience. To achieve true resilience, an organization should have mature sense, resist, and recover capabilities. It is important to note that implementation of all tools may not be a realistic option, since each of them requires a substantial investment of the organization's resources. Hence, some parity has to be established with regard to what capability needs to be developed at what stage. Hult and Sivanesan (2013) and Peter (2017) in their works were able to categorize the success factors for cyber resilience implementation.

On the basis of contemporary literature, the authors have identified four categories of success factors for cyber resilience implementation: people, process, technology, and management support. The people category of success factors directly deals with having the right people with the right skill set. The process category deals with having a mature, well-defined process for cybersecurity.

Table 12.4   Recover Tools

"Recovery" Category	Tools	Description
Redundancy	Device	Has redundant devices ready for quick switchover
	Network	Has multiple Internet Service Provider connections
	People	Trains people to take over each other's responsibilities
	Process	Enables the process to execute differently in the event of a disruption
	Data	Mirrors data storage in different locations using cloud computing
Continuity	Incident response plan	Creates a plan on how to respond to an incident
	Transportation plan	Creates a plan to transport the employees and equipment to the recovery site
	Site recovery plan	Plans to move the operations to cold site, warm site, or hot site
	Communication plan	Plans to ensure that communication happens effectively without creating panic
	Technology recovery plan	Plans to recover the technology components after an attack
	Testing and drills	Schedule frequent testing of the plans and record the results
	Review and update	Review and update plans based on testing results and change in the risk levels

The technology success factor deals with having the appropriate technological interventions to bring about resilience. Lastly, all contemporary researchers agree that cyber resilience requires extensive management support to thrive. Table 12.5 depicts the relationship between the tools of cyber resilience and the four categories of success factors.

Table 12.5 Cyber Resilience Implementation Success Factors

Cyber Resilience Components	Category	Impact of the Success Factor			
		People	Process	Technology	Management Support
Sense	Monitoring and detection	Low	Medium	High	Medium
	Collaboration	High	High	Medium	High
Resist	Defense in depth	Low	High	High	Medium
	Proactive defense	Low	Medium	High	Medium
	Reactive defense	Low	Medium	High	Medium
Recover	Redundancy	Medium	High	High	Low
	Continuity	Medium	Medium	Medium	High

12.4 Metrics of Resilience

In Section 12.3, we deliberated on various components that help organizations to develop cyber resilience. As part of the discussion, it is important to have a method to measure the resilience in an organization. Bodeau et al. (2014) identified the measurements of the proactive and reactive techniques for cyber resilience. They also created metrics to measure the flexibility of the architecture to accommodate a resilience technique.

Khan, Al-shaer, and Rauf (2015) and Zhang et al. (2016) focused on developing metrics to measure network resilience in the event network penetration attacks. Peter (2017) was able to bring in the cyber resilience angle to national security preparedness. His work is significant in establishing the need for collaboration for cyber resilience. Additionally, Linkov et al. (2013) provided a more comprehensive metric covering four categories, namely, physical, information, cognitive, and social across the various stages of a cyberattack. The metrics were spanned across four stages: plan, absorb, recover, and adapt. Their work provided great insights into the broad nature of tools that enable cyber resilience.

Ferdinand (2015) clearly identified five levels of cyber resilience maturity and was able to cross-reference the techniques that were needed to be implemented to reach each level of maturity. Hult and Sivanesan (2013) in their work were able to create an executive checklist for checking the cyber resilience implementation in an organization. The aforementioned literature was invaluable for the authors in creating the comprehensive metrics for cyber resilience listed in Table 12.6.

Table 12.6   Resilience Metrics

Rate your organization's implementation of the following cyber resilience tools using the below-mentioned scale: 1. Not implemented 2. Implemented on a trial basis 3. Implemented only for critical assets 4. Implemented for all assets 5. Implemented for all assets with periodic review	
Sense	
Monitoring and Detection	
1.	Device-level monitoring
2.	Network monitoring
3.	Anomaly detection
4.	SCADA
5.	IDS
6.	Staged attacks
7.	Threat hunting
8.	Desktop simulations
9.	White hat hacking
10.	System logs
Total score/10	
Collaboration	
1.	Knowledge management
2.	Leadership for security
3.	Institutionalization of security
4.	Emergency response teams
5.	Training
6.	Industry partnerships
7.	Delegate all assets and services to particular employees
8.	Identify external system dependencies
9.	Loop back from incident management
Total score/9	

(*Continued*)

Table 12.6 (*Continued*)   Resilience Metrics

Resist	
Defense in Depth	
1.	Risk assessment
2.	Policies for information security
3.	Segregation of duties
4.	Mobile device policy
5.	Background verification
6.	Inventory of assets
7.	Acceptable use of assets
8.	Return of assets
9.	Classification and labeling of information
10.	Management of removable media
11.	Disposal of media
12.	Access control policy
13.	Physical security perimeter
14.	Physical entry controls
15.	Cabling security
16.	Clear desk and clear screen policy
17.	Capacity management
18.	Protection of log information
19.	Securing application services on public networks
20.	Change management process
21.	User registration and deregistration
22.	Secure log-on procedures

(*Continued*)

Table 12.6 (*Continued*) Resilience Metrics

Resist	
23.	Secure development policy
24.	User acceptance testing
25.	Information security policy for supplier
26.	Security incident management
27.	Information security continuity
28.	Independent review of information security
29.	Identification of applicable legislation and contractual requirements
30.	Privacy and protection of personally identifiable information
Total score/30	
Proactive Defense	
1.	Segmentation
2.	Unpredictability
3.	Diversity
4.	Moving target
5.	Nonpersistence
6.	Substantiated integrity
Total score/6	
Reactive Defense	
1.	Deception
2.	Dynamic positioning
3.	Dynamic composition
4.	Adaptive response
Total score/4	
Recover	
Redundancy	
1.	Device

(*Continued*)

Table 12.6 (*Continued*) Resilience Metrics

Recover						
2.	Network					
3.	People					
4.	Process					
5.	Data					
Total score/5						
Continuity						
1.	Incident response plan					
2.	Transportation plan					
3.	Site recovery plan					
4.	Communication plan					
5.	Technology recovery plan					
6.	Testing and drills					
7.	Review and update					
8.	Risk assessment					
9.	Business impact analysis					
Total score/9						
Cyber Resilience Maturity						
		Nonexistent	*Immature*	*Basic*	*Reactive*	*Fully Mature*
Monitoring and detection		1	1–2	2–3	3–4	>4
Collaboration		1	1–2	2–3	3–4	>4
Defense in depth		1	1–2	2–3	3–4	>4
Proactive defense		1	1–2	2–3	3–4	>4
Reactive defense		1	1–2	2–3	3–4	>4
Redundancy		1	1–2	2–3	3–4	>4
Continuity		1	1–2	2–3	3–4	>4

(*Continued*)

Table 12.6 (*Continued*)   Resilience Metrics

Cyber Resilience Maturity

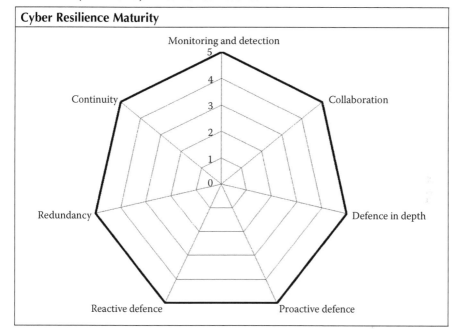

12.5 Conclusion

The changing importance of information systems necessitates the organizations to shift their focus from bulletproofing to recovery. Cyber resilience is a necessary evolution of cybersecurity that enables the organization to recover from disruptions with minimal impact. The contemporary treat–vulnerability matrix is evolving at a rapid pace, and this is forcing the organizations to transform their IT security infrastructure as well. Organizations have to focus on all the three components to effectively develop cyber resilience. Additionally, there are a wide variety of strategies and tools that will empower the organization. However, the organizations have to implement these strategies carefully and diligently; else, they may end up creating more gaps in their shield. It is also important to understand that the strategies and tools are not limited to technology solutions alone, rather they require the support of well-trained and vigilant stakeholders along with a robust process as well. The metrics discussed in this chapter provide organizations the ability to evaluate their cyber resilience levels. Literature points out that most organizations have reached only the first three levels of maturity.

While implementing cyber resilience, it is important to understand that the progression in the levels of maturity has to happen across all seven subcategories: monitoring and detection, collaboration, defense in depth, proactive defense, reactive defense, redundancy, and continuity. However, the progression in each subcategory can be independent of each other. Implementation of cyber resilience requires a structured approach with stringent timeline and appropriate resource allocation. Also the role of senior business and IT leaders will evolve with the progression of cyber resilience.

As a future research scope, the cyber resilience angle of national security preparedness could be explored. The cyber preparedness levels across various countries could also be explored. Researchers can also compare the cyber resilience awareness levels across industries to explore the differences among them. Also, the cyber resilience metrics could also incorporate the security requirements outlined in standards such as ISO 27001, ISO 22301, PCIDSS, and HIPPA.

References

Accenture, and Ponemon Institute LLC. 2017. "Cost of Cyber Crime Study." https://www.accenture.com/t20170926T072837Z__w__/us-en/_acnmedia/PDF-61/Accenture-2017-CostCyberCrimeStudy.pdf.

Acheson, Paulette, and Cihan Dagli. 2016. "Modeling Resilience in System of Systems Architecture." *Procedia Computer Science* 95: 111–18.

Agarwal, Pankaj K., Alon Efrat, Shashidhara K. Ganjugunte, David Hay, Swaminathan Sankararaman, and Gil Zussman. 2010. "Network Vulnerability to Single, Multiple, and Probabilistic Physical Attacks." In IEEE Military Communications Conference MILCOM, 1824–29.

Alcaraz, Cristina, Javier Lopez, and Kim Kwang Raymond Choo. 2017. "Resilient Interconnection in Cyber-Physical Control Systems." *Computers and Security* 71: 2–14.

Anguluri, Rajasekhar, Vijay Gupta, and Fabio Pasqualetti. 2016. "Periodic Coordinated Attacks against Cyber-Physical Systems: Detectability and Performance Bounds." In *IEEE 55th Conference on Decision and Control*, 5079–84.

Atoum, Issa, Ahmed Otoom, and Amer Abu Ali. 2014. "A Holistic Cyber Security Implementation Framework." *Information Management & Computer Security* 22 (3): 251–64.

Benameur, Azzedine, Nathan S. Evans, and Matthew C. Elder. 2013. "Cloud Resiliency and Security via Diversified Replica Execution and Monitoring." In *6th International Symposium on Resilient Control Systems*, 150–55.

Bodeau, Deborah J., Richard D. Graubart, and Ellen R. Laderman. 2014. "Cyber Resiliency Engineering Overview of the Architectural Assessment Process." *Procedia Computer Science* 28: 838–47.

Borum, Randy, John Felker, Sean Kern, Kristen Dennesen, and Tonya Feyes. 2015. "Strategic Cyber Intelligence." *Information and Computer Security* 23 (3): 317–32.

Brewer, Ross. 2015. "Cyber Threats: Reducing the Time to Detection and Response." *Network Security* 2015 (5): 5–8.

Carvalho, Marco, Thomas C. Eskridge, Larry Bunch, Adam Dalton, Robert Hoffman, Jeffrey M. Bradshaw, Paul J. Feltovich, Daniel Kidwell, and Teresa Shanklin. 2013. "MTC2: A Command and Control Framework for Moving Target Defense and Cyber Resilience." In *6th International Symposium on Resilient Control Systems*, 175–80.

Chaves, Andrew, Mason Rice, Stephen Dunlap, and John Pecarina. 2017. "Improving the Cyber Resilience of Industrial Control Systems." *International Journal of Critical Infrastructure Protection* 17: 30–48.

Cheese, Peter. 2016. "Managing Risk and Building Resilient Organisations in a Riskier World." *Journal of Organizational Effectiveness: People and Performance* 3 (3): 323–31.

Choo, Kim Kwang Raymond. 2011. "The Cyber Threat Landscape: Challenges and Future Research Directions." *Computers and Security* 30 (8): 719–31.

Clark, Michael, and Charles E. Harrell. 2013. "Unlike Chess, Everyone Must Continue Playing after a Cyber-Attack." *Journal of Investment Compliance* 14 (4): 5–12.

Collier, Zachary A., Daniel Dimase, Steve Walters, Mark Mohammad Tehranipoor, James H. Lambert, and Igor Linkov. 2014. "Cybersecurity Standards: Managing Risk and Creating Resilience." *Computer* 47: 70–76.

Comizio, V. Gerard, Behnam Dayanim, and Laura Bain. 2016. "Cybersecurity as a Global Concern in Need of Global Solutions: An Overview of Financial Regulatory Developments in 2015." *Journal of Investment Compliance* 17 (1): 101–11.

Cook, Allan, Helge Janicke, Richard Smith, and Leandros Maglaras. 2017. "The Industrial Control System Cyber Defence Triage Process." *Computers & Security* 70: 467–81.

Dacus, Chad, and Panayotis A. Yannakogeorgos. 2016. "Designing Cybersecurity into Defense Systems: An Information Economics Approach." *IEEE Security and Privacy* 14 (3): 44–51.

David, Carr. 2013. "Giving Viewers What They Want." The New York Times.

De Crespigny, Michael. 2012. "Building Cyber-Resilienceto Tackle Threats." *Network Security*, no. 4: 5–8.

Dowdy, John, Joseph Hubback, Dennis Layton, and James Solyom. 2010. "Can You Hack It? Managing the Cybersecurity Challenge." McKinsey.

Dwivedi, Anurag, Daniel Tebben, and P. Harshavardhana. 2010. "Characterizing Cyber-Resiliency." In IEEE Military Communications Conference MILCOM, 1304–9.

Eling, Martin, and Werner Schnell. 2016. "What Do We Know about Cyber Risk and Cyber Risk Insurance?" *The Journal of Risk Finance* 17 (5): 474–91.

Ernst and Young. 2017. "Global Information Security Survey 2016-17." http://www.ey.com/Publication/vwLUAssets/2017_GISS_Report_PDF/$FILE/REPORT - EY's 19th Global Information Security Survey.pdf.

Ferdinand, Jason. 2015. "Building Organisational Cyber Resilience: A Strategic Knowledge-Based View of Cyber Security Management." *Journal of Business Continuity & Emergency Planning* 9 (2): 185–95.

Florio, Vincenzo De. 2017. "Systems, Resilience, and Organization : Analogies and Points of Contact with Hierarchy Theory." *Procedia Computer Science* 109: 935–42.

Goldman, David, and Aaron Smith. 2016. "36,000 Verizon Workers Go on Strike." *CNN Tech*. http://money.cnn.com/2016/04/13/technology/verizon-strike/index.html.

Goldman, Harriet, Rosalie McQuaid, and Jeffrey Picciotto. 2011. "Cyber Resilience for Mission Assurance." In *IEEE International Conference on Technologies for Homeland Security*, 236–41.

Greenberg, Andy. 2017a. "New Group of Iranian Hackers Linked to Destructive Malware." *Wired*. www.wired.com/story/iran-hackers-apt33/.

Greenberg, Andy. 2017b. "Petya Ransomware Hides State-Sponsored Attacks, Say Ukrainian Analysts." *Wired*. www.wired.com/story/petya-ransomware-ukraine/.

Greenberg, Andy. 2017c. "Russia's Cyberwar on Ukraine Is a Blueprint for What's to Come." *Wired*. www.wired.com/story/russian-hackers-attack-ukraine/.

Herrington, Lewis, and Richard Aldrich. 2013. "The Future of Cyber-Resilience in an Age of Global Complexity." *Politics* 33 (4): 299–310.

Hoque, Nazrul, Dhruba K. Bhattacharyya, and Jugal K. Kalita. 2015. "Botnet in DDoS Attacks: Trends and Challenges." *IEEE Communications Surveys and Tutorials* 17 (4): 2242–70.

Hsu, Jeremy. 2017. "You Are the Target of Today's Cyberwars." *Wired*. https://www.wired.com/2017/03/you-are-the-target-of-todays-cyberwars/.

Huawei Technologies Co., Ltd. 2012. "Success Stories in the Energy Industry." http://e-file.huawei.com/in/marketing-material/onLineView?MaterialID=%7B6B98EF9C-877C-49A9-BCAB-59444157AA55%7D.

Hult, Fredrik, and Giri Sivanesan. 2013. "What Good Cyber Resilience Looks Like." *Journal of Business Continuity & Emergency Planning* 7 (2): 112–25. www.ncbi.nlm.nih.gov/pubmed/24457323.

International Organization for Standardization. 2016. ISO/IEC 27000:2016 Information Technology—Security Techniques—Information Security Management Systems—Overview and Vocabulary. ISO.org [Online]. Vol. 4.

Karabacak, Bilge, Sevgi Ozkan Yildirim, and Nazife Baykal. 2016. "A Vulnerability-Driven Cyber Security Maturity Model for Measuring National Critical Infrastructure Protection Preparedness." *International Journal of Critical Infrastructure Protection* 15: 47–59.

Katsumata, Peter, Judy Hemenway, and Wes Gavins. 2010. "Cybersecurity Risk Management." In IEEE Military Communications Conference MILCOM, 890–95.

Khaitan, Siddhartha Kumar, and James D. McCalley. 2015. "Design Techniques and Applications of Cyberphysical Systems: A Survey." *IEEE Systems Journal* 9 (2): 350–65.

Khan, Yasir Imtiaz, Ehab Al-shaer, and Usman Rauf. 2015. "Cyber Resilience-by-Construction." In Workshop on Automated Decision Making for Active Cyber Defense—SafeConfig, 9–14.

Kosek, Anna Magdalena. 2016. "Contextual Anomaly Detection for Cyber-Physical Security in Smart Grids Based on an Artificial Neural Network Model." In *2016 Joint Workshop on Cyber-Physical Security and Resilience in Smart Grids (CPSR-SG)*, 1–6. IEEE.

Kshetri, Nir, and San Murugesan. 2013. "EU and US Cybersecurity Strategies and Their Impact on Businesses and Consumers." *IEEE Computer* 46 (10): 84–88.

Kuru, Damla, and Sema Bayraktar. 2017. "The Effect of Cyber-Risk Insurance to Social Welfare." *Journal of Financial Crime* 24 (2): 329–46.

Lam, Dung, Erik Skiles, and Paul Grisham. 2013. "Simulation Tool for Evaluation and Design of Resilience Strategies." In *6th International Symposium on Resilient Control Systems*, 186–91.

Laudon, Kenneth C., and Jane P. Laudon. 2016. Management Information Systems: Managing the Digital Firm. Pearson Education Inc. Vol. 14.

Lemieux, Frederic, ed. 2015. Current and Emerging Trends in Cyber Operations: Policy, Strategy, and Practice. Palgrave Macmillan.

Linkov, Igor, Daniel A. Eisenberg, Kenton Plourde, Thomas P. Seager, Julia Allen, and Alex Kott. 2013. "Resilience Metrics for Cyber Systems." *Environment Systems and Decisions* 33 (4): 471–76.

Mansfield-Devine, Steve. 2017. "Threat Hunting: Assuming the Worst to Strengthen Resilience." *Network Security* 2017 (5): 13–17.

Martins, Goncalo, Sajal Bhatia, Xenofon Koutsoukos, Keith Stouffer, Cheeyee Tang, and Richard Candell. 2015. "Towards a Systematic Threat Modeling Approach for Cyber-Physical Systems." In Resilience Week, 114–19.

Masys, Anthony J., Nibedita Ray-Bennett, Hideyuki Shiroshita, and Peter Jackson. 2014. "High Impact/Low Frequency Extreme Events: Enabling Reflection and Resilience in a Hyper-Connected World." *Procedia Economics and Finance* 18: 772–79.

Matthews, Chris. 2015. "Walmart Loses $3 Billion a Year to Theft." *Fortune.* http://fortune.com/2015/06/05/walmart-theft/.

Meland, Per Hakon, Inger Anne Tondel, and Bjornar Solhaug. 2015. "Mitigating Risk with Cyberinsurance." *IEEE Security and Privacy* 13 (6): 38–43.

Miraglia, A., and M. Casenove. 2016. "Fight Fire with Fire: The Ultimate Active Defence." *Information and Computer Security* 24 (3): 288–96.

Morgan, Steve. 2016. "Cyber Crime Costs Projected To Reach $2 Trillion by 2019." *Forbes.* www.forbes.com/sites/stevemorgan/2016/01/17/cyber-crime-costs-projected-to-reach-2-trillion-by-2019/#1e96f2eb3a91.

Nazir, Sajid, Shushma Patel, and Dilip Patel. 2017. "Assessing and Augmenting SCADA Cyber Security-A Survey of Techniques." *Computers & Security* 70: 436–54.

Newman, Lily Hay. 2017a. "So, Uh, That Billion- Account Yahoo Breach Was Actually 3 Billion." *Wired.* www.wired.com/story/yahoo-breach-three-billion-accounts/.

Newman, Lily Hay. 2017b. "The Equifax Breach Was Entirely Preventable." *Wired.* www.wired.com/story/equifax-breach-no-excuse/.

Ning, Huansheng, Hong Liu, and Laurence T. Yang. 2013. "Cyberentity Security in the Internet of Things." *Computer* 46 (4): 46–53.

Nykänen, Riku, and Tommi Kärkkäinen. 2016. "Supporting Cyber Resilience with Semantic Wiki." In *12th International Symposium on Open Collaboration*, 35: 1–8.

O'Brien, James A., and George M. Marakas. 2008. Introduction to Information Systems. 15th ed. McGraw-Hill/Irwin. New York.

Pathak, Jagdish. 2005. "Risk Management, Internal Controls and Organizational Vulnerabilities." *Managerial Auditing Journal* 20 (6): 569–77.

Peter, Ada S. 2017. "Cyber Resilience Preparedness of Africa's Top-12 Emerging Economies." *International Journal of Critical Infrastructure Protection* 17: 49–59.

Pidd, Helen. 2012. "India Blackouts Leave 700 Million without Power." *The Guardian.* www.theguardian.com/world/2012/jul/31/india-blackout-electricity-power-cuts.

Pradhan, Subhav, Abhishek Dubey, Tihamer Levendovszky, Pranav Srinivas Kumar, William A. Emfinger, Daniel Balasubramanian, William Otte, and Gabor Karsai. 2016. "Achieving Resilience in Distributed Software Systems via Self-Reconfiguration." *Journal of Systems and Software* 122: 344–63.

Renaud, Karen. 2016. "How Smaller Businesses Struggle with Security Advice." *Computer Fraud and Security* 2016 (8): 10–18.

Rezvani, Mohsen, Verica Sekulic, Aleksandar Ignjatovic, Elisa Bertino, and Sanjay Jha. 2015. "Interdependent Security Risk Analysis of Hosts and Flows." *IEEE Transactions on Information Forensics and Security* 10 (11): 2325–39.

S´a, Alan Oliveira de, Luiz F. Rust da Costa Carmo, and Raphael C. S. Machado. 2017. "Covert Attacks in Cyber-Physical Control Systems." *IEEE Transactions on Industrial Informatics* 13 (4): 1641–51.

Sano, Fumikazu, Takeshi Okamoto, Idris Winarno, Yoshikazu Hata, and Yoshiteru Ishida. 2016. "A Cyber Attack-Resilient Server Using Hybrid Virtualization." *Procedia Computer Science* 96: 1627–36.

Schnell, Roger R. 2016. "Cyber Defence Triad for Where Security Matters." *Communications of the ACM* 59 (11): 20–23.

Shackelford, Scott J. 2016. "Business and Cyber Peace: We Need You!" *Business Horizons* 59 (5): 539–48.

Sharkov, G. 2016. "From Cybersecurity to Collaborative Resiliency." In ACM Workshop on Automated Decision Making for Active Cyber Defense, 3–9.

Simonite, Tom. 2017. "AI Could Revolutionize War as Much as Nukes." *Wired*. www.wired.com/story/ai-could-revolutionize-war-as-much-as-nukes/.

St-Germain, René, Faton Aliu, Eric Lachapelle, and Pierre Dewez. 2016. "ISO 22301 Business Continuity Management Systems." www.pecb.org/iso22301.

Stamford, Conn. 2017. "Gartner Says Worldwide IT Spending Forecast to Grow 2.7 Percent in 2017." *Gartner*. www.gartner.com/newsroom/id/3568917.

Symantec Corporation. 2016. "Internet Security Threat Report." Internet Security Threat Report. Vol. 21. http://e-file.huawei.com/in/marketing-material/onLineView?MaterialID=%7B6B98EF9C-877C-49A9-BCAB-59444157AA55%7D.

Thebeau, Danny, Benjamin Reidy, Ricardo Valerdi, Avinash Gudagi, Hemayamini Kurra, Youssif Al-Nashif, Salim Hariri, and Frederick Sheldon. 2014. "Improving Cyber Resiliency of Cloud Application Services by Applying Software Behavior Encryption (SBE)." *Procedia Computer Science* 28: 62–70.

Tran, Hiep, Enrique Campos-Nanez, Pavel Fomin, and James Wasek. 2016. "Cyber Resilience Recovery Model to Combat Zero-Day Malware Attacks." *Computers and Security* 61: 19–31. doi:10.1016/j.cose.2016.05.001.

Vlacheas, Panagiotis, Vera Stavroulaki, Panagiotis Demestichas, Scott Cadzow, Demosthenes Ikonomou, and Slawomir Gorniak. 2013. "Towards End-to-End Network Resilience." *International Journal of Critical Infrastructure Protection* 6: 159–78.

Vollmer, Todd, Milos Manic, and Ondrej Linda. 2014. "Autonomic Intelligent Cyber-Sensor to Support Industrial Control Network Awareness." *IEEE Transactions on Industrial Informatics* 10 (2): 1647–58.

Waters, Gary, Desmond Ball, and Ian Dudgeon. 2008. Australia and Cyber-Warfare. ANU E Press.

Wilson, Nigel. 2014. "Australia's National Broadband Network—A Cybersecure Critical Infrastructure?" *Computer Law & Security Review* 30 (6): 699–709.

Wolden, Mark, Raul Valverde, and Malleswara Talla. 2015. "The Effectiveness of COBIT 5 Information Security Framework for Reducing Cyber Attacks on Supply Chain Management System." *IFAC-PapersOnLine* 48 (3): 1846–52.

World Economic Forum. 2014. "Risk and Responsibility in a Hyperconnected World: Pathways to Global Cyber Resilience." World Economic Forum.

Yan, Jun, Haibo He, and Yan Sun. 2014. "Integrated Security Analysis on Cascading Failure in Complex Networks." *IEEE Transactions on Information Forensics and Security* 9 (3): 451–63.

Zhang, Mengyuan, Lingyu Wang, Sushil Jajodia, Anoop Singhal, and Massimiliano Albanese. 2016. "Network Diversity: A Security Metric for Evaluating the Resilience of Networks Against Zero-Day Attacks." *IEEE Transactions on Information Forensics and Security* 11 (5): 1071–86.

Chapter 13

Internet of Things (IoT) Deployment in Wearable Healthcare: A Sociotechno Evaluation

Gaurav Mishra
Development Management Institute (DMI)

Balakrishnan Unny
Institute of Management, Nirma University (IMNU)

Nityesh Bhatt
Institute of Management, Nirma University (IMNU)

Contents

13.1 The Internet of Things: Result of Digital Convergence

Digital convergence results in the integration of different components of computer technology and telecommunications technology into a single entity, i.e., information technology (IT) (Ogunsola 2005). Smartphone is the best example to elucidate the concept of convergence. Smartphones enable interactive voice and text communication in addition to synchronous and asynchronous multimedia communication capabilities. According to Mueller (1999), digital convergence happens when different forms of media are incorporated into one technology. For example, digital computer has integrated circuits, audio–video components, and uses different information theory models for functioning.

Technology improvements like enhanced data transmission and devices that have efficient computing capacity and improved data storage are important for technology convergence (Tiwari et al. 2006). In addition to these factors, Tufano and Karras (2005) included interactivity, self-configuration, and customization as significant factors for convergence. According to them, due to the increased processing capability of devices, users are becoming more comfortable in self-configuring applications. Users can configure various aspects, for example, they can add/remove/set alert for events on calendar, set notifications for content, and customize the user interface with respect to its look, feel, and layout of applications on their devices. Adoption of standards for data transmission is also seen as a precursor for convergence. According to Mueller (1999), the development of common protocols and technical standards is a result of synchronized acceptance of well-matched technology platforms by different stakeholders.

According to Finger (2010), convergence of technologies is the major contributor to the exponential growth of Information and Communication Technologies (ICTs) in different parts of the world. With the proliferation of such converged devices, the result is a completely new media ecology (Mueller 1999). The benefits of technological convergence are observed in domains from agriculture to health and business to infrastructure. For example, M-commerce is seen as coming together of IT and telecommunication technologies (Tiwari et al. 2006). The convergence of sensor and network technologies provide us the ability to measure, infer, understand, and communicate various critical indicators on a real-time basis. Technologies such as wireless sensor networks (WSNs), cloud platform, communication standards and protocols, radio frequency identification (RFID), etc. serve as the building blocks of this ecology (Roman et al. 2013).

Hence, we see that convergence of technologies support the development of a new ecosystem, and this chapter deliberates on how the convergence of technology has helped in the evolution of the Internet of Things (IoT). In addition, importance is laid on how the IoTs are applied in the health-care domain. It is well accepted that the IoT offers enormous benefits to various stakeholders. One of its applications can be remote monitoring of patients' health through healthcare wearable devices. Hence, a thorough understanding of the current trends in this segment is desirable for everyone interested in IoT deployment. However, the IoT remains in its introduction stage of product life cycle in the health-care field, especially in a developing country like India. Given the amount and sensitivity of health-related data, questions of security and privacy need utmost attention as these are being exchanged with other devices, people, and organizations. IoT deployment in healthcare raises numerous challenges such as identity management, interoperability, authentication, authorization, and management of several wearable connected devices. The chapter aims to elucidate various sociotechnical challenges of IoT deployment in health-care domain followed by possible solutions.

13.2 Internet of Things

With convergence of WSN technologies, open wireless technologies like Bluetooth, RFID, wireless fidelity (WiFi), telecommunication network, digital electronics, etc.; embedded devices are now able to exchange data with each other. This exchange of information among the various embedded computing devices is termed as IoT (Borgohain et al. 2015). The concept of "Things" in the IoT is generally used to reflect ordinary objects like televisions, watches, air conditioners, etc. The IoT results into an immensely distributed network of devices that communicate with people as well as other devices (Xia et al. 2012). They provide the benefit of creating a communication channel with all the entities in the network, supporting access to services ubiquitously. According to Ma (2011), the IoT has the following important characteristics:

1. Day-to-day "things" such as books, chairs, mobile phones, and foods can be instrumented (i.e., chip, RFID tags can be embedded, etc.).
2. Instrumented objects are connected as autonomic network terminals.
3. Autonomic terminals communicate with each other to make the pervasive service intelligent. As an example, the sensor nodes present on healthcare wearable devices can provide information related to the status of human body and provide reliable and real-time information to individuals, doctors, etc.

Realization of the IoT benefits is possible if ICTs integrate seamlessly with the real world of things. Through ICT usage in the "anytime" and "anywhere" mode, real world becomes more accessible in various domains as well as everyday scenarios (Uckelmann et al. 2011). However, integration of technologies shown in Figure 13.1 is crucial to materialize the advantages of IoT.

Some of the important or crucial technologies discussed in literature are as follows:

a. RFID: This technology is being used in many areas like retail, logistics, anti-counterfeiting, healthcare, and supply chain management. In simple terms, RFID works like barcode technology; however, it does not require a direct visibility of the monitored entities. RFID requires an interrogator, backend

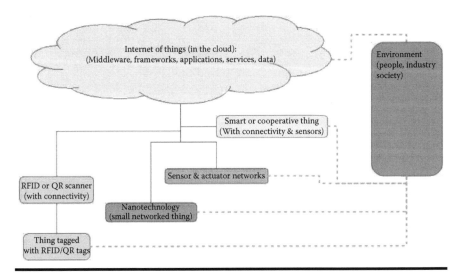

Figure 13.1 Components of IoT ecosystem (Coetzee et al. 2011).

system, and special tags for an entity tracking. Tags contain information about the item/asset. Interrogator communicates with the RFID tags, and backend system connects the interrogator with the centralized database. This technology has been there since long, but recently this technology has seen immense potential in the IoT due to its lower cost and increased capabilities (Sun 2012).

b. WSNs: It is a network of tiny low-cost devices equipped with sensors with a capability of taking measurements, storing locally, and communicating with each other (Bellavista et al. 2013). The most important advantage of WSN is that it makes interconnections quite easy and simple when compared with designing and implementing of wired connections. Ease of installation of WSNs reduces the cost and efforts for a large number of sensors (Ghayvat et al. 2015). WSNs find use in healthcare, where a number of discrete sensors provide different health parameters of individuals.

c. WiFi: In WiFi technology, the wireless network has an access point. This access point is the hub that provides connections to electronic devices, such as computers or mobiles phones, wirelessly. Most of us have used a WiFi network at home, company, institution, university, and many other places for the Internet services. Latest advances in WiFi technology have provided opportunities for a larger area coverage and has helped to extend the technology use in consumer electronic applications like video calling, streaming of videos and music, playing of games, exchange of data, etc. (Kaushik 2012). In addition, the cost and dimensions of WiFi chips have significantly decreased compared with their predecessors. WiFi may provide the communication fabric for the IoT applications and provide location-based services (Acer et al. 2015).

d. IoT Gateway: Due to lack of standard communication protocols, it is not easy to network the WSNs and mobile communication networks or the Internet with each other. Also, transmission of data from WSN to long distance is not possible due to the constraints posed by WSN's transmission protocols. To address this challenge, the IoT gateway is invented, which attempts to tackle the discreteness between WSNs, telecommunication networks, or the Internet and the diversity of protocols. It helps to bridge the available customary networks with sensor networks for better network communication. The IoT gateway helps in protocol conversion and device management (Zhu et al. 2010).

13.3 Applications of Internet of Things

IHS Markit forecasts that there will be 20 billion IoT devices in 2017. It is estimated that such devices will be 75.4 billion in 2025.[*] McKinsey estimates that the

---

[*] Information retrieved from www.ihs.com/industry/telecommunications.html, accessed on 2/10/2017.

total IoT market size will be USD 3.7 billion by 2020.* Gartner reports that the consumer segment is the major user of IoT with 5.2 billion units in 2017. It consists of approximately 63% of the total number of units in use.† Business Insider estimates that by 2019, the market of the IoT devices will be larger than that of the size of the mobile phones, computers, connected vehicles, and the combined wearable devices market.‡ McKinsey estimates that the total economic impact of the IoT will be greater in developed countries than in developing countries because of greater cost savings and better adoption rates§ (Please refer to Table 13.1).

Literature varied the applications of IoT in diverse domains. Figure 13.2 shows the heat map of key prospects of the IoT in different industries. Here, hotter shows the highest potential of IoT deployment. It can be reflected that health-care sector with "warm" category is still in the nascent stage of IoT usage.

Table 13.1 An Estimated Share of Economic Impacts of IoT, 2025

Settings	Advanced Economies (%)	Developing Economies (%)
Humans (wearable segment)	89	11
Homes	77	23
Offices	75	25
Retail environments	71	29
Vehicles	63	37
Cities	62	38
Factories	57	43
Others	56	44
Work sites	54	46
Overall estimates	62	38

---

* Refer to the report available on http://hk-iot-conference.gs1hk.org/2016/pdf/_04_Mc%20 Kinsey%20-%20(Chris%20Ip%20)%20ppt%20part%20%201%20_IoT%20-%20 Capturing%20the%20Opportunity%20vF%20-%2021%20June%202016.1pptx.pdf, accessed on 29/10/2017.
† Information retrieved from www.gartner.com/newsroom/id/3598917, accessed on 29/10/2017.
‡ Information retrieved from www.businessinsider.in/The-Internet-of-Things-Will-Be-The-Worlds-Most-Massive-Device-Market-And-Save-Companies-Billions-Of-Dollars/ articleshow/44766662.cms, accessed on 29/10/2017.
§ Source: www.mckinsey.com/business-functions/digital-mckinsey/our-insights/an-executives-guide-to-the-internet-of-things, accessed on 29/10/2017.

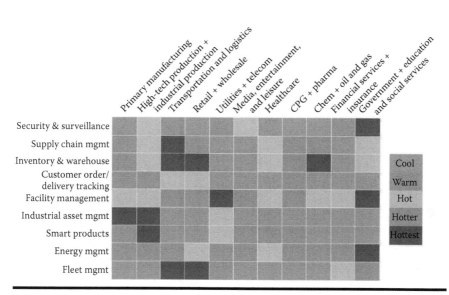

Figure 13.2   Heat map of the key IoT prospects in different domains (Pelino and Gillet 2016).

With the advancement and decrease in the cost of IoT technology, the possibility of including more and more objects into the IoT ecosystem is increasing. Through the IoT, it is possible to interconnect number of objects/entities, storing real-time data, and analyzing it for decision-making. Below are few examples where the IoT has been used successfully:

13.3.1 IoT in Business

Any business wants to have competitive advantage to survive in the competitive and dynamic market. The IoT can play a significant role in providing necessary and relevant data to businesses for better decision-making. As rightly pointed by Lee and Lee (2015), adoption of the IoT is rapidly gaining momentum in industry as technological, societal, and competitive pressures are driving them to innovate and transform. Real-time data and its processing have immense applications in manufacturing organizations, where the overall status of the machineries can be easily monitored using IoT. Through IoT, predictive maintenance is possible. Management will be in position to decide on replacement, repair, and preemptively follow maintenance of machineries before any major breakdown occurs. Companies can know the status of oil, brakes, engine, etc. along with the location of the fleet of vehicles used in logistics. As an example, in 2012, JCB India started using the IoT so that its customers are in constant touch with their machine by sending out real-time data and keeping them informed all the time. Through the system, in operations, users were able to collect important parameters for monitoring equipment usage, fuel consumption, status and health, and idle time. The system helped the organization in implementing product-as-a-service business models with no revenue leakage (Ramchandran 2015). In addition, information sharing and collaboration become efficient through the IoT. For example, managers can assign tasks to employees via an IoT-enabled mobile device. Insurance companies can set premium on car insurance based on the data on the driving behavior of the driver received through IoT-enabled devices in cars. Companies may use the location data of the customers to provide specialized services, such as alerting about the nearest retail store available to him/her.

13.3.2 IoT in Environment Monitoring

The IoT has been used widely for pollution monitoring, chemical hazard, earthquake and flood detection, weather forecasting, and precision agriculture. For example, Dubai Municipality, since 2012, uses a 14-station network comprising of air quality monitoring (AQM) stations to report and manage real-time data on air pollutants such as sulfur dioxide (from factories), carbon monoxide (from vehicles), ground-level ozone, and particulate matter.* In India as well, systems that provide real-time ambient air quality data have been implemented. For example, Delhi Pollution Control Committee provides real-time data on particulate matter in air for different regions of the Delhi city on their website.† The IoT has the potential to be used in the monitoring of varied environmental parameters. For example, we can monitor water level in lakes, dams, and rivers; air pollutant concentrations for cities; or for animal detection, detection of forest fires (Lazarescu 2013). Ridley Terminals Incorporation uses the IoT to prevent coal dust pollution. This system sends alerts to staff and management via SMS and e-mail whenever there is spontaneous combustion of thermal coal.‡ This prevents spread of fire by timely control and reduces losses occurring due to such events.

13.3.3 IoT in Automotive Domain

The IoT provides a new relationship between people and vehicles. As per the report by IBM, tomorrow's automotive disruptors are likely to be organizations that are able to integrate digital business with a new level of digital intelligence to create exceptional mobility experiences (IBM 2017). The IoT can detect the driving patterns of individuals that can be useful in saving lives. Using sensors on cars, real-time data on vehicle can be collected and accessed to improve in-car experience.

---

* Please visit https://d2pwrbx99jwry6.cloudfront.net/wp-content/uploads/Dubai-Municipality.pdf for more information, accessed on 8/10/2017.
† Please visit www.dpccairdata.com/dpccairdata/display/ITIJahangirpuriView15MinData.php for more details, accessed on 29/10/2017.
‡ Please visit https://d2pwrbx99jwry6.cloudfront.net/wp-content/uploads/Ridley-Coal-Terminals.pdf, accessed on 8/10/2017.

IBM has also reported about a Japanese auto manufacturer and identifies potential safety issues using advanced analytics to identify patterns and correlations between safety issues and root causes, allowing the automaker to find problems exponentially faster and more accurately. Vehicle tracking system is another application of the IoT that may help transportation fleet of a company by providing real-time information on the location aspects of a vehicle.

13.3.4 IoT in Home Automation

Products like Amazon and Echo Dot are changing the way we live. Through such systems, we are able to interact with small and large equipment, such as air conditioners (switching on/off, setting ambient temperature, etc.), lights (switching on/off, dimming, changing hues, etc.), controlling television, home theaters etc., both inside and outside our homes using mobile apps. Through products like Canary, Neurio, Connect Sense, etc., we can monitor temperature, humidity, security, power use, status of lighting, etc. Such devices are able to integrate electronic gadgets in a house with each other. With such incorporations, home devices are able to talk with each other, resulting in convenience, energy saving, and providing safety measures (Bhide 2014). Artificial intelligence and cloud computing are making these gadgets smart and responsive. For example, through Alexa (Amazon's cloud-based voice service), Echo Dot can stream music, provide answer to user's questions, suggest movies and its time, help in controlling home devices, and much more.

Under this backdrop, this chapter focuses on the IoT applications in healthcare. Therefore, from the following section, the authors discuss the IoT adoption in the context of healthcare with a particular focus on the reasons for their adoption and use. Though the IoT has the potential to offer enormous benefits in healthcare, the authors believe that it also faces many key challenges. The challenges such as identity management, interoperability, privacy, security, etc. (Khan et al. 2012) are covered in a greater depth in the context of healthcare.

13.3.5 IoT in Healthcare

The IoT can have one of the most promising applications in health-care domain. Markets and Markets estimate that the IoT health-care market is projected to grow to USD 158.07 billion in 2022 from USD 41.22 billion in 2017, at a compound annual growth rate of 30.8%.[*] In addition, they estimate that the market for global wearable medical devices will be USD 12.1 billion by 2021 from USD 5.3 billion in 2016, at a compound annual growth rate of 18.0%.[†] Major growth drivers of the

---

[*] Source: www.marketsandmarkets.com/Market-Reports/iot-healthcare-market-160082804.html, accessed on 29/10/2017.

[†] Source: www.marketsandmarkets.com/Market-Reports/wearable-medical-device-market-81753973. html, accessed on 29/10/2017.

IoT health-care market are evolution of artificial intelligence technology, rise in investments for the implementation of the IoT health-care solutions, and the penetration increase in connected devices in healthcare. Availability of real-time data for the purpose of monitoring or diagnosis can be crucial in saving a person's life. Given that the IoT has the potential to provide information about various health parameters from a number of interconnected sensor-based devices, lifesaving decisions can be taken not only by doctors but also patients. The advantages of the IoT in healthcare can also be leveraged in isolated or remote locations, where the presence of necessary medical facilities is not available for people who need constant medical supervision. There has been use of healthcare-related information systems since last few decades; however, such systems have restricted utility such as to store and view patient-related data. Analysis on such data is usually descriptive, such as knowing the number of visits made by a patient to the hospital, medications suggested, ailment symptoms, etc.

Most of such systems fail to provide real-time information about the patient health to doctors. With the IoT, there is immense possibility for transmission of data about a patient's condition to caregivers. With lower costs and good quality, wireless sensor based devices are available, which can detect various health-related parameters like blood pressure, heart rate, pulse rate, body temperature, etc. For patients, whose physiological status requires close attention can be constantly monitored using such noninvasive monitoring (Niewolny 2013). The IoT are being used in healthcare for better and efficient services. Niewolny (2013) describes a home health reference hub (refer to Figure 13.3) that enables collection and sharing of physiological information about a patient. The hub captures patient

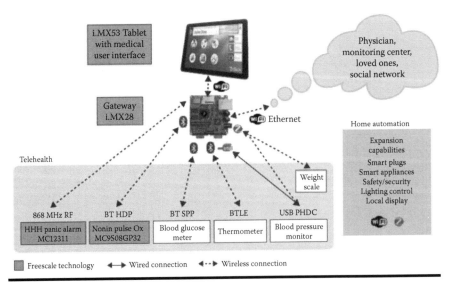

Figure 13.3 Home health reference hub.

data from different sensors and stores it in the cloud, where it can be accessed by caregivers.

Thus, we see that the IoT has uses in remote and real-time monitoring, clinical care, and early preventive care and medical emergencies.

13.4 IoT and Healthcare Wearable Devices

According to Gao et al. (2016), wearable devices are those devices that can be worn or mated with human skin to continuously and closely monitor an individual's activities, without obstructing the users' motions. Wearable devices are useful in unobtrusive monitoring of health-related parameters. Wearable devices may be embedded into textiles, in fashionable clothes or worn as mask to move voluntary muscles that have degraded due to medical ailments. Based on our literature review, healthcare wearable devices can be broadly categorized into "over-the-body" and "in-the-body" devices.

13.4.1 Over-the-Body Devices

Such devices are usually placed over the skin, worn on hands, arms, etc., or part of some external electronic gadgets. There are devices that can be laid as a patch on skin for monitoring and measuring a patient's heart rate, respiratory rate, skin temperature, and body posture. For example, Zio XT Patch,[*] developed by iRhythm, detects abnormal heart activity for two weeks and can be worn continuously. The data that is collected by the device is analyzed using a set of algorithms to provide necessary feedback. Wearable glucose monitoring devices are used to monitor glucose level continuously, and they seek to replace the need for users to rely on blood glucose meters. Some wearable devices use an accelerometer to gauge a user's activity level and help to alleviate pain in body parts.

13.4.2 In-the-Body Devices

These are placed inside the body as an implant to monitor and measure different health parameters. For example, some wearable devices are available to aid women to determine the time of ovulation and the most fertile period to conceive a child. The wearable device is inserted into the vagina, and then the biosensor monitors core body temperature throughout a woman's menstrual cycle. Through recent technological advancements, implantable devices are being used for better health monitoring, and in some cases, drugs or hormones are automatically released in the body based on analyzed data from the devices. For example, implantable skin

---

[*] For more information please visit: http://irhythmtech.com/products-services/zio-xt, accessed on 15/10/2017.

patches are available that sense arterial stiffening for heart attack related warnings. There are devices that can detect epileptic fits and automatically deliver drugs directly to affected areas of the brain.

It is observed that more impetus is being given to make wearable devices as small as possible so that the unobtrusiveness of such devices remains intact. In addition, emphasis is also on monitoring multiple vital parameters through a single device so that they provide a comprehensive bio/nonbiomedical data for analysis purpose. It can be rightly said that the IoT has undeniably immense opportunity for preventive, diagnostic, and recuperative healthcare. However, this development and deployment of IoT in healthcare is full of several challenges. In the next section, the authors discuss these challenges under the social, technical, regulatory, and managerial perspective.

13.5 Challenges of IoT in Healthcare

As every coin has two sides, the IoT applications in healthcare have positives and negatives. Most of the positives have been discussed in earlier sections; however, there are also some negatives that influence development and deployment of IoT-enabled wearable devices. Through literature review, the authors group such "negatives" into four broad categories: social, technical, regulatory, and managerial challenges. For smooth development and deployment of IoT in healthcare, strategies have been mentioned to overcome them. The major challenges in the IoT development and use are discussed as follows:

13.5.1 Social Challenges

According to Friedewald and Raabe (2011), possession of affordable devices, access to infrastructure and services and usability are important limiting factors in the adoption of IoT. However, factors such as awareness, cost of such devices, fear of technology, and resistance in adoption are also relevant for IoT-enabled wearable devices. Apart from these, legal and ethical challenges loom large on wearable medical devices. These factors have been discussed in detail later:

13.5.1.1 Awareness

Here, awareness is used in the context of healthcare wearable devices and individual's health consciousness. People's health and well-being are significantly affected by lifestyle factors such as smoking, hygiene, diet, and physical activity. These involve behaviors that are potentially controllable by the individual (Ryan et al. 2008). Hence, use of healthcare wearable device will be dependent on an individual's attitude toward health. It is likely that the person who seeks healthy lifestyle may use IoT-enabled devices.

13.5.1.2 Cost

The market for wearable technology is still at the stage of "early adoption" of Everett Rogers's diffusion of innovation trajectory (Sultan 2015). Hence, being in the early stage of innovation trajectory, IoT-enabled devices generally have high production costs driven by recently incurred design costs, frequent modifications, and low or unpredictable production volumes. Also in early stage of product life cycle, marketing costs may also be high. In addition, users have to bear an additional cost for repeatedly needing to learn new interfaces associated with the IoT (Costello et al. 2017). Therefore, the cost of wearable technologies might be high and may be a deterrent in its adoption. However, as these devices are early in their lifecycle, only early adopters may use such innovative products as they are likely to value performance over price (Solomon et al. 2000). In addition, according to Al Ameen and Kwak (2011), the cost of maintaining healthcare wearable devices may lay an extra financial burden on the person and the government.

13.5.1.3 Fear and Resistance in the Use of Healthcare IoT Devices

In their research on acceptance of WSNs by elderly people, Steele et al. (2009) concluded that there can be a lack of interest in using WSN systems due to the fear of not being able to interact with the system and the lack of confidence in them even though there are positive attitudes toward WSN systems. According to Schaar and Ziefle (2011), gender and level of technical experience have an influence on the adoption of technology. The authors point out that men are more willing to accept technology than women. Individuals with high technical experience are more likely to adopt technology in comparison with their low technical-experienced counterparts. Wearable devices inside human body may put psychological pressures on the mind of an individual (Al Ameen and Kwak 2011). In addition, fear related to privacy and security of data may also be a challenge in the adoption of healthcare wearable devices. There is also a social stigma attached with the use of healthcare wearables as people may feel pressured to adopt technology just to remain independent. In addition, some people may feel ashamed and view technology as an admission of dependence on wearable devices (Kang et al. 2010).

13.5.1.4 Less Social and Caregiver Contact

It is often believed that social contact is a sign of health in elderly patients. It is possible that monitoring technology could be used to replace caregiver–patient interactions. This may reduce the therapeutic aspect of social contact for the elderly patients, who are vulnerable to social isolation (Kang et al. 2010). Therefore, it is also important to ensure that technology is not a replacement of human care and does not contribute to the patient's isolation or does not threaten the trust in patient–physician relation (Lymberis 2003).

13.5.1.5 Legal and Regulatory Issues

The major challenges of legal issues come with the data generated through IoT devices. In literature, we did not come across examples where a robust legal framework is prevalent to define the actual ownership (who has the authority to delete, edit, and add information to data) and use of medical data generated by IoT devices. These reflect the intellectual property rights associated with the data. In the context, where the data is exchanged among different stakeholders at different places, the most pertinent issue is who owns the responsibilities and liabilities for the data collected from a person (Al Ameen et al. 2012), security, privacy, and its use. In addition, the devices also need to meet international quality standards to transcend international boundaries from consumer gadgets to medical devices. However, to avoid stringent regulations of a country, wearable devices are categorized as wellness/lifestyle tracking devices, which do not require rigid standards (Hiremath et al. 2014). Most countries do not have legal or regulatory framework to control development and use of healthcare wearable devices. Few regulatory bodies have touched upon a legal framework. For example, the Food and Drug Administration (FDA) in the United States of America (USA) issued a guidance document on the use of medical apps on mobile phones on September 25, 2013. In addition, FDA regulates wearable medical devices that consumers use. There is an approval process for the wearable medical devices. Only after being approved, such devices can be sold in market. FDA also focuses on how people can use these devices safely and effectively. There are countries like India, which have enacted the "IT Act"; however, there is no reference on the use of data collected through such devices. Certain conditions, such as emergency, disasters, or remote patient monitoring may require disclosure of information to other people to serve the patient in need (Al Ameen and Kwak 2012). According to Kang et al. (2010), medical care must be provided in accordance with state law even for providing care "remotely."

13.5.1.6 Security and Privacy

These issues include access rights to data and its analysis, how and when data is stored, security during data communication, and the governing policies (Meingast et al. 2006). Data collected from wearable sensors is vulnerable to data privacy concerns. Health-related data is sensitive as it may have users' absolute location and movement activities that compromise the users' privacy in case there is no safeguard against such information during the processes of storage or communication (Hiremath et al. 2014). Technologies used in the IoT may pose severe information security risks. For example, RFID may allow access to security-essential or competition-critical information due to lack of cryptographic procedures

(Friedewald and Raabe 2011). Personal health information exchange on the Internet exposes this data to more hostile attacks compared with the paper-based medical records (Meingast et al. 2006). In addition, there is also a conflict between security and safety. Too strict and rigid data access control may prevent the health-related data being accessed in time by legitimate medical staff, especially in emergency scenarios where the patient may be unconscious and unable to respond. On the other side, a loose access control scheme exposes data to malicious attackers (Li et al. 2010). There is often a possibility of monitoring the individuals without them being aware of it. The huge volume of data recorded by the sensors and communicated in different ways through networks may bring prejudice to the individual's private life (Popescul and Georgescu 2014).

Therefore, wireless communications, due to their remote access capabilities, are vulnerable to eavesdropping and masking attacks (Miorandi et al. 2012). Characteristics of the IoT such as global connectivity ("access anyone") and accessibility ("access anyhow, anytime") make them vulnerable to a number of attack vectors available to malicious attackers (Roman et al. 2013). For confidentiality, established encryption technology exists; however, such encryption technologies may not be feasible for the IoT technologies due to their limited computing power. Measures that can ensure authentication, confidentiality, and access control in the heterogeneity and mobility of "things" in the IoT will help build trust in them (Sicari et al. 2015).

13.5.1.7 Ethical Issues

Such issues mainly are the result of privacy and security challenges, equity in the access, health gap between rich and poor (and the associated life expectancy gap) as a result of the IoT use, trust, agency, and responsibility of errors (Brown and Adams 2007). Human and technology interaction are often complex in nature. In a digital age, society is generally divided based on access to technology and its use. Such division is related to availability of technology, socioeconomic status of individuals, skill set of a person to use the technology, etc. Similarly, the IoT are also subject to such divides. Hence, there will be people who will have access to the latest IoT devices, while some will not be in a position to use the devices due to several reasons. Those who have access to the IoT-based wearable devices will reap its benefits and avail better health-related decisions than the disadvantaged ones.

In literature, terms like "digital divide," "information rich and information poor," "haves and have nots," etc. are generally used to describe the biases in the access and use of ICTs. ICTs are used as an empowerment tool that helps in providing right information at the right time. "Access to information" may be seen as a right and therefore quite relevant for developing countries like India. Empowerment of the disadvantaged is a necessity to enhance their livelihoods. However, is access to the IoT-enabled health-care devices a necessity or a luxury? Well, the authors believe that the IoT is in the very early stage of product life cycle, the demarcation based on the "haves and have nots" may not hold unless this technology move ahead in the product life cycle.

The ethical question "who is to blame, and how will the consequent cost be covered?" may arise if the IoT healthcare devices go wrong and harm results (Brown and Adams 2007). Popescul and Georgescu (2014) believe that the digital divide will increase in the IoT, as it will be understood only by experts. They are also concerned whether there will be a fair distribution of benefits and costs as well as equal access to advantages leashed by the IoT.

Trust is another issue that is of concern, since the IoT ecosystem is characterized by different devices that have to process and handle the data in compliance with user needs and rights (Sicari et al. 2015). Device trust refers to the need to interact with reliable devices such as sensors and actuators. Daubert et al. (2015) discuss trust with reference to device, process, connection, and system. Device trust reflects the need to interact with reliable devices such as sensors and actuators. Processing trust relates to the need to deal with correct, meaningful, and errorless data. Connection trust relates to the requirement to exchange the right data with right service providers. System trust is associated with an expectation to use a dependable overall system by providing transparency to all involved stakeholders regarding workflows, processes, and underlying technology. Such matching between different stakeholders is generally based on trust relationships (Bandyopadhyay and Sen 2011).

13.5.2 Technological Challenges

Apart from social issues, technological issues also limit the use of the IoT in healthcare. The technological challenges range from data storage and management (e.g., physical storage issues, availability, and maintenance) and not limited to interoperability and managing heterogeneity alone. The major technological challenges that are seen as impediments in the use of IoT for healthcare are as follows:

13.5.2.1 Software and Algorithm

According to Sundmaeker et al. (2010), there is a lack of a common software fabric underlying how the software in different environments can be integrated to function as a composite system. Other challenge is how to build an integrated application out of a large collection of heterogeneous software modules using open middleware. There is also a need for encryption algorithms that are energy efficient. There is also a requirement for intelligent algorithm to trigger activities from multiple events (such as group observations or sensor readings) rather than just a single event. For this, the algorithm must correlate among different events (Bandyopadhyay and Sen 2011). This may also require transformation of raw sensor data in some way or other for integrated analysis. Often these algorithms will have to consider correlation among events that may possibly require transformation of raw sensor data. Moreover, it is expensive to transmit enormous volume of raw data in heterogeneous network, so the data compression and data fusion provision of IoT should be in place so as to reduce the data volume (Qin et al. 2014).

13.5.2.2 Hardware

If the IoT has to provide a standard set of functionalities, there are some stringent requirements on the hardware capabilities of the devices (Miorandi et al. 2012) such as necessity of miniature devices and increased functionality. Often, there is a requirement to upgrade hardware whenever there is change in protocols and designs for high performance in case of scalable algorithms. Such need to upgrade hardware has to be minimized as it would resist various stakeholders in adopting the IoT. There is also a need for energy-efficient devices that require low power, as power and energy storage can be crucial for the use of IoT in healthcare. Microbatteries with enough energy to power devices and energy scavenging technologies that let them collect power from their operating environment are the need of the hour (Sundmaeker et al. 2010).

13.5.2.3 Sharing of Resources

According to Qin et al. (2014), there is a need for shared provisioning of network and sensor resources across multiplicity of applications for efficiency. In the heterogeneous and complex IoT ecosystem, different user-defined tasks may run simultaneously with differentiated quality requirements in terms of reliability (packet loss), latency, jitter, and bandwidth. Therefore, there are chances that these applications are often developed, deployed, and triggered in an uncoordinated manner. Hence, there is a need to coordinate and optimize sharing of resources in such a complex and networked heterogeneous environment. Data and service sharing infrastructure can address several application scenarios. For example, anomaly detection in sensed data can be shared between several applications to reduce computing load on a single device (Gubbi et al. 2013).

13.5.2.4 Interoperability

Interoperability addresses the need for a synched environment, where various heterogeneous devices and platforms are able to talk to each other and provide seamless services. In the present context, most of the wearable devices have their own standards for interoperability, and hence, such specific standards may not integrate different IoT devices. For the IoT, all the devices in the ecosystem should be able to intercommunicate with each other at any given time. This is important because information available on one device may be useful to other devices in the same environment. According to Korzun et al. (2013), device, service, and information interoperability are important in the IoT ecosystem. Device interoperability relates to technologies for seamless device discovery and networking with each other.

Service interoperability is about the technologies for heterogeneous devices to discover services and use them. Information interoperability relates to technologies and processes for seamless exchange of information between devices without a need to know interfacing methods of the entity creating or consuming the information. The overall objective of interoperability is to provide an environment where devices can be deployed in a way to allow them to blend with other IoT devices around them seamlessly (Gubbi et al. 2013).

13.5.2.5 Availability of Search Engine Technologies

Extrapolating the status of the IoT devices several years into the future, the magnitude of sensor-based devices will be more than currently existing webpages (Ostermaier et al. 2010). The IoT would require the development of lookup/referral services for linking information in a way that respects both the privacy of individuals and confidentiality of information (Sundmaeker et al. 2010). Other aspects relate to finding relevant information using search engines. Even though hundreds of general search engines are available, finding relevant and valid health information remains difficult due to the structure and size of the Internet (Ilic et al. 2003). With growing number of devices in the near future, the network traffic will be difficult to manage both in terms of the number of accesses to the devices and of the number of queries received by the search engines (Nitti et al. 2014).

13.5.2.6 Standardization

As we have seen in the previous sections, IoT devices have to be of low cost and should require less power. Due to such nature of devices, they are often disabled for long times (sleep periods) to save energy. Therefore, the networks formed by these devices have different traffic patterns, high packet loss, low throughput, frequent topology changes, and small useful payload sizes (Ishaq et al. 2013). Hence, the integration of IoT devices into the Internet introduces many challenges, as many of the existing Internet standards were not designed for them. Standards are necessary in the IoT as there is a need for bidirectional information exchange among things in the ecosystem. Therefore, it is important to have standards like architecture standards, security standards, data and information processing standards, communication protocol standards, and service platform standards (Chen et al. 2014). In the present context, there are not many standards available for information interchange on the IoT devices and even those that are available are at an abstract level or proprietary in nature. For example, ISO/IEEE 11073 standards are available. They are normally used for bedside monitoring in hospital environments, to wearable, multisensor monitoring systems designed for home healthcare (Yao and Warren 2005). IEEE 802.15.4 standard are there for low-power devices that communicate less data in a short range. If standards for information interchange are available for the IoT ecosystem, then the issues related to interoperability, security, and privacy can be reduced considerably.

Table 13.2 depicts a comparative assessment between in-the-body and over-the-body IoT sensors from the perspective of social and technological challenges discussed in previous sections.

Table 13.2   Comparison of in-the-Body and over-the-Body Social and Technological Challenges

Challenges		*In-the-Body IoT Sensors*	*Over-the-Body IoT Sensors*
Social	Awareness	Low	Comparatively high
	Cost	High	Comparatively low
	Fear and resistance	High	Comparatively low
	Legal and regulatory issues	High	Comparatively low
	Security and privacy	High	Comparatively low
	Ethical issues	High	Comparatively low
Technological	Software and algorithms	Not available for an integrated solution	Not available for an integrated solution
	Hardware	Design, development, and deployment of sensors is challenging	Design, development, and deployment is comparatively easy
	Interoperability and standardization	Lack of interoperable components and standards	Lack of interoperable components and standards

13.6 Strategies to Overcome Sociotechnological Challenges

The sociotechnological challenges discussed in the previous sections have to be addressed so as to enhance their adoption, thereby guaranteeing equitable and seamless services through wearable healthcare. There are many social challenges that cannot be addressed completely but can be reduced to a considerable extent. To reduce the effect of social isolation and stigma of wearable healthcare in elders, it will be an appropriate approach to present the technology to them as a useful, helpful option and as a way to promote safety. In addition, wearable healthcare should be adopted before it is needed, as an option, which could avoid stigmatizing older persons. Also, it is recommended that the wearable devices are as small as possible so as to make them literally invisible and sync easily with the day-to-day activities of elders. For example, these devices can be built into clothing (Kang et al. 2010). This would help in minimizing feelings of dependency, anxiety, and fear in elders.

Digital divide in the use of the IoT devices cannot be overcome only by reducing the cost of such devices or by increasing access to them. It requires a holistic approach by not only individuals but also other stakeholders such as hospitals, government, and private organizations. Skills have to be enhanced, attitudes toward such devices have to be changed, and policy measures toward communication standards, privacy, and security aspects have to be undertaken.

Changes in attitude toward healthcare IoT devices can be there if people understand the usefulness of such devices. Gao and Bai (2014), in their study on adoption of the IoT devices concluded that usefulness is the primary determinant of one's use of the IoT while ease of use, trust, and enjoyment are secondary determinants. In addition, they also conclude that social influence is a major determinant in the use of IoT. Therefore, it is necessary for the IoT service providers to focus on social influence for greater adoption of the IoT technology.

According to Prayoga and Abraham (2016), if people are provided with resources and support such as Internet access and elaborate information to use the device—combined with their tendency to relate the wearable healthcare device's usage to their personal problem, they will be more likely to perceive the device as useful. The IoT practitioners can also take benefit of earlier adopters of the IoT services, whose views and reviews may generate positive social influence on subsequent adoption behavior (Wiedemann et al. 2008). The overcoming of the slowing factors needs a coordinated effort of the IoT practitioners to stimulate interest in potential final users and, in parallel, to boost the evolution of readers, software, and devices toward a more interconnected aspect (Amendola et al. 2014).

Technological challenges too need coordinated efforts by the IoT community. According to Sundmaeker et al. (2010), through consensus processes involving the IoT practitioners, it will be possible to develop standardized semantic data models and ontologies, common interfaces, and protocols. These may be initially defined at an abstract level and then with example bindings to specific cross-platform, cross-language technologies. Semantic ontologies can help to overcome issues resulting from human error or differences and misinterpretation due to different human languages in different regions of the world. To make the devices tightly coupled, an ontological knowledge representation, supporting localized agreements and personalization, is a requirement. Interoperability issue can also be taken care by such mechanisms. It is necessary because the knowledge processors that run in the IoT devices and coordinate in various service scenarios are often loosely coupled (Korzun et al. 2013). As IPv4 addresses, which is a 4-byte addressing system, are decreasing at a fast rate, it is recommended that IPv6 addresses, which are 128 bits, are used to address all the IoT devices. IPv6 can define 10^{38} addresses, which may be enough to identify any object that is worth to be addressed (Atzori et al. 2010).

Bandyopadhyay and Sen (2011) recommended use of service-oriented architecture to support interoperable machine-to-machine and thing-to-thing interaction over a network as it helps to organize the web services and makes it a virtual network. To address the issue of heterogeneity, "Information Driven Sensornet Architecture" is recommended, as protocol designers have to consider only the "information exchanges" with respect to a network protocol. Responsibility of packet creation and buffer provisioning are delegated to the architecture. Because of this, network protocols are simpler and require less memory (De Poorter et al. 2011). Other benefit of the architecture is that it can connect objects directly without any gateway, interpret an incoming packet type and drop unrecognized packets, and support communication between devices that uses different protocols (Rehman et al. 2016).

With respect to data security and privacy, one of the ways to handle the issue is to have concrete security and data governance rules for health-related data access. Charani et al. (2014) elaborate on the need for data governance rules for mobile phones in organizations. Similarly, rigid data governance rules might be applicable in the access and use of data collected from healthcare IoT devices. There is a need to have stringent policies to protect sensitive personal health information as it becomes available electronically (Meingast et al. 2006). Users should be made aware of how the data trails being left by the healthcare devices are stored and used. This would not only be ethical but also help build trust of people in such devices. Framed rules should guide the process of data collection, defining its ownership, storage, use (update, delete, and dissemination) and anonymizing the collected data.

It is recommended that systematic and consistent monitoring of new technologies on their impact on privacy is carried out. There is also a need for role-based access control and security, which may result in the reduction of the network complexity and cost of security administration. In healthcare, role-based control can be done using encryption, which is useful to ensure the security of data and help prevent eavesdropping. Encryption both at hardware and at software level may ensure the highest level of security (Meingast et al. 2006).

13.7 Conclusion

As discussed, the IoT has an immense potential in healthcare; however, implementation challenges are also not less. Data and privacy challenges are at the forefront, given the sensitivity of information associated with the medical data. In developing countries like India, the economic impact of IoT can be materialized if there is a comprehensive strategy toward adoption of IoT technologies. Given that social and technological challenges do not come under the purview of a single stakeholder, all the stakeholders of the IoT community require a coordinated effort. To address security and privacy aspects, public and private players have to come under one roof. Governments may address the privacy and security issues of IoT-related data by formulating stringent data governance rules. In India, the honorable Supreme Court has regarded privacy as the fundamental right of a citizen. The court establishes that the private zone privacy, which relates to the personal data shared during the use of credit cards, social networking platforms, income tax declarations, etc., should be used for the purpose for which it is shared by an individual. Given this context, and especially in relation to health-care data, it is imperative for the Government of India to frame privacy laws so that there is accountability and liability for leakage and misuse of data by any person or organization. In addition, the healthcare wearable devices should come under strict regulations for approval and use. The approval process should focus on whether the medical wearable device is safe for use by common people. For this, health and IT departments of government have to function in sync to frame such monitoring and evaluation processes. In addition, emphasis should be there to monitor the data protection and security aspects of the device. The process should ensure that the technical standards used for data communication between devices are safe and secure.

Medical wearable devices manufacturing organizations also have a responsibility toward data protection. These organizations should ensure that the components used in the medical wearable devices are safe to use and reliable. In addition, the organization should adhere to existing privacy laws and act in accordance with them. Research and development should be an ongoing process to consistently improve data protection technology. Service providers also play a significant role in reduction of privacy and security challenges. They are the true custodians of users' data. Service providers with respect to data management require effective quality measures in accordance to the privacy and security laws of a country. At an individual level, we should be aware of how our data will be used by the service provider.

Social stigma associated with the medical wearable devices may be overcome by the government, hospitals, nongovernment organizations, doctors, and individuals. Through everyone's effort, an enabling environment can be created for the adoption of medical IoT devices. In addition, to reduce the impact of digital divide, the IoT community may create mechanisms for creating awareness on the use of wearable devices to reduce resistance in the use of technology. Doctors, nongovernment organizations, and wearable device users may socially influence others to allay fears of using medical wearables. Though the cost of such devices is reducing, however, the present cost is beyond the reach of people in developing countries like India. Hence, developing countries should engage in government–industry partnerships for social and medical researches/social research for cost reduction of wearable devices. As we are aware that these devices are early in their life cycle, the earlier steps will be important in creating trust of users in medical wearables and thereby foster smoother adoption.

References

Acer, Utku Günay, Aidan Boran, Claudio Forlivesi, Werner Liekens, Fernando Pérez-Cruz, and Fahim Kawsar. "Sensing WiFi network for personal IoT analytics." In *Internet of Things (IOT), 2015 5th International Conference on the Internet of Things*, Seoul, South Korea, pp. 104–111. IEEE, 2015.

Al Ameen, Moshaddique, and Kyung Sup Kwak. "Social issues in wireless sensor networks with healthcare perspective." *International Arab Journal of Information Technology* 8, no. 1 (2011): 52–58.

Al Ameen, Moshaddique, Jingwei Liu, and Kyungsup Kwak. "Security and privacy issues in wireless sensor networks for healthcare applications." *Journal of Medical Systems* 36, no. 1 (2012): 93–101.

Amendola, Sara, Rossella Lodato, Sabina Manzari, Cecilia Occhiuzzi, and Gaetano Marrocco. "RFID technology for IoT-based personal healthcare in smart spaces." *IEEE Internet of Things Journal* 1, no. 2 (2014): 144–152.

Atzori, Luigi, Antonio Iera, and Giacomo Morabito. "The Internet of Things: A survey." *Computer Networks* 54, no. 15 (2010): 2787–2805.

Bandyopadhyay, Debasis, and Jaydip Sen. "Internet of Things: Applications and challenges in technology and standardization." *Wireless Personal Communications* 58, no. 1 (2011): 49–69.

Bellavista, Paolo, Giuseppe Cardone, Antonio Corradi, and Luca Foschini. "Convergence of MANET and WSN in IoT urban scenarios." *IEEE Sensors Journal* 13, no. 10 (2013): 3558–3567.

Bhide, Vishwajeet H. "A survey on the smart homes using Internet of Things (IoT)." *International Journal of Advance Research in Computer Science and Management Studies* 2, no. 12 (2014): 243–246.

Borgohain, Tuhin, Uday Kumar, and Sugata Sanyal. "Survey of security and privacy issues of Internet of Things." International Journal of Advanced Network Applications, vol. 6, no. 4 (2015). 2372–2378.

Brown, Ian, and Andrew A. Adams. "The ethical challenges of ubiquitous healthcare." *International Review of Information Ethics* 8, no. 12 (2007): 53–60.

Charani, Esmita, Enrique Castro-Sánchez, Luke S. P. Moore, and Alison Holmes. "Do smartphone applications in healthcare require a governance and legal framework? It depends on the application!" *BMC Medicine* 12, no. 1 (2014): 29.

Chen, Shanzhi, Hui Xu, Dake Liu, Bo Hu, and Hucheng Wang. "A vision of IoT: Applications, challenges, and opportunities with china perspective." *IEEE Internet of Things Journal* 1, no. 4 (2014): 349–359.

Coetzee, Louis, and Johan Eksteen. "The Internet of Things-promise for the future? An introduction." In *IST-Africa Conference Proceedings, Gaborone , 2011*, pp. 1–9. IEEE, 2011.

Costello, Richard W., Alexandra L. Dima, Dermot Ryan, R. Andrew McIvor, Kay Boycott, Alison Chisholm, et al. "Effective deployment of technology-supported management of chronic respiratory conditions: A call for stakeholder engagement." *Pragmatic and Observational Research* 8 (2017): 119.

Daubert, Joerg, Alexander Wiesmaier, and Panayotis Kikiras. "A view on privacy & trust in IoT." In *2015 IEEE International Conference on Communication Workshop (ICCW), London* , pp. 2665–2670. IEEE, 2015.

De Poorter, Eli, Evy Troubleyn, Ingrid Moerman, and Piet Demeester. "IDRA: A flexible system architecture for next generation wireless sensor networks." *Wireless Networks* 17, no. 6 (2011): 1423–1440.

Finger, G. "Digital convergence and its economic implications." Development Bank of Southern Africa, 2010. https://www.dbsa.org/EN/About-Us/Publications/Documents/Digital%20convergence%20and%20its%20economic%20implications.pdf. Accessed on 10/10/2017.

Friedewald, Michael, and Oliver Raabe. "Ubiquitous computing: An overview of technology impacts."

Gao, Lingling, and Xuesong Bai. "A unified perspective on the factors influencing consumer acceptance of Internet of Things technology." *Asia Pacific Journal of Marketing and Logistics* 26, no. 2 (2014): 211–231.

Gao, Wei, Sam Emaminejad, Hnin Yin Nyein, Samyuktha Challa, Kevin Chen, Austin Peck, et al. "Fully integrated wearable sensor arrays for multiplexed in situ perspiration analysis." *Nature* 529, no. 7587 (2016): 509–514.

Ghayvat, Hemant, Subhas Mukhopadhyay, Xiang Gui, and Nagender Suryadevara. "WSN-and IOT-based smart homes and their extension to smart buildings." *Sensors* 15, no. 5 (2015): 10350–10379.

Gubbi, Jayavardhana, Rajkumar Buyya, Slaven Marusic, and Marimuthu Palaniswami. "Internet of Things (IoT): A vision, architectural elements, and future directions." *Future Generation Computer Systems* 29, no. 7 (2013): 1645–1660.

Hiremath, Shivayogi, Geng Yang, and Kunal Mankodiya. "Wearable Internet of Things: Concept, architectural components and promises for person-centered healthcare." In 2014 4th International Conference on Wireless Mobile Communication and Healthcare - Transforming Healthcare Through Innovations in Mobile and Wireless Technologies (MOBIHEALTH), Athens, pp. 304–307. IEEE, 2014.

IBM. The Cognitive Effect on Automotive Unleashing Exceptional Experiences from an Abundance of Data, 2017. www-01.ibm.com/common/ssi/cgi-bin/ssialias?htmlfid=GBE03870USEN&. Accessed on 08/10/2017.

Ilic, Dragan, T. L. Bessell, C. A. Silagy, and S. Green. "Specialized medical search-engines are no better than general search-engines in sourcing consumer information about androgen deficiency." *Human Reproduction* 18, no. 3 (2003): 557–561.

Ishaq, Isam, David Carels, Girum K. Teklemariam, Jeroen Hoebeke, Floris Van den Abeele, Eli De Poorter, et al. "IETF standardization in the field of the Internet of Things (IoT): A survey." *Journal of Sensor and Actuator Networks* 2, no. 2 (2013): 235–287.

Kang, Hyun Gu, Diane F. Mahoney, Helen Hoenig, Victor A. Hirth, Paolo Bonato, Ihab Hajjar, et al. "In situ monitoring of health in older adults: Technologies and issues." *Journal of the American Geriatrics Society* 58, no. 8 (2010): 1579–1586.

Kaushik, Shailandra. "An overview of technical aspect for WiFi networks technology." *International Journal of Electronics and Computer Science Engineering (IJECSE, ISSN: 2277-1956)* 1, no. 1 (2012): 28–34.

Khan, Rafiullah, Sarmad Ullah Khan, Rifaqat Zaheer, and Shahid Khan. "Future internet: The Internet of Things architecture, possible applications and key challenges." In 2012 10th International Conference on Frontiers of Information Technology, Islamabad, pp. 257–260. IEEE, 2012.

Korzun, Dmitry G., Sergey I. Balandin, and Andrei V. Gurtov. "Deployment of smart spaces in Internet of Things: Overview of the design challenges." In *Internet of Things, Smart Spaces, and Next Generation Networking*, Edited by Balandin, Sergey, Sergey Andreev, and Yevgeni Koucheryavy, pp. 48–59. Springer: Berlin and Heidelberg, 2013.

Lazarescu, Mihai T. "Design of a WSN platform for long-term environmental monitoring for IoT applications." *IEEE Journal on Emerging and Selected Topics in Circuits and Systems* 3, no. 1 (2013): 45–54.

Lee, In, and Kyoochun Lee. "The Internet of Things (IoT): Applications, investments, and challenges for enterprises." *Business Horizons* 58, no. 4 (2015): 431–440.

Li, Ming, Wenjing Lou, and Kui Ren. "Data security and privacy in wireless body area networks." *IEEE Wireless Communications* 17, no. 1 (2010).

Lymberis, A. "Smart wearable systems for personalised health management: Current R&D and future challenges." In Proceedings of the 25th Annual International Conference of the IEEE Engineering in Medicine and Biology Society (IEEE Cat. No.03CH37439), Vol. 4, pp. 3716–3719. IEEE, 2003.

Ma, Hua-Dong. "Internet of Things: Objectives and scientific challenges." *Journal of Computer Science and Technology* 26, no. 6 (2011): 919–924.

Meingast, Marci, Tanya Roosta, and Shankar Sastry. "Security and privacy issues with health care information technology." In 2006 International Conference of the IEEE Engineering in Medicine and Biology Society, New York, NY, pp. 5453–5458. IEEE, 2006.

Miorandi, Daniele, Sabrina Sicari, Francesco De Pellegrini, and Imrich Chlamtac. "Internet of Things: Vision, applications and research challenges." *Ad Hoc Networks* 10, no. 7 (2012): 1497–1516.

Mueller, Milton. "Digital convergence and its consequences." *Javnost – The Public* 6, no. 3 (1999): 11–27.

Niewolny, David. How the Internet of Things Is Revolutionizing Healthcare, 2013. www.nxp.com/docs/en/white-paper/IOTREVHEALCARWP.pdf. Accessed on 15/10/2017.

Nitti, Michele, Luigi Atzori, and Irena Pletikosa Cvijikj. "Network navigability in the social Internet of Things." In 2014 IEEE World Forum on Internet of Things (WF-IoT), Seoul, pp. 405–410. IEEE, 2014.

Ogunsola, L. A. "Information and communication technologies and the effects of globalization: Twenty-first century "digital slavery" for developing countries – myth or reality." *Electronic Journal of Academic and Special Librarianship* 6, no. 1–2 (2005): 1–10.

Ostermaier, Benedikt, Kay Römer, Friedemann Mattern, Michael Fahrmair, and Wolfgang Kellerer. "A real-time search engine for the web of things." In *Internet of Things (IOT), 2010*, Tokyo, pp. 1–8. IEEE, 2010.

Pelino, Michele, and Frank E. Gillet. The Internet of Things Heat Map, 2016-Where IoT Will Have the Biggest Impact on Digital Business. Forrester, 2016. www.cloudera.com/content/dam/www/marketing/resources/analyst-reports/forrester-the-iot-heat-map.pdf.landing.html. Accessed on 29/10/2017.

Prayoga, Tommy, and Juneman Abraham. "Behavioral intention to use IoT health device: The role of perceived usefulness, facilitated appropriation, big five personality traits, and cultural value orientations." International Journal of Electrical and Computer Engineering 6(4): (2016): 1751-1765.

Popescul, Daniela, and Mircea Georgescu. "Internet of Things – Some ethical issues." *The USV Annals of Economics and Public Administration* 13, no. 2(18) (2014): 208–214.

Qin, Zhijing, Grit Denker, Carlo Giannelli, Paolo Bellavista, and Nalini Venkatasubramanian. "A software defined networking architecture for the Internet-of-Things." In *Network Operations and Management Symposium (NOMS), Krakow, 2014 IEEE*, pp. 1–9. IEEE, 2014.

Rehman, Sadiq Ur, Iqbal Uddin Khan, Muzaffar Moiz, and Sarmad Hasan. "Security and privacy issues in IoT." International journal of communication networks and information security 8, no. 3 (2016): 147.

Roman, Rodrigo, Jianying Zhou, and Javier Lopez. "On the features and challenges of security and privacy in distributed Internet of Things." *Computer Networks* 57, no. 10 (2013): 2266–2279.

Ryan, Richard M., Heather Patrick, Edward L. Deci, and Geoffrey C. Williams. "Facilitating health behaviour change and its maintenance: Interventions based on self-determination theory." *European Health Psychologist* 10, no. 1 (2008): 2–5.

Ramchandran, S. IDC Manufacturing Insights #IN250976, May 2015. www.wipro.com/documents/insights/innovative-use-cases-for-the-adoption-of-internet-of-things.pdf. Accessed on 08/10/2017.

Schaar, Anne Kathrin, and Martina Ziefle. "Smart clothing: Perceived benefits vs. perceived fears." In 5th International Conference on Pervasive Computing Technologies for Healthcare (PervasiveHealth) and Workshops, Dublin, pp. 601–608. IEEE, 2011.

Sicari, Sabrina, Alessandra Rizzardi, Luigi Alfredo Grieco, and Alberto Coen-Porisini. "Security, privacy and trust in Internet of Things: The road ahead." *Computer Networks* 76 (2015): 146–164.

Solomon, Rajeev, Peter A. Sandborn, and Michael G. Pecht. "Electronic part life cycle concepts and obsolescence forecasting." *IEEE Transactions on Components and Packaging Technologies* 23, no. 4 (2000): 707–717.

Steele, Robert, Amanda Lo, Chris Secombe, and Yuk Kuen Wong. "Elderly persons' perception and acceptance of using wireless sensor networks to assist healthcare." *International Journal of Medical Informatics* 78, no. 12 (2009): 788–801.

Sultan, Nabil. "Reflective thoughts on the potential and challenges of wearable technology for healthcare provision and medical education." *International Journal of Information Management* 35, no. 5 (2015): 521–526.

Sun, Chunling. "Application of RFID technology for logistics on Internet of Things." *AASRI Procedia* 1 (2012): 106–111.

Sundmaeker, Harald, Patrick Guillemin, Peter Friess, and Sylvie Woelfflé. "Vision and challenges for realising the Internet of Things." *Cluster of European Research Projects on the Internet of Things, European Commission* 3, no. 3 (2010): 34–36.

Tiwari, Rajnish, Stephan Buse, and Cornelius Herstatt. "From electronic to mobile commerce: Opportunities through technology convergence for business services." (2006).

Tufano, James T., and Bryant T. Karras. "Mobile eHealth interventions for obesity: A timely opportunity to leverage convergence trends." *Journal of medical Internet Research*, 2005;7(5):e58. doi:10.2196/jmir.7.5.e58

Uckelmann, Dieter, Mark Harrison, and Florian Michahelles. "An architectural approach towards the future Internet of Things." In *Architecting the Internet of Things*, Edited by Uckelmann, Dieter, Harrison, Mark, Michahelles, Florian (Eds.), pp. 1–24. Springer: Berlin and Heidelberg, 2011.

Wiedemann, Dietmar G., Tobias Haunstetter, and Key Pousttchi. "Analyzing the basic elements of mobile viral marketing-an empirical study." In 7th International Conference on Mobile Business, Barcelona , pp. 75–85. IEEE, 2008. pp. 75–85. doi: 10.1109/ICMB.2008.41

Xia, Feng, Laurence T. Yang, Lizhe Wang, and Alexey Vinel. "Internet of Things." *International Journal of Communication Systems* 25, no. 9 (2012): 1101.

Yao, Jianchu, and Steve Warren. "Applying the ISO/IEEE 11073 standards to wearable home health monitoring systems." *Journal of Clinical Monitoring and Computing* 19, no. 6 (2005): 427–436.

Zhu, Qian, Ruicong Wang, Qi Chen, Yan Liu, and Weijun Qin. "IoT gateway: Bridging wireless sensor networks into Internet of Things." In IEEE/IFIP International Conference on Embedded and Ubiquitous Computing, Hong Kong, pp. 347–352. IEEE, 2010.

Chapter 14

IoT-Based Privacy Control System through Android

Ravika Gupta
G.G.S. Indraprastha University

Gulshan Shrivastava
National Institute of Technology Patna

Rohit Anand
G.G.S. Indraprastha University

Tina Tomažič
University of Maribor

Contents

14.1 Introduction

With the advancements in technology taking place over the years, there has been a rapid transition in the way people communicate. Large numbers of people are getting inclined towards the use of wireless technology, merely because of its numerous advantages over the existing wired technology. Envisioning wireless technology's current potential, its further development and diffusion in various applications depend on a range of factors such as speed, cost, performance, and efficiency required in specific applications. In this regard, wireless technology has been proved beneficial and has provided a strong base for home automation. "smart home" (Azni et al. 2016) is a rapidly growing concept among the people nowadays. Energy is a crucial aspect that is to be taken care of; hence, energy management is an important parameter that is governed by smart home automation technology. In addition to energy management, there are quite a lot of other advantages that are provided, which includes security, surveillance, access control, lighting, and entertainment. One of the biggest advantages that smart home automation provides is that of access control. With the help of various software and user-friendly interfaces that can be controlled with the help of a mobile application, it is now possible to control and access various devices and appliances situated in far-off places or remote areas.

This concept of managing various gadgets has proved beneficial to the public in terms of cost and energy as total home control is provided on a single interface, available in the form of one-touch control containing different icons, thus making it user-friendly and easy to recognize the devices on mobile devices, tablets, or wall touch screens. Total energy management can help achieve efficiency in automation by automating devices such as air conditioners, thermostats, pumps, and fountains for temperatures, lightning intensity (Gioia, Passaro and Petracca 2016), and control of solenoid valves for sprinklers in lawns and gardens based on time duration and occupancy. Sensors can be used to automate lighting in an area by sensing motion detection, schedule, door openings, alarms, sunrise, sunset, etc. Hence, automation can help greatly in generating energy savings by reducing outrageous bills and therefore can help reduce energy expenditures to a great extent. It has been proved that dimming a light by 10% can save 10% of the energy and can double the life of the bulb. This also ensures the longevity of the devices and reduces rampant wastage of power when the devices are functional, especially when not needed.

This chapter deals with the implementation of wireless home control system with the help of Global System for Mobile Communication (GSM). It also illustrates how the concept can be extended to applications such as guard alert systems, flood alert systems (Asmara and Aziz 2011; Soliman et al. 2013), intrusion detection and notification alerts, and security systems, thus preventing any unauthorized access to the devices. Security is the prime concern in all sectors of today's world. For this reason, surveillance and security automation have gained large importance. Now, day and night supervision is done by the cameras installed at various locations within premises. Burglar and fire detection are possible by sensing intrusions, fire, smoke, and other hazardous objects. When an emergency situation arises, the owner is informed immediately with the help of notifications in the form of a call or short message service (SMS). Electronic locks also restrict the access and admission to specifically designated areas.

Internet of Things (IoT) has paved the way for the various wireless technologies for remote sensing and controlling. Technologies such as GSM, Bluetooth (Minoli, Sohraby and Kouns 2017), ZigBee, and Wi-Fi have been used in smart home automation, making it possible for the user to control his appliances from a remote location, without the need for him to be actually physically present near the device. Home automation or intelligent/smart home (SH) refers to the automation of daily work performed by the electrical devices used in homes. Therefore, home automation systems (HASs) should take care of the factors such as interoperability, security, scalability, and accessibility.

This chapter investigates the various methods by which different appliances in a home environment can be effectively controlled and accessed over the network. SH applications based on IoT are implemented by interfacing Arduino microcontroller with GSM module that is used to monitor the working of the devices with the help of a mobile Android application, built on a Massachusetts Institute of Technology (MIT) app developer.

Past researchers have made various attempts in this respect. Raza et al. (2017) used Bluetooth Low Energy (BLE), also known as "Bluetooth Smart" that guaranteed low-power consumption. Davoli et al. (2016) focused on the integration of Wi-Fi nodes hosting HTTP resources, into a Web of Things Testbed. The concept of IoT was implemented by Bahl et al. (2016) using Ethernet, which has many advantages including high speed, stability, and low cost.

In this study, an attempt has been made to make the system more efficient in terms of accessibility over a wider coverage range and has ensured to maintain the aspect of "privacy" and "security" at its best, by enabling the user to control the functioning with the help of a mobile application that sends the command to the GSM modem, by making use of SMS and calling features associated to it.

14.2 Related Work

It is well known that wireless technology has been proved to be very useful in home environments. Many attempts have been made in this field to implement the IoT-based wireless control systems (WCSs).

Sriskanthan et al. (2002) proposed the use of Bluetooth wireless technology that proved to be advantageous in terms of less hardware requirement as it can be embedded in various appliances and can successfully be a part of the networking environment to communicate. The model consists of a remote, a mobile host controller, and various home appliances. It also incorporates error detection and correction facility at the Bluetooth level.

Kho et al. (2005) exploited the Bluetooth technology, where it can manage only a limited number of analog and digital devices when interfaced with a microcontroller or a processor. This research also throws light on Bluetooth-enabled Electrocardiography (ECG) monitoring systems.

Wijetunge et al. (2008) have proposed the use of Bluetooth technology to handle and manage the working of the appliances and other devices. These authors have made use of a microcontroller and have interfaced it with the personal computer, through which the control and management of devices have been provided. The major advantage of using the Bluetooth module is that it does not involve any service charges, such as the GSM module. But the drawback is that the Bluetooth module provides a limited range of coverage, beyond which it is nonoperational. The use of a smartphone to control the working is also not done, which provides limited accessibility.

Wasi-ur-Rahman et al. (2009) stated that any sort of intrusion or a rise in temperature is conveyed to the user by sending an SMS with the help of a GSM module. Asmara and Aziz (2011) demonstrated a "flood alert system" using the GSM module. Madan and Reddy (2012) described the GSM-Bluetooth-based light controller and remote monitoring system. The major objective is to minimize the power consumption.

Kalaikavitha and Gnanaselvi (2013) emphasized majorly on the security aspects. The chapter shows the implementation of secured login using the mobile phone. It uses encryption techniques and helps to increase the overall security of the system. It is also beneficial to the users as it prevents any unauthorized access.

Soliman et al. (2013) proposed an architecture to elucidate the prominent features that are provided by the concept of "SH Automation." This architecture reduces the intervention of humans and helps in easy access, control, monitoring, and management of home appliances. The approach focuses on the use of embedded intelligence in sensors and actuators.

Aneiba and Hormos (2014) explained the implementation of Wi-Fi technology in mobile robots for operation and control purposes, where the robotic module wirelessly communicates with the operator. The GIX or "Gone In eXchange" algorithm is used, which ensures secure communication as it makes use of encryption and decryption techniques at the transmitter and receiver ends.

Caldo et al. (2015) explained the design and construction of a switch control system based on Wi-Fi technology, which can be put to use in home control system to control and access various appliances via the local area network (LAN) or the Internet. The use of Wi-Fi technology in comparison with other technologies is undoubtedly advantageous as it guarantees cost-effectiveness, robustness, high bandwidth, and coverage range.

Sun et al. (2015) have put forth the idea of a Wireless Control System (WCS) which is basically designed on the Arduino platform to mitigate the structural vibrations and other ground motions that occur during the natural calamities, such as earthquakes. It has various advantages over the wired systems, such as easy installation and low maintenance cost. It also offers a feedback control mechanism.

Collotta and Pau (2015) have proposed a fuzzy logic-based mechanism that makes use of (BLE, a concept in which the sleeping time of the devices is calculated and analyzed, making it energy efficient. Baghyalakshmi et al. (2015) described the design and integration of Ethernet gateway with other sensor networks. The use of Ethernet gateway has replaced the need of a PC, which was used for centralized logging purpose. Kusriyanto and Putra (2016) proposed an SH by making Arduino Mega as the server as well as the control center by using an Ethernet shield and a local area network. It uses the network router as the main component. The system is able to monitor and record the power consumption for home appliances.

Alaa et al. (2017) made various attempts by using the various technologies, such as Bluetooth, Wi-Fi, GSM, and Ethernet. It is quite evident over the past few years that IoT has successfully paved its way through SH technology. This has led to enormous energy conservation and has provided numerous benefits to a common man in day-to-day life. Along with this, there are a few challenges associated, such as safety, privacy, data management, and reliability. In this chapter, the authors have made use of liquid sensors and GSM technology. The sensors can detect high level of water and can be quite effective to be installed in flood-prone areas. The GSM module is used to intimate the user of any abnormal water rise and is useful to prevent any potential loss of life and property.

14.3 System Architecture and Proposed Methodology

After having a deep insight into the previous work, this chapter proposes the use of GSM module (SIM 900A) as the wireless communicating device. Arduino microcontroller is interfaced with the GSM module, which is further connected to a relay. Various home appliances are controlled, monitored, and accessed with the help of a simple SMS that is sent by the user. For maintaining privacy and building a secure system that can easily be accessed by the user from any geographical area, the chapter also proposes an Android application, which is built on MIT App Inventor2.

The programming is done on Arduino IDE platform. Overall, the proposed model ensures reliability, security, and privacy control without the physical presence of the user at the location.

Hardware requirements include Arduino UNO microcontroller, GSM module, and relay through which various devices are connected. The basic structure consists of the hardware components shown in Figure 14.1.

14.3.1 ATmega328P Microcontroller (Arduino Uno)

Arduino is an open-source platform, which provides user-friendly hardware and software Arduino (2015). Arduino Uno contains an 8-bit high-performance ATmega328P Reduced Instruction Set Computer-based microcontroller, which can be programmed according to the need of the application. Its bus and registers can handle eight parallel signals. It operates at 5 V of input power and has memory needed to store programs and other parameters required for its functioning. The clock frequency of 12 MHz is provided, which means that nearly 3×10^5 lines of C program can be executed in a second.

Three types of memory are present:

A. 32 kb flash memory: It is nonvolatile in nature and is used to store the application by the user onto the chip.
B. 2 kb static RAM: It is volatile in nature and is usually used to store the local variables while the application is running. It is lost once the module is reset or is powered up.
C. 1 KB EEPROM: It is nonvolatile and is used to store data that is required for further processing.

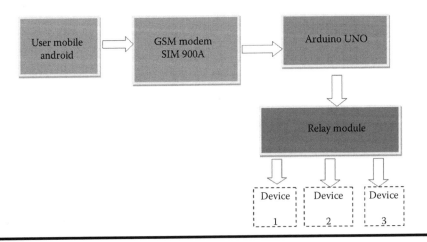

Figure 14.1   Basic structure and architecture.

Arduino UNO consists of one serial communication port (COM port), which allows the Universal Serial Bus (USB) cable to upload sketches onto the chip that can be monitored by using Arduino Serial Monitor window on the Arduino Integrated Development Environment (IDE). To use the serial COM port, the following header file is included:

```
SoftwareSerial.h
```

The chip contains 6 analog and 14 digital I/O (Input/Output) pins, thus making it versatile for controlling devices. It also contains an USB port, a power jack, and a reset button used to configure the module. Arduino boards are commercially available in assembled form, or they can be assembled easily if available in the form of the kit, as shown in Figure 14.2.

14.3.2 SIM 900A

GSM module (SIM 900A in this case) serves the purpose of accepting a SIM card and functions analogous to a mobile phone. It communicates in the frequency band of 900 MHz. It requires a 12 V power supply. The basic function of the GSM modem is to send and receive SMS from the mobile station. Interfacing of GSM and Arduino enables the controller to communicate with the end user over the mobile network. SMS is sent by the mobile user, which is received by the GSM module installed in the desired location. The received message is stored in GSM memory, and the task is performed according to the instructions

Figure 14.2   Arduino UNO.

provided by the user in the SMS. Both the user and the GSM should have a valid subscription.

Serial communication takes place between the GSM module and Arduino. The Tx (i.e., transmitting) pin is connected to the Rx (i.e., receiving) pin of GSM, and the Rx pin of GSM is connected to Tx pin of Arduino. The ground is made common. This way, the soft serial connection is established between the two interfacing devices.

A variety of GSM modules available have their own specifications. Some of them include SIM 900A, SIM 800, GSM+GPRS, etc. In this work, SIM 900A has been used since it is simple to interface with Arduino, as shown in Figure 14.3.

GSM is one of the most popularly used mobile communication systems throughout the world. It was invented in 1970 at Bell Laboratory. It makes use of time division multiple access techniques, where time slots are allotted to every user for communication to provide the data rate of 120 Mbps.

GSM architecture consists of the mobile station, the base station subsystem, and the network subsystem. Some of the prominent features offered by the GSM module are as follows:

■ Fixed dialling number
■ Encryption techniques to ensure secure transmission
■ Real time clock
■ SMS service
■ Integrated Services Digital Network (ISDN) and Public Switched Telephone Network (PSTN) compatibility
■ Mobility and phonebook management
■ Spectrum efficiency

Growing popularity among the people to make use of GSM (in a mobile phone) in security and automation is due to the easy access of appliances with the help of a device, i.e., a mobile phone, which is 24 hours with every person nowadays.

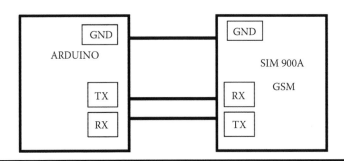

Figure 14.3   Pin connection between Arduino Uno and SIM 900A.

14.3.3 Relay Module

Relay module is essentially an electromechanical switch operated either mechanically or electronically. It comprises an electromagnet and contacts that perform the switching mechanism. Relays are used in various industrial applications so as to improve the efficiency of the devices. It is primarily used when a low-voltage signal is used to drive high-voltage circuits and to perform time delay functions.

A few applications of relay module are as follows:

■ Relays play a vital role in the realization of the logic function.
■ They are used for time delay functions, such as delay open and delay close.
■ They are used to control high-voltage and high-current circuits with the help of low-voltage and low-current signals.
■ They help in fault detection and isolation.

The different contacts in the relay module are as follows:

A. Normally open (NO)/make contact: When the relay is activated, the circuit is closed, and when the relay is deactivated, the circuit is open.
B. Normally closed (NC)/break contact: It is opposite to NO contact. When the relay is activated, the circuit is open, and when the relay is deactivated, the circuit is closed.
C. Changeover contact: It is used to control NO and NC contacts having the same terminal.

Selection of relay is also important and depends on the following things:

■ Contact protection and coil protection must be taken into consideration to prevent circuit arcing
■ Whether the contact is NO or NC
■ Current and voltage readings
■ Switching interval
■ Break before make contact or make before break contact

14.4 Program Flowchart

The flowchart (Figure 14.4) shows the basic flow of steps and the algorithm followed while controlling the functioning and working of various devices and appliances. The first step is to decide and set the baud rate at which the microcontroller and the GSM module will communicate with each other. The smartphone is kept ready, i.e., the application is successfully logged in and the details entered by the user are verified. It ensures that only the authenticated users are having access to the devices. The devices then send the ready signal, when they are

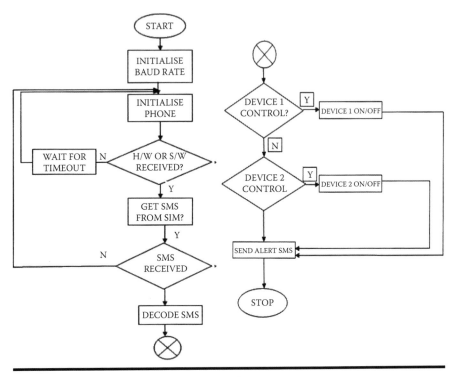

Figure 14.4   Flowchart to control the device.

powered up. The Light-Emitting Diode(LED) blinks for a few seconds at regular intervals. This shows that the GSM module is now ready to communicate with the Arduino (ATmega328P). To control a device or a home appliance, i.e., to turn it ON/OFF, the user selects the desired option in the mobile application and is sent to the GSM module. The SIM card installed in the GSM module receives the SMS sent by the user of the mobile application. The keyword is searched in the text message by the GSM module. It is programmed with the help of the search algorithm. Once the keyword is found in the message, it is decoded, and the particular device is turned ON/OFF accordingly. If the SMS is not received, GSM module keeps itself ready at all times to receive the message from the user.

14.5 Model of Home Automation System

In this model, the mobile station of the remote user is wirelessly connected to the GSM mobile over the network. Home automation control system is connected to the GSM module (Figure 14.5). The chapter proposes two major subsystems that are a part of the home automation control system: application control subsystem and security control subsystem. They are discussed in Sections 14.5.1 and 14.5.2.

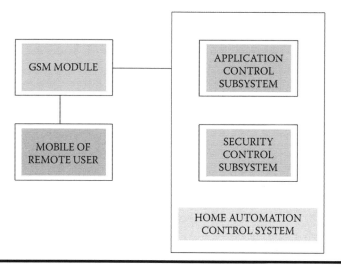

Figure 14.5   Two major subsystems of home automation control system.

14.5.1 Application Control Subsystem

This subsystem is basically used to control and access the various devices and applications by the user.

14.5.2 Security Control Subsystem

This subsystem takes into consideration the security aspects in home automation. It includes devices such as electronic locks, guard alert systems, and other security systems that can be employed in homes, offices, and other institutions.

14.6 Implementation of Wireless Control System Using GSM Module

In this chapter, microcontroller ATmega328P is interfaced with GSM modem (Das and Saikia 2015). GSM modem is controlled with the help of "AT commands." AT commands are the standard commands that are governed by the European Telecommunications Standard Institute in GSM 07.07, GSM 07.05, V.25ter, and T.32. These commands are the instructions that are given to the GSM modem. "AT" literally means ATtention. It is usually used as a prefix to the commands, indicating the modem about the start of a command line. AT commands are used to interact with the computer machine and get access to information and services, for instance, SMS, fax, calling, or information related to the SIM card.

The structure of AT commands comprises three parts: AT followed by a command and then the line terminator. When interfaced with the Arduino, a successful AT command sends an "OK" acknowledgment on the serial monitor, while an unsuccessful command will report an error. There are three types of AT commands:

- **Test command:** Its role is to verify the command's existence and the range of the subparameters.
- **Read command:** Its role is to check the current value of the parameter or subparameter.
- **Set command:** Its role is to set a new value to the parameter. If the command is satisfactory, it sends "OK," else a detailed error report indicating the fault is sent to the user interface.

AT commands can also be categorized into two parts:

1. **Basic commands:** These commands perform the basic functions and do not begin with a "+" sign. Few basic commands are shown in Table 14.1.
2. **Extended commands:** These commands perform advanced functions. They begin with a "+" sign. All GSM-based commands come under this category. Few extended commands are listed in Table 14.2.

Table 14.1 Basic AT Commands

Command	Meaning
ATD	Makes a call to a particular number
ATA	Answers the incoming call
ATH	Disconnects a remote user from the GSM module
ATO	Returns to online data state

Table 14.2 Extended AT Commands

Command	Function	Syntax
AT+CMGF	Sets up the SMS mode	AT+CMGF=<mode>
AT+CMGS	Sends SMS to a particular phone number	AT+CMGS=serial number
AT+CSMS	Selects message service	AT+CSMS=<service>
AT+CMGW	Stores a message in the SIM	AT+CMGW="Phone number"> Message to be stored Ctrl+z

The commands related to the text mode are shown in Table 14.3. Some other AT commands are shown in Table 14.4.

Arduino library provides various serial communication functions. Few of them are listed as follows:

- **Serial.begin ():** It is used to get the number of bytes or characters that are available at the serial port and are ready to read.
- **Serial.write ():** It is used to write binary data to the serial port. Data is written in the form of bytes or collection of bytes. Write () will return the number of bytes written.

Table 14.3 Text Mode AT Commands

Command	Function
AT+CMGF	Message format
AT+CSCA	Address of service center
AT+CMGL	Lists message
AT+CMGR	Reads message
AT+CMGS	Sends message
AT+CMGW	Writes message to memory
AT+CMGD	Deletes message
AT+CMSS	Sends message from memory
AT+CSAS	Saves settings
AT+CRES	Restores settings

Table 14.4 Miscellaneous AT Commands

Command	Function
A/	Re-executes command line
AT?	Commands help
AT*C	Starts SMS interpreter
AT*T	Enters SMS Block Mode Protocol
AT*V	Activates V.25bis mode
AT*NOKIATEST	Tests command
AT+CESP	Enters SMS Block Mode Protocol

- **Serial.read ():** It is used to read the incoming serial data. It returns −1 if data is not available to the serial port.
- **Serial.available ():** It is used to write the binary data to the serial port. The information is sent in the form of bytes or a collection of bytes.

14.7 Android Application

The chapter deals with two different parts: hardware implementation and Android application. As the technology is gradually evolving over the years, people look around for ways that provide an easy method to complete their work. An Android application is a helpful tool, which can be installed in mobile phones, tablets, or wall touch screens. It provides a user-friendly graphical user interface, with the help of which it is possible for the person to have ubiquitous access and control of their devices (Azni et al. 2016). The devices that are connected to the network with the help of IoT can be monitored and regulated at any instant of time just by a few clicks. It also ensures the security with a given premise as it also prevents any unauthorized access to a particular device or to any restricted area by installing it in door locks. In this way, it also saves a lot of time and energy.

Android, founded by Andy Rubin, is an operating system that has evolved from Linux and is undoubtedly the most widely used operating system in smartphones and tablets. Later, Google acquired Android Inc. in October 2005. Normally, Java programming language is used to create Android applications. Software Development Kit application has tools that are used for compiling and creating ".apk" extension files, known as Android packages (Shrivastava and Kumar 2017).

MIT App Inventor 2 is an online free-of-cost platform, which can also be used to create Android applications. It runs online and hence can be accessed by the user from any browser. It does not make use of Java programming language and is quite simple to understand. It is based on the connection of various logic blocks. It is a visual programming environment that can be nearly understood by everyone. It is indeed a great time saver than many existing complex development environments. Instead of generating an error report after all the blocks are connected and compiled, MIT App Inventor 2 platform does not allow two blocks having a different structure to connect to each other. For instance, the text block cannot be connected if the function asks for a number block. This feature makes it an easy block programming language, which is based mostly on the logic used by the developer.

MIT App Inventor 2 platform can be useful to develop applications that serve a variety of purposes. Applications can be built related to games, home automation, location-based applications, and educational applications. Applications controlling robots or SMS applications can also be developed on this platform.

The application will serve as a low-cost, low-power consumption, wireless control HAS to its users. It works in real time and is useful to monitor and control the devices installed in far and remote locations (Ding, Zhao and Ma 2009; Lim and

Ryoo 2004). Therefore, it is a convenient, fast, and effective method. Because the application can be successfully installed in a smartphone, it is portable too. This is one of the biggest advantages.

ATmega328 microcontroller is the core of this WCS (Arduino 2015). The sensors can be installed and can provide the data continuously to the microcontroller. Threshold limits are preset by the user and depend on the application. The microcontroller can be programmed by the user to meet the need of the application or the task. For example, temperature sensors can be installed in an office that continuously measures the outside temperature value and is received by the microcontroller. These temperature sensors are equipped with meteorological webs. If the data received by the sensors is above the preset threshold value, the controller sends a HIGH output signal, increasing the temperature of the air conditioner. The closed-loop air conditioning system can be installed in buildings, schools, and offices, which can reduce the energy consumption and human effort. The application builds on MIT App Inventor platform that can be easily comprehended with the help of logical programming blocks as shown in Figure 14.6.

The programming blocks of App Inventor clearly indicate the working of the application. With the rapid growth in the mobile communications seen over the years, more and more people are inclined to use their smartphone that can perform a variety of tasks. This mobile application comes as a handy tool that can easily be designed to automate home appliances effectively. In the absence of smartphone, MIT App Inventor has the feature of "Emulator" that serves the exact purpose of a smartphone.

14.8 Cost Analysis

The project is coded in Arduino IDE. It uses the instructions from C/C++ programming language. The program is compiled by the compiler and is dumped into

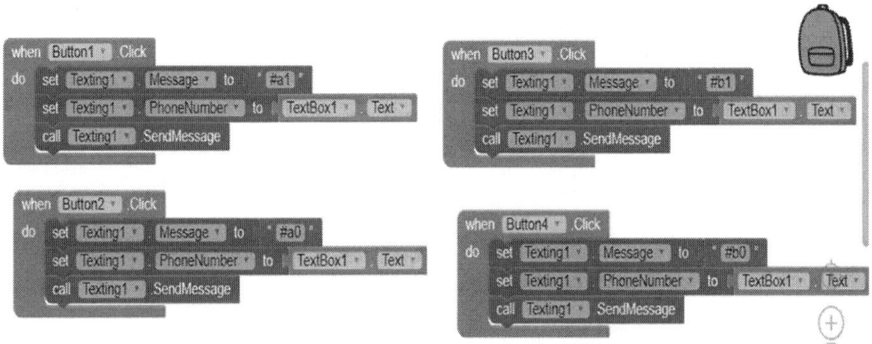

Figure 14.6 Programming blocks.

the microcontroller's memory, where it is stored for further execution. The components used are Arduino UNO, GSM SIM900A, relay module, jumper cables, adapter, and USB cable.

It can be seen that the concept of IoT in the HAS has greatly helped to reduce the overall cost of the project.

14.9 Existing Work

14.9.1 Smart Sensors

The term "smart sensor" refers to the integration of sensors with an interfacing unit. The sensor is an electronic device that may be used to sense or retrieve data from the environment. It sends the data to the controller where it gets processed. Smart sensors are capable of performing a two-way communication and are also able to perform logic functions (Healy, Newe and Lewis 2008). Its most basic task is to sense any physical, biological, or chemical input and to convert it into a digital form so that it can be processed accordingly. The combination of an actuator and a sensor is called a smart sensor (Cook and Holder 2011; Pande, Solanke and Panpatte 2017). Two basic components are present in a smart sensor:

a. Network Capable Application Processor
b. Transducer Interface Module

A few features of the smart sensor are listed as follows:

■ Installation is easy.
■ It is small in size; hence, it does not require much space.
■ It works well with all types of signals.
■ It can be designed to sense various parameters, such as pressure, temperature, smoke, humidity level, and water level in irrigation systems (Rajpal et al. 2011; Zhou et al. 2009). Therefore, it possesses multisensing features.
■ It is cost-effective. The use of smart sensors can be used to reduce the overall cost of the project, since it reduces the hardware cost and the need for multiple testing at various stages of the project.
■ It provides computational features that allow the user to obtain the statistical measurements, such as average, deviation, and variance for a given set of data.
■ It possesses self-calibration property by which it is able to adjust the output obtained from the desired value.
■ It ensures high reliability and high performance, i.e., it is efficient.
■ It reduces the number of connecting cables and other hardware required as nowadays smart sensors are available as an independent module that makes it much easier to interface.

Home security can further be enhanced using the wireless technology by installing a number of sensors (Sun et al. 2015). A smart house system can have the following sensors integrated into its structure so as to increase the monitoring:

A. **Door sensors:** These are installed on the entry and exit doors. They are used to detect the presence of any unwanted person within the given premises. This ensures safety and does not require continuous monitoring by humans.

B. **Door contacts:** Sensors can be installed at door contacts. Once the contact is broken, a signal is sent by the sensor and information is received by the owner on his control panel or mobile application. It is useful to protect the home from burglary.

C. **Motion-activated sensors:** As the name suggests, these sensors are used to detect any motion and presence of an intruder.

D. **Glass break sensors:** These sensors are used to detect the breakage of any glass. They can be installed in window panes. If the glass breaks, sensors inform the owner about any intrusion. These sensors help to ensure security and safety. They are also used to protect the property. They are sometimes also referred to as "shock sensors," as they are able to sense the high frequencies generated by the breakage of glass.

A general architecture of HAS using sensors is shown in Figure 14.7.

14.9.2 Smart Locking System

Gone are those days when people used to keep duplicate keys for their workplace or homes. With the technology progressing at an ever-accelerating pace, door locks

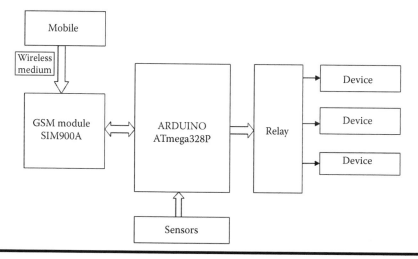

Figure 14.7   General architecture of HAS using sensors.

can be designed keyless on the concept of the IoT (Gioia, Passaro and Petracca 2016; Minoli, Sohraby and Kouns 2017). These locks can be monitored by the user on their smartphone or tablets. Smart locking system (Enderle, Pruehsner and Hallowell 1998) can be installed in homes or in offices so as to provide the users with a refined means of having access control.

Few features of the smart locking system are as follows:

- Door access can be provided to other people with the help of mobile phones by providing virtual keys.
- Smart door locking system can make use of "proximity sensors" that can detect the presence of the owner and can automatically lock/unlock the doors.
- Information regarding the use of locks, such as the time at which it was accessed and for how long is notified to the owner. It provides a complete activity log.
- Scheduling feature is available that works best in the absence of the owner.

Smart locking system (Das and Saikia 2015) allows the user to enter the premises only after entering the correct password in the secure login. A person is given access only if correct login details are provided. If the password entered by the user matches exactly, the door opens and the person is given access. With this, the owner is also notified of the access. These security systems can be installed in homes, offices, banks, educational institutions, and places that require restricted access.

14.10 Comparison and Implemented Results

The comparison table between the different technologies on the basis of maximum capacity/data rate and typical distance range may be shown as Table 14.5.

GSM-based WCS is successfully implemented. The overall hardware of the system is shown in Figure 14.8. It is clearly seen that the system is ready to respond to the owner's instructions to control any of the household devices. The user has the access to the devices with the help of a mobile application.

Further, the screenshot of the mobile application designed for two devices is shown in Figure 14.9.

Table 14.5 Comparison of Various Technologies

Feature	Bluetooth	GSM	Wi-Fi	Ethernet
Maximum data rate	21 kpbs	9.6 kbps	54–600 Mbps	10 Mbps–100 Gbps
Typical coverage range	Up to 100 m	35 km	Up to 250 m	Up to 100 m

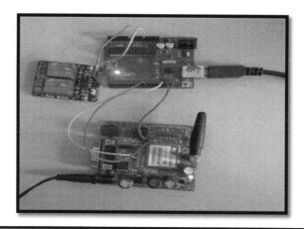

Figure 14.8 Overall hardware of GSM module interfaced with Arduino.

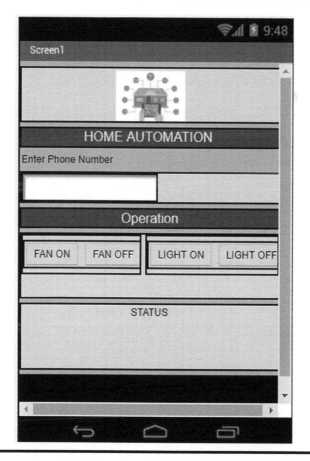

Figure 14.9 Mobile application designed for two devices.

14.11 Conclusion

In this chapter, privacy control in home or commonly referred to as "SH" based on the concept of IoT has been implemented. It is a well-known fact that home automation has been and is still continuing to make people's life more convenient. The basic objective of this chapter is to address the aspect of "security" and "privacy" efficiently. The research involved the interfacing of Arduino microcontroller with GSM module, to which various home appliances can be connected with the help of relay. The main advantage of accessibility is provided by building a mobile application, through which various devices can be controlled and monitored by the user.

The previous attempts made in this regard make use of various communicating devices, such as Bluetooth, Ethernet, or Wi-Fi to ensure wireless transmission of data. However, the use of these technologies differs in a multitude of aspects, such as bandwidth and coverage range. Also, the use of GSM technology does not require the physical presence of the user at the installed location of the system, as the control and access of devices are possible with the help of SMS.

There are numerous advantages of home automation using wireless technology. Home automation saves a lot of time of the user. It has made possible to control, access, and monitor various gadgets and appliances installed at homes, offices, and institutions and industries, without being physically present at that location. It also improves the standard of living and is also an extremely useful tool for the elderly. The concept can be extended effectively to implement guard alert systems and automated locking systems. This is also useful to prevent any sort of unauthorized access and security breach. It significantly reduces the power consumption and manpower requirement compared with the existing nonautomated systems. Arduino, GSM, Wi-Fi, Bluetooth, and Android application-based home control and automation systems provide the user with user-friendly means of operation. It also saves quite a lot of energy and thus results in reduced electricity bills. This way, it also contributes to the economy. A HAS does not use the old switching mechanism and is therefore quite efficient. It protects from short circuits that occur while using traditional wall switches in the appliances or loads.

A few of the limitations associated with the system implemented include low reliability, as it involves connectivity problems that may arise at the service provider's end. This may disrupt the flow of transmission, and hence, the probability of the occurrence of delay is quite high. This issue can be resolved by making use of higher end technologies, such as wireless sensor-based mobile technology that provides lower power consumption and system cost efficiency.

14.12 Further Scope

An attempt was made in this chapter to integrate ATmega328P microcontroller with the GSM module. This led to the design of a wireless control HAS that can be installed to monitor, control, and access various home appliances and gadgets over the network. It also features security aspect and can detect intrusions or any unauthorized access.

The work can be made more security oriented by adding a few features. The complexity of the system can be increased and be made more reliable and efficient by interfacing a number of sensors and motion detectors. Image processing and facial techniques are also used to detect and intimate the people about any possible threats and increase their safety.

The following points are suggested in this regard for further scope:

- Instead of using the communicating device as GSM module, Wi-Fi module can be used in its place. This will provide a wide coverage range. In addition to this, it has an added advantage that connection will be free from frequent mobile network failures or delays that occur during the transmission of data.
- Status of the device should be updated at regular intervals, which will help to keep the owner informed about the working appliances.
- This concept of automation should not be restricted just to homes, but rather should be extended to implement in offices, schools, and institutions.
- It should be noted that the WCS implemented in this project gets the power supply from the public source. A better approach will be to have an independent power source that can be in the form of solar or battery. This will ensure that the system is not dependent only on the public power supply and is functional at all times, even in case of a power failure.

References

Abhinav Rajpal, Sumit Jain, Nistha Khare, and Anil Kumar Shukla. "Microcontroller-based automatic irrigation system with moisture sensors." In Proceedings of the International Conference on Science and Engineering, pp. 94–96. 2011.

Adel Aneiba, and Khaled Hormos. "A model for remote controlled mobile robotic over Wi-Fi network using arduino technology." In *Frontiers of Communications, Networks and Applications (ICFCNA 2014—Malaysia), International Conference on*, Kuala Lumpur, Malaysia, pp. 37–4. 2014.

D. Baghyalakshmi, Sukant Kothari, Jemimah Ebenezer, and S. A. V. SatyaMurty. "Ethernet gateway for wireless sensor networks." In *Wireless and Optical Communications Networks (WOCN)*, 2015 *Twelfth International Conference on*, pp. 1–5. IEEE, 2015.

Dae-Young Lim, and Young-Jae Ryoo. "Development of remote monitoring system for cold-storage." In *Industrial Electronics Society, 2004. IECON 2004. 30th Annual Conference of IEEE*, vol. 3, pp. 2252–2254. IEEE, 2004.

Daniel Minoli, Kazem Sohraby, and Jacob Kouns. "IoT security (IoTSec) considerations, requirements, and architectures." In *Consumer Communications & Networking Conference (CCNC), 2017 14th IEEE Annual*, pp. 1006–1007. IEEE, 2017.

Diane J. Cook, and Lawrence B. Holder. "Sensor selection to support practical use of health-monitoring smart environments." *Wiley Interdisciplinary Reviews: Data Mining and Knowledge Discovery* 1, no. 4 (2011): 339–351.

E. Kalaikavitha, and Juliana Gnanaselvi. "Secure login using encrypted one time password (OTP) and mobile based login methodology." *International Journal of Engineering and Science* 2, no. 10 (2013): 14–17.

Egidio Gioia, Pierluigi Passaro, and Matteo Petracca. "AMBER: an advanced gateway solution to support heterogeneous IoT technologies." In *Software, Telecommunications and Computer Networks (SoftCOM), 2016 24th International Conference on*, pp. 1–5. IEEE, 2016.

Himshekhar Das, and L. C. Saikia. "GSM enabled smart energy meter and automation of home appliances." In Energy, Power and Environment: Towards Sustainable Growth (ICEPE), 2015 *International Conference on*, pp. 1–5. IEEE, 2015.

J. D. Enderle, W. Pruehsner, and B. Hallowell. "First year experience at the University of Connecticut with NSF design projects to aid persons with disabilities." *Biomedical Sciences Instrumentation* 35 (1998): 253–258.

Jifeng Ding, Jiyin Zhao, and Biao Ma. "Remote monitoring system of temperature and humidity based on GSM." In *Image and Signal Processing, 2009.* CISP'09. 2nd International Congress on, pp. 1–4. IEEE, 2009.

Luca Davoli, Laura Belli, Antonio Cilfone, and Gianluigi Ferrari. "Integration of Wi-Fi mobile nodes in a Web of Things Testbed." *ICT Express* 2, no. 3 (2016): 96–99.

Mario Collotta, and Giovanni Pau. "Bluetooth for internet of things: a fuzzy approach to improve power management in smart homes." *Computers & Electrical Engineering* 44 (2015): 137–152.

Md Wasi-ur-Rahman, Mohammad Tanvir Rahman, Tareq Hasan Khan, and S. M. Lutful Kabir. "Design of an intelligent SMS based remote metering system." In *Information and Automation, 2009.* ICIA'09. International Conference on, pp. 1040–1043. IEEE, 2009.

Medilla Kusriyanto, and Bambang Dwi Putra. "Smart home using local area network (LAN) based arduino mega 2560." In *Wireless and Telematics (ICWT), 2016 2nd International Conference on*, pp. 127–131. IEEE, 2016.

Michael Healy, Thomas Newe, and Elfed Lewis. "Wireless sensor node hardware: a review." In *Sensors, 2008 IEEE*, pp. 621–624. IEEE, 2008.

Moataz Soliman, Tobi Abiodun, Tarek Hamouda, Jiehan Zhou, and Chung-Horng Lung. "Smart home: Integrating internet of things with web services and cloud computing." In *Cloud Computing Technology and Science (CloudCom), 2013 IEEE 5th International Conference on*, vol. 2, pp. 317–320. IEEE, 2013.

Mohd Nor Azni, L. Vellasami, A. H. Zianal, F. A. Mohammed, N. N. Mohd Daud, R. Vejasegaran, N. W. Basharudin, M. Jusoh, Ku Azir, and PL Eh Kan. "Home automation system with android application." In *Electronic Design (ICED), 2016 3rd International Conference on*, pp. 299–303. IEEE, 2016.

Mussab Alaa, A. A. Zaidan, B. B. Zaidan, Mohammed Talal, and M. L. M. Kiah. "A review of smart home applications based on Internet of Things." *Journal of Network and Computer Applications* 97 (2017): 48–65.

N. Sriskanthan, F. Tan, and A. Karande. "Bluetooth based home automation system." *Microprocessors and Microsystems* 26, no. 6 (2002): 281–289.

Priya H. Pande, Nileshwari N. Solanke, and Sudhir G. Panpatte. "Security system using Arduino microcontroller." *International Advanced Research Journal in Science, Engineering and Technology* 4, no. 3,(2017): 107-110.

Rionel Belen Caldo, Derrick Castillo, Joseph T. Seranilla, Jose Maria T. Castillo, Ivan Carlo C. Largo, Marie Antonette T. Latayan, and Michael Gabat. "Development of Wi-Fi-based switch control system for home appliances using android phone." In *Humanoid, Nanotechnology, Information Technology, Communication and Control, Environment and Management (HNICEM), 2015 International Conference on*, pp. 1–6. IEEE, 2015.

S. A. Arduino, "Arduino." Obtenido de Arduino Mega: http://arduino.cc/en/Main/arduinoBoardMega (2015).

S. P. Wijetunge, U. S. Wijetunge, G. R. V. Peiris, C. S. Aluthgedara, and A. T. L. K. Samarasinghe. "Design and implementation of a Bluetooth based general purpose controlling module." In *Information and Automation for Sustainability, 2008. ICIAFS 2008. 4th International Conference on*, pp. 206–211. IEEE, 2008.

Shahid Raza, Prasant Misra, Zhitao He, and Thiemo Voigt. "Building the Internet of Things with Bluetooth smart." *Ad Hoc Networks* 57 (2017): 19–31.

Shikhar Bahl, Peeyush Chandra, Vandana Rathore, Alka Shukla, and Akash Garg. "Wireless ethernet for IoT: A case study." In *Intelligent Systems and Control (ISCO), 2016 10th International Conference on*, pp. 1–6. IEEE, 2016.

Shrivastava, G. and Kumar, P. "Privacy Analysis of Android Applications: State-of-art and Literary Assessment." Scalable Computing: Practice and Experience, 18, no. 3(2017): 243–252.

T. K. Kho, Rosli Besar, Y. S. Tan, K. H. Tee, and K. C. Ong. "Bluetooth-enabled ECG monitoring system." In *TENCON 2005 2005 IEEE Region 10*, pp. 1–5. IEEE, 2005.

Vini Madan, and S. R. N. Reddy. "GSM-Bluetooth based remote monitoring and control system with automatic light controller." *International Journal of Computer Applications* 46, no. 1 (2012): 20–28.

Wan Adlin Harris Wan Mohd Asmara, and Noor Hafizah Abdul Aziz. "SMS flood alert system." In *Control and System Graduate Research Colloquium (ICSGRC), 2011 IEEE*, pp. 18–22. IEEE, 2011.

Yiming Zhou, Xianglong Yang, Liren Wang, and Yibin Ying. "A wireless design of low-cost irrigation system using ZigBee technology." In *Networks Security, Wireless Communications and Trusted Computing, 2009. NSWCTC'09. International Conference on*, vol. 1, pp. 572–575. IEEE, 2009.

Zhuoxiong Sun, Shirley J. Dyke, Francisco Pena, and Alana Wilbee. "Development of Arduino based wireless control system." In SPIE Smart Structures and Materials+ Nondestructive Evaluation and Health Monitoring, pp. 94351D. International Society for Optics and Photonics, 2015.

Chapter 15

Digital Signature and Its Pivotal Role in Affording Security Services

Sushree Bibhuprada B. Priyadarshini
Institute of Technical Education and Research

Amiya Bhusan Bagjadab
Veer Surendra Sai University of Technology

Brojo Kishore Mishra
C. V. Raman College of Engineering

Contents

15.1 Introduction to Digital Signature

The chapter is devoted to defining the *digital signature* (*DS*), its trends, relevance, the security services provided by it, and the various schemes associated with *DSs* as well as some of the relevant applications of *DS*. Basically, signature represents a combination of letters or figures written in a distinguished way that acts as a form of identification while conjointly authorizing a document or a formal letter. Each and every one of us is quite familiar with the notion of signature. Basically, the signature of a person on a document affirms that the "document" originates from an appropriate source. A signature is basically a proof to the recipient that the received document is authentic, i.e., it comes from the right sender.

Consider a biodata document signed by a specific person. If the signature pertaining to the document is authentic, it confirms that the biodata is truly genuine. Consider a person A who sends a message to another person B. While receiving the message from A, B should make sure that it has come from A. In this regard, B can interrogate A to sign the concerned document electronically. The electronic signature affirms the credibility of A as the true consigner of the message. Such signature is referred to as "*DS*" by Kahate (2005).

The process of DS takes place in the following manner: When A is the sending agent and B is the recipient, A encrypts the message using the corresponding *"private key"* and thereafter transmits the encrypted message to B. Then B being the receiver of the message unravels the message with the aid of A's *public key*. Since A hides the message with its own *private key*, his/her intention is to hide the contents of the desired message to be sent to B. Now if the decryption by receiver B becomes successful, then B can make sure that the message was indeed sent by sender A. Since B decrypts the message by using A's *public key*, this is obvious that the initial message was encrypted by the *private key* of the concerned sending agent A. This is due to the fact that a particular message encrypted by a *private key* can only be decrypted with the corresponding *public key* and vice versa.

The entire mechanism of *DS* is illustrated in Figure 15.1. A and B denote the respective sender and receiver of a plain text message. In the beginning, A encrypts the *plaintext* to be sent with his own private key. Here, the encrypted message is regarded as the *ciphertext*. Then the message after encryption, i.e., the cipher text, is sent to the receiver B across the network. Later on, on receipt of the message from A, the receiver B decrypts the message received from A with A's *public key*. Now after decryption, the original *plaintext* is obtained at the receiver B. The entire process is portrayed in Figure 15.1.

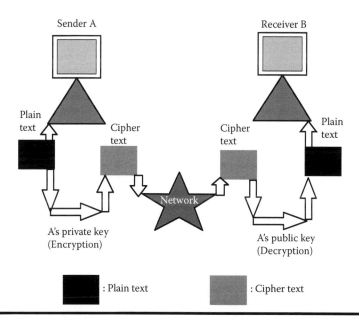

Figure 15.1   Fundamentals of DS mechanism.

15.2 Trends of Digital Signature

In 1976, Whitfield Diffie, an American cryptographer, and Martin Hellman, an American cryptologist, first described the concept of DS strategy. The duo exclusively inferred that such methods are based on the functions that are back entrance to "one-way permutation." This thing is also elaborated by Diffie and Hellman (1976) and Lysyanskaya (2002). Thereafter, Rivest, Shamir, and Adelman (1978) put forward the Rivest–Shamir–Adleman (RSA) algorithm that can be utilized to generate *"primary DSs."*

In this context, the leading first extensively retailed "software package" to tender the *DS* was Lotus1.0, discharged in the year 1989 that made use of the RSA algorithm. Distinct alternative DS methods were rampantly constituted after RSA. But the primeval were Lamport signatures (1979), Merkle signatures (1990), and Rabin signatures (1979).

15.2.1 Lamport Signatures

Lamport scheme was envisioned in 1979 and was named according to its founder Leslie B. Lamport (born: February 7, 1941), an American computer analyst. The Lamport signatures are also referred to as "Lamport one-time signature scheme." It is basically a technique for furnishing DSs.

Lamport signatures might be assembled from any cryptographically guarded "one-way function," normally a "cryptographic hash function." In lamport signatures, a key pair known as "lamport key pair" is used, i.e., a "private key" along with a corresponding "public key." To create the private key, the person who wants to send the message (i.e., the Alice) adopts an arbitrary number producer for generating 256 "pairs of arbitrary numbers" (total = 2×256 = 512). Again every number is of 256 bits size, i.e., a total of = 2×256×256 bits. This is the private key that is to be stored by Alice in a safe place. Again for creating the public key, Alice hashes every 512 arbitrary numbers in the private key, thereby generating 512 hashes, individually 256 bits of size. Such 512 numbers form the public key, which is shared by him/her with the universe.

Whenever Alice intends to sign her message, she "hashes" the message to a hash sum of 256 bits. Later on, considering every bit present in the hash, she chooses any one number from the "concerned pairs of numbers," which encompasses her private key based on the value of the desired bit. In this connection, considering the bit to be 0, the initial number is determined while considering the bit as 1, and the second number gets selected. Likewise, 256 random numbers are generated. Every number is again 256 bits long. Hence, the comprehensive size of her signature will become 256 ×256 bits. Such arbitrary numbers represent his/her signature, and he/she discloses it along with the message. Here, only the private key of Alice is used, and this ought not to be used further. The rest of the 256 random numbers that were not availed need to be demolished. This is because every optional signature reiterating the private key halves the level of security that may generate "false" signatures out of those in future.

Later on, the recipient, i.e., Bob, wishes to authenticate the sender's signature of the received message. Bob too now hashes the message to attain a "256-bit hash sum." Afterward, Bob adopts the bits in the corresponding hash sum to dis-cry "256 of the hashes" in Alice's *public key*. He chooses the hashes in similar way that Alice has selected the arbitrary numbers for the concerned signature. In this context, if the first bit of the message hash evaluates to be 0, he selects the initial hash within the initial pair and so on. Now, Bob hashes 256 arbitrary numbers in Alice's signature, which provides him 256 hashes. Now, if these 256 hashes completely match the 256 hashes he received from the public key of Alice, at that time, he makes sure that the signature is alright. If not, at that point, he infers that the received signature is faulty.

It should be noted that before Alice publishes the signature pertaining to the message, nobody is aware of the "2×256" arbitrary numbers in the concerned "private key." Therefore, nobody is capable of forming an applicable list of 256 arbitrary numbers for the signature. Further, as soon as Alice publishes the signature, remnants are still ignorant of the rest of the 256 random numbers, and therefore cannot generate signatures that are corresponding to the rest of the "message hashes." However, the problem in Lamport's signature is that every Lamport key is deployed for signing a "single message."

Further, in combination with "hash trees," a single key can be employed for a number of "messages";, thus, composing the Lamport scheme is an effective DS approach. Basically, a hash tree is a "persistent data structure" that can be used to implement sets and maps. They are basically aimed at replacing the hash tables in case of purely functional programming. Fundamentally, a hash tree stores the hashes of its keys referred to as strings of bits in a tree, the actual keys as well as the optional values stored at the final nodes of the corresponding trees. A generalized Lamport one-time signature scheme saves the storage space effectively. Basically, the proposed approach is employed for signing a lengthy message by hashing the message before signing for making the proffered approach more effective.

15.2.2 *Merkle Signatures*

This scheme was given by Ralph Merkle in the late 1970s. It acts as a substitute to conventional DS algorithm. The benefit of using such algorithm is that it is in contrast to quantum computer principles. Such Merkle scheme is dependent upon "Merkle signature scheme" and represents a DS approach based on hash trees and Lamport signature schemes. Here, the hash trees of secure hash function are also referred to as Merkle trees or hash trees. The benefit of using the Merkle signature approach is that this is considered to be resisting opposed to the quantum computer strategies. However, the Merkle signature approach relies on the presence of defended hash functions. Such thing causes the Merkle signature strategy: too conformable and opposing to quantum reckoning. Moreover, the Merkle signature represents a *"one-time signature"* strategy having restricted signing abeyant.

15.2.2.1 Key Generation

The Merkle signature strategy is used for signing a restrained count of messages with a public key. Further, the count of probable messages becomes the power of two. Thus, the probable count of messages is denoted as $M=2^m$. Furthermore, the initial phase is to generate the public key "pub" to induce the M private/public key pair (X_j, Y_j) for some one-time signature strategies such as Lamport's signature strategy. Further, every $1 < j < 2^m$, $h_j = H(Y_j)$ gets substituted. Considering the hash value h_j, a hash tree gets constructed while pacing the 2^m values as leaves. Further, recursive hashing is carried out to generate the desired hash trees.

Suppose $a_{j,k}$ indicate the node belonging to the tree having a height j and a left–right location k. Then, the hash values $h_j = a_{0,j}$ represent the leaves. In this context, the charge for every inner node pertaining to the tree represents the "hash" corresponding to the "concatenation of its children." As an illustration, $a_{1,0} = H(a_{0,0}||a_{0,1})$ and $a_{2,0} = H(a_{1,0}||a_{1,1})$. Likewise, a tree having 2^m leaves along with $2^{m+1}-1$ nodes gets constructed. The private key involved in the Merkle signature strategy is the whole set of (X_j, Y_j) combinations. However, sole among the crucial problem represents that the size of the concerned private key calibrates linearly with the count of messages to be communicated. The public key pub denotes the root of the concerned tree $a_{m,0}$. Here, the respective public keys are needed to be contrived as public beyond breach of any immunity, despite those are kept as secret to minimize the size.

15.2.2.2 Signature Generation

For signing any message MS by utilizing the Merkle signature strategy suggested by G. Becker (2008) the concerned endorser selects a key combination(X_j, Y_j),and he/she signs deploying the one-time signature scheme. Subsequently, optional information is added to it for justifying that this was really one of the actual key combinations to some degree than the nascent one procreated through a counterfeiter. At the outset, the concerned signer selects a (X_j, Y_j) combination that was not formerly employed for signing any alternative message and employs a "one-time signature strategy" for signing the message, thus giving rise to the signature and the respective public key.

The signer, generally, includes the corresponding intervening nodes belonging to Merkle tree, such that a verifier will establish $h_j = a_{0,j}$, used for computing the public key $a_{m,0}$at the root of the destined tree. Further, the path pertaining to the concerned hash tree from $a_{0,j}$to the root be m+1 nodes, namely,$A_0, A_1, A_2, ..., A_m$, with $A_0 = a_{0,j} = H(Y_j)$ as the leaf and $A_m = a_{m,0} = $ pub as the root. Further, A_j is the child of A_{j+1}. For the verifier to estimate the next nodeA_{j+1} inured the antecedent, they have to be aware of the alternative child of the A_{j+1}, i.e., the "sibling node" pertaining to the node A_j, which is referred to as *authen$_j$* such that$A_{j+1} = H(A_j||$authen$_j)$.

Thus, m nodes *authen₀, authen₁,..., authenₘ₋₁* are needed so as to construct $A_m = a_{m,0} =$ pub from $A_0 = a_{0,j}$. The figure shows an "authentication path." The nodes *authen₀, authen₁,..., authenₘ₋₁,* the Y_j, and the "one-time signature" *sign'* in sync form the signature "MS" using the Merkel signature strategy. Here, *sign'* = (*sign'* ‖ Y_i ‖ *authen₀, authen₁,..., authenₘ₋₁*).

15.2.2.3 Signature Verification

The receiver knows the public key pub, the message M, and the signature *sign'* = (*sign'* ‖ Y_i ‖ *authen₀, authen1..., authenₘ₋₁*). In the beginning, the recipient checks the one-time signature sign of the message MS employing the one-time *public key* Y_j. If *sign'* becomes a valid signature of MS, the recipient reckons $A_0 = H(Y_i)$ by hashing the public key of a one-time signature. For $k = 1, 2,..., m-1$, the nodes of A_k of the *path* gets enumerated along $A_k = H(A_{k-1} \| authen_{k-1})$. If A_m becomes equal to the public key pub of the Merkel signature strategy, the signature becomes credible.

15.2.3 Rabin Signatures

The "Rabin signature strategy" is a technique of DS that was initially proffered by Michael O. Rabin in the year 1979. This scheme was the first to belong to the hardness of falsification precisely to the integer factorization. This scheme is popularly used in most of the elementary courses of cryptography due to its obviousness and clear-cut feature in previous public key cryptography. The Rabin signature strategy is closely related to the Rabin cryptosystem. Basically, the "Rabin crypto system" is an asymmetric cryptographic technique, and the problem on which this scheme relies has been proved as hard as integer factorization.

The strategy entrusts on collision-defiant hash function" as follows:

$$H : \{0,1\}^* \rightarrow \{0,1\}^k \tag{15.1}$$

15.2.3.1 Key Generation

- The signer S selects prime numbers p and q, each of which has the size of k/2 bits as well as substitutes the product n=pq.
- Afterward, S selects b in {1, 2,..., n}.
- Now the public key is represented by (n, b) and the private key by (p, q).

15.2.3.2 Signing

- For signing a message MS, the concerned signer S chooses the arbitrary padding U as well as estimates H(MSU).
- S thereafter construes x(x+b) = H(MSU) mod n. In case there exists no solution, S selects a new pad U as well as retries.

- If H is genuinely arbitrary in nature, the awaited count of efforts becomes 4.
- The signature on MS is the combination (U,x).

15.2.3.3 Verification

- Let MS be the given message and (U,x) be the signature.
- Now the verifier V estimates x(x+b) as well as H(MSU) and verifies that they both are same.

15.3 Digital Signature Standard

The DS standard (DSS) is defined in "Federal Information Processing Standards Publication (FIPS)" series of the "National Institute of Standards and Technology." FIPS represents a formal array of publications related to regulations and protocols endorsed and annunciated beneath the foundations of the Federal Information Security Management Act (FISMA) of 2002.

This DSS itemizes a series of methods that can be employed for generating a DS. Basically, the DSs are utilized to detect the illegitimate changes to data as well as to validate the integrity of the "signatory." Moreover, the receiver of the concerned signed data can also employ the DSas proof in professing to a third party that the signature is indeed produced through the "claimed signatory," which represents the non-repudiation as the concerned signatory and cannot measly refuse the signature later on.

15.4 Relevance of Digital Signature

DS is a relevant technique used nowadays to provide message authentication, non-repudiation as well as message integrity.

15.4.1 Role of DS in Message Authentication

Basically, message authentication is a defensive measure in which the sender of a particular message gets verified for each of the issued messages. In the process of DS, a signing algorithm is utilized by the sending agent for signing the document to be sent. Afterward, the signature along with the message is sent to the receiver. After receiving the sent message, the destined receiver uses the verifying algorithm to make sure that the received message is communicated by the concerned sender. Then the result is verified, and if found to be true, then the received message is accepted; otherwise, it gets rejected. Such technique is regarded as "message authentication."

15.4.2 Role of DS in Message Non-repudiation

"Message non-repudiation" ascribes a state of pursuit where the originator of a message will not be capable of successfully challenging the authorship of the message sent by him/her. Generally, DS affords message non-repudiation if a trusted third party is used. In this context, the credible third party, i.e., the trusted third party, represents the individual that promotes intercommunication between the two desired parties who both trust the third credible party of interest. Fundamentally, the credible third party inspects all disparaging transaction communications between both the corresponding parties.

15.4.3 Role of DS in Message Integrity

Message integrity represents the validity of the transferred message. Basically, message digest (MD) is a cryptographic hash function retaining a string of digits generated by a one-way "hash formula."

Fundamentally, a cryptographic hash function represents a unique class of hash function, which has specified features that enable it to be competent enough for cryptography. Moreover, it is an analytical algorithm that traces the data of arbitrary size to a bit string of stable size. This means that a hash function that is refined to be a one-way function is impossible to be inverted. Further, the major features of an ideal cryptographic hash function are as follows:

- The cryptographic hash function has deterministic characteristics so that a particular message always gives rise to the same hash.
- This becomes expeditious for reckoning the hash value for a particular disposed message.
- This is not preposterous to produce a message from its corresponding hash value, excluding trying of all probable messages.
- A slight modification to a specific message must vary the hash value so broadly that the new hash value emerges unrelated with the older hash value.
- This becomes quite impracticable to realize two different messages with equal hash value.

15.5 General Deliberation on Digital Signature

A DS represents an electronic correspondent of "written signature." Such signature is capable of affording the affirmation that the defending signatory has signed the required information. Further, a DS can be utilized for detection in case the information has been changed after it has been signed. This is accomplished for detecting the integrity of the corresponding signed data. Such guarantee can be checked whether the concerned data was received in a transmission or retrieved from the concerned storage. Further, a perfectly realized DS algorithm that confirms the prerequisites of the standard can afford such favor.

A DS algorithm fundamentally comprises a signature generation process and a signature verification process. A "signatory" needs the procreation procedure for producing a DS on the concerned data. Moreover, a verifier uses the phenomenon of verification to justify the validity of the desired signature. Every signatory possesses a public as well as a private key, and the signatory is the proprietor of the corresponding key pair. The private key is employed in the signature formation strategy. This means the private key is, basically, employed in the signature production strategy. In this context, the key pair holder is the mere entity who has been accredited for using the private key to produce the desired DSs.

To restrain the rest of the entities from asserting to be the key combination proprietor and employing the private key for furnishing the "fraudulent signatures," the private key has to be kept secret. The endorsed DS algorithms are intended for preventing the foe that is ignorant of the signatory's private key from producing a similar signature as the signatory on a distinct message.

As such, signatures are constructed with the goal that they can't be counterfeited. A number of optional terms are utilized in such regulations to adduce to the scrivener or key pair holder. An individual that wishes to create DSs later on might be known as "intended signatory" before the checking of the signed message. Here, the signatory is known as the "claimed signatory." The public key is employed in the course of signature endorsement. In this context, the public key may not be put up secluded; however, its probity must be kept up. Anybody can check an accurately signed message while employing the corresponding public key.

For twain of the signature procreation as well as averment mechanism, the signed data, i.e., the message, gets changed to a rigid length form of the message by utilization of an "authorized hash function." In this context, both the initial message and DSs are made accessible to the concerned verifier. Further, the verifier needs the guarantee that the public key to be employed for validating a signature pertains to the desired entity which affirms to have produced a claimed signatory, i.e., the DS. Here the verifier needs certainty that the signatory is the real possessor of the private/public key pair utilized for producing as well as verifying the DS. Moreover, a requisite of an owner's integrity as well as public key can be actualized so as to afford such warranty.

A verifying agent too needs the confirmation that the key combo proprietor particularly owns the private key interrelated with a public key. The public key denotes an analytically valid key. By procuring such assurances, the verifier gains the certainty that if the DS can be appropriately verified using the public key, the DS is correct, i.e., the key pair owner really has signed the desired message. Further, the DS validation includes both the analytical verification of DSs and gaining of proper assurance.

Let us discuss some of the reasons behind such assurance. If the verifier does not get the certainty that a signatory is the real owner of the actual concerned key pair, the public integral is used for checking the signature. The dispute of fabricating a signature is diminished to the predicament of wrongly asserting the identity. If a verifier does not need the certainty that the concerned president is really the proprietor of the particular public key, it is utilized for analytically checking the signature of the concerned message. Afterward, the booming signature substantiation affords the warranty that the message has not been changed as it has been signed; however, it does not give the assurance that the particular message originates from the president (which means the concerned verifier has the certainty of the integrity of the data; however, the proper validation of the source lacks).Moreover, in case the public key utilized for verifying the signature is not analytically true, the arguments utilized for establishing the cryptographic firmness of the signature algorithm may not be applied.

Further, the owner cannot be the mere party that can produce the signatures that can be checked with the public key. In case a public key framework cannot afford certainty to a verifier of the fact that the holder of a key combo has introduced, the notion of a private key relates to the public key of the owner, and later on it may be feasible for an entity to get its identification attached to a public key that can be used by any other party. Afterward, the "unscrupulous entity" can demand to be the fountainhead of particular messages signed by the other party of interest. It may so happen that an "unscrupulous entity" has to attain the dominion of a particular public key, which is being selected having the main aim of permitting the testament of a signature on a particular message itself. Broadly, a key combo necessary for a DS approach may also be utilized for the schemes rather than the DSs (such as for the key formulation). But a key combo necessary for DS production as well as verification as described in such type of regulation will not be applicable for any alternative intent. Further, a large count of steps is necessary for enabling DS production and averment to happen according to this standard. Every party that produces DSs can carry out the initial setup process.

Before the acceptance of a DS, i.e., to justify the DS to be correct, the verifier should have (1) certainty of the signatory's asseverating identity, (2) certainty of the credibility of the domain parameters, (3) certainty of the authenticity of the public key, and (4) certainty that the contended signatory really attains the "private key," which has been utilized for producing the DS during the time the signature has been produced.

15.5.1 Message Digest

A MD is basically a "fingerprint" or a "summary" of a message according to Kahate (2005). Fundamentally, MDs are formed for maintaining the integrity of a piece of data or media to uncover modifications and transformations to any part of a message. They are a type of cryptography that uses hash values, which can urge the copyright owner of any changes enforced to their work. DS also ensures message integrity if the digest of the message gets signed in lieu of the message itself.

15.5.5.1 Requirements of MD

The requirements of MD are as follows:

a. For a specific message, it is very easier to find its concerned MD.
b. For a particular MD, it is very hectic to find the original concerned message.
c. For any two given messages, if we estimate their MDs, both the MDs must be different from each other.
d. If any two messages generate the same MD, then collision is said to take place.

15.5.2 MD5 Algorithm

MD5 is basically an MD algorithm that was proposed by Ron Rivest. The initial MD algorithm was known as message digest. The next version of the algorithm, i.e., MD2, was developed. However, it was seen to be a weaker algorithm. Later on, Rivest developed MD; however, due to a serious failure, it was not at all released. Soon, Rivest developed the MD4 algorithm. Subsequently, in due course of time, MD5 was developed.

MD5 is a very fast algorithm, and it generates 128-bit MDs. In the beginning, some initial processing is carried out, and the corresponding input text gets processed in 512-bit blocks, which are again segregated into 16-bit and32-bit sub blocks. As a result, the output results in a 128-bit MD.

15.5.2.1 Working of MD5

The various phases involved in the functioning of MD5 algorithm are as follows:

a. **Phase 1—padding:** In this step, padding bits are added to the initial message. The main motto behind the current phase is to get the length of the initial message equal to the value that is 64 bits lesser than any accurate multiform of 512. Suppose the length of the initial message is 1000 bits. Then, a wadding of 472 bits gets appended so as to form the length of the message equal to 1472 bits. This is because, if we append 64 to 1536, it becomes a multiple of 512. Hence, after the padding, the initial message has a length of 448 bits, 960 bits, 1472 bits, etc. Further, the padding comprises a single 1 bit succeeded by as many 0s as needed. Moreover, the padding length has the value between 1 and 512.
b. **Phase 2—length appending:** After the addition of padding bits, the next aims to estimate the initial length of the corresponding message as well as append it toward the terminal of the message. Now remove the padding bits. Now the length of the message is estimated. Moreover, the length of the initial message can be represented as a 64-bit value. Further, such 64 bits gets added to the end of the initial message plus the wadding. However, the

condition is that if the dimension (i.e., length) of the concerned message super cedes 2^{64} bits, at that time, only the low-order 64 bits of dimension is considered. Hence, dimension mod 2^{64} gets estimated.

c. **Phase 3—segregating input into 512-bit blocks:** After the padding length phase, the input message is segregated into blocks of 512 bits in length.

d. **Phase 4—computing chaining variables:** In this phase, four variables known as chaining variables get computed: A, B, C, and D. Every one of such variables represents a 32-bit number.

e. **Phase 5—processing blocks:** After all the computations are done, the proper algorithm commences. There exists a loop that lopes for as many 512 numbers of blocks as in the concerned message. The systematic process is summarized as follows:

- Model the four chaining variables into four respective variables. Now x=A, y=B, z=C, and l=D. The algorithm considers the combination of x, y, z, and l as a 128-bit single register, say xyzl.

- Segregate the recent 512-bit block into 16 sub blocks. Hence, every sub block retains 32 bits.

- Again there exists four rounds. All the 16 sub blocks are processed in every round. The inputs to every round are as follows:
    ■ All 16subblocks
    ■ Variables x, y, z, and l
    ■ Some constants denoted as *t*
        Single MD5 operation can be analytically denoted as follows:

$$x = y + ((x + \textit{Process } P(y,z,l) + M[i] + T[k]) <<< s) \qquad (15.2)$$

Where
x, y, z, and l are the chaining variables
T[k] is a constant
<<<s is circular left shifting by s bits
Process P is a nonlinear Boolean operation on y, z, and l.
The values of process Pin case of various rounds are listed in Table 15.1.

Table 15.1   Process P in Every Round

Round Process P
Round 1: (y AND z)OR ((NOT y) AND (l))
Round 2: (y AND l) OR (z AND (NOT l))
Round 3: y XOR z XOR l
Round 4: z XOR (y OR(NOT l))

15.5.3 Secure Hash Algorithm

Secure hash algorithm (SHA) was established by the National Institute of Standards and Technology and NSA. SHA functions with any input message that is lesser than 2^{64} bits in length. Moreover, the output of SHA is an MD that is 160 bits in length, which is 32 bits greater than the MD produced by MD5.

15.5.3.1 Working of SHA

SHA works as follows:

a. **Phase 1—padding:** The terminal of the initial message padding is added so that the length of the message is 64 bits shorter of a multiple of 512.
b. **Phase 2—appending length:** The length of the message, except the length of the padding, is now estimated and gets added to the ending of the padding as a 64-bit block.
c. **Phase 3—segregate the input into 512-bit blocks:** Afterward, the input message is currently segregated into blocks, each having a length of 512 bits. Such blocks act as an input to the processing of the corresponding MD.
d. **Phase 4—initializing the chaining variables:** Here five chaining variables A–E get initialized.
e. **Phase 5—processing blocks:** In this step, the steps are normally similar to MD5.
   - The chaining variables A–E are copied to x, y, z, l, and w. The combination is called xyzlw and is regarded as a single register for retaining the final along with the intermediate results.
   - The 512-bit block gets divided into 16 sub blocks, each of which comprises 32 bits.
   - SHA consists of four rounds, and every round has 20 individual phases. Every round considers the 512-bit block, the register xyzlw as well as the constant K[t]. Now the contents of the register xyzlw get updated using the steps of SHA algorithm.
   - SHA consists of four rounds, and each round comprises 20 iterations, and hence a total of 80 iterations,

Analytically, iteration comprises the operations as follows (Table 15.2):

$$xyzlw = (w + Process\ P + s^5(a) + W[t] + K[t]), x, s^{30}(y), z, l \qquad (15.3)$$

where
    xyzlw is the register made up of five variables

Table 15.2   Process P in Every SHA-1 Round

Round Process P
Round 1 (y AND z)OR ((NOT y) AND (l))
Round 2 y XOR z XOR l
Round 3 (y AND z) OR (y and l) OR (z AND l)
Round 4 y XOR z XOR l

Process P is the logical operation
s^t is circular left shifting of 32-bit subblock by t bits
W[t] is a 32-bit value derived from a recent 32-bit subblock
K[t] is one among the five "additive constants"

15.5.4 Message Authentication Code

Its concept is very similar to that of MD. In case of MD, no cryptographic process occurs; however, message authentication code (MAC) needs both the sender and the receiver to be aware of a shared "symmetric secret key" that acts as the basic ingredient in the formation of MAC.

Let us consider a sender P who wishes to communicate a message MS to a recipient Q. Now the following process occurs:

1. Both P and Q share the symmetric secret key K that is unknown to anybody else.
2. P estimates the MAC by using the key K for the message MS.
3. Afterward, P reports the initial message MS and MAC H1 to the corresponding recipient Q.
4. When Q receives the message, Q too uses K for estimating its own MAC H2 over message MS.
5. Now Q compares H1 with that of H2. If both match, Q infers that the original message MS has not been altered during the transition.
6. If H1≠H2, Q rejects the concerned message while considering that the original message was changed during the transit period.

Importance of MAC:

■ MAC gives assurance to the desired recipient that the concerned message is not changed.
■ The recipient is sure that the message indeed came from the actual sending agent.

15.5.5 Hash-Based Message Authentication Code

Hash-based MAC(HMAC) is basically used for reusing the already existing algorithms. Hence, it performs its work with any of the MD algorithms.

15.5.5.1 Working/Operation of HMAC

Suppose
  MSD: the MD/hash function in use
  MS: input message whose MAC is to be estimated
  l: total count of blocks in the desired message
  B: total count of "bits" in every block
  k: "shared symmetric key" to be used in HMAC
  ipadd: a string 00110110 reduplicated B/8 number of times
  opadd: a string 01011010 reduplicated B/8 number of times

Step 1. Compute the length of k as B
    The algorithm initiates with three possibilities, depending on the length of the key k. Three cases are encountered here.
    i. Length of k < B
        In this situation, expand the key k for making its length equal to the count of bits in the initial message block (B). Therefore, we append 0 bits as needed to the left of k.
    ii. Length of k = B
        In this situation, no action has to be taken, and we have to proceed to the next step 2.
    iii. Length of k > b
        Here, we need to spruce k for making its length equal to the count of bits in the initial message block (B). Afterward, k is passed through the MD algorithm H.
Step 2. XOR k with ipadd to generate S1
    The resulting output of step 1 is XORedand ipadd for generating variable S1.
Step 3. Appending M to S1
    Initial message MS is added to the terminal part of S1that was estimated in step 2.
Step 4. MD algorithm
    The chosen MD algorithms such as MD-5 and SHA-1 are applied to the output obtained from step 3. Suppose the output of this operation is H.
Step 5.XOR k with opadd generates S2. Afterward, k is XORed with the opadd for generating available known as S2.
Step 6. Appending H to S2

The MD H estimated in step 4 is now added to the terminal of S2.

Step 7. MD algorithm

The MD algorithms such as MD5 and SHA-1 are now applied to the output pertaining to step 6. Now this is the MAC obtained finally.

15.5.6 Rivest–Shamir–Adleman and DSs

RSA is implemented for accomplishing the DSs. Suppose the sender P wishes to send a message MS to recipient Q along with the corresponding DS estimated over the message MS.

Phase 1. The sender makes use of SHA-1 MD algorithm for estimating the MD (MD1) over the original message MS.

Phase 2. Subsequently, the sender P encrypts the concerned MD with his private key. In this context, the output of the process is regarded as DS.

Phase 3. Sender A sends the initial message M along with the concerned DS (DS) to the corresponding desired recipient B.

Phase 4. After the receiver Q gets the original message MS and the sender A's DS, q makes use of the same MD algorithm that was implemented by P and estimates its own MD MD2.

Phase 5. The receiver Q now makes use of the sending agent P's public key for decrypting the DS. Afterward, Q compares the two MDs as follows:

MD2: that was estimated in phase 4.

MD1: that was retrieved from P's DS in phase 5

If MD1–MD2, the following things occur:

Receiver Q accepts the initial message MS as correct and unaltered message from sender P. Receiver Q is currently sure that the message has been received from the sending agent P and not from anybody else.

15.5.7 DS Algorithms and DSs

DS algorithm (DSA) represents a federal information processing standard for the DSs.

Let us explain the concept of DSA:

P: a prime number having length L bits, where L is basically a multiple of 64 between 512 and 1024.

Q: a 160-bit prime factor of (p−1)

$g = h^{(p-1)/q} \mod p$, where $h < (p-1)$ and $h^{(p-1)/q} \mod p > 1$

x: a number less than q

$y = g^x \mod p$

H: MD algorithm SHA-1 normally

In this context, p, q as well as g are public. Hence, they can be sent freely across the secured network. For x being the private key, y represents the corresponding public key. Suppose the sender of the message intends to sign the message m and communicate the signed message to the intended recipient. Now the ensuing situation occurs as follows:

The sender first produces a random number k. Further, k < q.

The sender of the message now estimates:

$$r = (g^x \bmod p) \bmod q$$

$$and \ s = (k^1(H(m) + xr)) \bmod q$$

Here, the r and s values represent the signatures of the sending agent. Such values are then sent to the corresponding receiving agent under consideration.

$$w = s^{-1} \bmod q$$

$$u1 = (H(m) * w) \bmod q$$

$$u\,2 = (rw) \bmod q$$

$$and \ v = ((g^{u1} * y^{u2}) \bmod p) \bmod q$$

If v = r, it means the signature is now checked; otherwise, this gets rejected.

15.6 Blind Digital Signature

The concept of "blind signature" was proposed by David Chaum. It is a type of DS where the content of the concerned message gets blinded or disguised before being signed. Again the corresponding signature gets substantiated in public against the initial unblended message in the way of a general DS. Basically, the blind signatures are generally deployed in "privacy-related protocols." In such scenarios, the message author as well as the signer are distinct parties. To realize such a signature, the message is initially blinded by merging the message with a "blinding factor." Then the blinded message is communicated to a signer, who thereafter signs it employing a "standard signing algorithm." Afterwards, the emerging message and the blinding factor are verified against the public key of the concerned sender. In such a strategy, the final outcome, i.e., the message or signature of the blind signature approach, is the same as that of the conventional signing protocol.

15.7 Undeniable Digital Signature Scheme

Undeniable DS scheme is another approach that comprises three major parts: a signing algorithm, a verification protocol, and a disavowal protocol. In this context, the signing algorithm makes the sender to sign the message. The verification protocol uses the challenge-response mechanism that involves the sender to verify the signature. Such schemes prevent duplication of signed message without the approval of the sender. There is always a one-to-one correspondence between a document and the DS.

15.8 Applications of Digital Signature

The major application of DS is in signing the certificates issued by the certification authority. Basically, the DS is used for providing message authentication, non-repudiation as well as message integrity in real-life practical applications as discussed earlier.

15.9 Conclusions and Future Directions

DSs are versatile technologies that have attained a huge range of popularity in various industries such as engineering, architecture, and healthcare. Basically, at the time of applying the DS, a cryptographic operation binds the digital certificate as well as the data to be signed into one unique fingerprint. Basically, the DS acts as a viable alternative to conventional signatures that not only speeds up the document delivery but also reduces the paper wastage while conjointly decreasing the overhead costs.

The advantage of DS is what makes DS as a viable replacement to wet ink signatures. Such technologies are quite helpful and popular in the global DS software market and quite beneficial while maintaining message non-repudiation, message authentication as well as message integrity. Such active features of DSs can enable it to operate as an online equivalent to passport in every sphere of life as a direction towards future research.

References

G. Becker. 2008. Merkle Signature Schemes, Merkle Trees and Their Cryptanalysis, Seminar 'Post Quantum Cryptology' at the Ruhr-University Bochum, Germany.

W. Diffie and M. Hellman. 1976. New directions in cryptography, *IEEE Transactions on Information Theory*, IT-22(6):644–654.

A. Lysyanskaya. 2002. *Signature Schemes and Applications to Cryptographic Protocol Design*, Massachusetts Institute of Technology.

A. Kahate. 2005. *Cryptography and Network Security*, Tata MC Graw Hill, Pennsylvania.

R. Rivest, A. Shamir, and L. Adleman.1978.A method for obtaining DSs and public-key cryptosystems (PDF). *Communications of the ACM*. 21(2):120–126. DOI:10.1145/359340.359342.

L. Lamport. 1979. Constructing DSs from a One-Way Function, Technical Report CSL-98, SRI International.

R. Merkle. 1990. A certified DS, In Gilles Brassard, ed., *Advances in Cryptology – CRYPTO '89*, vol. 435. Lecture Notes in Computer Science, Spring Verlag, Berlin, 218–238.

M. O. Rabin. 1979. Digitalized Signatures as Intractable as Factorization, Technical Report MIT/LCS/TR-212, MIT Laboratory for Computer Science.

Websites

https://en.wikipedia.org/wiki/Non-repudiation (accessed October 5, 2017).

https://encyclopedia2.thefreedictionary.com/message+integrity (accessed October 5, 2017).

https://en.wikipedia.org/wiki/Digital_signature (accessed October 5, 2017).

https://en.wikipedia.org/wiki/Lamport_signature (accessed October 9, 2017).

https://en.wikipedia.org/wiki/Security_level (accessed October 11, 2017).

https://en.wikipedia.org/wiki/Hash_tree_(persistent_data_structure) (accessed October 11, 2017).

https://msdn.microsoft.com/en-us/library/windows/desktop/ff801752(v=vs.85).aspx (accessed October 5, 2017).

http://www.sciencedirect.com/science/article/pii/S0096300304004783 (accessed October 13, 2017).

https://en.wikipedia.org/wiki/Merkle_signature_scheme (accessed October 13, 2017).

https://en.wikipedia.org/wiki/Rabin_signature_algorithm (accessed October 14, 2017).

https://en.wikipedia.org/wiki/Rabin_cryptosystem (accessed October 14, 2017).

https://en.wikipedia.org/wiki/Digital_Signature_Standard (accessed October 14, 2017).

http://nvlpubs.nist.gov/nistpubs/FIPS/NIST.FIPS.186-4.pdf (accessed October 5, 2017).

https://en.wikipedia.org/wiki/Cryptographic_hash_function (accessed October 14, 2017).

https://www.lifewire.com/cryptographic-hash-function-2625832 (accessed October 14, 2017).

https://en.wikipedia.org/wiki/Blind_signature (accessed October 14, 2017).

https://en.wikipedia.org/wiki/Undeniable_signature (accessed October 13, 2017).

Index

Page numbers followed by *f* indicate figures; those followed by *t* indicate tables.

Printed and bound by CPI Group (UK) Ltd, Croydon, CR0 4YY

24/10/2024

01778284-0009